Once I Was a Princess

ONCE
I WAS A
PRINCESS

A Mother's Worst Nightmare

JACQUELINE PASCARL

MAINSTREAM
PUBLISHING
EDINBURGH AND LONDON

This revised edition, 2007

First published in Great Britain in 1999 by
MAINSTREAM PUBLISHING COMPANY (EDINBURGH) LTD
7 Albany Street
Edinburgh EH1 3UG

ISBN 9781840182774

A catalogue record for this book is available
from the British Library

Typeset in Sabon
Printed and bound in Great Britain by
Cox & Wyman Ltd, Reading

For my children Iddin and Shahirah
I love you millions, billions, trillions and infinities;
and I always will

This is an account of how the Islamic religion was taught and explained to me by a particular royal family, in a particular nation and at a particular time – it is not meant as a blanket indictment against Islam, nor is it completely indicative of all Muslims. I believe that all religions have an intrinsic goodness. Harm comes with the interpretations and prejudices wrought by individuals skilled in political and sociological manipulation.

Preface

When it was first suggested that I write a book about the turmoil of my life since the kidnap of my children in 1992, I was convinced that I was incapable of writing and shuddered at the very thought. But gradually I realised that one day Iddin and Shahirah would need to know the truth about what had happened to them, and the reasoning behind the decisions I have made in my life. Fortified by my children's need to know yet with much apprehension, I sat in front of my computer and began to draw the fragments of my life together into some sort of coherent account. To write one's autobiography at the age of thirty does indeed seem ludicrous, even to me; yet I had no other choice but to do so for them.

Sometimes it became far too painful to continue writing. On those days I took to my bed and simply willed the world to go away; on others, the proverbial anvil would fall from the sky and I would have to put the book to one side and enter the fray yet again to do battle for Iddin and Shahirah. However, out of this confusion came the realisation that it was also good for me to finally peel all those layers of hurt away and find out what sort of woman I had become because of the strange experiences I had had. I have learned that one of the most important things to do in one's life is to turn a negative into a positive, and I hope that my children will be able to do this in their own lives even though I can't be there to show them how.

'We live in hope . . .'

Prologue

The screaming is terrifying, filling my whole head with its volume, drowning me in waves of panic, smothering me with its despair. I feel arms around me and hear words, a voice. But I can still hear the screaming, still feel the terror, even as I'm shaken awake and I realise the shrieks are mine – this is a nightmare, my nightmare, the one I have nearly every night, the thing that makes me too scared to go to bed at night and too petrified to close my eyes during the day.

My children, my little ones, with their huge grins, cuddly bodies and spindly legs, don't ever smile in the nightmare; instead they stare with blank eyes at the mirrored walls in front of them. Incarcerated in separate bedrooms with no windows or doors, they sit on their beds and I watch as their mouths form the word 'Mummy'. But the words I hear aren't synchronised with their lips and they call my name over and over again, with anguish and confusion in their voices. I try to break through the glass wall, to scream to them that I'm coming, that I love them, that it will be all right, but they don't hear me. The children just keep crying out my name.

Then the laughter starts: derisive, cruel and so familiar. I know to whom it belongs: my former husband. Yang Amat Mulia (HH Prince) Raja Kamarul

Bahrin Shah ibni Yang Amat Mulia (HH Prince) Raja Ahmad Baharuddin Shah. Or, more simply put, Bahrin.

My dreams now are like horror films on a continuous loop. Always the same and always so real. As I become conscious in my rescuer's arms, I babble incoherently, trying to relate the details of my terror so I can recruit him into the madness too. And still my comforter holds me and rocks me as I sob and shake, reassuring me as my conscious and subconscious minds reconcile themselves in the wee small hours of the morning. It is, after all, only a dream . . . a nightmare . . . my living nightmare . . . my payment for the choices I made when I was seventeen years old. The price I pay, and my children, Iddin and Shah, pay, because once I was a princess.

One

I have been told on good authority that my earliest memory can be fixed at the age of seven months. I can remember the shadows on the walls of my mother's bedroom as dusk fell, and the uniquely Aussie summer evenings as the neighbours watered their gardens on a hot night, the fragrance filtering through the open windows and venetian blinds. The focus of Mum's room was the hulking white dressing-table mounted by a round bevelled mirror on which stood china trinket dishes, her rosary beads and her precious transistor radio. Mum slept in a single bed, one of two which were placed on either side of the room and topped with pale plum-coloured candlewick bedspreads, the sight of which always made me feel a little sad when I was growing up – they seemed as tired and faded as Mum.

I distinctly recall being placed on the bed opposite the window, and I remember my mother's face looming above mine as she nervously attempted to change my nappy. It was a face which I would come to equate with distance and illness during my early childhood: dark blonde hair pinned up, blue eyes and a very Gallic nose, seldom close enough for me to touch or explore with my chubby fingers. This particular evening has often sprung to mind when, over the years, I have contemplated nappy pins. It has left me charitably open to the concept of disposable nappies with their sticky-tape fasteners. You see, during the nappy-changing operation my mother managed to insert a large nappy pin through one side of my flesh and out through the other, fastening the garment most securely whilst I released a loud scream. This in turn panicked my young mother. She plonked me down and went in search of help, leaving me on her bed with the offending sharp item still fastened through my stomach. During this lull in the excitement I remember ceasing my howls long enough to realise the pain wasn't so bad after all, but I certainly wasn't going to put up with it for very long, so, inhaling deeply, I started to scream again. I was still screaming as my nanna arrived on the scene to part me from my mother's 'tailoring'. In fact, after the notorious nappy-pin episode, I can safely say that my relationship with Mum was pretty much downhill all the way.

I was born in the Jessie MacPherson Hospital in Melbourne, Australia, on 5 July 1963, at precisely 8.48 a.m. I know that my mother was definitely there, but couldn't say who else was present to welcome me. I think the moment Mum saw me, all her illusions about what her baby would look like were shattered. As a blonde, blue-eyed Anglo-Saxon Australian, she expected me to resemble her – wrong. Very unlikely, considering my father was Chinese. Instead she got a brown-eyed, brown-haired squaller who bore no resemblance to any of the other babies in the hospital nursery and was certainly not a future candidate for a Pears soap advertisement.

Mum had met my father, Chuan Huat, when he was a flashily dressed overseas student from Malaya, as it was then known. I fear he sounds as if he dressed like a cross between Charlie Chan (in white suits and shoes) and an Asian Marlon Brando, apparently even riding a motorbike at one stage of their courtship. After a protracted year's romance, my parents finally tied the knot in September 1962. I have calculated that I was probably conceived during the honeymoon. Family legend has it that my father wed without the consent or knowledge of his parents back in Penang, Malaya, who were less than pleased when they discovered I was on the way. I entered my father's world on schedule, whereupon he duly left mine five days after I was born.

Unfortunately, I know very little about my father's personality or foibles as he departed in such haste, never to return to Australia. The pretext for the exit was that his brother was on his deathbed; I must add that my uncle did in fact pass away shortly after Father's return to Malaya. I suspect, however, that Father had probably had his fill of Mum's histrionics and decided to cut his losses. He stayed in Melbourne just long enough to cast his eyes over me and bestow my name. I have speculated over the years about my gender vis-à-vis Father's decision to 'shoot through'. I have always wondered whether my lack of 'dangly bits' underneath the swaddling finally pushed him over the brink – or should I say over the tarmac.

Poor Mum went into a decline which probably began her long dalliance with prescription drugs. Into the breach stepped my nanna: Irene Rosaleen Pascarl. Nanna was a tiny powerhouse of tenacity, keeping us together as best she could and, in hindsight, probably abrogating Mum's maternal instincts and rights in the process.

Nanna's childhood and upbringing is a unique story of Aussie life in the years following Australia's Federation in 1901. She was born one of four children to Phoebe Ann Clarissa and her Irish husband. My great-grandparents met when young Mr Stafford, just off the boat from Galway in Ireland (although a copy of their marriage certificate notes that he was born in

Warnambool – a ruse used to cover up the fact that he had no legal identity papers as a citizen of the colony), obtained work as a 'jobbing carpenter' on Phoebe's parents' estate. At fifteen my future great-grandmama was a rebellious and pampered miss and the only daughter of the house. Descended from English and French aristocracy, which included at least one duke and a Marshal of France, they were a family for whom the usual route to Australia in the early 1800s, via convict deportation, did not apply. Her forbears (in the younger son tradition) had taken up voluntary administrative postings in England's newest colony. The commotion of Phoebe's precociously amorous stirrings at the age of fifteen and subsequent bolt from the parental home in the company of Mr Stafford, a mere employee of unknown origin and age, had enormous repercussions within the family but remained a closely guarded secret for decades.

Marrying her Irish lover minus a parental blessing or dowry significantly affected the success of Phoebe's marital union. When the marriage eventually turned sour, my nanna, Irene, was placed in foster care along with her brothers, Gordon and Lionel, and baby sister, Eileen. Her mother, Phoebe, returned to her wealthy parents' home from where she had eloped. She eventually remarried bigamously and had no contact with her daughter, my nanna, until Nanna was in her early twenties. Phoebe's second husband never knew of her first 'fruitful' marriage or of the children she had given up. It was a scandal efficiently buried under the weight of money and influence.

Attitudes have changed enormously since Nanna and her siblings were placed in foster care before the First World War. Then the young family was split up, with Nanna and Uncle Gordon being placed with one Catholic family and Uncle Lionel being given to another.

Baby Eileen, it was decided by the authorities, would be raised by a well-to-do Anglican couple, which ensured that, with the religious prejudices of the era, she was completely cut off from my nanna until she was in her twenties. The gap left by the social structure of the day was too wide ever to bridge and the two sisters never really became close. What an irony it was that religion was to play such a dramatic role in the upbringing of children whose background was Jewish, French Huguenot, English and Irish.

Nanna's childhood can only be described as brutal. As a tiny girl she became nothing more than an unpaid flunky to her foster family: scrubbing floors at five in the morning, washing, cooking and caring for the menagerie of horses and livestock kept in the garden, as well as attending school and caring for the younger children in the clan. She was often beaten and seldom treated as a member of the family. At fourteen they put her to work in a factory making boxes, with her meagre wages going to her foster mother.

When Nanna was almost twenty, having made the transition from box-maker to milliner, she met my grandfather at a church dance cum football social. Romance blossomed between the pair and a very, very long engagement followed. Relatives tell me that Grandpa was also making sure that he was sowing his wild oats in as many fields as possible. It's amazing how much acreage he covered without my nanna twigging. When they finally married, just before the Second World War, they had been 'stepping out' for over ten years. They had decided that Grandpa would try to build their dream house while Nanna concentrated on building up the contents of her 'hope chest'. I used to tease Nanna that her it must have been warehouse-sized after a decade. Mum was my grand-parents' only child; they separated when she was fifteen and, except for my parents' wedding, never saw each other again.

By all accounts, my mother and grandmother had a volatile and uncomfortable relationship – in these days of psycho-trauma counselling and the understanding society has about the damage that child abuse and the lack of parental nurturing has on a young child, it's patently obvious that Nanna was ill-equipped to 'mother' and nurture when her own demons were still howling.

Nanna had always had 'aspirations' for her only child. My mother was thrust into radio performing at an early age on the *Swallows and the Juniors Show*. She had singing lessons, elocution classes, frothy lace dresses, ringlets and a private, if impoverished, Catholic ladies' college education.

Following Nanna's lead, my mother left school quite young and took up a job as receptionist/typist with a small chemical firm in the city, where she remained until she married Father when she was twenty-one. Although she had been living in a 'hostel for young ladies' in Footscray for a couple of years, she had never cooked a meal or organised a home and was still apparently a virgin when she embarked on married life with Father. He had always been cared for by either his mother or servants until he came to study in Australia and I understand that he was not a virgin.

My parents had never spent any long period of time together before they married, and certainly never shared a bed. Domestic problems loomed from day one of the marriage, but what they couldn't comprehend in each other they simply patched over with party after party after party, making sure they were always either out on the town or surrounded by friends. This plan for domestic bliss developed a major hitch when my father's allowance from his oil-tanker-owning family dried up and they discovered that one and one invariably makes three if contraception isn't used.

So the sartorially elegant, and formerly wealthy, young man had to leave university and get a job in a paint factory to support his pregnant wife and the lifestyle to which they had become accustomed. My parents found the realities of married life and the pressure of cultural differences great fodder for arguments and recriminations. By the time I was born, the days of the marriage were already numbered – numbered at five.

Two

With my father's hasty departure from Australia, my life settled down with Nanna in charge. My first birthday was marked by a beautiful cake iced with a duck made by my godmother, Auntie Connie, who, along with Uncle Kevin, my godfather, was to remain my only link with normality, and a haven of fun, throughout my childhood.

My second birthday was marked by the 'death' of my mother. Mum had been ingesting quantities of prescription drugs since Father departed, but this time one of them didn't agree with her. She had decided, on this particular day, to pay a visit to her former employers and was sitting down sipping coffee and chatting when she collapsed on a desk. Mum's heart had stopped and, as she wasn't breathing, her friends threw her into a car and sped around the corner to St Vincent's Hospital. It took over seven minutes to revive her, during which time she was pronounced clinically dead.

Mum had had an embolism, a condition in which a blood clot and an air bubble travel to the brain (or sometimes a lung), causing death. In my mother's case, her 'death' and subsequent revival left her with a scar on the left temporal lobe of her brain, knocking out her capacity for speech and certain higher intellectual functions, as well as leaving her with epilepsy. As she recovered, she had to learn how to write and use a knife and fork again, and it was found that she had lost certain facets of her memory as well. When Mum returned home, the first of the *grand mal* seizures began. Mum's fits happened without warning. She would collapse on the floor and jerk uncontrollably, her eyes rolling back in their sockets. She would grind her teeth and sometimes bite her tongue in the process. Nanna had to try to learn to deal with Mum's fits as well as care for me.

From the time my mother's epilepsy and mental instability took hold, I spent long stretches of time and the majority of my holidays on my godparents' dairy farm, which nestled in a valley surrounded by the heights of the Gippsland ranges, dotted by lone ghost gum trees, white bark reflecting the harsh light of midday. The nearest neighbours lived miles away, and the mail was delivered once a week, dropped into an old milk can which served as a letterbox, nailed to the front gate, a thirty-minute walk from the house. Days were spent happily milking cows and mucking out dairy sheds, making hay and following Uncle Kevin on my short, chubby legs up steep hills and along well-worn cattle trails in search of lost livestock. Climbing and playing hide and seek in the orchard of plum and apple trees with my adopted dog Tuppence, also a strange hybrid like me – part whippet and part fox terrier – filled my days and insulated me from my mother's drug-induced haze.

As I grew older I began to realise that Mum would probably always be different from the mothers I saw on the television screen. There would be no mother and daughter baking sessions, nor could I expect her to play games with me. I could only daydream about a world where mummies brushed their little girls' hair and read them storybooks at bedtime.

By the time I reached the age of four, Mum existed solely in a shadowy world of constant illness where days, or even weeks, would go by without my catching a glimpse of her. The door to her room with its high chrome handle would remain firmly closed, only opening to admit my nanna as she scurried to and from the sick-room.

My place was with Nanna in our bedroom, next door to my mother's. It was a small, rectangular shoebox of a room with a single window, the only source of natural light, looking out onto a wooden paling fence. My grandmother's bed was directly under the window, which she refused to open between 4 p.m. and 8 a.m. during the winter months as she was convinced that the night air would go straight to my chest and give me a chill. She was a firm believer in the danger of a 'chill'. One of her pet phrases was 'Be careful you don't get a chill', whereupon she would warn me of the dire consequences should I catch one in the kidneys. Much to my horror, I have found myself shaking my head gravely and warning my own children about the dangers of 'the chill', always feeling a secret twinge of guilt at echoing my grandmother's sentiments, even though I don't really believe them.

At the foot of our beds, along the wall, stood two enormous and ornately carved wardrobes in which all of Nanna's treasures were stored. From these stores she could produce the most amazing things to keep me busy on rainy days. Her stockpile of haberdashery items, left over from her days as a shopkeeper, provided endless diversions. There were boxes and trays of buttons fashioned from mother-of-pearl, leather, wood and gold filigree, some intricately carved into the shape of flowers, others just the plain and ordinary type. I would sort them into sizes, shapes and colours for her, sometimes attaching them to pieces of cardboard that she had hoarded with this use in mind; other times I'd thread the buttons up as temporary jewellery for myself. I probably sorted and re-sorted the same buttons scores of times without realising that Nanna had purposefully jumbled them up again to give me something to occupy a boring afternoon.

Then there were the fox furs, leftovers from Nanna's 'chic days' in the thirties and forties, smelling strongly of mothballs and decay. I was allowed to drape them about myself and sashay around the house feeling very glamorous. They had an odd way of fastening – their mouths and heads had been converted with a peg-like arrangement to clip securely onto the tail of the fox, enabling the lady of fashion to fling the whole carcass around her shoulders, leaving the still-attached limbs to dangle around the arms and chest of the wearer. This was, my nanna assured me, the very height of elegance 'in her day'. I often wondered how the lady of fashion avoided dipping the paws of the deceased animal in the soup or leaving a trail of claw marks in the butter as she reached across the buffet table.

When I was small, the same wardrobes that housed Nanna's treasures used to appear to me in the most terrifying nightmares, flapping their doors and bearing down on me ready to swallow me up, their cavernous interiors hungry for little girls (or so I thought at the time). I would wake up shaking with fright and jump into Nan's bed, snuggling up to her for warmth and comfort. I always refused to tell her what had caused my terror – somehow I reasoned that the wardrobes would overhear and get even angrier and more determined to catch me if I told her. Even now, I still have a strong aversion to open wardrobe doors.

Between our bed-heads was Nanna's dressing-table. It was cluttered with an eclectic mix of knick-knacks and religious paraphernalia: holy pictures of the Sacred

Heart and Virgin Mary, rosary beads, china dishes, crystal bowls and lace doilies. From the mirror hung gaudy brocade pincushions holding Nanna's collection of brooches, a unique hanging letter-holder fashioned from an old ice-cream container held together with raffia, and a poignant-looking crucifix.

So this was my world at the age of four. To a child of that age the parameters seemed enormous: our orchard garden at the back of the house was my haven of exploration and adventure and our front garden a buffer zone against 'the world'. And by the age of four I really did need a buffer zone against life's harsh judgements.

I was a child born of the sixties, an era I now understand as an adult to have been a time of enormous social change and upheaval: birth control, the Vietnam War, the Beatles and the rebellion of youth. But for me, all that meant very little. For me the sixties and early seventies did not spread their freewheeling mentality into our ghetto of rigid suburbia – at least, not in any tangible way that affected me or mine.

Three

Until I started school aged four, I had never really played with other children or mingled in large groups. Because of my mother's epilepsy our family remained almost entirely isolated in what would have seemed to an observer to be a very friendly and tightly interwoven community. And I suppose that it was, in its own way, a community of like-minded people who baked cakes and babysat for each other, but for whom the consequences of world events and social change barely registered.

For the ten years we lived in Blyth Street, Murrumbeena, my nanna never addressed the neighbours as anything but Mrs So-and-so or Mr So-and-so, and in return she remained Mrs Pascarl. Our female neighbours seemed to wear their married titles as badges of honour; none of them worked outside the home, and all appeared to be content with their laminex tables, and meat and three veg for dinner. I was never to know if they had individual personalities or opinions on anything of import. They seemed content to fade behind the breadwinners of the family, scrub their children and attend church every Sunday. But somehow they encapsulated a social goal for me, a safety zone which marriage appeared to make obtainable, almost an anonymity behind the title 'Mrs' which made them fit in.

And anonymity and social acceptability were assets I was to prize highly from a very early age. With school came the terrible realisation that I was 'different'. 'Different'. That terrible, ominous pronouncement, which to most children can mean the distinction between receiving that coveted invitation to a birthday party or having someone to play with in the schoolgrounds during lunch, and spending the lunch hour sitting on a bench alone and friendless, yearningly observing the other children playing.

No matter how diligently Nanna wound my hair into torturous bunny rags every night to give me Shirley Temple ringlets or walked me to church every Sunday, I was still different in the eyes of our predominantly white Anglo-Saxon community. Through their own ignorance they equated my presence, my features and my mother's marriage as a personal insult aimed at the narrow confines of their insular existence. In those years of the Vietnam War I bore a close, if somewhat hazy, resemblance to the 'yellow' enemy which they saw killing our Aussie soldiers every night on the six o'clock news. It was so easy for them to assume that my mother was some sort of traitorous radical who had married my father in order to taint the local racial purity. And that I, in turn, would infiltrate their children's games and contaminate them in some way.

How could they have known, or even understood, that the focus of their racial hatred was part of a family whose members had served and fought for Australia in both world wars; that my family had first arrived in Australia in 1801, as part of an exploratory expedition, and had always prided themselves on being at the forefront, helping to build a young nation; or that I was the only one in the family with any Asian blood? But should any of this have made a difference? Did my bloodlines and antecedents matter so much that to defend myself I should have carried around a family tree and worn my Uncle Gordon's Anzac medals to school? Would they have acted as a shield? I think not.

Children invariably carry their parents' ignorance, prejudice and hatred to school with them; to this I can attest from first-hand experience. Teasing happens to most kids at some stage during their school years, perhaps because someone is clumsy or has a tooth missing, perhaps because of his or her name; usually the tormenting runs its course and peters out after a short while. This was not so in my case.

From Prep to Grade Four I was systematically and repeatedly jeered at and bedevilled. As I walked home from school, up the steep hill to our house, most nights I would lead a procession of schoolchildren behind me. To the casual glance we probably appeared to be playing follow the leader, but we weren't; the children of the neighbourhood were following me like an angry mob venting its bloodlust on a symbol, rather than the cause, of its vexation. In summer I could expect to have rotten plums, spitballs and abuse hurled at me. One bright spark composed an interchangeable ditty about me which they chanted in unison over and over again: *Chinese, Japanese, dirty knees, money please* or *Chinese, Japanese, stinky piss, one of this*, along with attendant obscene gestures, shoves, slaps and curses.

In winter it would be the same rhyme but instead of rotten fruit and water, I was on the receiving end of mud, rocks and muck from the wet gutters. Nothing I did dissuaded them from heckling and humiliating me. Certainly Nanna's intervention at the school only worsened the kids' attitude to me: they labelled me a 'dobber' and the teasing increased. At one stage a parent actually wrote to the school requesting that their daughter's desk be moved away from the 'coloured' girl.

So I retreated into a world where I was equal; to places and times I alone controlled. I found refuge in books and dancing.

Four

Books showed me the world. They made life accessible and provided knowledge and goals – as well as a perfectly attainable escape. The written word took me into the realms of fantasy and showed me how to use my imagination and how to temper fiction with facts. They gave me a common ground to communicate with my teachers, but they also set me even further apart from my peers: I was labelled a 'teacher's pet'.

I had no desire to be a 'pet': I just wanted knowledge. Reading has always made me feel like a thirsty sponge; even at eight or nine years old, I felt I was unable to read and absorb all a book had to offer at a fast enough pace. Books dispelled my loneliness; they always have and they always will. Books are precious items to be treasured and preserved. They are a lasting and truer reflection of our sociological history and changing times than any other means of record. Try and explain that to a fellow nine-year-old.

There was also my ultimate escape: dance. I danced whether I was feeling sad or happy; movement gave me the ability to restore myself to myself and shut out the children who called me ugly and foreign. When I danced 'I' was there. As I grew up I found that dancing for myself, by myself, was more gratifying than performing for others. The music would swirl around me and through me, and it didn't matter if the steps were classical ballet, jazz or combinations of Swahili swaying and tap-dancing, all that mattered was the privacy and fulfilment I found in the music and the dance. It is still like that for me now: I hear a piece of music and immediately envision steps for it.

But that self-awareness was many years off from the primary school student. I was happy when I danced; I didn't analyse it much further. Encouraged by Nanna, I learnt any form of dance that was available, memorised routines from old musicals on television and did a mean Charleston under Nanna's tuition.

Dancing was something I didn't discuss with anyone as I was growing up; it was there, I was there, and I suppose the two of us just matched up. I made the prudent decision that I would hide as much as possible about myself from the other children at school – I didn't trust them not to turn my interest in dance into fodder for more tormenting. Besides, I had no particular friend, in fact I had no friends at all. During the entire seven years I attended primary school, I was invited to only five birthday parties. I still remember the children's names: Leonie, Maryanne, Kevin, Cathy and Katrina.

How I longed to be included with the 'golden children', to be part of the in crowd, to excel in sport and to be congratulated for doing something worthwhile for the school – but that was completely unrealistic: bats, balls and me simply didn't click. I was always the last kid to be picked for a team. As everyone else lined up for selection, the team captains haggled among themselves about the amount of handicap points to which they were entitled should they be unfortunate enough to have to include me on their side.

One sunny and mild spring day, I got the chance to actually play during a game of baseball. I can't remember how that occurred; usually everyone on my team was extremely careful that I only neared the playing field during half-time to serve the oranges. The pressure on me to hit the ball with the bat was intense: the air pulsed with trepidation and the disdain of those assembled; from the corner of my eye I noted a nun crossing herself discreetly; a projectile puke flashed through my thoughts as a means of escape.

I was quaking in my shoes and my stomach was in knots as instructions and reminders were shouted to me from the sidelines by my teammates. From what they were yelling at me I gathered that I was expected not only to make contact with the ball by using the bat, which I deemed entirely ridiculous due to its minuscule size, but also to throw the bat and run to the base. In my mind, throwing the bat assumed the importance of a medal at the Olympics. It was obviously taken seriously by my fellow players and so, with this in mind, I stepped up to the pitch. I swung the bat and hit the ball. I really did; never before had I ever achieved this feat. Then I threw the bat as instructed – straight into the crowd of players behind me.

After they had all recovered from their injuries some days later, it was decided by the nuns that it would be best if I stuck to oranges in the future.

Five

Nuns. My school was run by the Presentation Order of Sisters – brides of Christ minus the domestic chores of marriage and the discarded clothes on the floor. Black-mooded and black-dressed, they didn't walk but glided along the school corridors like legless apparitions of piety. With their wimples, veils and rattling rosary beads, they endeavoured to patrol our minds as well as our souls. The nuns were sacrosanct, never wrong, and supposedly embodied all the goodness of the Virgin Mary, as well as all the answers and remedies to combat the temptation into sin of any facile and weak-minded child.

It was an extraordinary day when the Principal, Sister Philomena, announced to us that henceforth we were to address her as Sister Rosemary and that the other nuns were also changing their names. More shocks followed the ensuing Monday when the Sisters appeared wearing legs and what seemed to be visible indications that they possessed hair. But the exposure of the nuns' anatomy did nothing to slow the pace of our indoctrination; classes continued as normal in preparation for our First Confessions and Holy Communion. I spent my nights in great agitation trying to come up with a good crop of sins with which to regale the parish priest on this momentous occasion.

But, try as I might, I couldn't come up with anything juicy, so, like any good Catholic, I decided the most expedient way out of the situation was to tell some whoppers in the confessional and make everyone happy. However, Father Murphy smelt a rat and turned me in to Sister Philomena; I was convinced that she was going to send me to hell immediately with a tattoo on my forehead marking me as one of the great sinners of all time. What I got instead was a 'fire and brimstone' lecture on the evils of the blood that ran in my veins and a sound strapping. Nanna was mortified. She prayed for my redemption. I prayed for my release.

Great rays of sunlight struck me – for a lonely child it was like a divine revelation. For that one glorious day of sin I was considered a normal kid by the others in my class. If sin could bring me social acceptance (sort of like Mary Magdalene, I reasoned), what then was achievable through really calculated wickedness? I embarked on a mission to find out.

First I decided that whispering in church would be a pretty hefty sin. This was made a little difficult, though, as I had no friend to whisper to. Next I tried singing strange sounds during choir practice, but that didn't improve my social life either, so I resolved to ask questions. Such questions as what was a virgin, and how did we know that wine and bread became the body and blood of Christ? Then I launched my pièce de résistance – I argued with the nuns about the posters of aborted babies fixed to the doors of the church. The result was a stormy-faced priest calling on Nanna to discuss my future at the school.

Father Murphy explained that while it was acceptable that I should seek knowledge and strive to improve my mind, theological arguments, debate and rabble-rousing at the age of nine was not the sort of behaviour conducive to my continued enrolment at their school.

The upshot was that I was silenced from conjecturing about the mysteries, and to me what seemed the great hypocrisy, of Catholicism, and found that I was required to pay lip-service to the mysticism and dogma spouted at the school.

My campaign to gain popularity hadn't worked; however, it had served a purpose – my blind acceptance of authority, and of a teacher's word, was dispelled for ever. A questioning stickybeak with a propensity to be a pain in the proverbial had been launched.

Six

Through sheer necessity I was a precocious child. It became obvious over the ensuing years that my grandmother was not equipped to deal with some of the situations arising from my mother's illness. She tended to go into a flapping panic at the wrong moments. During one convulsion, Nanna thrust a spoon into Mum's jaw to prevent her biting her tongue, breaking Mum's front teeth off in the process. I had to learn, and I had to learn quickly, how to give Nanna whatever practical assistance she needed during my mother's epileptic fits: straightening Mum's limbs, putting a wet flannel between her teeth or just rolling and half-dragging her into a safer position on the floor as she convulsed. Then I'd set off for school.

As time progressed, Mum's condition was stabilised to a certain extent by medication, and she decided to resume some social activities. On her friend Lily's suggestion, this led to voluntary hostessing at the 'Catholic' Stella Marus Seaman's Club at Melbourne's dockside. It also led to a succession of 'pen pal' seafarers: Anton, Felix, Carl and Ashley. None of whom I liked, not because of any jealous feeling, but because my mother made it clear that I had to sit on the knee of any of her special friends to whom I was introduced. It made me feel like a sideshow doll on a stick, an amusement for these strange men to whom the smell of the sea still clung and the veneer of control was flimsier than plastic wrap. Mum's choice of activities eventually became a bone of contention between the women of my family; it exacerbated their bickering and arguments, causing quite a few to degenerate into violent tussles, as well as triggering Mum's protracted and frequent absences from Blyth Street.

I remember approaching my tenth birthday with a feeling of expectation. To me, it seemed that reaching double figures signified the beginning of the end of my childhood. A feeling of optimism and change had permeated Australia with the election of the Labor government in December 1972; that feeling spilled over into our house. Nanna told me that because of Gough Whitlam's win and his new position as Prime Minister, we'd be considerably warmer that winter. I hadn't understood what she'd meant, until I was tucked up beneath the new gold wool blankets purchased with the pension bonus she'd received from the new government. With the naivety of youth I continued to hero-worship Whitlam for many years. I may not have agreed with his politics, but for me he hovered as a champion of the ordinary person because of those blankets. It wasn't until years later that I realised he hovered because he was full of hot air.

Nanna was a lot like those blankets; warm, comforting and all-enveloping, she shielded me from the realities of life, scrimping and saving to keep us clothed and fed. But there were some things that even Nan couldn't protect me from, and one of those was Mum.

Children can find familial upheaval difficult to handle at the best of times; what happened in my tenth year was more of an eruption than an upheaval. Suddenly Mum was an in-patient at a psychiatric unit. No warnings, no signs, she was just there. For months. I was told she needed to withdraw from prescription drugs that were damaging her liver. But I knew something else was going on. I had no concept of this 'group therapy' thing Mum kept telling me about, I was just unhappy and confused at having to make conversation once a week with a woman who was now even more of a stranger than she'd been before. It was also patently obvious that she was extremely hostile to Nanna. I feared my visits to her in the hospital. I hated to be confronted by the other patients who shuffled along the corridors, or darted furtive glances at me whilst I sat in the cafeteria with my mother. They seemed like tortured souls, tight-lipped and tragic, their angst apparent even to a child. Somehow this hospital for people with 'problems', or 'mind sickness', as my mother described it, was to its inmates both a refuge and a prison.

Mum checked into the 'unit' with perfectly coiffured hair and high heels; she left resembling a refugee from Woodstock: barefoot, with her long hair flowing down the back of the obligatory kaftan. She'd also decided that it was time to play happy families, but for that a 'daddy' was needed. And she had him in tow.

Roger Barrantes had been in and out of psychiatric hospitals for years. He was in his late thirties, lanky, with a large hooked nose and dirty hair. His eyes had met Mum's across a crowded group-therapy session and that was that. Mum and Roger arrived at our home and promptly announced to Nanna that she was no longer a part of 'our' family and would have to find accommodation of her own within twenty-four hours. Svengali-like, Roger seemed to have mesmerised my mother, and she acquiesced to his every pronouncement. Then they dropped the other bombshell: I was going with them to their new love nest.

Nanna found a tiny flat in Carnegie, a suburb adjoining Murrumbeena, whilst Mum moved us into a small one-bedroom flat with a kitchenette and minuscule bathroom which overlooked the railway line and provided a cacophony of scheduled trains chugging at fairly regular intervals. I was devastated. Suddenly the only constant in my life had been banished. I was instructed that I was forbidden to see or even speak to my grandmother; Mum explained to me that Nanna was to blame for every single thing which had gone wrong in her life.

Apparently Mum viewed this sudden domestic upheaval as a blow struck for independence. My mother was a fool, even I could see that. She was just swapping one form of dependency for another. I barely knew my mother and I certainly had no desire to know Roger any better than I already did. I blamed him and Mum's psychiatrists for her illogical behaviour. She seemed to constantly glance at him for approval and validation, and was incapable of making an independent and resolved decision on anything without Roger's assent.

The first night in the new flat was one of the most bewildering, miserable and frightening of my life. I realised that with Christmas fast approaching it would be impossible to see Nanna. I had never spent Christmas without her and she would be alone. I didn't understand why I was needed to complete this bizarre plan of my mother's, or why Roger was so insistent on taking me with them. Nothing seemed to make sense any more as I lay bunched up in a ball beneath the floral sheet Nanna had sewn a couple of months before. I just sobbed and sobbed and sobbed. I must have been crying so much that I didn't hear Roger open the door and come in.

He sat down on the right side of my bed and placed his hand on my calf. He said that they had agreed that he would be the best one to calm me down and relax me. He said that I was being very uncooperative and making this whole situation more difficult for Mum than it need be. He said that I must do as he told me; that he was here because Mum wanted him here and that I had to cooperate with him. He told me that he was a microbiologist and a physicist and practically a doctor, except that he hadn't done the final exam – and that I must do exactly as I was told.

Roger was to repeat this declaration about his education and qualifications to many other people over the passing years – yet it was all lies. He had never even completed university. The truth, as I know it, is that he once worked as a laboratory cleaner for a large ice-cream company and that that was the only stable job he was ever able to hold down.

As I lay there sobbing, he told me that my Nanna was mentally sick and I would be better off without her. He said he knew what was best for me – and that Mum trusted his judgement and wanted him to put me to sleep. Then he ordered me to lie flat on my back so he could relax me properly. When I didn't do as I was told, he said again that I was not cooperating and that this was my home now and I must obey. When I finally did roll onto my back he ordered me to keep my eyes closed tightly and not allow any part of my body to move whilst he 'massaged' me. And then he began to touch me. He started at my feet, and kept talking as his hands continued up my legs, telling me that now I was being cooperative.

I lay there as stiff as a board with tears coming through under my lashes as he stroked me. My mind raced at a thousand miles a second; my brain spun round and round until I felt dizzy. Inside my head I could hear myself screaming and screaming and screaming at him to stop. Why was he doing this? Why was Mum sitting in the lounge next door and letting him do this? The spinning in my head got worse and I realised I had to get to the bathroom, had to get away. I flung him from me as hard as I could and lunged for the bathroom door, slamming it shut behind me. I heard his voice through the door as I was vomiting into the toilet bowl. He said, 'Don't worry, you'll get used to my relaxation techniques. Your mother has.' When I finally came out of the bathroom, the bedroom was empty. Only my bed appeared wrong and out of place. Even with Teddy, Panda and Lambkin sitting on my pillows, I knew that my bed was no longer the safe haven it had always been. I also understood my new life: I was part of a package deal; my mother had traded me for a mate.

I had been right about my tenth birthday: it was the beginning of the end of my childhood.

Seven

This new domestic arrangement continued for a couple of months: Mum and Roger sharing the fold-out couch in the lounge, with me 'safely' tucked up in bed in the adjoining room. Roger 'visited' me to say goodnight a couple of times each week, always reiterating that I must learn to cooperate with the new family rules. My mother was merely there, existing on the periphery of the whole scenario, nodding and smiling vaguely in my direction. A distracted 'seeker of self', she acknowledged only the pleasantly palatable facets of life around her and abrogated all her responsibilities to Roger, continually referring any questions to him for resolution.

By midsummer their domestic arrangement had obviously lost some of its appeal for Roger, as he abruptly stated that he was heading up to Mooroopna in Northern Victoria to find employment fruit-picking. With Roger gone, my mother completely disintegrated. Her anguish at his departure made her incapable of even the simplest of tasks. She would spend hours on her bed sobbing and wailing, agonising about Roger's safety and mental well-being. Her main concern seemed to be his apparent inability to handle his own finances. She told me that Roger had a history of literally burning money, be it pension cheques or cash. That and his deep-seated hatred of his family and a few minor sexual disorders were only some of the problems my mother told me he had received psychiatric treatment for over the years. I really had no particular desire to be in possession of these snippets of information; they certainly didn't engender a feeling of confidence in my mother's choice of partner. These revelations, I decided, were just too complicated for me to fathom. I was, after all, only ten and a half and I just couldn't understand why, out of all the men on earth, Mum had chosen one who had a penchant for making monetary bonfires.

During this period Mum treated me more like a contemporary girlfriend than her daughter; on bad days I became the mother and she the child. It was probably a good thing that I was on summer holiday, so I could be with her twenty-four hours a day. I did all the banking and all the shopping, whizzing up to the local shopping centre on my two-wheeled scooter, preparing the meals as best I could (grilled lamb chops and mashed potatoes were my speciality) and paying the bills. On a couple of occasions when Mum's hysterics became too much for me to handle on my own, I had to resort to telephoning the doctor to come and calm her down. Other times a slap across the face would suffice.

It was during this phase that my mother revisited her past, when one of her seafaring pen pals resurfaced. An enormous mountain of a man, Ashley, who claimed his background was Burmese, English and some equally exotic ethnicity, spent a couple of nights crammed into my mother's bed, lurching through my bedroom in the middle of the night on his way to the bathroom. It didn't last long, though. The liaison spiralled into a public commotion late one afternoon when the police were summoned to remove the temporary lover as I played downstairs at a neighbour's flat, Mum screaming allegations to all and sundry that Ashley had tried to strangle her. Quietly, I had my doubts – strangulation had been one of my mother's favourite statements about my tiny nanna as well.

Mum clung to her ideal of Roger as her knight in shining armour, anticipating his return with every day on the calendar, waiting eagerly for the postman to bring word from her errant fruit-picker. And then, as suddenly as he had departed, he returned. The pattern of our strange existence immediately fell back into place. In Roger's opinion I was still 'uncooperative' and spoiling the wonderful family life we could all have together. He now openly derided Mum's opinions or wishes and castigated her for her stupidity, which only seemed to make Mum more adamant that the sun shone from his nether regions. She would brook no criticism of Roger from me or her friends, remaining resolute that he was the only person on the earth who had the answer to everything.

Eventually I completed primary school and it was time to embark on my secondary education. Roger ruled that I was not to attend high school with any of my contemporaries, enrolling me instead at a ladies' college some distance from our flat. I lasted all of a term and a half there, refusing to dissect animals in science and playing truant to visit Nanna secretly. I was utterly miserable but unwilling and unable to confide even in her – I couldn't increase her worries any further. She loathed Roger already and was bewildered by Mum's rejection. I simply sought solace in her warm lap as I laid my head there and drew comfort from her hands stroking my forehead. What was happening at home was too alien and shameful to tell Nanna – I instinctively knew I needed to preserve one thread of my childhood intact, one escape hatch to which I could bolt.

I soon realised that if I was ill, Roger would leave me in peace and I also wouldn't have to attend school. I began consuming chocolate laxatives at a great rate.

My mother had no idea why I seemed to develop chronic diarrhoea, nor did she wonder why Roger was so ill-tempered when I was sick. Unfortunately, on one occasion I ate a whole box of laxatives and made myself a little too ill, which led to the discovery of the empty carton amongst my clothes. Roger promptly announced to my mother that I had tried to commit suicide. I wasn't that stupid: if I had wanted to kill myself I certainly wouldn't have chosen diarrhoea as my method of exit.

The upshot of his pronouncement was my mother's conviction that I needed to see a psychiatrist. Mum obtained a referral for us to see a consulting psychiatrist with rooms in the suburbs of South Yarra and Richmond. Before our first session, Roger and my mother sat me down on the small backless stool which sat in front of the dressing-table and lectured me from 8 p.m. to after 3 a.m. on the consequences of my divulging any part of what they were doing to me in the privacy of the tiny flat in which we shared the same oxygen. Prison for lying girls, mental institutions and broad-sweeping adult disbelief at my ingratitude were thrown at me until they considered I was prepared for my first appointment.

Once a week on a semi-regular basis for around eighteen months, I would sit with my mother in the psychiatrist's dimly lit suite of rooms and watch her falling to pieces and in tears, bemoaning the fate that had saddled her with an 'uncooperative' child. Uncooperative was the catchword of our 'family', used to describe my unwillingness to participate in Roger's intimacies but never, ever defined verbally by my mother. The doctor would occasionally throw an obtuse enquiry my way regarding how I felt about my mother's distress at my uncooperative behaviour. More often than not, I would answer monosyllabically. How this doctor expected me to unburden myself in Mum's presence is beyond me. His lack of empathy as a clinician still astounds me – he seemed more intent on castigation than on finding the truth. All the signs and indicators of sexual and emotional abuse were there in my behaviour and in my reticence, but not once did he ever indicate to me that he had a shred of suspicion or concern for the obvious strangeness of my parental relationships. What was even more bizarre was his insistence that I make a financial contribution of one dollar fifty of my pocket money per session so my mother could continue to complain about me. All the while at home the abuse continued. The doctor failed me and he failed his profession. I wonder how many other children he nodded sagely at whilst remaining selectively blind and deaf to their cries for help.

Eight

Inevitably I sought refuge in independence, obtaining a part-time job after school hours as a house model and sales assistant with the Myer department store chain. Outside modelling assignments for jewellery and swimwear also came my way – at thirteen I was reasonably adept at passing myself off as fifteen or sixteen years old. Working was something I did enjoy and the modelling was fun but, unlike my fellow part-timers, the cash I earned wasn't for frittering away on whims or fancies: it was an economic necessity. I became almost financially independent due to my work; at home I was soon expected to buy not only all my own clothing but also my own food, as well as contribute a portion of my pay towards electricity bills and rent. Roger and Mum eventually made demands for monetary compensation for their role as parents too. Over the preceding time, as a retaliation by Roger for my 'uncooperativeness', food, television, telephone privileges and my allowance had been withdrawn. As a rule, the money wasn't handed to them directly – on most occasions I was ordered to pay the nominated sum directly into Roger's telephone betting account at the TAB. The irony of the situation was that whilst too young to legally place a bet on a horse, it was acceptable for me to pay funds into a gambling account.

As a teenager, completing school was never my burning ambition. I was far more interested in obtaining an education. I found the school system stifling, and the naivety of my peers maddening. For me to even attempt an explanation of my home environment to any of them would have been both an impossibility and a folly. How could teenagers from 'normal' families have comprehended the circus I called home? It would have been akin to explaining the dietary requirements and rituals of the inhabitants of the Seventh Interplanetary Sector of the Venus Black Hole Belt: there was simply no point of reference or common ground. I was as alien to them as they were to me. But for all that, I coveted their seemingly safe, structured and simplistic lives. So part way through Year Ten I discarded the textbooks for good. There seemed to be no other way to gain my release from Mum and Roger than to find my feet in the world.

Dancing still remained my intensely private pleasure, one which I guarded closely from my mother because of her attitude to Western influences on me. For all of my life, Mum was determined to push me towards my Asian roots. Never content to let me grow up as me, she would take every opportunity to tell me that I didn't fit in to Australian society, that I failed to blend visually, and that she was sure I would be completely at home mixing with overseas students from Asia. Not once did she ever discuss, acknowledge or encourage my love of ballet. She even actively vetoed my activities, forbidding me to socialise with other Aussie teenagers in favour of various Asia–Australia family associations. The only dance classes she encouraged me to attend regularly, making a point of becoming involved by being nominated for the parents' board, were the classical Balinese and Javanese classes run in conjunction with the Australian Indonesian Association. This involvement with Indonesians gave my mother the chance to do what she really excelled at: reinventing my racial and family heritage. Mum had a disconcerting habit of trying to make me fit in with whatever Asian group of people was present in the room at the time. I would suddenly find that, according to Mum, I was half Indonesian, Chinese, Thai or Malaysian, depending on who was there. Conveniently she would concoct fictitious relatives for me in Sumatra, Peking or anywhere else; it was really quite exhausting being internationally interracial.

Like most young girls growing up, I idolised particular movie actresses and hoped I would resemble them as an adult. Audrey Hepburn, Vivien Leigh and Katharine Hepburn were my special favourites. Beautiful, elegant and vivacious, they also had a core of intelligence and passion. What a blow it was when I finally had to face the fact that I would never look like my idols. It also came as a shock. I felt Australian, I certainly thought Australian, I was Australian, but on the outside I would always be packaged differently. That's a difficult thing for a teenager to come to terms with. Adolescence is hard enough, but a variance on the stock physical expectations of society can be excruciating. And without parents to encourage me just to be me, my self-esteem and security plummeted further.

I met my father in 1977. It would be our first and only meeting. Stricken with throat and nose cancer, he was dying. I fantasised for days that he would rescue me from Roger and Mum, whisk me into his arms and make me belong. His faceless figure loomed large in my dreams, offering me a key to myself, promising a piece of my identity forbidden for so long by Mum. I felt as though my chest were wide open, ready to receive the part of myself that had been missing forever. I was bursting with questions for him; finally I hoped to be able to understand why I was who I was, and why I was there. I yearned for him to tell me that he had wanted me to be born. He never did.

I arrived in Singapore with Mum in tow. She had refused me permission to travel with a cousin, insisting that it wasn't appropriate for me to meet my father alone. (The price I paid for that trip was very high for a fourteen year old – the night before our departure, Roger and Mum had so severely abused me, I found myself in hospital having a general anaesthetic to remove a foreign object they had inserted into my resistant body as both of them held me down. Roger sang a strange ditty as it happended; Mum warned me that if I told my doctor, I would never meet my father.) It was the day Elvis Presley died.

Walking across the tarmac in the sweltering Singaporean heat made me wonder how anyone lived there. The humidity was oppressive and I found myself surreptitiously gasping for air as we entered the terminal. My relatives collected us from the airport and deposited Mum and me at my uncle's home, where my father was waiting.

Father stood up as I entered the room. In his arms he held two enormous stuffed pandas, obviously meant for me. As I began to make my way across the room towards him, Mum thrust herself in front of me and strode up to Father, voicing a strident 'hello'. I think he was taken aback to see her there. What's more, she had certainly changed from the willowy young woman she'd been years before. She now weighed in excess of fourteen stone and had a faded and bitter face. When he turned to me, my heart stopped. I was poised for a declaration of love from him, expectantly waiting for some sort of instant and intimate bond to become evident, but there was none. Instead it was apparent that he had imagined

I would be a tiny child, hence the soft toys, but much to his dismay I was five foot tall and well into puberty. Our first words were awkward and stilted – we were, after all, total strangers.

The whole visit was a fiasco, a nightmarish opportunity for my mother to flex her manipulative skills. Mum never willingly left me alone with Father. She was adamant in her refusal to allow me just to sit next to him as he drove us on various shopping expeditions, instead claiming that right as her own, prattling along inanely, seemingly without a care in the world, as though Father were a tourist guide. Father indicated many times that he wished to have some time alone with me but Mum made that impossible. I felt as though I were trapped in a surrealistic portrayal of the shattered family, bound by a mother whose mouth threatened to envelop us all.

Father tried to develop some common ground between us through shopping, buying me mountains of clothes, jewellery and treasures for my bedroom at home. We were both delighted to find that we genuinely liked the same foods and had the same shaped feet (duck-like). He also organised the design and making of my first formal gown, asking that I put it away and remember him when I was finally old enough to wear it, stipulating that when I eventually did, I must wear white gardenias in my hair. He said that their perfume would be as intoxicating as the beauty he knew would come my way. Father managed to tell me this in a rare snatched moment when my mother wasn't present. It will always remain my most treasured memory of him. It came from his heart, stranger to stranger, but father and daughter for just the briefest of heartbeats.

And then he was gone from my life again. No time for me to ask all those questions I had formulated and kept locked up inside me. My mother terminated our presence in Singapore with such paranoid abruptness that I was left wondering if I had ever been there at all. Her reasons? She was convinced Father was about to sell me into the 'white slave trade', as she put it, and because Roger wanted us home immediately. She packed our bags and fled secretly, insisting I wear a disguise in the taxi in case Father was having us followed. On arrival at the airport, she telephoned my father's family to let them know of our departure. There was no time left for farewells and I wasn't able to say goodbye to my father.

I never saw him again. Six months after my departure from Singapore I received a telephone call informing me that he was dead. He had been a virtual stranger but, with the news that he was gone, I felt as if a tiny bud of promise deep inside me had withered away forever.

Nine

In the months after Father's death I drifted from one thing to another, barely studying, and socialising more and more with older people. I became enmeshed with a group of university students who treated me like their mascot, although they did assume I was older than my fifteen years. I was, on reflection, desperately searching for a place to fit in, trying to find an identity for myself or the picture of myself which I wished to show to the world. I thought being older would facilitate that. My mother seemed to have few qualms about my social activities – in fact, if anything, she actively encouraged me to begin dating Asian students in their twenties, telling me that my true niche was with them and not with 'pure Australians'. Fortunately none of them took advantage of my pseudo-maturity and I managed to remain, by choice, firmly virginal in most areas.

The exception to the 'Asian mandate' was Peter Wallace, a medical student, who was to become my first real male friend, and who remains one of my very close and loyal friends. Throughout the years Peter has been a shoulder to cry on and sometimes my conscience when he thought I needed one. Peter was virtually the only friend I trusted enough to bring home; things had degenerated so much over the preceding years it would have been difficult to mask the truth of the situation there. Peter never questioned me about Roger and Mum's peculiarities, even making no comment about the toilet having no door. Roger had taken the door off its hinges soon after we moved into the house, on the pretence that the dog needed a place to sleep. All it did in practice was make it easier for him to watch me during the moments when we all require privacy. It was a situation in which I felt humiliated and more violated than ever.

By this stage of my life, dancing was probably the only thing keeping me sane. I adopted a motto, 'When in doubt, dance', and dance I did, any type of dance. As long as I was moving, I could obliterate everything from my mind. I took classes in Greek, Croatian, Javanese, tap, jazz, flamenco, Balinese, Chinese, Malay, contemporary and classical dance. But it was with ballet that I felt my soul was clean. The purity and the discipline was comforting and the music the stuff of pure fantasy and enchantment. I would use any pretence to get away from home to attend classes. Mum would reiterate that ballet was not for me – that I didn't have the right shape and that I was too Asian in appearance to look right on stage. 'Stick to something where you fit in,' she said, 'stick to Balinese.' Attending class became a clandestine operation and something which, yet again, I didn't discuss for fear of either ridicule or curtailment.

To supplement my income further I obtained work promoting and doing publicity for various airlines and trade fairs, as well as marketing imported costume jewellery for a Singaporean company. It was convenient to take advantage of my Asian side to gain a foothold in promotions and it worked to my advantage when I later decided to get a full-time job.

I started my stint with the Melbourne office of Malaysian Airlines in 1979, having been offered the position by the station manager. I was employed as their receptionist, as well as being in charge of tourism information and public relations for travel fairs. (To this day I still bless Nanna for organising and financing my attendance at summer secretarial school where I learned to touch-type – that skill has stood me in good stead over many years and allowed me to feed my family.) When the time came for me to fill out the staff information file, I gave my birth date as 1961, making me two years older than I actually was. Ironically that was the only time anyone questioned my age – they remarked that they thought I was much older than my fabricated years!

On my sixteenth birthday I was legally old enough to move out of home, which I did with great alacrity and satisfaction, finding sanctuary with three friends in their house in staid Armadale. I will always be very grateful to them for taking me in with no questions and a great deal of tolerance.

A week or so earlier, things had come to crisis point with Roger. He had become more invasive and insistent with his demands on me, entering my bedroom in the middle of the night when Mum was asleep. Clad only in singlet and Y-fronts, he attempted to begin his old trick of wanting to help me 'relax'. He revolted me. I had had enough. 'No more!' and 'Not again!' filled my head with a deafening roar, blocking out his stern words and threats. This time something snapped inside my brain. I struggled with him, fighting to pull myself upright on the bed. It was as though I were watching myself from across the room as I instinctively clasped my fists together like a club and brought them crashing down on his skull with as much force as I could muster, screaming at him to get out. It felt so good to finally hit back, and I felt so satisfied as I heard him groan and leave my room for the last time. I knew then that Roger would never dare touch me again. It was over.

Ten

Flowers, flowers and more flowers. Bahrin had arrived in my life. One day I had a steady if monotonous job, a complacent boyfriend and the centre of my secret life – my dancing. The next I was being wooed under seige by a master of the art who was extremely skilled and equipped with the determination and single-mindedness of an Olympic long-distance runner. Bahrin (or his alias Shah Ahmad, his name during his student days in Melbourne) had decided that he must acquire me by hook or by crook. Apparently I had piqued his curiosity, as well as his interest, when he had seen me perform during one of the Australian Broadcasting Commission's promenade concerts at the National Gallery. He was able to ascertain that we had mutual acquaintances, whom he questioned casually for details about me. Armed with information about my workplace, he began his campaign.

His first strategy was launched in the form of a seemingly chance meeting after work in the vicinity of my office. Bahrin dropped the names of some people I knew and mentioned that he had seen me dance, and that he had met me briefly a couple of years earlier. He told me that he was studying architecture at Melbourne University and was in his fourth year. Small talk and names formally exchanged, we both proceeded to go our separate ways. Although feeling mildly flattered, I gave the encounter very little thought and hurried on to my dance class. I had no inkling that this was only the beginning, as far as Bahrin was concerned.

The next day at noon, there stood Bahrin beside my desk, his arms laden with pink carnations. He proposed that we lunch together. I was very surprised to see him. He was better looking than I had remembered, slim, swarthy-skinned and quite tall, with terribly thick black hair and enormous, if slightly prominent, black eyes that waited expectantly for my reply. I politely declined his invitation. He took my refusal nonchalantly. Handing me the flowers, he said, 'That's all right, I'll just keep coming back until you say yes.' He turned quickly on his heel and departed, leaving me totally bewildered.

I soon discovered that he wasn't joking. For most of September 1980, Bahrin would turn up at my office as regularly as clockwork, armed with carnations and an invitation to lunch – and I would just as regularly decline. But my resolve was weakening. At seventeen, this sort of sustained attention was dazzling. I remember feeling as though I were the most captivating girl in the world. And so I finally capitulated and allowed him to take me to lunch.

Bahrin chose the Hopetoun Tea Rooms in the Block Arcade as the venue for our first date. The 'Block', a true Melbourne institution with its Victorian grandeur, intricate mosaic floors, frescoed vaulted ceilings and chiming clock, was a place I was quite familiar with – I had visited the arcade many times with Nanna and knew its history as the place to promenade during the roaring twenties. As we discussed inconsequential things over our meal of gourmet sandwiches, it became apparent and mildly flattering, if a little surprising, that Bahrin knew quite a lot about me already, having diligently made his investigations through my friends.

He also knew that I had very few family ties and that I was sharing a house in Armadale, an inner Melbourne suburb not unlike Notting Hill. He told me that he liked me very much, that I was beautiful and he would like to take me to dinner and to a disco. I explained that I was already dating someone and that I wouldn't go out to dinner with him. Bahrin let that subject drop and instead began to tell me a little about himself.

He was twenty-six, an only child, and had been raised by his maternal grandfather in Terengganu, Malaysia. Because of our respective grandparents' influence on our lives, he was eager to draw parallels between us and talked at length about his grandfather's wisdom. He went on to add that he had studied at the elite Geelong Grammar – the school also attended by Prince Charles – before beginning Architecture at Melbourne University. And all the while I sat there listening to him speak, mesmerised by his dark eyes looking into mine and the low tones and gentleness of his voice. Occasionally I added a comment, but I was quite content simply to sit watching his slender fingers play unconsciously with the edge of the lace tablecloth. After we parted under the clock at the General Post Office I felt almost euphoric, and that strange feeling of well-being stayed with me for the remainder of the day. I wondered what would happen next.

It didn't take long for my musings to be satisfied. I rapidly learned that Bahrin did nothing by halves.

The next lunchtime that Bahrin (or Shah, as I knew him then) appeared at my office, he took it for granted that I would be joining him, and he was right. It was as if being with him were the natural progression of my life. We continued to meet every day for another month at the Hopetoun Tea Rooms, where we would chat and discuss superficial things. He showed a polite interest in my dancing through no more than courtesy, I think, but just enough to continue to hold my attention. During our lunchtime rendezvous he would talk earnestly about his love of architecture and the types of projects he hoped to build one day – all the while looking unblinkingly into my eyes in a way that gave me the sensation that we were completely alone and not in the middle of a crowded café. Then one day he dropped his bombshell. He told me that he was divorced. Bahrin explained in a perfectly plausible and believable manner that he had been manipulated into marriage by a girl named Fauziah, the adopted daughter of Tun Faud Stephens, the late Chief Minister of Sabah (Borneo) in Malaysia, that the marriage had lasted only one year and that during that time she had been unfaithful to him, finally leaving him for her lover – an Australian gardener. Bahrin said he felt completely humiliated and disillusioned, as he had married in defiance of his family's wishes and had been proven very wrong, very publicly.

I should have realised that at seventeen years old this scenario was well beyond my comprehension. I should have stood up and walked out of his life then, when I still had the chance, or at the very least I should have wondered why his wife had felt the need to have an affair so soon after marriage. But I didn't. Instead I looked into his pleading eyes and felt indignant and affronted for him. A tiny voice in my head vowed never to hurt or humiliate him like Fauziah had; I knew what it was like to feel deserted. Reading me like a twenty-foot billboard, he pushed home his advantage, persuading me to rescind my edict against evening dates. My fate was sealed from the moment I agreed.

He continued to be totally charming, courting me in a well-bred, British sort of way, with a wonderful intensity but the utmost consideration for my feelings and my needs, and absolutely no indication at all that there was any kind of sexual desire within him. We ate in intimate restaurants, took walks in the Botanic Gardens, went to the latest movies and the trendiest discos and shopped together – shopping for designer clothes was one of his passions. In fact, whilst he was romantic in the extreme, Bahrin seemed almost asexual in the rest of his behaviour. It was a trait which at that time I found comforting and non-threatening, for although I wasn't an innocent by this stage, I had in the past always tried with difficulty to control the physicality of my sexual relationships with other boyfriends. Bahrin's gentlemanly behaviour and 'non-demands' came as a relief and gave me a conviction that this relationship could become serious.

Around the same time, a career in dance became more than just a daydream for me: it crystallised into a glimpse of a possibility. Apparently, at one of the performances at the National Gallery I had been marked down as a candidate for an audition with a major dance company. This was the culmination of an unspoken aspiration. My secret life was merging with my everyday life; it promised the chance of fulfilling everything I had ever dreamed of.

I tentatively mentioned my news in passing to Bahrin. It seemed barely to register with him, so I decided not to make very much of it at all. It was becoming obvious that he viewed my passion for dance as as mere whimsy, rather quaint and pretty as a hobby but not anything important. However, I began to train in earnest, picking up extra classes whenever I could, dieting rigorously and worrying a lot.

Eleven

It was a soft spring evening, well before dusk, as I hurried from the office with my rehearsal bag over my shoulder. I was heading directly to an extra class in pas de deux, a discipline in which I had decided I needed further work if I really wanted this audition opportunity; Bahrin was to pick me up afterwards so we could go out to dinner. The studio was quite crowded and through the windows I could see people milling about in the forecourt outside, occasionally trying to peer in through the windows to catch a glimpse of us warming up at the barre. With the music coming from the cassette player standing on top of the piano, the teacher (not our regular instructor, but a 'fill-in') began to run through the combinations for our centre work. My usual partner was waiting to pair off with me. We were working on a series of lifts that we had practised in the preceding sessions. The first required my partner to lift me very high above his head and then bring me down in time to the music into a 'swan dive' pose. With a quick toss, I was meant to finish with my legs up high in the air, my hands and face almost touching the ground, and supported by my partner.

We worked our way through the first seven bars of the music. I was above his head and then he brought me down with the toss, but instead of grabbing my inner thigh and anchoring me there securely he miscalculated, grabbing my crotch and getting such a shock in the process that I found myself dropped like a hot potato – straight onto my right knee. I was trying not to cry although the pain was terrible, but I was still able to flex my leg and walk so I assumed it wasn't anything major. I thought I'd just slipped my kneecap and it would pop back in again. With regard to injuries, in those days dancers in Australia were very careless. It was, and still is, common to continue to perform with stress fractures and injured muscles. I viewed the accident as just one of those things. I didn't blame my partner, it was just bad luck.

Bahrin appeared quite perplexed when he arrived to fetch me and saw that I was limping and that my knee was starting to swell. It was obvious that a night on the town was out of the question. Instead of going to a restaurant he took me back to his house in Carlton, a lovely double-storey terrace house painted cream with terracotta trimmings and a wrought-iron picket fence. Amidst ice packs for my knee and Randy Crawford background music, we ate Chinese takeaway food from cartons by mellow lamplight and chatted about inconsequential things. And then it happened. Bahrin leaned over and kissed me deeply for the first time. Up until that moment his kisses had been almost perfunctory and certainly not unrestrained, but something had changed that night and we soon found ourselves upstairs in his bedroom.

Our first time was pleasant but not particularly passionate, which I related more to my injured knee than any expectations on my part. In any case, I was more interested in the feelings of intimacy and affection that sex can bring than in unbridled sexual romping. I didn't go home that night; he was insistent that I should not leave.

In the morning, when I woke, my knee had swollen up like a huge balloon, and I hobbled into the office limping severely. Warning bells started to go off in my head as I realised that this knee injury might be more serious than I had thought. After X-rays and consultations with a doctor later that afternoon, my worst fears were confirmed – I had fractured my right kneecap. I knew immediately that any potential career as a dancer I might have had twenty-four hours earlier was gone.

I didn't have the luxury of time – auditions like this simply wouldn't wait, and I suspected that interest in me would dissolve immediately with the knowledge that I had a gammy knee. Recuperation from this sort of damage was painfully long and complicated and there was no guarantee of a return to full mobility and strength.

In the days that followed, it was easy to resign myself to my shattered dreams. If anything good had come from growing up the way I did, it was that I had learned to take nothing for granted and to just 'go with the flow'. My deep depression was somewhat tempered by the distraction of a new, and very romantic, romance. Bahrin was attentive and tender during this period, and I was beginning to believe that I was in love with him. With our affair blossoming, we decided – or rather Bahrin did – that I should take up residence with him in Carlton. The idea of 'playing house' appealed to me at the time so, with the callousness of youth, I packed my bags and moved out of my shared house in Armadale, with very little explanation proffered to my housemates.

I had little or no comprehension of what a domestic, conjugal relationship should be like; my only sources of reference were sketchy at best. *The Brady Bunch*, *Bewitched*, *My Three Sons* and *The Sullivans*, I am embarrassed to say, gave me the fictional, and not terribly factual, examples of live-in domesticity to which I aspired. In all of these television families the man of the house was the sun around whom all others revolved – not a very feminist attitude for the 1980s, I do admit, but the best I had to go on. In any case, they proved to be the ideal role models for me. As far as Bahrin was concerned, any other type of behaviour would have been an aberration. So I settled down to rival Doris Day in the 'make your man happy' stakes.

It was so extraordinarily simple to throw myself headlong into the relationship with Bahrin. When all my visions of dancing had melted away, replaced by uncertainty and lack of direction, it was as if he were the only life-preserver in reach. I looked at Bahrin and saw only what I wanted to see. You see, I fooled myself and I fooled Bahrin, but mainly I fooled myself into believing I was in love, when I had no concept of what love was.

Twelve

In love with the idea of being in love. Doesn't that conjure up a painful picture: a generalised thumbnail sketch of teenage love and many early relationships? I know it's the description which best fits my entanglement with Bahrin in the closing months of 1980. Nothing in my life seemed to matter as much as he did; tomorrow and the future were just like 'once upon a time' – words that existed in the vocabulary but I couldn't define. Reality was then and there, not somewhere down the track.

Bahrin was scheduled to return home to Malaysia, on his annual summer break, sometime in mid-November, a few weeks after I had moved in with him. We decided that I should take my Christmas holidays over there too, so we could have a wonderful vacation together and he could show me 'his' Malaysia. It didn't occur to me that that was a term to be taken literally.

There was one flaw with the plan, however; although working for the airlines entitled me to free overseas air travel, I didn't possess a valid passport. Being under-age meant that to obtain a passport I needed my mother's signature on the application form – a problem in itself. Mum refused point-blank to sign, citing the old 'white slave trade' line to make her point. She was, at the time, already furious with me. I had recently stopped paying a weekly 'storage' fee to her for my old toys and books, left behind at her house when I made my bid for freedom months earlier. I wanted to collect my possessions and move them into my new home, but she and Roger wanted payment for them before they would allow me to do so. Eventually I had to retain a lawyer to act as an intermediary between my mother and me. It had become impossible to conduct a lucid and civilised conversation with her about anything, and only the threat of legal action and the promise of financial compensation convinced her to sign my passport application. These humiliating and demeaning machinations within my family made me fantasise more and more about what I labelled a 'normal' home life. In the back of my mind it became a major goal in life: I longed to find a niche of respectability and security that didn't have a cash price, and I suppose I began to identify Bahrin as the key to that desire.

Bahrin seemed to take all my familial wrangling in his stride; he didn't blink an eyelid, he just told me it was imperative that I get a passport at all costs so we could be together. When I once tentatively tried to explain my mother's behaviour to him, he said that he had no interest in my former home life and that we would make our own lives.

What an odd couple we made, even early on. Both from dysfunctional families, but neither of us willing to admit or even recognise that we lacked the basic relationship skills to build from. Frankness seldom figured in our conversations; polite and genteel language was our unspoken rule. I never even told Bahrin about Roger's abuse – I felt far too ashamed and contaminated to even think about what had happened when I was growing up, let alone verbalise it to anyone. I simply compartmentalised all the hurt and revulsion into a corner of myself and tried to forget and move on.

In those first weeks of living together, Bahrin occasionally gave me glimpses of his own vulnerability, when, with very little warning, he would turn the conversation around to describe the kind of parenting he had experienced when growing up. It wasn't ever a case of him criticising his mother, father or grandfather, just the things he said about the way he wanted to have his own family one day, outlining the sort of mother he wanted for his children, and the personal parental care that he felt was so important for a child. He wanted the closeness of an Aussie clan; he wanted the 'ideal' family straight off the cinema screen. It's frightening that I didn't see anything wrong with Bahrin wanting a fantasy life based on fictional characters.

I was passionate myself about the way I wanted to bring up any children I might have. A husband and family were the most important commitments I could envisage myself ever making. When Bahrin questioned me nonchalantly about my thoughts on babies and marriage, I answered quite truthfully, if a bit too idealistically, that I believed marriage was for ever and that I would never relinquish my children to someone else to care for. Bahrin fairly bridled with pleasure at my answer – apparently I had passed some sort of test.

One afternoon – it happened to be the day of the Melbourne Cup, when all Australia takes a holiday and the nation pauses for a horse race – we'd gone for a drive in the rain. Pulling over to the side of the road and stopping the car by the edge of a park, Bahrin suddenly started to speak without pause. He began to tell me, in a very matter-of-fact voice, about his childhood. As he went on to describe the events soon after his birth, he became increasingly intense. He explained that he was the first-born grandson in his family, the product of an arranged marriage, with strong royal bloodlines on both sides stretching back five or six generations. His mother, Tengku Zaleha, a princess of Terengganu and one of the favourite daughters of the Sultan, was wed at the age of fifteen to a complete stranger, his father, Raja Ahmad. He was a minor prince from the House of Perak, a military college graduate and man about town, aged twenty-three. (My mother-in-law later confided in me that she was absolutely terrified on her wedding night, was completely ignorant about sex and, even years afterwards, could never bring herself to do more than sneak a terrified peek at her husband's body, a situation which existed right up until their divorce.) Bahrin's birth had been eagerly awaited by the Sultan, his grandfather, who had once served as King of Malaysia. Since the country obtained independence from Great Britain in the 1950s, Malaysia's kings have been elected by the rulers from amongst themselves to serve on a five-year rotational basis.

Preparations had been made for his mother's one hundred days of 'lying in' at the old palace, Istana Maziah, by the mouth of the Terengganu River, and a British doctor was specially retained to be in charge of the delivery. The long-awaited grandson made his appearance just as the sun rose to its zenith and the Muslim call to prayer reverberated across the country. It was a Friday, the holiest day of the Islamic week, and a day seen as fortuitous for the birth of a child. All this Bahrin related to me in serious tones.

As Bahrin described the circumstances of his birth to me, sitting in his tiny Honda Civic with the rain running down the windows, the implications of what he was telling me gradually began to sink in. He wasn't, as I had been led to believe, just the plain old overseas student called Shah Ahmad. He was not perhaps quite as ordinary, or at least his family weren't quite as ordinary, as I had expected. It also explained the large photograph of the elderly gentleman and lady ensconced on thrones which I had come across when I was cleaning up the mantlepiece in his study. They were his grandparents.

He went on to say how his grandfather had decided from the moment of his birth that he wanted to raise the newborn in the confines of his establishment, independently of his parents. He told me how his mother had never physically cared for him, breastfed him nor changed a nappy; all this was taken care of by his nanny, Zainab, in the nursery wing of the Sultan's palace. Here, in later years, he was joined by his younger boy cousins, Zainol and Ihsan, with much the same sort of parental arrangements as his own: parents living in a separate house within the palace compound, with decision-making and parental care relinquished to the ruler. None of the new parents involved seemed to have raised any objections to this arrangement; no one ever questioned his grandfather. Bahrin painted a picture of his childhood as both lonely and indulged, with isolated incidents of rebellion swiftly quashed by either his nanny or the Sultan himself.

As Bahrin continued with his outline of his family's dynamics, I scoured my memory for anything I knew about the Malaysian royal family but couldn't come up with anything. I knew that in India, royal princes were a dime a dozen and that the label 'royalty' was virtually meaningless in this day and age, not necessarily indicating a style of living or wealth; but where Malaysia was concerned I was ignorant. Having a passion for European history, I really equated what I considered 'true' royalty with that continent: diplomacy, treaties, science, architecture, art, ballet, culture, law, legends, mythology, great battles, the Renaissance and international intrigue all belonged and warranted identification with Europe, not with Asia. I just couldn't get these revelations into perspective sitting in a damp car – did this change things between us? Was he hinting I should curtsey? I simply wasn't able to fathom the meaning of what he had told me; I needed time to work it out. Besides, what had become glaringly obvious during this conversation was that Bahrin had had a really sad and isolated childhood, lacking the cuddles and type of love I'd been lucky enough to receive from my nanna. In my book, that was a more significant and immediate problem than the other new information I had been given.

Luckily, a few days later, before I was called upon for some sort of reaction, my apparently royal suitor departed for his break in Malaysia without the subject being raised again.

Thirteen

Free. Or so I thought as the aircraft took off from Melbourne Airport on the first leg of my journey to Malaysia. As I peered down at the receding and familiar skyline of the city, my thoughts raced ahead to the exotic destination printed on my ticket.

It was Christmas Eve and I was jammed into an Alitalia jumbo jet along with three hundred other passengers, most of whom were bound for Rome and family. Not me, though; I knew my itinerary by heart. I was only travelling as far as Singapore, where I was scheduled to connect with a flight on to Kuala Lumpur, the capital of Malaysia. This leg of the journey will always remain in my memory as completely unique due to the odd behaviour of the Italian cabin crew. Meals were virtually flung at the poor passengers in double-quick time almost immediately after take-off, and the trays collected just as speedily. The cabin lights were switched off and the crew disappeared. No matter how many people rang for assistance, no one materialised to answer their calls. After about two hours, most of my fellow travellers gave up trying to get the flight attendants' attention and went to sleep. However, I was still thirsty and moderately curious. I wondered where all the staff had gone and decided to investigate. Wandering up the aisle, past the sleeping figures in their seats, I arrived at the curtained-off first-class section of the aircraft from where sounds of music and revelry seemed to be emanating. Sneaking a look between the curtains, I saw all of the crew in the middle of a raging party. A beaming Latin steward caught sight of me and yanked me through the opening and into the midst of the proceedings. Paolo, I read from his name tag, demanded to know where I was going and what I did for a living. Learning that I also worked for an airline, he and his friends insisted I stay up front and join the Christmas party in progress. I had a wonderful time, singing carols in Italian and drinking champagne all the way to Singapore. The other poor passengers had no idea what a great bash they'd missed.

I vaguely remember floating across the tarmac at Changi Airport, giggling tipsily and singing 'Jingle Bells' as I bade goodbye to my new friends, and only just making my connecting flight to Kuala Lumpur.

By touchdown in Malaysia, I was very sober and very nervous. What if Bahrin had changed his mind and wasn't there to meet me? What if this trip was all a big mistake? I should have gone to France and Scotland, as I had planned originally. What if? What if? And then it was too late for what ifs. Before I had more time to think, I was cleared through customs and immigration with a wave and, after crossing the open-air arrivals hall, I saw Bahrin and launched myself into his arms. I hardly noticed that his arms didn't encircle me in return, but I did see his pleased smile and my anxiety disappeared. It was 1 a.m. on Christmas morning in a strange country. Everyone was speaking in an indecipherable tongue and, even at that time of night, it was stinking hot and humid. But I was welcome and expected – nothing else really mattered.

As we drove to his father's house, through the muggy and pungent night air, one of the first things Bahrin said to me was that I must never touch him in public again, at least not whilst we were in Malaysia. He gently, but firmly, told me that my behaviour had been offensive by Muslim standards and I must be careful not to repeat my mistake. I silently resolved not to mention my in-flight Christmas celebration or my new friends. I didn't know it but my indoctrination had subtly begun.

The way to Bahrin's father's house took us via the city of Kuala Lumpur, which appeared to be a mixture of shanties and high-rise modern buildings, sometimes side by side. The floodlit colonial grandeur of another era – whitewashed facades, balustrades and minarets, echoes of the days of the 'Raj' – vied for space along the crowded motorways, overshadowed by the pristine and sterile Hiltons and Holiday Inns indicative of a thriving tourist trade. The street lighting became sketchier the further we progressed into the suburbs through the maze of streets, and it was difficult to make out anything in great detail. Occasionally the tantalising aroma of food from a street vendor wafted through the car window, only to be replaced seconds later by the stench from an open drain or a pile of rotting garbage beside the road. Then, without warning, the highway started to climb and it began to feel as if we were entering a jungle. Lush vegetation and overhanging vines made a canopy over the route of the car, blocking out all but the vaguest glimpses of the moon.

As we continued along the narrow winding track, Bahrin began, rather dispassionately, to detail his father's domestic arrangements. His father, Raja Ahmad, was a 'bachelor' residing with his Chinese mistress, Lina, a nurse. This was an ideal arrangement which served its function well, he assured me. Lina did not attend social occasions with her lover, nor did she expect to, and she was not acknowledged formally by any of the members of his family; however, it meant his father had someone to clean the house and do the washing and Lina, in turn, had somewhere cheap to live in a better part of town. I refrained from asking about mutual respect and love; this was Bahrin's turf, and the customs, I supposed, were different. I did understand that, but I would learn to bite my tongue very often from that night.

With this information under my belt, we came to an abrupt halt at our destination on Federal Hill. Raja Ahmad's home had a tired and slightly run-down air to it. The two-storey residence provided by the government was set back into the hill and seemed to be on the verge of reclamation by the surrounding vegetation. As I made a scanty inspection in the glare of headlights, whilst Bahrin fumbled with padlocks and keys, I couldn't help wondering if the bars and grilles on the windows and doors were to keep intruders out or people in.

Inside, the house seemed damp, mouldy and unused. Bahrin snapped on the lights in the rooms as we walked through. We could have been in the home of a big game hunter; stuffed eagles adorned the sideboards and tiger pelts, heads still attached, carpeted the floor. A cobra, rearing and poised to strike, gave testimony to the skill of the local taxidermist and the bad taste of the owner. Bahrin barely had time to show me my room and explain that we could not share a bed overtly before the crunch of gravel outside signalled his father's homecoming.

Raja Ahmad immediately struck me as jovial and very much the worse for wear as he listed into the house supported by his girlfriend, Lina. In his late forties, he had the bearing of a retired military man and the paunch of a dedicated beer drinker. A thick mop of black curly hair surmounted his bearded face and barely contrasted with his deeply tanned skin, acquired after hours on

the golf course. Bahrin's father welcomed me heartily
in his clipped, slightly British accent and promptly
retired to bed with Lina, leaving Bahrin and me alone
except for the stuffed carcasses and the buzz of the
ceiling fans.

Fourteen

Our sojourn in Kuala Lumpur sped by in a haze of nightclubs, sightseeing and get-togethers with Bahrin's cousins, a few of whom I had already met in Melbourne. Suddenly I was a member of the 'in set' as Bahrin and I joined his cousins and their friends; they were the hedonists of Malaysia, the young royals who prowled the nightclubs to boogie and drink their way from disco to disco, always professing boredom. We'd arrive en masse in a flurry of luxury cars, dressed in the highest of fashion and expecting the VIP treatment, which was always forthcoming. Safely isolated from the realities of mixing with the plebeians, the young royals accepted the fawning and gratitude as a matter of course.

But Bahrin's cousins seemed pleased to accept me into the fold. They were the perfect hosts: charming, sophisticated, eager to make me welcome and quick to fulfil any desire I had to sightsee or shop. The girls puzzled me somewhat; they had a frenetic quality about them, an intensity of purpose when it came to fun. They always talked about Kuala Lumpur, Singapore or London as if any time spent in those cities were borrowed and illicit. Later, when I saw them within the confines of the palace, walking placidly behind their parents, I would come to understand this attitude. Gone were the miniskirts, strapless dresses and hair gel, replaced with long flowing garments and suitably downcast eyes.

Terengganu. It's a word that rolls off the tongue sensuously with the promise of lush vistas and pearl-white beaches. The travel brochures predicted giant leatherback turtles, coconut trees, endless sandy coastlines, azure blue seas and a cultural richness passed down through many generations.

And that's where we were heading. Bahrin had decided that the best way to show me 'his' Malaysia was by travelling to his home state by car; that way I could see the countryside and we could break the six-hour trip in the resort town of Kuantan, in the state of Pahang, by spending a few days at the Hyatt Hotel. We had a wonderful time in Kuantan. It was to be the only romantic holiday we were ever to have together. Bahrin temporarily rescinded his edict on public physical contact and we walked along the beach hand-in-hand, snatching kisses in the sand dunes and splashing and rolling around in the sea together. It astounded me that Bahrin was quite unwilling to enter the water any deeper than his knees; he had never learnt to swim, and deep water terrified him. Notwithstanding his strong Islamic stance later, Bahrin had no qualms then about my wearing bathing suits in public. I have dozens of photographs which he took of me on the beach with his treasured Pentax camera; he particularly liked me to pose bare-shouldered with my hair out loose and blowing in the wind, as he snapped off a roll of film.

At sunset we would sit on the hotel terrace overlooking the ocean, sipping our drinks, Bahrin with his Bacardi and Coke with a twist of lime – 'not too much ice,' he'd say – and me nursing whatever colourful cocktail he had chosen for me that evening. Gazing at one another, we would discuss the day in a lazy way and make half-hearted plans for the next, never anything too strenuous and never anything that would take us far from our idyllic retreat among the sand and the palms. Our talks seldom turned to the second leg of our journey on to Terengganu. It was as if neither of us wanted to end our time in limbo. Instead, I lay awake at night next to Bahrin, listening to the waves hit the beach and worrying about my inevitable meeting with his mother.

And then one morning it was time to gird my loins and sally forth to meet Tengku Zaleha, daughter of a sultan and a king, devout Muslim, divorcee and pilgrim to the holy city of Mecca. So far during this holiday I had danced with a crown prince or two, hobnobbed with Bahrin's cousins and met a couple of his aunts and uncles, but up until this point nothing had seemed quite as daunting as the prospect of my first contact with Yang Amat Mulia Tengku Hajjah Zaleha Puteri binti Almarhum Duli Yang Maha Mulia Sultan Ismail Nasiruddin Shah, the mother of my boyfriend.

Bahrin suggested that I should wear something very demure for the second leg of our trip. I had sewn two approximations of Malay traditional garb, at his suggestion, and brought them with me from Melbourne. It was decided that the purple outfit was the right choice for his mother, the simple *baju kurung*. Translated literally it means 'the dress cage' and it consisted, in this case, of a long, floor-length purple skirt and a purple-and-white geometric patterned A-line knee-length over-blouse, made in soft voile with sleeves reaching to the wrists and a high, rounded neck-line.

With my hair parted in the middle and falling loosely down my back at Bahrin's behest, dressed 'appropriately' and not quite ready to go, I watched the bellboys from the steps of the hotel as they loaded our bags into the car. I took one last look around me, back down to the palm-lined beach, thinking wistfully that it would be heaven just to lie on the sand for days and days more. As I imagined lazing on the beach I was optimistically planning a return visit to beautiful Kuantan. I didn't understand then that the past can never be recaptured and revived, that everything changes and we move on to other pleasures and hopes. Sometimes the past is sweetened by the passage of time, but that sweetness can sour like a rotting tooth, decaying memories and rebuking us for our naivety. I got into the car and, with a final glance over my shoulder, turned to greet the future I didn't know I had.

Fifteen

It took an hour and a half to reach the Pahang/
Terengganu state line, driving along a chaotic
thoroughfare bordered on one side with squalid villages,
jungle and rice fields and on the other by the glimmering
South China Sea. We shared our route with an odd
assortment of vehicles: rickety trucks, timber lorries
carrying enormous logs cut from the rainforest, and
luxury cars jockeying for lead position with motor
scooters – often with a family of five balancing
themselves precariously from handlebar to pillion like
some sort of circus act – goats and bicycles. Crossing
the border into Terengganu, I noted that there were
fewer people on the roads and that the jungle was more
abundant and greener than I had seen earlier. I found
it strange trying to adjust my mind to the fecundity of
my surroundings; shade upon shade of green, splashes
of bright tropical flowers, creepers and vines seemed at
odds with my expectations of the great outdoors. The
tropical jungle was beautiful but incongruous to me,
like a painted scenic backdrop rolled out for my benefit.
I was used to our Australian summers: the dry brown
grass of Gippsland and the tiny wild orchids that pop
up in a flash of defiant colour amongst it; the
expansiveness of our open rolling plains dotted by
eucalyptus trees with their dull khaki leaves and

greyish-white bark, and the rich, unique perfume of the Aussie bush.

Gradually, villages began to dot the roadside at closer intervals as the highway widened out into a double carriageway on the outskirts of the Kuala Terengganu township. During the drive, Bahrin and I had conversed little, listening instead to the music tapes he had brought along; but, as we started to approach a large structure on the left, Bahrin almost imperceptibly straightened his back, raised his chin higher and slowed the car to a crawl as he launched into an explanation of the ten-foot-high, mile-long concrete fence we were passing. It was, apparently, the Istana Badariah, Badariah Palace, home of his uncle, the Sultan: Duli Yang Maha Mulia Sultan Mahmud ibni Almarhum Sultan Ismail Nasiruddin Shah. As we drove by I caught a glimpse of a large building that was painted a pale grey colour. Armed sentries stood guard at the main gate and a flag flew high on its pole, one of many lining the entrance boulevard. Bahrin explained that the grounds of the palace were very large and incorporated a golf course, clubhouse, badminton hall and tennis courts. Bahrin also added that he had grown up behind those formidable walls. It was a fact merely stated, without a tinge of nostalgia, as though it were some inconsequential detail. I wondered if that was because as a 'royal' he had been brought up to expect a new reign to take precedence over the old. Or did he resent being disenfranchised from his old home? I wondered, but I asked nothing; I didn't think it was my business to pry. I recognised that I was well and truly out of my depth. So, right then and there, I mentally instructed myself to go with the flow, not offend anyone and be guided by Bahrin in all things; this seemed the most sensible and logical thing to do, and was probably the only way I was likely to survive the approaching minefield of cultural and royal etiquette. That, and a lot of finger crossing.

Bahrin reached across and squeezed my hand affectionately before he turned our car into a driveway just down the road from the palace. We had reached our destination and, for propriety's sake, I had been billeted with his aunt and uncle in the house next to his mother's.

Down the drive we went until we turned a sharp corner. All I could see in front of me was a mass of greenery, almost entirely obscuring the house from view. What I could glimpse left me with the impression of a roofline that seemed to be a mix of every known architectural style and of owners who valued their privacy.

The home of Yang Amat Mulia Tengku Seri Paduka Raja, Tengku Ibrahim, Bahrin's maternal uncle and younger brother of the Sultan, and his Chinese wife, Rosita, was decorated in the style of the US television series *Dynasty*. Hand-carved doors guarded the entrance to the mansion, and the obligatory verse from the Koran, the Muslim holy book, also carved and picked out in gold filigree, surmounted the lintel. These Koranic verses were meant to protect the inhabitants of a house from evil spirits and to show a family's devotion to Allah.

Inside, gleaming parquet and marble floors were scattered with priceless Chinese and Persian rugs. Reproduction crystal chandeliers dominated some rooms, which were air-conditoned, whilst in others the ceiling fans whirled above antique lacquered screens and mirrored walls which bounced back one's reflection a dozen times. The decorating style was a bewildering mixture of the very kitsch and the very expensive. Some corners of the house were devoted to entire themes – Italian nouveau, with gilded palm trees and lots of glass tables, or Japanese, incorporating antique kimonos hanging from the walls and a water garden. The house was luxurious but not really in the best of taste. Unlike many houses I was to see during my time in Terengganu, the family's living quarters at Auntie Rosita's were very European in both furnishing and feel: large squishy sofas and tubs of plants filled the three main reception rooms, and they featured Western bathrooms. Although not all had hot water, they did have the luxury of pedestal-type toilets, even if there was a lack of lavatory paper.

The house has since been renovated and extended again, adding new wings and upper storeys as well as a fibre-glass inground pool shipped over from Australia in one solid piece.

I was greeted warmly by Bahrin's aunt, whom I had already met in Kuala Lumpur, and his cousins, Nasiruddin and Alina, both of whom were also studying in Melbourne. Auntie Rosita was wearing a long batik kaftan in hot pink covered in large flowers, which, I found out later, was the 'at home' uniform for many members of the royal family. Quite a difference from the short designer garments, high heels and perfectly coiffured hair I had seen Auntie Rosita wear in the capital. Both her stepchildren and her own daughter, Suzi, were clad in jeans, each with a Walkman slung around the neck and adorned with masses of gold and diamond jewellery.

I learnt then and there that etiquette required all shoes to be removed before entering someone's house; it made quite a sight watching a group of visitors scrambling around at the front door looking for a missing sandal.

My luggage was whisked away by an elderly manservant as I was guided to the dining-room for afternoon tea. I felt shy and very overwhelmed amongst these relative strangers. Thankfully, Bahrin didn't bolt as immediately as he'd planned. Catching sight of my beseeching face, he forestalled his departure just long enough to chat briefly and gulp down a drink. But his mother was waiting to greet him so, in what seemed like the flicker of an eyelid and a flurry of leave-taking, he was gone, leaving me gazing after him as though I were Dorothy watching the Yellow Brick Road being jack-hammered and covered in black tar.

Sixteen

With all the servants Auntie Rosita and Tengku Ibrahim had living in – cook, two maids, elderly manservant/ butler, serving boy and two chauffeurs – I was surprised that Bahrin managed it. 'It' was a midnight visit to my ground-floor guestroom on the night of our arrival. Bahrin had organised for his cousin Nasiruddin to unlock one of the doors for him at an appointed time and relock the same entrance after he had departed. That way he was able to slip into my bed without his family being any the wiser. Appearances, I was soon to understand, meant far more to the royal family than the actual truth.

'M' day finally arrived. Decked out again in my most 'suitable' clothing, I was escorted by Bahrin across the garden compound which separated the residences, to his mother's home next door.

During the 1960s, Bahrin's grandfather decided to build houses for his favourite children. He set about subdividing a large portion of the palace grounds, laying private roads to link the houses and installing drainage and electricity. Each of his children and grandchildren was presented with an identical dwelling: a standardised three-bedroom house with servants' quarters, set on half a hectare of land and built from brick with cement-rendered walls. Every building was painted white to reflect the British colonial influence and verandahed to combat the torrential monsoon rains.

As the accommodation needs of each favoured descendant grew apace with the financial gains they reaped from the valuable rainforest timber concessions and gas and oil discoveries in the state, so too did the homes. In some cases, what had started off as a modest suburban house evolved into a ten-bedroom mansion.

As we walked the two hundred yards to Tengku Zaleha's, Bahrin explained that the area where the family lived was referred to colloquially as Kampung Istana, meaning 'the palace village'. But from what I saw it was hardly a village.

Tengku Zaleha's home, a simple and fairly new brick home with verandahs on two sides, painted off-white with the window trims picked out in apple green, was a far more modest and less forbidding building than her brother's. On Bahrin's signal I removed my shoes as gracefully as I could and entered the house, which was dimly lit and quite austere.

Bahrin's mother sat primly on the edge of a couch in the living-room, giving me a smile which didn't quite reach her eyes and extending a hand to me in welcome whilst remaining seated. In Malaysia women don't shake hands with a strong hand clasp; it's really a touching of palms, a slight encompassing of one another's fingers. Luckily I had been coached by Bahrin and quickly took her right hand and touched my nose and lips to the back of it in homage, sketching a sort of bobbing-bending curtsey just as I had been instructed. Her face seemed to unfreeze a little at this, and I caught just a glimmer of relief as her eyes met mine again and she nodded her acknowledgement. Years later, Tengku Zaleha was to tell me that she had also been nervous about our first meeting and relieved when she realised that I knew how to behave with decorum and was not the 'barbaric white girl' she had feared. Attired in a pink silk *baju kurung*, white muslin headscarf, barefoot and wearing frosted pink lipstick, she struck me as someone who didn't quite live in the real world, and she always reminded me of an ageing English duchess who couldn't quite understand that 'horseless carriages' were here to stay.

The language barrier proved to be a difficulty. Tengku Zaleha had once been conversant in English but had let it lapse, and she was too shy to begin using that language again for fear of ridicule. So although she often comprehended what people were saying in English, she chose not to converse in that tongue. So we sat, Bahrin, his mother, Auntie Rosita, a cousin or two and I, sort of nodding, smiling and holding a stilted conversation. 'Where were you born?' came the question through Auntie Rosita from Tengku Zaleha. 'Do you work, and where?' cousin Alina asked for her aunt, followed by 'How old are you?' at which point Bahrin interjected, hurriedly asking his mother, in a tone a little sharper than his usual, if he had mentioned that my father was originally from Penang.

It irked me that Bahrin felt it necessary to circumvent questions about my age, although I had understood his instructions and his reasons – even if I didn't entirely agree with them. Bahrin had explained that all his younger cousins gave him the title of 'Abang', meaning older brother, which was a form of respect, and that should his cousins learn my true age of seventeen (which meant that I was far younger than most of them), it would be embarrassing for him. Our relationship could be construed as Bahrin being attracted to a teenager who was not a Muslim and not legally an adult. So he asked me to lie about my age to his family. 'Anyway,' he'd said, 'it's no one's business except our own.'

More 'getting to know you' conversation continued to roll politely around the room as the bilingual ball was tossed into the air by Tengku Zaleha or me, forwarded on its way by willing helpers, each eager to take on the role of language decoder. We must have resembled spectators at a tennis match: all heads turned right, all heads turned left, as phrases were interpreted back and forth across the room. This definitely wasn't a relaxing afternoon tea where one could let one's hair down; it was more like torture by tea and cakes.

What really broke the ice between Bahrin's mother and me was a huge box of Cadbury's milk chocolates. I had brought a dozen boxes of chocolates from Australia, just in case I needed 'thank you' gifts, and I gave Tengku Zaleha one. She couldn't contain her delight or the mischievous smile which broke through our communication barrier. Over that sizeable Cadbury's selection, we identified each other as fellow chocoholics and began to be friends.

So with the ordeal of formal introductions and obligatory chitchat over, Bahrin and I were excused and, accompanied by a cousin as chaperone, we took a spin around the Kuala Terengganu township. Later that evening, at his uncle's home, Bahrin congratulated me, saying that I had 'done very well' at my meeting with his mother. I couldn't help thinking that he sounded as if I had accomplished some undercover mission behind enemy lines – I waited for the medal but it wasn't forthcoming, so I just smiled uncomprehendingly.

A year later, when I had become more familiar with Muslim customs, I realised that when an Islamic man takes a girl to meet his family, particularly his mother, it's a definite indicator that he's contemplating marriage. Members of the opposite sex don't just drop into each other's houses and visit with each other's parents unless the relationship is serious. His poor mother: she knew what was going on in Bahrin's mind well before I did; perhaps she simply assumed that I knew too.

My memories of that first visit to Terengganu seem to run into one another and circle round and round in my head – I can recollect 'scenes' with the clarity of a photograph, but a lot of the inconsequential hour-by-hour events have receded into the files of my mind. It may also be because I let myself be seduced by Bahrin's family. I saw behaviour then, in the early days, that I suppose I chose to gloss over, letting the good aspects outweigh the less palatable facts of their lives. At seventeen, I didn't rock the boat. At thirty, I'll make tidal waves if the need dictates.

Over the first two weeks of January 1981, Bahrin and I hopped between Terengganu, Kuala Lumpur and Singapore at a head-spinning pace. In Terengganu I saw the sights, in Kuala Lumpur we partied hard and in Singapore we shopped till we dropped.

It was in Singapore that I first met the Sultan of Terengganu, Bahrin's maternal uncle, along with his second wife, Sharifah Nong, mother of his eldest son, Mizan, the Crown Prince, or Raja Muda, and the majority of his children. I already knew and liked Mizan, who in those days was a very easygoing, unpretentious young man prone to shyness. His combination of Arabic and Malay genes gave him a rugged handsomeness and brooding dark eyes. He always had a warm if somewhat tentative smile for me and was far better at the basic domestic chores around the house than Bahrin. It was not unusual for Mizan to be found mopping the floor or cooking a simple meal when he visited Bahrin and me in our Melbourne home. I felt quite sorry for him because I knew he hated Geelong Grammar, Bahrin's old school, where he had been sent to complete his schooling. Not academically brilliant, he found the going hard and the isolation of the boarding school contributed to his misery. But as a Crown Prince and probable future king of Malaysia, he had very little choice about the mapping out of his life. His career, where he lived and whom he married as his official wife were all decisions to be made for him, or were faits accomplis.

I had already met the other royal children, Mizan's sisters and brothers, in Terengganu. The girls, Farah, Anna and Ima, ranged in age from fifteen to twenty-one. Farah, the eldest, was reed thin, with a delicate heart-shaped face and voluptuous lips; a chatterbox like her mother, she loved nothing more than a good gossip and had a penchant for decking herself out with masses of jewellery and paying extravagant compliments, which I found very disconcerting.

Anna, on the other hand, was outwardly quieter and much preferred to sit back and observe the goings-on rather than join in the conversation. Stunningly beautiful with long black hair, Anna had a smouldering sensuality about her; fine-boned like her elder sister, her air of fragility masked a spine of steel and a bitchy and somewhat petulant nature.

The tomboy and youngest daughter of the Sultan's family was Ima. Ima was a female version of Mizan, her brother, with the same dark eyes and chiselled features. She wore her hair defiantly short in a boyish style and, unlike her sisters, was anything but fragile. She always seemed far more at ease in jeans than the traditional and stifling Muslim garments she was obliged to wear in public or around her father, the Sultan. She was known to be more at home kicking a soccer ball than playing the dutiful princess, and I would often catch sight of her eyelids lowering to mask her rebellious streak.

The two younger boys of the royal clan were greatly

overshadowed by their elder siblings and, as a result, seemed to gravitate towards mischief like moths to a flame, constantly getting into strife and taking any opportunity to play practical jokes on poor unsuspecting innocents. Ten-year-old Tengku, 'Baby' to use his nickname, was a particularly loathsome child, the type of kid that makes birth control a really attractive proposition. He was sadistic to animals and apt to lie or manipulate any situation to his advantage. 'Baby' took extreme pleasure in tormenting his younger half-brother, Tengku Adik, sometimes punching, pinching and hitting him to get a reaction.

And so, to my first audience with HRH The Sultan of Terengganu. Sultan Mahmud and his family were taking a brief holiday in Singapore, staying with their retinue at the Goodwood Park Hotel, which is owned by the world's richest man, the Sultan of oil-rich Brunei. More Raffles than Raffles, the Goodwood Park was arguably the best five-star hotel in Singapore. Discreet, understated but infinitely elegant, the lobby of the establishment seemed calculated to temper one's exuberance from the outset. Bahrin and I made our way along a long corridor to the private suite usually reserved for the hotel's owner but which, out of courtesy, had been made available to the Terengganu royals.

As my feet sank into the deep silky carpet lining our progress along a hallway almost twice the width of a small bedroom, we came across a scene to rival any frenzied sale day at Harrods, Bloomingdales or Harvey Nichols. Shopping bags adorned with labels like Christian Dior, Giorgio Armani and Yves St Laurent were stacked high against the walls, spilling their contents onto the floor: numerous boxes of ladies' shoes, Wedgwood china, two or three bicycles and a small electric car. Members of the Brunei royal family had been shopping. I was in awe; I was looking at the spoils of an orgy of unbridled spending. This was serious and devoted consumerism – and, being Muslims, the Bruneians didn't even celebrate Christmas.

Bahrin and I were ushered into his uncle's presence through a suite of beautiful rooms, some hexagonal with full-length bay windows, by a liveried footman decked out in the standard-issue palace uniform of white jacket and trousers, *sampin* – men's sarong worn around the waist over trousers – and black velvet *songkok*, a brimless oval fez-like hat, trimmed with the royal insignia.

After a few minutes, Farah and Mizan joined us; their conversation and manner was normal and relaxed, with Farah holding forth on the joys of shopping in Singapore.

Suddenly all the jollity in the room evaporated – we were in the presence of the Sultan. A fairly tall man of bulky proportions, he didn't smile as I dipped my curtsey, made my *angkat sumpah*, palms of hands pressed together and raised to the forehead in obsequiousness, and kissed his outstretched hand whilst semi-kneeling. The Sultan thankfully gave me little more than his perfunctory attention as I attempted to blend into the woodwork. His demeanour seemed vague, as though he operated in another dimension. Bahrin told me later that his uncle had not been the same since his heart condition had been diagnosed, spending a considerable amount of the year trying both traditional and offbeat medicine to ensure his longevity.

After his brief appearance in the reception room, during which his two eldest children fidgeted nervously and shifted from side to side with downcast eyes, his number two wife, Sharifah Nong, bustled in to join us. She was swathed in silk, her eyes were rimmed in kohl and her hands were a mass of diamond, ruby and emerald rings, two to a finger; around her wrists snaked gold bangles and a platinum-set diamond Piaget watch. Hung around her neck was an abundant collection of long solid-gold chains, diamond pendants and engraved lockets with the Arabic symbol for Allah. All of this jewellery clanked and jangled as she proceeded to lower herself onto the couch beside me. She was like a very large chattering whirlwind, a woman whose personality could overwhelm all around her with her lack of discretion. Bombastic in the extreme, it wasn't hard to understand her daughters' enthusiasm for gossip – it was their mother's lifeblood.

I was immediately pronounced 'pleasing to the eye', in need of fattening up and so much fairer in skin colour and with nicer hair than Bahrin's first wife, Fauziah, whom she said she hadn't liked. All this Auntie Sharifah Nong managed to say within the first two minutes of our meeting. I wondered what she would have said if she had known me better or had had more time with me. She said that she knew we would be good friends. I could hardly wait.

Having met Bahrin's family, been inspected and passed, more or less, it was soon time for me to head home to Melbourne and normality. The morning of my departure, Bahrin and I were lazing in bed together at his father's house when he turned to me out of the blue and remarked that he was having a ring made for me. An engagement ring. He hadn't proposed – he pronounced.

Bahrin swept away any questions I had, any queries about our future or any uncertainties on my part, with the line: 'Don't spoil this by talking about it, just go home and wait for me.' So I did. I boarded the plane that afternoon, not realising that I was setting a pattern in our relationship which would never be broken – the pattern of my total obedience.

Seventeen

Upon my return home to Australia, and during the following weeks whilst I waited for Bahrin to rejoin me, life settled down into its casual pace again. There were times when I truly wondered if I had really been to all those exotic locations. My existence seemed so normal and I revelled in my solitariness, opting to walk from my city office through the still-bright summer sunshine to the house in Carlton, pottering in the tiny back garden, and taking the odd ballet class to keep myself limber. It was probably the first time in my life that I made an attempt at enjoying my own company. I often wonder what would have happened if Bahrin had never come back to Melbourne to collect me. But then, on the other hand, perhaps my confidence emanated from the security of being involved with him. I'll never know for sure: my life is too far along its path now to ponder alternative teenage routes.

He was home, bearing engagement ring, romance and my future.

The ring he presented with flair on the night of his homecoming during a candlelit dinner at Tsindos Bistro, 'our special restaurant', and the words: 'Three diamonds – I . . . Love . . . You.' I suppose my acceptance of the ring was my tacit agreement to wed – it didn't occur to me at the time to say 'yes' as there was never a question posed.

The romance he provided in abundance, as though he had a 'how-to-woo' manual in his back pocket. There were intimate lunches when we discussed nothing at all, long drives with music drowning out any attempts at conversation, pleasant, undemanding lovemaking and flowers, lots and lots of flowers.

Flowers were truly my downfall, and Bahrin was a master at providing the cliff. I arrived home on 14 February 1981 to find the front door covered in carnations and ribbons. As I turned my key in the lock and entered the house, more flowers greeted me, banked in disarray at the foot of the stairs around a greetings card which read 'Happy Valentine's Day'. Tied to the banisters of the staircase were red roses, one for each balustrade, winding up and around out of sight. I followed the floral trail, collecting them as I ascended until, as I reached the top floor, my arms were struggling to contain the blooms. Behind the door, hung with still more roses and marked 'I Love You', sat Bahrin quietly and nonchalantly, as though it were quite a natural thing to purchase what seemed like the entire contents of a florist's shop.

But for the rumble of traffic, the house was silent. Bahrin looked up at me as I tried to stammer my appreciation. He shot me one of his fleeting grins and flippantly said, 'Well, what did you expect? You are going to be my wife.' I knew that I couldn't compete with a reply – so I kissed him.

As our affair moved apace, I found myself out of touch with more and more of my close friends. My new life revolved entirely around my new-found love; so much so that I hardly registered that my circle of friends was now made up of Bahrin's cousins or university mates, and that they themselves could be counted on the fingers of one hand.

We rolled into the month of March with little thought of anything bar Bahrin's crucial end-of-year finals. It was Sunday, 8 March; Bahrin and I had been watching television in the study after dinner when he turned to me and dropped his bombshell: 'You know next week is my uncle's coronation and Mizan's installation, and I really should be there.' Then, more hurriedly, he added, 'I think that we should both go back to Terengganu for the coronation and get married at the same time.'

I sat on the living-room floor as exclamation marks ricocheted around my brain, grappling for words, my thoughts racing. We had never set a date for a wedding before now. I'd always assumed that we would talk about this sort of thing after he had graduated; being engaged was fun and, as I was taking the pill, we didn't have to worry about babies arriving before we wanted them. I finally managed to splutter, 'But I'm still only seventeen.'

'So you've only been playing around with me, have you?' Bahrin shot back angrily. 'Do you think that I would take just anyone home to meet my mother? I've been serious about you from day one,' he added. 'I knew that you'd make the perfect wife for me. Why are you finding excuses now?'

'But it's in seven days . . .' I replied, stalling for time. 'I can't legally marry you, I'm under-age.' And then, rather stupidly, 'I haven't got a wedding dress.'

These comments only served to inflame the tenor of the conversation. 'What do you think being part of a royal family means? I can fix all that. I can make all that legal. I can organise everything. All I have to do is ring Malaysia.' He continued: 'I'm the only person who has ever offered you the chance to fit in. You don't fit in here in Australia, you don't belong and you don't look like them . . . I can make you part of a family for the first time in your life and all you're trying to do is find fault with it,' Bahrin screamed at me. 'It won't matter what you were or who you were before you married me, no one in Malaysia will dare think of you as anything less than a member of my family. All you are here is a Eurasian half-caste. You've said yourself what a terrible time the Australians gave you at school, how you felt unhappy all the time growing up – well, it won't happen in Terengganu. For the for first time you'll have a real family. I'm offering you the protection of everything I have, of everything my family is, and all you can do is find fault, look for obstacles.'

I had never seen him angry before and it frightened me. Maybe he was right. Maybe I didn't belong in Australia. Maybe I could find a sort of racial purity, and future for my children, by marrying him; then they wouldn't go through the agony of being different, like me.

I just didn't know what to say. I started to cry, trying to explain everything that frightened me, all my uncertainties, but he wouldn't listen. He just kept yelling his accusations at me, stripping down all my carefully built-up layers of self-protection and confidence, laying bare all my vulnerabilities and exposing all my fears.

'Where are you going to go now? What are you going to do?' Bahrin asked.

'What do you mean?' I countered.

'Well, you don't think we can continue to live together and not get married, do you? I won't live with a slut. I'm a Muslim and, so far, just living together has meant me living in sin. It can't go on. I have given you enough time to grow up, now I'm giving you the chance to be someone, to fit in for the first time in your life, to have a family, and you don't want it. I love you but now I'm telling you: we either get married or we break up,' he railed.

I couldn't lose him. I was so terrified of being on my

own now. I loved him, I didn't want to end up like my mother. Maybe he was right. I just didn't know any more – I was so confused I felt dizzy. I kept weeping as he continued to harangue me.

At one point I blurted out that I knew that Muslims could have more than one wife; after all, his own uncle, the Sultan, had at least two wives at once. I didn't want him to be married to anyone else. 'I couldn't stand it,' I cried. I wanted my marriage to last, I told him. I didn't believe polygamous relationships were right, I wouldn't compete with another woman. 'I won't share – ever!' I told him vehemently.

By way of an answer he snatched up the Koran, the Islamic holy book, which he kept on the mantelpiece in the study, went down on his knees and swore that he would never ever take a wife other than me and that we would be together until we died. He swore in the name of Allah and on the holiest book of his religion. It was a sacred oath, he assured me, one that he was bound to by his religion. Bahrin was later to repeat this holy oath, again with the Koran in his hand, in the presence of, and at the request of, his mother on at least three other occasions during our marriage.

I had to capitulate. He was so adamant that he would walk out of my life for ever if I didn't marry him the following week. I just gave in. I didn't have the strength to quarrel any more and I couldn't risk losing him because I thought we should wait.

He made love to me as soon as I'd surrendered, telling me that he would never leave me, vowing that he'd love me for ever and promising over and over that everything would be all right now that we were in agreement.

Later Bahrin told me he had decided that we shouldn't have sex again before we were officially married; that we should keep ourselves pure before our wedding night but continue to share a bed. It sounded a lot like shutting the stable door after the horse had bolted, but who was I to argue?

I was only the bride.

Eighteen

I looked at my reflection in the mirror as I sat before the dressing-table and made my evaluation. I saw large eyes rimmed with kohl, shiny dark hair draped with filmy chiffon and hands that fidgeted nervously with the silver-backed brushes laid out before them. On my right breast was pinned my precious diamond brooch, given to me by my father. It stood out well against the dark maroon lace of my gown.

It had taken a full night's sewing with a friend to complete on time, a lunch hour of frenetic shopping to find the matching lingerie which I wore beneath my dress, and an hour to wash my hair and apply my make-up.

The image I saw in the mirror was not what I had imagined all those hazy years ago when I conjured up visions of my future; in those daydreams I held lilies and gardenias and was resplendent in white.

It was seven o'clock in the evening, I was in a foreign country, and I was to be married in a few minutes' time.

The seven days leading up to this moment had evaporated like ice thrown on a bonfire. A tornado of shopping, sewing, travel arrangements and just downright hysterical mayhem had left me little time to ascertain the exact details of the ceremony itself. I left them to Bahrin, which seemed more appropriate under the circumstances. He had proved true to his tirade: when he wanted wedding preparations made, he simply picked up the phone.

Seated in the first-class section of the aircraft for our journey to Malaysia, my mind kept turning to my nanna; we had spoken to her the previous night and told her of our wedding plans. Nanna had said nothing to discourage us, only saying that she wanted me to be happy. She did have reservations about the speed at which everything was happening, and she was disappointed that she wouldn't be there to see me married. But Bahrin explained to her that, so as not to interfere with his uncle's coronation, this was only going to be a simple registry-office-type wedding; we would, he said, have a proper ceremony later, one with all the trimmings, which she could attend.

Sitting next to the man I was about to marry, I couldn't help but secretly agree with Nanna. I too was disappointed that she wouldn't be at our wedding and that the planning was all out of my hands. But this was the way Bahrin wanted it, and I didn't want to lose him. I was sure that I wanted to spend the rest of my life with him – just like in the fairy tales.

Fairy tales aside, there were some details that even Bahrin had not yet covered. A couple of hours into the flight, he began to run over the agenda for our wedding, the next evening. The actual wedding would take place in the Malay language, he said, with a good measure of Arabic thrown in. I would be expected to speak a certain phrase in that language, as well as in Malay. It would be simpler and less confusing for me, Bahrin explained, if he taught me those phrases now, during the flight, as getting the tongue around Arabic was difficult for a novice learner.

So, in between the meals and by skipping the movie, I learnt my first Arabic phrase, phonetically and by mimicking Bahrin: '*Wah Ash Hah Do Allah, Mohamad Arrr Rasool L'Allah Law.*' I repeated this over and over again like a broken record. 'There is but one God, Allah, and Mohamad is his prophet,' Bahrin translated. This phrase would get me through, he promised; it was all that was needed, the rest was easy. I asked him what the significance of the words were and he replied, 'Just on paper you'll need to become a Muslim. No one from my family is legally allowed to marry a non-Muslim. Anyway, it's only a formality, it doesn't really mean much, and it doesn't matter if you don't believe it.'

We stayed overnight that Saturday at Bahrin's father's house in Kuala Lumpur, before continuing on to Kuala Terengganu for the nuptials. Raja Ahmad was not invited to our wedding; it was tacitly agreed that his attendance was not an option due to the rift caused by his divorce from Bahrin's mother, Tengku Zaleha, years earlier. The next day he toasted our happiness in Tiger brand beer and sent us on our way with a couple of bawdy jokes and promises to see us on our way back to Melbourne in six days' time.

By the time we finally arrived at our destination I was absolutely exhausted and I can't honestly remember feeling any joy at the thought of our impending union. I had reached the stage where I just had a sense of fatalistic anticipation towards it all. Taking stock of myself in the mirror in the bathroom, I looked more like a dishevelled marathon runner than a blushing bride – a bride who had less than three hours to produce a blush.

Tengku Zaleha ushered me into the master bedroom of her house so I could freshen up. She had obviously gone to great pains in the short time she had been given to convert the bedroom into a bridal suite, Malaysian style. The furniture was new, made from mahogany and very ornate in design. The bed featured intricate carving in a floral design highlighted in gold, the bed-head was padded with canary yellow brocade to match the curtains and other soft furnishings. It was not the type of decor I would ever have chosen for myself, but I did appreciate Tengku Zaleha's thoughtfulness and tried to communicate that to her before she left me alone.

After a few minutes Bahrin asked me to rejoin him in the dining-room. The furniture had been cleared to one side with the dining table at one end of the room. Sitting at the table were two men, absorbed in making entries in a large official-looking register and shuffling papers from side to side. They paid me scant attention as I first entered the room. Their attire was like nothing I had encountered in Malaysia so far: full-length long-sleeved dresses, rather like a priest's cassock, but in pale-coloured cottons with trousers underneath, and turbans on their heads. They were Imams or religious men, equivalent to vicars or preachers, empowered to marry people, give religious instruction and interpret Koranic law. When Bahrin introduced me to them I proffered my hand to shake, but neither Imam returned the gesture and they both stared pointedly at my futilely outstretched hand. Bahrin diffused the awkward moment by explaining to me that these gentlemen were there to organise our marriage. Neither of the Imams spoke English or seemed particularly fazed by the fact that I spoke no Malay, so Bahrin had to interpret.

I caught my name, followed by the word 'Yasmin', during a brief conversation in Malay between the men. 'Yasmin' was the name Bahrin had chosen for me to use on official documents after our marriage, and the name we had agreed the Malaysian public would know me by.

With a slight nudge, Bahrin prompted me in low tones. 'You say what I taught you,' he said.

So obediently, and a little nervously, I repeated what

he had taught me on the plane: '*Wah Ash Hah Do Allah, Mohamad Arrr Rasool L'Allah Law.*'

'Sign here,' and 'Sign there,' Imam Ali said in Malay, gesturing at the register and smiling for the first time as I put my signature alongside the Arabic squiggles in the leather-bound book.

'What do I do now?' I asked, turning to Bahrin as he began to leave the room.

'Get dressed for our wedding,' he replied as I followed him into the corridor. 'Oh, and put your hair up for me. It looks more elegant that way.'

Nineteen

The voice of the muezzin calling the faithful to sunset prayers cut through my musings as I sat in my bridal clothes before the dressing-table. There was a knock on the door and Bahrin entered. He was dressed in the traditional male costume of *baju melayu*, a loose, long-sleeved, high-necked shirt without a collar, fastened down the front with jewelled studs, and baggy silken trousers worn with a brocade skirt wrapped around the waist. He had a black velvet *songkok* on his head. I watched his reflection advance on me in the mirror and thought how dark and handsome my soon-to-be husband was.

In his right hand I noticed a red velvet box, which he opened as he stood beside me. Inside was a heavy diamond necklace designed in the shape of orchids and leaves, set in white gold and platinum. The matching earrings and bracelet were just as ornate as the necklace and just as heavily encrusted with diamonds of varying sizes.

'You look beautiful, Yasmin,' Bahrin told my image in the mirror. 'These are for you. You can wear them now. My mother chose them. They're my wedding present to you. I asked her to organise them when I rang. You'll need proper jewellery to wear now you're going to be my wife. Put them on for the wedding.'

'Wear all of them now?' I said, thinking how pleased I had been with my attire before he came into the room and how perfect and understated I thought my father's brooch looked against the dark red lace of my dress.

'Yes. Do you like them?' he asked me.

I hesitated before answering him. I would have to lie. I couldn't hurt his feelings by telling him the truth – by telling him that I loathed large gaudy jewellery.

'They're absolutely beautiful,' I lied, 'but they're too much. You didn't have to buy me something like this. I would have been happy with a wedding ring. These weren't necessary.'

'Jacqueline, you're going to be my wife – of course they were necessary,' he said as he placed his hand on my shoulder and spoke into the mirror. 'I'll see you soon.'

'What happens now?' I asked, not wanting to be left again.

'Well, you just converted to Islam with the Imams, so now we can get married. Everything's almost ready,' he replied.

'But what about me being under-age?'

'That's taken care of,' Bahrin assured me. 'My uncle, Sultan Mahmud, has the power to stand as your legal guardian. He's the religious head of our state and he's given his proxy permission to the Imams to marry us.'

He exited the room with a smile.

Twenty

It was dark outside when Tengku Zainah, Bahrin's aunt, came to fetch me. From along the corridor the sound of Arabic chanting filtered through the open bedroom door.

Adjusting my veil, I was led by Tengku Zainah across the hall and into another bedroom, which was devoid of furnishings, save for the plush Persian carpet on the floor. She indicated that I should be seated on the rug and showed me how to sit demurely with my feet tucked over to one side as she deftly arranged my skirts so that no skin was visible. Another two or three of Bahrin's aunties and female cousins joined us, lining one side of the room.

Presently a turbaned figure I recognised as one of the Imams from earlier in the evening came through the door of the room.

'*Saya terima*,' he said to me.

I nodded politely to him and smiled.

'*Saya terima*,' he repeated again in a slightly exasperated tone.

Confused, I nodded and smiled again.

Tengku Zainah giggled nervously and gesticulated with her hand.

'*Saya terima*,' I said, finally comprehending what was expected of me.

When the words passed my lips, an almost audible sigh emanated from the other women in the room. I was obviously on the right track.

The Imam then thrust a document in front of me. It was entirely written in Arabic squiggles save for the figure '25' on one line. Somehow a pen found its way into my hand. I must be meant to sign it, I thought, but where?

A pointing finger from Tengku Zainah saved me any further confusion as, with a sense of achievement, I affixed my name to the place indicated. The Imam departed as soon as he had my signature, followed by Tengku Zainah. Left in the room and still waiting to be married, I looked around me for signs of approval or moral support and was greeted with beaming smiles and nods from the women of Bahrin's family.

'Ah, one brownie point for Jack,' I thought. 'I've got his family smiling at me.'

There was a rustle at the door as Bahrin entered and beckoned to me. 'Well, come on, Yasmin,' he said as he stood in the doorway.

'Is everything ready for the ceremony now?' I asked him.

'What do you mean ceremony?' Bahrin said quizzically.

'Don't be silly,' I responded. 'How much longer will it take?'

'But we're already married,' he told me.

'We can't be married yet – I haven't gone through a ceremony with you or made any wedding vows. In fact I have hardly even seen you tonight,' I managed to squeak under my breath to Bahrin.

'We don't do that,' he explained patiently, as though I were a halfwit. He led me into the hallway. 'I made my vows in the dining-room and married you. You said "*saya terima*" in here and accepted your bride price.'

'My bride price?' I hissed, trying very hard not to explode.

'Yeah, the twenty-five dollars that was written on the marriage certificate you signed. The legal amount is only supposed to be fifteen dollars in the State of Terengganu but you are worth the extra money,' he joked. 'Come on, everyone is waiting for us, come and have some satay – I ordered it for our wedding supper because I know it's your favourite,' he added as he set off towards the living-room, with me scurrying behind.

By this time I was totally bewildered. Apparently I was neither present nor necessary at my own wedding. Talk about feeling superfluous: all dressed up and nothing to do, a bride with no wedding to go to and no role to play.

In fact, the whole supper passed in a blur. Comments flew over my head in Malay with only the occasional English interpretation being made for my benefit. I gathered that most of the discussion was about the children Bahrin and I would have, and was quite complimentary to me. Talk also turned to the Crown Prince's installation the next morning, which all the royal family would be attending. I, as a wife of a prince, albeit a brand new one, was also expected to attend.

Our guests departed fairly early, taking the Imams along and leaving just the servants and Tengku Zaleha in the house with us.

Bahrin indicated that it was time to say goodnight, so, turning to his mother, I smiled and bent forward, kissing her on the cheek in gratitude. She was very startled by the physical contact but patted my cheek and chuckled at me, bidding us goodnight as she entered her bedroom.

Twenty-one

'Well, I'm a married woman now,' I smiled to myself as I reached behind my head and freed my hair from its pins.

Bahrin had disappeared into the bathroom, leaving me time to slip into the pale pink nightgown and wrapper I'd purchased especially for our wedding night. Pure silk, and cut on the bias with insets of lace, it had cost the earth, but I hadn't cared – I wanted to look beautiful for Bahrin.

When he finally emerged from the bathroom wearing short summer pyjamas he didn't utter a word; he seemed to observe me as though he'd never laid eyes on me before. It made me feel I was being evaluated by a stranger.

And then he smiled at me – but the smile didn't quite reach his eyes.

As Bahrin moved towards me I tried to lighten the strange mood that hung in the air around us. Rising from the stool, I smiled and reached out my hand to him. He moved into my arms, quickly tilting my head back for what I thought would be a kiss. I felt his hand wind itself into my hair, felt the pressure of his fingers against my skull and relaxed as I heard him murmur, 'My beautiful, beautiful wife.'

The tugging increased on my hair as he wound it

tighter and tighter around his wrist; suddenly he yanked my head and snarled into my face, 'You belong to me, do you understand? You belong to me!'

'Don't, you're hurting me, darling,' I told him as I tried to squirm free. In answer he just forced my head further backwards and grabbed the hand I was trying to use to extricate myself. 'Please, you're hurting me, this isn't funny. Let me go!' I implored.

'I can do anything I want with you – you belong to me,' he hissed in my ear as he shoved me viciously backwards over the edge of the carved bed end.

I had started to sob so he slapped me and ordered me to be quiet. Somehow he had managed to pin my arms above my head as he tore at the lacings of my nightie. It was as though I were an object, not someone he loved. The sharp points of the bed were cutting into my back, sending shooting pains along my spine and making me whimper and cry out for him to stop. But he wouldn't and he didn't – his answer was to slap me again, hard across the face, and order me to shut up.

Then he began to rape me, to force my body. 'This wasn't how it was meant to be!' my brain screamed.

I was crying, but I couldn't scream out for help. I didn't want people bursting in and seeing us like this. I was afraid of Bahrin, but I was more afraid of being humiliated.

'Please don't, you're hurting me,' I pleaded with him, but he wouldn't listen, he wouldn't stop.

Over and over again as he ripped into me I could hear him whispering in my ear, telling me I had to understand, telling me that I belonged to him, telling me that I was his wife, that I was his beautiful, beautiful wife. My mind switched to autopilot, blanking out his face. His eyes looked at me but didn't see. Everything was just one blur of pain and panic and disbelief.

When Bahrin was finished he shoved me roughly to

the floor, telling me that I looked a mess and should clean myself up. His face was closed and cold as he settled himself comfortably in our marriage bed, like someone who had just diligently completed a distasteful but necessary task. There was nothing for me to say or do – my mind had rusted over, none of my thoughts flowed coherently and my reasoning capacity was overwhelmed by the desire to throw up, which I did heavingly when I staggered into the adjoining bathroom.

Washing my face at the basin, I fought down the urge to retch again as I saw, reflected in the small mirror above, the imprints of his grip on my wrists and the red slap marks on my face. My whole body felt torn and filthy. I twisted stiffly and gingerly ran my fingers down my back to register the places where the carvings of the bed end had scraped and bruised the flesh. My nightgown, purchased in expectation of a dream-like honeymoon, was no longer wearable – it was as tattered as my hopes,

I don't know how long I sat on the toilet seat crying. I didn't attempt to analyse Bahrin's attack fully – I couldn't face his reasons and I couldn't understand where my gentle boyfriend had gone. 'Maybe it was the pressure of the wedding,' I tried to rationalise. Maybe it was a mental aberration. I wasn't able to deal with it then – it was too much. 'It'll be all right,' I chanted to myself repeatedly. 'It'll be all right, we'll work it out.' But first I just had to get on with the matter of being.

The lights were already extinguished as I made my way across the room from the bathroom. I hardly dared draw a breath in case it woke Bahrin. I needn't have worried. He had rolled onto his left side and was snoring loudly. After changing my gown I slid beneath the sheet as far from his body as possible. 'I mustn't cry,' I thought, 'musn't cry,' as I drew my knees up to my chest and tried to calm my breathing. 'I'm a married woman now.'

Yes, I was a married woman. I was a seventeen-year-old married woman who'd apparently been taught an important lesson – if only she knew what the lesson was.

Twenty-two

My first day as a member of the royal family started at 4.30 a.m. when Bahrin and I were roused by a servant knocking on the door of our room. As I awoke, I turned cautiously to my new husband, not knowing what to expect. Despite my trepidation, his smile was quick, if somewhat distracted; his mood bore no similarity to the black and vicious behaviour of the night before. It seemed that as far as he was concerned, the most challenging and worrisome problem facing our brand new marriage was getting his bride through the day's royal agenda without her making a social gaffe. Mizan's installation as Crown Prince of Terengganu dictated that all senior members of the royal family be present for the ceremony, including its greenest recruit.

No mention was made by Bahrin of our less-than-perfect wedding night. I refrained from broaching the subject; in fact the whole episode had taken on a surreal quality which left me confused and wondering if I had imagined it all – but I hadn't. The welts on my back were enough evidence to assure me that what had occurred was more than a nightmare. I was so devastated that I wasn't able to be confrontational; I couldn't deal with it yet, I had to get through the day. I was married to this man. I had to get through a coronation. I had to meet all his family and I didn't speak the language.

What happened the previous night would never happen again, I told myself. I resolved to lock it all away, compartmentalise the memory and the fear, leave it until another day when I had the strength to work out what I had done wrong. Meanwhile I would hide my hurt and bewilderment behind polite smiles whilst trying harder to please him. After all, Bahrin had been continually telling me since our arrival in Malaysia, 'Appearances are everything.'

Much to my consternation, I ended up attending Mizan's installation ceremony as a Crown Prince resembling a five-foot-three-inch Christmas tree. Both Bahrin and his mother were adamant that I must be attired in the correct 'court dress'; this called for me to don my red lace wedding *baju kurung* and all the jewellery that Bahrin had presented to me the night before.

Whilst I dressed for my first official function, Bahrin cajoled, coached and issued instructions to me on etiquette and protocol. His words flew by my head as I struggled to tame my hair. 'Make sure to kiss the hand of every older member of my family, it's very important,' he said first.

'Don't look any man directly in the eye unless he's a member of the family and keep your eyes downcast as you walk along,' directed the light of my life as I nodded in feigned comprehension. If I look down, how can I see where I'm going? I was tempted to retort.

'Never cross your legs unless you can keep your ankles together,' I was instructed by my husband. That conjured up the strangest mental image, making me glad that I was still limber.

'Don't ever offer your left hand to anyone,' Bahrin snapped sternly. I decided that I had better stick my left hand behind my back at all times. Actually, until I got the hang of keeping the offending appendage out of sight, my gait suffered a one-sided imbalance.

'Keep your voice low and never talk loudly in public,' was issued next.

'Make sure that you never walk past a seated person at your full height, stoop and extend your right hand in front of your body as you do so and try to lower you head to their level.' That description reminded me of Charles Laughton in *The Huncbback of Notre Dame*. Thank goodness I was not that tall, otherwise I'd end up with a permanent hump.

'Don't take such big steps when you walk and try to keep your legs together at all times,' was translated by Bahrin for his mother. That one left me thinking that they should just give me a pogo stick and be done with it, then I could just hop along next to them, keeping my knees together.

'You can only sit when senior members of the family are seated first. Don't sit down first, unless of course they aren't royal then you can sit before they do, as they can't sit down until you do.' I only hoped that everyone wore name badges with their rank clearly displayed, or understood this protocol thing better than I did.

'Don't wriggle or move around in your seat too much or talk to me – there will be television cameras in the palace for the ceremony,'

'Great,' I thought, 'a video record of my humiliation.'

And lastly, 'Don't be nervous, you look beautiful, just follow all of my instructions and you'll be fine.'

If you insert batteries in my back you can operate me by remote control, I longed to quip, but didn't quite have the gumption.

So less than twelve hours into our marriage we set off for the Istana Maziah, Maziah Palace, accompanied by Tengku Zaleha and the twelve million butterflies in my stomach. 'How and where does a new princess throw up?' I pondered as the car pulled out of the compound, veil loosely in place over my hair.

The roads into the centre of town were congested and colourful, temporary archways had been erected to span the thoroughfares at regular intervals. Embellished with portraits of Sultan Mahmud and his first wife and consort, HRH Tengku Ampuan Bariah, the arches were concoctions of painted plywood and coloured light bulbs which flashed and winked whilst proclaiming the greatness of the ruler and wishing him long life and prosperity. Sponsored by business interests and government bodies, they vied with each other in their gaudiness. Bunting and flags flew from all the lampposts and the whine of sirens heralded the arrival of foreign diplomats, royalty and politicians.

Our driver deposited us at the gates of Istana Maziah, the gracious Georgian-style palace built during early colonial days by Bahrin's great-grandfather, Sultan Zainal Abidin, and now reserved solely for investitures, coronations, weddings and state banquets. Originally the main royal residence, it had been renovated and extended during the late seventies in a style which jarred badly with the elegance of the original architecture. Painted in the traditionally royal colours of bright yellow and white, its awnings and porticos were festooned with fairy lights and the parade grounds transformed into an outdoor roofed dining area for the general public who would be fed as an act of magnanimity as we, the invited guests, dined in air-conditioned comfort within.

As we approached the main doors Bahrin pointed upwards to the fourth window from the left on the second storey. 'That's the room where I was born,' he told me proprietorially. Interested in this new piece of information and longing to enquire further but not given the chance, I followed meekly and a little nervously as Bahrin and his mother entered the palace through the main vestibule.

Overstuffed Italianate reproduction furniture was dispersed around the perimeter of the foyer. Large crystal chandeliers and light fittings were suspended overhead, illuminating the portraits of the past sultans and the intricate plasterwork of the walls.

I could feel dozens of eyes turn towards me inquisitively and hear the speculative whispers as we made our way up the broad staircase to the second floor. The doors to the throne room were of massive proportions and appeared to be at least six inches thick. They were beautifully crafted in *kayu chengai* wood, the rich red-brown timber divided into panels and carved with the Terengganu coat of arms intertwined with flowers and scrollwork.

The throne room itself was the size of two ballrooms and able to seat around fifteen hundred people. Plushly carpeted in canary yellow, its opulent ornamentation made the rest of the palace seem understated. The walls were entirely panelled with latticework carvings, with the relief highlighted in gold leaf. The ceiling was one vast expanse of plaster foliage concentrically framing the chandeliers which reflected the light through their prisms and onto our faces below. Pale olive-green leather-upholstered chairs were placed in precise rows in blocks of one hundred. The higher-backed chairs were reserved for members of the family and the foreign ambassadors, who wore either dress uniform, national costume or morning dress complete with winged collar and waistcoat. The women, clad in either full evening dress or traditional costume and dripping in jewels, were an incongruous sight at 8 a.m.

The seating arrangements had been meticulously planned. Each chair was labelled, with the names typed neatly on cards topped by the royal crest. Mine read: 'The Lady Yasmin Tengku Bahrin'. In the last twenty-four hours I had been reinvented. As far as the protocol people at the palace were concerned, Jacqueline no longer existed.

High-backed thrones upholstered in bright yellow velvet surmounted a dais and were reached by ascending seven symbolic steps. They stood beneath a canopy of gold and yellow *songket* brocade. A lower platform at right angles to the thrones, and set slightly apart, was reserved for the Sultan's uncles and brothers. Opposite and slightly towards the middle of the hall was another dais, this time reserved for the members of Nobat, the royal orchestra.

The trumpeting of the Nobat horn and the beating of the drum heralded the entrance of the Sultan and his consort, Tengku Ampuan. The royal salute given by the three-foot-long noteless trumpet was deafening and quite unnerving. It echoed around the chamber like a cross between an elephant call and a bugle blast.

All the assembled guests rose to their feet as the royal couple and various footmen and attendants came into the room. They remained standing until Sultan Mahmud was seated. The proclamation of primogeniture was read and the Crown Prince, Mizan, was formally presented and publicly acknowledged as heir to the throne after he had made his obsequious homage to his father and stepmother.

Mizan looked slightly nervous but very stiff-backed in his bearing. He was dressed. from head to toe in a traditional *baju melayu* and yellow *tanjok*, or crownless turban, trimmed with diamond brooches and dress studs. The royal costume was completed by a ceremonial *kris* or dagger tucked into his *sampin* at the waist, yellow socks and highly polished black loafers. The other senior males of the various royal families wore similar costumes in varying hues, as well as sashes over one shoulder and medals denoting either rank or royal awards.

Tengku Ampuan Bariah and the Sultan had not yet

been formally crowned; that would come later in the week as a culmination to the seven days of festivities. Therefore they were obliged to limit their attire to the elaborate yellow *songket* costumes of their rank, but without the new coronation crowns which had been designed and made by Queen Elizabeth's jewellers in London. Even so, Tengku Ampuan's tiara of white diamonds was quite magnificent, as was her necklace and accompanying jewellery.

The detailed presentation and investitures took well over three hours to complete; no vows or proclamations were spoken by the Crown Prince to the Sultan during this time; no eye contact, no nods of encouragement passed between the two, only the pressing of Mizan's lips to the back of his father's hand as he knelt before him as a mark of feudal allegiance. Of all those gathered in such grandeur, Tengku Ampuan Bariah alone allowed herself a warmth of eye and tiny smile to us all as the senior royal party exited at the completion of the ceremony, accompanied by their attendants and the strains of the Nobat horns.

As I stood next to Bahrin and my mother-in-law in the foyer downstairs after the ceremonies, I surreptitiously uncrossed my fingers and breathed a sigh of relief. I had made it through my first royal function without a hiccup. People were milling about all around us. I caught brief glimpses of Auntie Rosita and Tengku Ibrahim in the crowd and waved a discreet hello. Other faces were making their way determinedly across the foyer in our direction. An older couple in full court dress greeted Bahrin and his mother. Following their lead I also stooped to kiss their hands with deference and smiled uncomprehendingly as the conversation continued in Malay above my head.

I felt a small touch on my sleeve and turned to find a rotund and jolly-looking woman beaming at me. 'Ah yes, I know what to do,' I thought. Stooping, I quickly kissed her hand and curtsied.

I was puzzled by her giggling reaction and realised that a lot of heads had turned my way. Bahrin, catching sight of what had just transpired, jerked my right hand away and hissed under his breath, 'What did you do that for? She's not royalty, she's only a wife of a Datuk, a knight!'

'Well, how was I to know?' I whispered back as my blushes became red hot. 'She looked like an auntie.'

With a venomous look Bahrin warned me, 'Don't do that again. You just embarrassed me in front of all these people.'

Well chastened, I attempted to blend with the wallpaper until our car arrived. Retorts stuck in my throat and frustration gnawed a pit in my stomach. I resolved never to make a gaffe like that again. I couldn't stand it when Bahrin got angry with me – I had to find a way of making him proud of me by fitting in completely.

A sketchy one hour's instruction on protocol and etiquette was obviously not going to be enough to get me through the minefield of Malaysian society.

The remodelling of Jacqueline had begun. Outwardly Lady Yasmin Tengku Bahrin was about to take her place.

Twenty-three

The remaining festivities for the Sultan's coronation followed each other at a breakneck pace until each day blurred into the next. Ceremonies, firework displays, banquets and religious rituals ensured that there was very little time for discussion or intimacy between Bahrin and me during the remaining five days of our stay in Terengganu; instead, we circled each other with the utmost courtesy and a detachment usually reserved for working colleagues, rather than spouses. We lay in bed at night exhausted by the day's demands, separated by an expanse of cool crisp sheet that neither of us seemed willing or able to breach.

Five days of uncertainty, insecurity, icy-cold etiquette and unfamiliar protocol ensured that I remained malleable and eager to please my new family.

Because of the many public engagements we were obliged to attend, my wardrobe, or lack thereof, suddenly took on an importance bordering on the ridiculous. It caused a great deal of consternation when Bahrin and his aunties discovered that I had only one formal *baju kurung* to wear for official occasions. As a result, hasty arrangements were made with three different dressmakers for them to complete and deliver (within twenty-four hours) suitable garments for me to wear during coronation week. Luckily, each of the women in Bahrin's family had a private hoard of fabric lengths put away for future use, and it was from these stores that bolts of silk chiffon, lure threaded crêpe and crêpe de Chine were found for my dresses. I felt a little like an oversized Barbie doll as Bahrin's mother and his aunts draped lengths of material against my face and discussed designs with the tailors.

My one set of newly acquired daimonds would have to do, although it was pointed out to me that 'society at large' would notice that I was in a parlous state in terms of my jewellery box. Apparently, I would have to collect more serious ornamentation and cajoling Bahrin was the key, I was told by my new aunts. Until I had the usual array of 'opera' length pearls with matching earrings and bracelet, as well as a set of sapphires or rubies, life would be incomplete, they told me in in all seriousness. Meanwhile, it was decided my naked neck and ears would be adorned by a pair of Tengku Zaleha's elegantly designed diamond solitaire earrings of so many carats I was nervous lest I lose them. I was very grateful for my new in-laws' care and attention, but felt a twinge of guilt as I couldn't help pondering if they were doing it for me or to ensure that I didn't embarrass the family.

During the final days of our lightning-quick visit to Terengganu, Bahrin and I attended the *Istiadat Bersiram*, or ceremonial bathing ritual, of the new Sultan and his consort. It was an outdoor spectacle held in Istana Maziah's grounds at mid-morning and, unlike the installation of the Crown Prince and the coronation ceremony the next day, owed nothing to Western influences or twentieth-century social custom. The centuries-old ritual incorporates traditional Malay cultural practice and the Islamic tenets of purity and cleanliness, symbolising that their new ruler will begin his reign with a purified body and soul.

We arrived at Istana Maziah about twenty minutes early. The sky was cloudless and very blue as we took our designated seats on the palace lawns. In front of us stood a domed rotunda hung with magnificent awnings of yellow silk which were drawn back, leaving its sides open to the breeze. Through the pillars of the rotunda, just beyond the palace fence, the river, rippled by current, flowed out into the South China Sea, where I caught a glimpse of fishing boats moored in the shallows and bobbing gently up and down. For a split second I longed to join them in the coolness of the waves. I quashed that errant thought firmly as we all sat in the full sun waiting for the appointed hour to come around. With the temperature nudging one hundred degrees and the humidity high, tiny beads of perspiration began to cover my face, and my newly made court dress of deep purple chiffon fully lined in royal blue and bordered with pale pink and cream camellias stifled me. I fought the urge to lift my skirts for some relief. My neck felt sticky beneath the borrowed jewels, seeming to protest against so much glitz donned before nine in the morning.

The other guests chatted gaily with one another, brightly clothed and decorated, dress uniform sashes and gold braid, ceremonial decorations and top hats, silks and brocades all in abundance. A military band played on the opposite side of the quadrant, all cymbals, drums and brass. Bahrin and I sat in silence.

Suddenly the whole town seemed to come to a standstill as the Nobat horn blared out across the grounds; its unearthly trumpeting reverberated through my chest as a wave of movement signalled the start of the royal procession from the palace doors. We all rose and turned to watch its progress along the yellow carpet which had been rolled out for the occasion.

All this pageantry and pomp was what I'd married, I realised for the first time with alarm and a hollowness beneath my ribs – even as green a royal as I could picture these endless ceremonies stretching into the rest of our lives. For now, though, the newness made it fascinating to witness.

The first things that I caught sight of, over the sea of people, were the bright yellow satin umbrellas atop ten-foot mahogany poles. Tasselled round the edges, gold threads glinting in the sun, they were borne by uniformed lackeys and positioned above the heads of the Sultan and Tengku Ampuan to signify their royalty and protect them from the sun's harsh glare. Their entourage was huge: handmaidens in white and red *baju kurung* and wearing the royal insignia; men-at-arms and standard-bearers decked out in red *songket* and carrying the symbols of royal office, solid gold ceremonial *kris*, or dagger, sword and seal; military and police adjutants in dress uniform; and the members of the Nobat orchestra in black *baju melayu*, playing their instruments as they walked.

The royal couple themselves were dressed simply, by Malaysian standards, in paper-thin cream-silk ensembles which, on closer inspection, had been trimmed from neck to hem with small twenty-four-carat-gold medallions sewn in diamond patterns. His Royal Highness wore a plain *tanjok*, or crownless turban, as he walked with measured step, his military training evident in the set of his shoulders and the focus of his eyes which were 'parade ground' correct. No discernible flicker of emotion crossed the Sultan's face as he walked slightly ahead of his wife towards the dais, his jaw set square and his lips held firmly together. Whatever thoughts passed through his mind as he prepared to ascend his father's throne were kept strictly guarded and in check.

Once in position under the dome, Sultan Mahmud and his wife were surrounded by courtiers who, holding what resembled lengths of sheeting, screened the couple like a shower cubicle during the bathing ritual. Litre after litre of water, to which fresh limes had been added for their mystical cleansing properties, doused the fully-clothed couple. Poured from large brass urns according to a centuries-old tradition, the water ran in rivulets over the faces of the royals and down the steps of the rotunda. Protection from ill-wishers and evil intent was ensured by the contents of those jugs and the pith of the limes which clung to their hair. I watched, mesmerised by this ancient mysticism, vague parallels to papal coronation coming to mind amidst an Islamic/Asian enclave of royalty and superstition. When the symbolic rites were over, the Chief Imam joined the Sultan's entourage on the dais and, lifting his palms upwards, exhorted Allah to protect and guide the new ruler in the years to come. The long draperies of the dome were then drawn to allow the saturated Tengku Ampuan and Sultan to change their clothes in privacy.

Attired in dry robes of white *songket*, and wearing heavy and ornate solid gold jewellery, the royal procession then retraced its steps and disappeared inside the palace to the strains of the Nobat and shouts of '*daulat tuanku*', or 'long live the King'. I stayed in my seat as the other guests began to mill around and exchange pleasantries. I had the feeling that I had just been hurtled back in time, that what I had just witnessed was a throwback to a culture and a simplicity of belief long since abandoned. For all their outward sophistication and penchant for any new technological advances, I was beginning to understand that Bahrin's family still counted on, and trusted in, the 'old ways' to ward off evil and ensure harmony.

I would discover many contradictions of religion, legend, superstition and modern science the more I got to know my new family. I had a lot to learn.

Twenty-four

Life quickly swung back into the realms of normality as soon as we got home to Melbourne, leaving Bahrin's princely family and aristocratic strictures as a memory thousands of miles distant. We bounced along superficially, playing the parts of the carefree young marrieds, shopping, partying, studying and working. One noticeable effect of my new status as a married woman was the change in attitude towards me by my boss at Malaysian Airlines. Suddenly he was more polite and tended to talk to me as if we were sharing some private joke to which I had been made privy by my marriage to a 'royal'. It was a strange situation to be in; on one hand I was an employee on the lower rungs of the company and on the other I was the wife of someone my manager was obliged to treat as a VIP.

As Bahrin was in the final year of his architecture course, our schedules always involved coordinating his study times with our outside interests, none of which I can claim were intellectual or thought-provoking. By mutual consensus (Bahrin's decision and my acquiescence), I did not resume my ballet classes. Our leisure time was spent shopping in the trendier 'designer' parts of town. Bahrin had a fascination with men's fashion and passed a considerable amount of time poring over magazines like *GQ*, *Vogue* and *Playboy* (which he maintained he collected solely for the articles). As far as clothing went, for Bahrin only the best would do. The best shoes, ties and fabrics would leave him in paroxysms of delight and rapture. Money was no object when kitting himself out in the stores. Friday nights and Saturday mornings would usually see us strolling hand in hand along Melbourne's shopping boulevards in search of the perfect trouser cut or right collar size for him. Bahrin's reaction to designer clothing was almost sensual; he would stop and stroke a silk shirt as if it were the holy grail. His passion for elegance and dapper dressing led him to be considered a valued customer at several stores dealing in imported Italian and English goods. Paul Smith, Hugo Boss, Burberry and Valentino were his weaknesses. My penchant was for shoes and home furnishings. It was great fun deciding on my 'nesting materials' and drooling over Bahrin's *Architectural Digest* magazines to decide on colours and styles.

I threw myself wholeheartedly into the happy homemaker role and really enjoyed trying to learn how to cook. Together we would make early-morning visits to the local produce market on Saturdays to buy the week's supply of food. Bahrin seemed to enjoy the novelty of grocery shopping with me, although he had an almost anthropological curiosity about the whole process of purchasing ingredients and cooking meals. 'Spaghetti bolognese experimental' was one of my most successful forays into cooking. Bahrin ,with great gusto, would savour my meat sauce with its base of red wine, herbs and garlic. Dietary arrangements were not an issue; despite being a Muslim, he had no qualms about recipes containing alcohol and even admitted to having eaten bacon and eggs with relish when attending Geelong Grammar School.

Growing up in the palace had never exposed Bahrin

to any of life's daily necessities or chores. We were like children exploring the adult world and, thanks to Bahrin's inheritance and earlier dividends from royal holdings, our buying power was enormous and our enthusiasm unlimited. Looking back now, I recognise that this domesticity was never Bahrin's reality, it was only an interlude away from the discipline of being royal.

Curiosity and active contribution are two very different things. My new husband never made any attempt to enter our kitchen other than to help himself to the drinks in the fridge, but he would stand at the arched doorway that led into the living-room making appreciative noises about the aromas wafting from the pots simmering on the stove. Domestic equality and a sharing of responsibility were not in my vocabulary then. I was content to handle all those chores and not question his role in the household department. I finally had a family and a place for myself. I was playing house and felt gratitude to my husband for my new self-image as wife and homemaker. The abused child had been safely camouflaged and put away.

In the first months of our marriage we had a very romantic side to our relationship which would see us dining at 'our' restaurant, Tsindos, to celebrate our weekly anniversary. A candlelit dinner followed on some occasions by a jaunt to our favourite disco, a movie or a spontaneous bouquet of roses from him would complete the illusion that we were the 'ideal couple'. I must be honest and admit that in those early days I was very happy. I didn't question any facet of our relationship; to me Bahrin was always right, and the perfect man. Our wedding night was never referred to, nor was our future discussed at any length. Intimately, we had a pleasant and warm relationship, if somewhat lacking in consuming passion; quite sporadic, it was always gentle. I didn't expect any more at my age; the days of the women's movement and equal rights had skimmed over my head and hardly registered as anything relevant to me. I had chosen marriage both as a natural progression of an early permanent relationship and for its security. I look back now and view 1981 as the halcyon days with Bahrin; they bore very little resemblance to what was to come. But for the early period of our marriage I was in love with the idea of being in love.

Our social circle was insular and compact. Bahrin's cousins were our main companions, all of whom seemed to speak with him in some private code, even when conversing in English, a kind of royal shorthand of shared experiences and illicit musings about what the consequences would be if the family knew of their Western antics. There were no trusted confidants or friends in his life when I met him, just acquaintances and fellow students with whom he socialised but whom he kept at arm's length. The friends I had had prior to our marriage seemed to fade into oblivion. Bahrin didn't make things easier for me; it was difficult to maintain friendships when he made it quite clear that the only contact with people should be through him and at his instigation. He was adroit at creating situations with no leeway for compromise; arrangements would be made and presented to me as faits accomplis. I saw nothing odd about this. My whole universe revolved around his wishes.

Recently, I resumed a friendship with an old and dear girlfriend from my pre-Bahrin days. Shirley finally enlightened me about what had really happened to my old cohorts. As an example, one evening in the autumn of 1981, Shirley and another friend knocked on the door of our Melbourne house with the intention of dropping in for a coffee. They wanted to catch up on all my news and, as they hadn't seen me since my wedding, hear about our plans and check on how I was. Bahrin answered the bell and seemed at pains to open the door only a fraction. Shirley could hear music blaring through our house and smell a roast cooking. She also managed to catch sight of my large handbag just inside the door and assumed I was also at home. Upon requesting to see me, they were informed by Bahrin that it wasn't a convenient time to visit and that I was, in fact, out. When she pressed him to nominate a time when they could come back to speak to me, Bahrin told her very politely that he 'really didn't think that it was a good idea'. He told them that I had decided to make a new life with him and that 'really, quite frankly' I now moved in different circles from them, having made my choices when we married, coming to the decision to cut all old ties. Ordinarily, he said, members of his family's staff would have made my new situation and status clear, but as we were living in a foreign country it fell to him to define my position. From what Shirley has told me, and after she compared notes with several other mutual friends, she wasn't the only friend of mine who was treated in that manner and actively discouraged by Bahrin.

Peter Wallace, my close friend, also had his reservations about Bahrin right from the beginning. Prior to my 'engagement' trip to Malaysia, Peter, who was on his way to Thailand to take up his placement in their refugee camps as part of his fifth-year medical elective, made a stopover en route in Terengganu, where he spent several days as a guest at Bahrin's house. Being protective, he wanted to check out my new boyfriend for himself. He says that he left Terengganu after his brief sojourn feeling that there was much more to Bahrin than met the eye; knowing that I, being extremely headstrong and stubborn, would refuse to listen if he tried to dissuade me from becoming further involved with Bahrin, he kept his own counsel.

In 1981, the Islamic fasting month of Ramadan fell in the cold winter month of June. Fasting from the hours of sunrise to sunset during the month of Ramadan is observed by Muslims as penitence for their sins of the past year. No liquid or food of any kind may be consumed during these times. Sex must be abstained from and any form of bodily gratification such as ear cleaning or nose scratching is also forbidden. Menstruating or pregnant women are exempt from this practice but must make up the deficit in fasting days at some later date. The infirm are also excused. For Bahrin, the fasting month consisted of only the final four days; to me this had little significance and seemed more to be a by-product of the arrival of his Aunt Zainah and two of her adult children, Diana and Zainol.

Aunt Zainah had decided that she wished to holiday in Melbourne and see some of the city where two of her sons and various nieces and nephews had been sent to complete their education. Her daughter, Diana, who accompanied her, was a student at the London Polytechnic. The youngest in the family and probably the most Westernised, she was vivacious and had a good sense of humour. We hit it off immediately, which was fortunate as Bahrin considered Diana the closest thing he had to a sister. Diana appeared to be very independent and continually clashed with her mother's ideas on education, decorum and dress. For their stay with us I had pulled out all the stops, cleaning the house from top to bottom and stocking the refrigerator till it was groaning with food.

Viewing me as somewhat of a novelty for my 'Australian-ness', Aunt Zainah, who had been present at our wedding, exuded an affection and warmth for me that was to continue for all the years of my marriage to Bahrin and beyond. For a Malaysian woman in her late forties, and a princess to boot, she had an endearing tendency to giggle nervously at anything new or unfamiliar to her. As we had no common language, I did a lot of my communication with her using an English/Malay dictionary and Bahrin and his cousins as interpreters. This way I was able to ascertain that Tengku Zaleha, my mother-in-law, had been receiving my letters and that they were much appreciated; in fact they were much appreciated by her sisters and courtiers too, as she would pass them around for discussion.

I had made a decision after my return home that I would try my utmost to forge some sort of relationship with Bahrin's mother and decided that the best way to show her that I was trying hard to learn her language would be to write her a weekly letter. So, armed with a dictionary and an extremely basic and new knowledge of a few key words, I would sit down to compose my notes with a view to making a good impression. In my letters I would try to describe our daily lifestyle and what her son and I were up to. My efforts had the literacy of a six-year-old and my syntax was non-existent, but the thought was there. After a few months Tengku Zaleha began to reply in her childish hand. She used very basic and easy-to-grasp vocabulary which I could decipher with the use of my trusty dictionary. She also began to style herself 'Mak', the term used in Bahrin's family for 'Mum', so I knew that I was on my way to being accepted. Bahrin, on the other hand, never wrote to his mother and seldom telephoned her unless he had instructions about finances or shares. He was amused by my efforts but said he couldn't really understand why I bothered.

On the final day of the fasting month, Hari Raya, and in the company of his aunt and cousins, I discovered a new facet of Bahrin's personality that frightened and disturbed me. As part of a celebration for the end of Ramadan, Bahrin opted to take his relatives to Inflation, a nightclub and discotheque in central Melbourne. It was a busy night with people packed into the club from wall to wall. Aunt Zainah was thrilled to be on such an adventure but drew the line at actually taking to the tiles and dancing to the beat. She kept repeating that she was 'being very daring and modern' coming out with all us youngsters and swearing us to secrecy lest her brother, the Sultan, find out.

About two hours after our arrival, I saw a familiar face amongst the throng of bodies on the dance floor. Leaving, Bahrin to nurse his Bacardi and Coke, and first explaining to him that I thought I saw a friend on the other side of the floor and wanted to say hello, I picked my way slowly through the crowd.

I was very pleased to find that I had been right; I had recognised my friend Simon even without my spectacles on. As I said hello I gave him an affectionate hug and a peck on the cheek, which he returned happily. I hadn't seen him for almost two years and I filled him in on my marriage, my career and my decision not to dance any more and the reasons why.

After chatting excitedly for a few minutes, I returned to our table to find Bahrin seething with rage, his colour high and his eyes bulging out of their sockets. Grabbing hold of my wrist, he pushed me before him up the staircase leading to the exit level of the building, hissing the words 'slut' and 'whore' as we went. Managing to wrench myself from his grip, I whirled around to face him just as we reached the middle landing and caught a slap across my face in the process. That first blow was followed by another which knocked me to my knees. Confused as to what had triggered his attack, I struggled to make sense of the torrent of abuse flowing from his mouth. I was a 'slut' and a 'disgusting little bitch' who had embarrassed him in front of his family.

'Only sluts throw themselves at strange men and kiss them in public,' he berated me as I managed to move out of his reach and up a step.

'Do you mean Simon? But I've known Simon since I was ten, I was friends with his five sisters,' I tried to explain.

'You're just a filthy Australian slut like all of these bitches here,' he railed, as though he hadn't heard me.

Suddenly what had always been socially acceptable behaviour, what had always been considered polite contact between friends by Australian society, was being categorised as uncouth, filthy and illicit by my husband.

'I've done nothing wrong. Simon's an old friend and, besides, he's gay,' I pleaded. But he was beyond listening as he dragged me by the wrist through the foyer of the nightclub, past the curious faces of other patrons and down the steps into King Street, where he bundled us into a cab and left his family behind. I was crying by now, trying to get as far away from him in the taxi as I could, as he shot me withering glances and gripped the arm-rest until his knuckles turned white. Once home and inside the front door, he began to tongue-lash me again; I was 'worthless, nothing, a slut and a bitch', he screamed at me, kicking furniture, knocking over stacks of books and swiping his drafting pens and materials off his desk as I cowered in a corner of his study.

I couldn't stand it. I couldn't handle his being furious with me, couldn't cope with his abuse and anger. I was afraid that he would never stop. I groped in my mind for a way to temper his outrage and silence his shouting, afraid of what else he might do to me. Then I remembered what day it was: remembered that it was Hari Raya, the end of the fasting month, and the one day in the Islamic calendar when Muslims were bound by their religion to forgive any sins or slights against them which were professed by another.

Sliding onto all fours at Bahrin's feet and touching my forehead to his shoes, I sobbed out my remorse for anything I had done to anger or displease him and reminded him that it was Hari Raya. Haltingly, I spoke the prescribed words of penitence, '*saya ma'af zahir dan batin*', as I cried and remained on the floor. My relief was immense when he ceased his tirade, began to regulate his breathing and relaxed his shoulders. He appeared to be somewhat mollified by my penitence, but I kept out of striking distance as I sat upright on the floor at his feet. I flinched as Bahrin reached down to take my elbow. Drawing me upright before him, he said in a cold tone, 'Now you have to kiss my hand to show you respect me as your husband.' I complied, hoping that this would end his fury; it did, changing his countenance from hostile to benevolent within a matter of seconds and leaving me holding my breath in anticipation of what he would do.

His next words truly fazed me.

'Darling, you must think before you say or do something that could annoy me,' Bahrin chided me. He went on in a gentle and controlled tone, 'I have to get angry with you when you do something that's wrong. You have to learn.'

By now all I wanted to do was keep the peace. I was frightened and, as I tentatively murmured how sorry I was for what I had done, I felt as if I were balancing a pyramid of eggs on the end of my nose, hoping that my remorse would stave off any further eruptions of displeasure, but ready in case my tone was not the right one to mollify him. In a secret recess behind my heart, I was seething with rage and disgust at myself for not standing up to him and maintaining my innocence; and rage and disgust at Bahrin for making me apologise for a crime I hadn't committed.

*   *   *

The fifth of July would mark my eighteenth birthday. Bahrin decided we could have a party to celebrate the occasion, but only if I were circumspect and referred to it as my 'coming-of-age birthday' and not my eighteenth when talking to his friends. He ordered my favourite triple chocolate and mousse cake from Paterson's Bakery in the shape of a key and I spent hours taping music and preparing finger food.

Bahrin chose my dress for the party from a shop called Digby's: hot fuschia-pink georgette, calf-length with long sleeves and beading across the bodice. I thought it was terribly sophisticated, if a little old for me. He had wanted me to wear my hair up in a bun for the party but I managed to cajole him into letting me wear it out long and curled without receiving too much disapproval from him.

Not one of my own friends came that night. The guests consisted of his university mates, lecturers, a few of my workmates from Malaysian Airlines whom Bahrin thought might be suitable guests, one of my former teachers and Bahrin's cousins. The champagne I drank that evening only heightened my feelings of being a stranger at my own birthday celebration and made me a little fuzzy about just exactly how old I was meant to be that night. Bahrin's cousins knew I was eighteen, the people from my office thought I was twenty and his university friends assumed I was twenty-one. When it came time to sing 'Happy Birthday' there was a great deal of confusion, adroitly glossed over by Bahrin and barely remembered later.

I slept fitfully that night, my dreams a confusion of images, myself at seven, eighteen and fifty all merging into each other as I looked in the mirror and didn't recognise the reflection, seeing only a figure with no face.

Twenty-five

In the latter half of 1981, Bahrin and I worked hard together to ensure that he finished his honours thesis for his architectural degree. Many nights I would arrive home from the office a little after him, we'd eat dinner and watch an hour's television and then we'd knuckle down to the real work at hand. Bahrin perched on his stool in front of the drafting table, working on the scale models of his building designs, as I sat cross-legged on the study floor with a typewriter balanced precariously atop a planter box, transcribing Bahrin's thesis notes into legible material. It was a companionable period for us. We talked pleasantly about his ideas for the Victorian State Library student competition and of the buildings he would design when he was qualified. He would ask my opinion on the model of the library which was taking shape from the sheets of white construction cardboard we had dragged upstairs and which he painstakingly glued, cut and photographed as it progressed.

The model was beautiful: porticoes, corridors filled with natural light and intricately cut windows and rooflines – a simplicity of design which was approachable rather than mausoleum-like. I became very adept at holding fiddly bits and pieces for Bahrin while he glued sections or cut doorlines with a razor-sharp Stanley knife.

As the university was only a stone's throw from the house, some evenings, weather permitting, we would jog round the athletics track and then scoff ice creams on the way home or stop off at our favourite café in Lygon Street for pasta and gelati. As long as I made sure not to annoy Bahrin, everything was peaceful.

For the wedding of Prince Charles and Lady Di, Bahrin and I decided to invite a couple of friends over for a royal wedding picnic to coincide with the live television broadcast of the event. Interest in and enthusiasm for the wedding was high in Australia, if in many cases rather tongue in cheek. In others, a closet fascination with all the pomp and ceremony such an occasion brings encouraged unbridled media coverage and headline stories every day. Pubs with royal monikers such as the Prince of Wales or the Royal Arms held wedding parties on their premises which were so successful it was standing room only. People seemed caught up in the fairy-tale quality of the impending union and a naive secret belief in the Cinderella syndrome.

During our picnic in front of the television we sipped champagne and orange juice and ate smoked salmon on toast as we sat huddled on the floor together under the watchful gaze of a portrait of Bahrin's grandfather, the late Malaysian King. We joked and laughed that evening, caught up in the gaiety and optimism reflected by the British crowds on the TV screen. Like many of the 500 million people around the world who watched the broadcast beamed internationally by satellite, we were eager to see the bride trip demurely up the aisle and the prince transform her into a Royal Highness before they floated together out of the cathedral as husband and wife to live happily ever after. It was odd to watch another young girl being inducted into a royal family. I remember sending her a silent 'good luck' and hoping that her protocol training was going to be more complete than mine had been three and a half months earlier.

We made a lightning trip to Malaysia in August of that year, stopping off in Kuala Lumpur to belatedly purchase a wedding ring for me. Bahrin chose a cluster of twenty-two diamonds in a flower shape, set in yellow gold. As it was far too big and ornate a design to escape anyone's notice, I enjoyed flashing it in the sunlight to see it sparkle, although it took me ages to get used to its weight and I was forever clunking into door frames and getting it caught up in my clothing or hair. (I could never countenance jewellery that large now – I prefer little or none at all.)

Along with my new acquisition came a new rule: Bahrin said that whilst I was in Malaysia, I must wear my ring on the right hand rather than the usual left of Western custom. To me it made little difference as my wedding ring bore no resemblance to a Western-style marriage band, a fact which disappointed me somewhat. When I voiced that misgiving to Bahrin, he replied that his family would think he was some sort of cheapskate if he only gave me a gold band rather than a diamond ring. Privately I couldn't see that it was their business, and it seemed ridiculous to worry about their likes and dislikes on the matter of my wedding ring. Bahrin and I continued on to Terengganu a day or so later. We were making the trip to organise some of the finer details of our impending *Bersanding*, or formal wedding ceremony, planned for the new year. Having had only the equivalent of a registry service, we were now obliged to wed in the traditional royal fashion with all due pomp and protocol. To begin with, this entailed choosing the colour, design and weave of the silk *songket* fabric which had to be woven for our wedding costumes well in advance, as it would take several weeks to complete the quantity of material needed for the traditional royal garb.

We were chauffeured close to the factory in one of the family cars, then we picked our way on foot between the goats and the chickens roaming free amongst the banana and coconut groves that dotted the village. A large concrete well centred between the houses was the only water supply for the ten or so families living there. To me it seemed strange that there was no grass visible anywhere – for all the lush greenery of the surrounding jungle, there was not one blade of grass to be found. Children played in the dirt and in the shade beneath their houses, barefoot and grubby. Dressed in cheap cotton dresses or singlets and bare-bottomed, they scrabbled around boisterously, a mixture of all ages. Like any other children, they ranged from the very timid and shy to the brave and cheeky ones who looked at us forthrightly and grinned. The contrast with the opulent and orderly lifestyle of Bahrin's family shocked me greatly. Here the toilet was the spinach patch a few feet from their homes, their kitchens open to the flies. A refrigerator was unheard of; those things existed only as a picture in a magazine. Bahrin passed all these sights by without a single flicker of his eyes showing that the squalid conditions that these people lived in had even registered. He just walked on, straight and tall, immaculately attired in clothes that had probably cost more than what this entire village spent in food in a month, until we reached the factory.

It was hot and very sticky in the tiny wooden house which stood on stilts in the middle of the fairly isolated village and doubled as the *songket* factory. Together we sat on a woven grass mat of variegated colours, the rhythmic click clack of the looms punctuating our conversation. Second only to fishing as an income generator for the small community, *songket* weaving was a skill often passed down from generation to generation. This particular community of artisans had been supplying *songket* to the royal family for more years than anyone could remember.

Looms slung with half-finished fabrics lined the walls, hues of blue, red and sombre black indicating the diversity of commissions that the establishment accepted. Most of the young female weavers observed us surreptitiously, barely keeping their curiosity in check as we pored over samples and photographs with their supervisor. I shot a friendly smile at one or two of the girls, which they returned shyly with a muffled giggle before immediately pretending to be engrossed in their work. The weavers were aged between thirteen and twenty, dressed in full *baju kurung* and wearing veils which obscured their hair and neck, leaving only their faces, hands and feet uncovered. Dressed as they were in the sweltering heat, I imagined that they must have been very uncomfortable in the badly ventilated building.

After much discussion, we finally decided on deep maroon red *songket* shot with black and incorporating a modern geometric pattern in gold thread. Fifteen metres would be delivered in plenty of time to the tailor who would transform the fabric into our traditional bridal clothes. A price was mentioned by the supervisor which seemed very reasonable to me but Bahrin was intent on haggling over the cost. I felt very embarrassed that he would try to beat them down on the price considering the weeks it would take to complete the commission. But Bahrin prevailed and we departed having struck what I considered an unholy bargain.

Once settled back into the air-conditioned comfort of our car, I began to pump Bahrin carefully for information and his opinions on the village we had just left. According to him, the average wage in that community was somewhere in the region of two hundred

Malaysian ringgit a month, or about thirty-two pounds sterling. Most villages were no better or worse than the one we had been to; most had no electricity or running water, let alone sewerage. 'They know no better, they're happy the way they live,' pronounced Bahrin. 'They're only *orang darat*, rural people, hillbillies. Don't worry about their lives, to them that's normal. Anyway, they're not your concern,' he said firmly, closing the topic to any more questioning.

It began to occur to me then that my husband was blinkered, by choice, to the poverty which contrasted so blatantly with his family's affluence. I was beginning to understand that the gap between the 'haves' and the 'have nots' in Malaysia was not in fact a gap but more of an unbridgeable chasm, pristine on one side and suppurating on the other.

Bahrin's mother openly showed her pleasure with me during this visit, arranging a girl's tête-à-tête and ensuring that there was someone on hand to interpret. She and I discussed her views on the wedding clothes and she gave me a list of items to purchase in Australia for the *Hantar Belanjar*, or bridal gifts, that the couple are traditionally expected to exchange as a form of dowry and goodwill. Tengku Zaleha also told me that my grandmother was more than welcome at the wedding and that the royal family expected to see her there. As a signal to other members of her family that she accepted me as her daughter-in-law, she presented me with diamond solitaire earrings which had been her favourite pair and asked me to wear them immediately. It made me extremely happy that she openly accepted me; all the letter writing and courtesy had been a good idea and it was easy and natural to like her right back as she was a gentle and unassuming woman. Her warmth engendered a feeling of optimism about my new marital situation which had been lacking up to this point. And it made me more confident that I had at least one relationship with another woman in a strange country to count on, albeit a tenuous one.

Twenty-six

The sum total of my life was assembled before me in thirty-six tea chests, itemised, wrapped and numbered. Everything that was me and everything that was mine was in those boxes. Panda, Teddy and Lambkin had been stowed carefully, ready for the day when my child could find comfort in their worn and bedraggled fur. Eighteen years of books, too precious to leave behind, were crammed into other boxes alongside cherished photographs, ballet shoes and the more mundane trappings of my new domesticity. Our Christmas tree and decorations were on their way to warmer climes as were our feather quilts and winter clothing. If I had to live in Malaysia, Australia was going with me.

It was November 1981 and I was leaving my country with hardly a qualm. My future was with my husband, and for all intents and purposes, and as Bahrin had led me to believe, we were planning simply to transplant our Australian life to Malaysia. The reality of such a momentous move did not hit home for several months. The flurry of preparations, logistics, house sales and packing left little time for contemplation, nor was I astute enough at eighteen to envisage a shift in continents as more than an interesting exercise in organisation and travel.

I was married to Bahrin and my place was with him.

Marriage, as far as I was concerned, was for ever. If things between us had not magically become more intimate or intellectually melded from the moment I became his wife, time would fix that, I reasoned optimistically. I had been rather idealistic when we married. I imagined that the mere fact that I was his wife would bestow on me some invisible key to unlock his innermost thoughts and feelings, that he would open up to me and we would enrich our lives together by sharing all and discussing everything under the sun. But by the time I had been through six months of married life I began to make excuses for his lack of warmth, his withdrawn moods and the wall which marriage seemed to have thrown up between us. 'It will take time,' I used to tell myself. 'One morning I'll open my eyes and the warmth I felt from him will return for good. It's all a matter of time and trust.'

If I close my eyes hard, I can picture events and conversations from those first months of living in Malaysia. They flash by like two-dimensional postcards pegged to a conveyor belt. If I focus harder, those individual scenes begin to emerge from their flatness and take on a depth of colour and sound which draws me back into the past. I see myself almost as a third person, as a mannequin being shaped and modelled into the perfect wife, a fitting fixture for all royal events, not in control of my own likes and dislikes, tastes or opinions. I seem eager to please, ready to be re-educated; a bystander to my own existence.

I see a teenage girl, veiled, bejewelled and bewildered, sitting in solitary state upon a throne. Ceiling fans whirl smoothly above the heads of the guests who sit before the girl observing her demeanour intensely for a hint of brazen behaviour or a glance of unmaidenly mirth, but there is none. She sits still, eyes downcast, hands in her lap, waiting. A stout matron advances towards the throne, her long skirts rustle as she accepts a saucer of holy water in which rests a golden whisk. An attendant leans forward, turning the girl's hands over to reveal the large henna-stained circles which brand her palms. Each of her ten fingertips and nails is stained a brownish red as well; she'd sat motionless for hours earlier that day, her hands and fingers encased in a mixture resembling wet tea leaves to achieve this effect and bring her to this moment in her new life.

The *Istiadat Berinai*, or henna ceremony, a symbol of purity, dictates that she be blessed to ensure fertility. Her status as a bride is heralded by her henna-stained hands, her stiff *songket* garb and the heirloom veil of heavy silk and gold thread. A solid gold tiara resembling a sunburst anchors the veil in place. It feels heavy and its unyielding support band cuts into her scalp just above the right ear. She must submit to the *Berinai* ritual with complete detachment, removed from the proceedings around her – as if she were chiselled from stone.

The stout, opulently dressed matron flicks holy water over her with the golden whisk, but the girl on the throne barely stirs as the droplets hit her face, drip down her chin and land with inaudible plops on her outstretched hands. She sits stoically as matron after matron repeats the motions of the blessing, never flinching, just staring straight ahead.

Later, alone in her bedroom, the girl peers into the mirror at the exotic stranger reflected there. Dark eyes rimmed with kohl, red 'beestung' lips, the face of a stranger playing a role, the face of Yasmin. She tilts her head from side to side almost quizzically and wonders where Jacqueline has disappeared to, now that Yasmin has arrived. And all she feels is numbness.

How hard it is to find the words to describe my other self, the girl on the bridal throne, the ravenous bride fainting with hunger and heat amidst the well-fed guests at her own wedding. It all seems so far away, so remote and divorced from the woman I am now.

The day after the *Berinai* ceremony was our *Istiadat Bersanding*, or formal wedding. One thousand guests, give or take a few score, had been invited for the occasion. Pavilions had been erected in the grounds of our new home in Terengganu by the state public works department to accommodate the guests. Hung with state flags, royal bunting and hundreds and hundreds of coloured lights, the house and gardens resembled a fairground; all that was missing was the ferris wheel. The workmen, having first removed all the furniture, installed our bridal thrones and dais beneath a canopy of silk strewn with gold filigree leaves and small golden beads sewn in place by willing courtiers. Palace officials arrived with boxes of pure gold ornaments, trays and royal insignia.

In a rear courtyard, three days before the actual wedding feast, the palace caterers set up their huge cooking pots, from which tantalising aromas emanated. A horde of ladies – Bahrin's cousins and aunts, as well as the wives of palace officials – arrived in the days leading up to our *Bersanding* to assist in the flurry of preparations essential to a royal wedding.

Over the course of forty-eight hours, fifteen hundred eggs had to be hard-boiled and dyed red for inclusion in the *bunga telur*, literal translated as 'egg flower', the traditional commemorative gift presented to each guest. These varied from wedding to wedding; in our case, the *bunga telur* had been chosen with great care by a team of Bahrin's family over a number of months. Elegant gold and silver filigree baskets, each containing one hard-boiled egg dyed red, were trimmed with narrow yellow and white ribbons which secured a printed card with our names, the date of our marriage and a thank-you message. A symbol of fertility, these ornaments were prized souvenirs in Bahrin's country and generally considered a mark of social status and sophistication, a yardstick by which to gauge the merit of the host family. It was quite common practice for Malaysians to collect dozens of them in a lifetime and display the *bunga telur* in their china cabinets, with souvenirs from royal weddings taking prominent positions in the display. China eggcups served the same purpose and were distributed to the dozens of village people and servants' families who also attended our wedding informally but were kept away from the aristocracy by barriers both physical and social.

On the morning of our *Bersanding*, the *Hantar Belanjar*, or exchange of bridal gifts, took place. Royal custom dictated that Bahrin and I exchange thirteen trays of gifts each. The bridegroom's gifts to his intended must include a tray of betel nut (the traditional chewing plant with a mild narcotic effect), cash, something sweet to eat and an article of clothing, to symbolise that he will be able to provide all the necessary creature comforts for her. The gifts, on silver and brass trays, are exchanged in a formal ceremony akin to the acceptance of a dowry by both parties and are laid out for inspection by all members of the respective families and evaluated on artistic presentation and worth. Bahrin himself chose most of his gifts to me as well as their presentation: a dress length of sheer black silk chiffon from France, strewn with gold glitter and folded ornately to resemble a large flower; diamond jewellery; black silk evening shoes; a range of Jean Desprez perfumes and bath oils; ten thousand ringgit in cash, cleverly designed and crafted into a miniaturised traditional house on stilts; a gold metal evening bag shaped like a shell; and a tray of betel nut with all the necessary accoutrements for its consumption – clippers, bowl and box.

In return, my gifts to Bahrin had been chosen with care on the advice of Tengku Zaleha: a set of architectural coffee-table books detailing historic buildings and structures around the world (my own choice); a briefcase made from fine burgundy leather and matching wallet and belt; an emerald solitaire ring; antique *songket* fabric; and a set of Pino Sylvestre, his favourite cologne. Following the solemn acceptance of these gifts according to Malay tradition, the stage was set for our 'public marriage'.

For the centuries preceding the arrival of Islam to Malaysia, these traditional practices of *Hantar Belanjar* and *Bersanding* were the only acknowledged forms of marriage throughout Malay society. Therefore even though Bahrin and I had already been legally married under Islamic law, the social significance of our 'second wedding' could not be ignored.

As tradition dictates, on the day of her *Bersanding*, the bride has to be isolated from all outside influences bar the women of her family. This meant I found myself banished to my bedroom far away from all the fascinating preparations that were taking place outside. I was supposed to give myself up to the luxury of being pampered and groomed for my big moment as the centre of attention. All I could think of was how to get some food into my stomach. Every time I caught the attention of a passing servant or relative to beg for some sustenance, they would smile, nod and promise that my meal would be arriving on a tray soon. After eight hours had gone by, I really began to doubt my proficiency in the Malay language. I knew that I had a long way to go before I was fluent, but I was pretty sure that my desperate pantomime of hunger and my rumbling stomach had been enough to convey my near starvation.

By 7.30 p.m. I was almost ready for the formal ceremony. Peeking through the curtains of my room, I could see the guests arriving in a fast and steady stream and I could hear the military band beginning to play. Periodically Bahrin's mother and aunts would come in to check on the progress of my toilette and my nerves, and oversee my dressing, but still no one thought to bring me any food.

I had caused consternation in the family by opting to arrange my own hair and apply my own make-up, rather than hire a professional make-up artist. It was strange enough wearing all the traditional finery without being at the mercy of a traditional stylist. About that I was adamant – I would be wearing my own face.

Bahrin was proud of his royal heritage and truly loved the richness of his race's culture. He had chosen all my bridal accoutrements himself and had set his mind on the most authentic and antique style of dress for me. Tall on elegance and antiquity, short on comfort and practicality.

My bridal costume was incredibly ornate, but most of all it was incredibly uncomfortable and heavy. On my feet I wore gold Charles Jourdan evening shoes with four-inch stiletto heels to give me added height (the only concession to the twentieth century), and around my ankles were heavy twisted gold anklets that jangled as I moved. My dress was made from the maroon *songket* we had ordered months before, fully lined and tailored into a *baju kebaya*, a knee-length jacket with turn-back collar and wraparound skirt. Tight and figure-hugging, it was sweltering to wear in the thirty-five degree heat and humidity. Underneath, I wore the customary full-length strapless corset-brassiere which was boned and padded to give the correct silhouette to the bridal garment and totally precluded any of the normal bodily movements of a woman – bending, breathing or sitting with any modicum of comfort. In fact, it reminded me of the backboards young Victorian girls were made to wear to improve posture.

Around my neck and across my chest was fastened a large *kalong*, or necklace, of gold discs linked by chain and falling in three tiers. Both my wrists were encircled by bracelets which matched my heavy anklets and my fingers were weighted down with borrowed rings set with diamonds, rubies and emeralds.

My hair was pinned into a huge bun at the nape of my neck and supplemented with artificial hairpieces to increase its bulk until it resembled a large football. Twenty *bunga goyang*, quivering flowers in gold and mounted on tiny springs to increase their shimmering effect, were inserted into the back of my hairstyle at the direction of the gaggle of ladies who had come into my dressing-room to assist in my transformation.

The main bridal headpiece was lowered carefully onto my head and secured ruthlessly with so many hairpins I could have kept a chain of hairdressers supplied for a year. Made of gold filigree and tiny hidden springs beneath layers of tooled flowers, the bridal headdress was shaped like an open fan and tinkled and quivered with my every move. The final touch to this confection was the brow piece, a band of beaten gold and filigree work. It spanned my forehead and pressed tightly into my temples, resting just above my eyebrows. The whole outfit was absolutely breathtaking, like something out of the pages of an anthropological book on medieval costumes.

And so the time arrived for me to join Bahrin on the bridal thrones for our *Bersanding*. Escorted on either side like an invalid, I took tiny steps along the red carpet and mounted the dais to sit on Bahrin's left. Neither of us even glanced at the other as this was forbidden; the bride and groom are expected to keep absolutely straight faces and not raise an eyebrow. We were flanked on either side by attendants in court dress, the daughters of courtiers who had been seconded to us as bridesmaids and two palace matrons who were to supervise the proceedings.

A huge tiered yellow wooden stand, used only for royal weddings, had been sent from the palace. Shaped like open stars, each tier had been filled with yellow-tinted sticky rice into which the royal family's heirloom *bunga telur* had been arranged. Two centuries old, these *bunga telur* in solid gold were formed into the shape of flowers, complete with stems and stamens and from the centre of each hung a coloured egg.

In days gone by, as most Malay marriages were arranged, the *Bersanding* was the first time a bride and groom would see each other. This was part of the reason for the constraints placed upon the bridal couple whilst sitting in state – it was probably to discourage a look of horror passing between two strangers.

Our marriage blessings were bestowed by the senior members of Bahrin's family, starting with the Sultan and Tengku Ampuan, in a similar ceremony to my *Berinai* of the night before. This time, however, we were both showered with holy water, followed by handfuls of uncooked rice for fertility and prosperity. This procedure was repeated by about twenty other VIPs, including the Dowager Tengku Ampuan, the state's Prime Minister and his wife, Bahrin's parents, aunts and uncles and my darling nanna, whom we had brought out from Australia for the occasion.

After all of our thousand or so guests had filed past to see us sitting in state, it was time for us to pay our formal respects and homage to the Sultan and Tengku Ampuan. It was only about two hundred yards from the dais but that two hundred yards proved to be my undoing. Just as I was about to make my curtsey and kiss their Highnesses' hands, the world began to spin and suddenly everything went black. The combination of hunger, nerves, heat and the weight of the bridal costume had given me a migraine and made me pass out. I must have made a stunning picture crumpled on the floor. I came to shortly afterwards, just as they were holding a drink against my lips to revive me.

Bahrin was very concerned about me, as were all of his family. I don't think the Sultan knew what to make of my fainting spell, though – women in his family just didn't faint in public, and certainly not at their own weddings. I felt a lot better after they allowed me to sit awhile in the air-conditioning, but it wasn't more than ten minutes before everyone began to whisper that I must greet the rest of the guests and cut the wedding cake.

I can't remember with any great clarity how I managed to stand up for the hour it took to greet each of the guests individually – or what on earth I said to them, as the vast majority were total strangers – but, according to the photographic evidence, I did. Bahrin eventually guided me to the open-sided pavilion where our wedding cake stood so we could fulfil our final obligation of the evening – cutting the three-tiered, bright yellow cake, which was covered in hideous icing-sugar flowers.

I think that cake was a definite omen of the future of our marriage: it had turned rancid in the heat, right down to the very last inedible crumb.

We were woken up the next morning by the ringing of an alarm that just wouldn't stop. Twenty minutes later we finally located its source. Some wit had set an alarm clock to ring at 7 a.m. before wrapping it and delivering it as one of our wedding gifts. The parcel was right at the bottom of the mountain of presents which completely filled our guestroom and flooded out into the corridor. Luckily the cavalry arrived in the form of Bahrin's immediate family, who had come to join in the gift opening.

By the time all the presents had been opened, Bahrin and I had enough appliances to open a well-stocked chain store. We received, give or take a few gifts: thirteen china tea sets, nine irons, twenty-seven clocks of varying styles including the ringing alarm clock, which was a white porcelain seventeenth-century reproduction, a battery-operated timepiece topped with gold doves, fifteen sets of bed linen, thirty-two pieces of Pyrex cookware, four brass trays, one canteen of solid silver cutlery in a setting for twenty-four, seven coffee sets, two Mistral cooling fans, twenty-two lengths of dress fabric, twelve men's prayer sarongs, six ladies' batik sarongs, fifteen pieces of silver tableware, a silver posy bowl, two brass portable handwashing urns, a silver picture frame and a large round leather jewellery box by Lanvin, twenty lengths of *songket*, four Islamic verses from the Koran to hang above doors, five or six presentation boxes of perfume and men's cologne, a dozen place mats, a Noritake dinner set, matching his and hers gold Lanvin watches, a reproduction 1920s telephone, assorted crystalware, four prayer rugs, six sets of baby clothes (in anticipation or encouragement), at least £10,000 in cash. There was also a large assortment of gold jewellery, diamond jewellery and a set of sapphire and diamond jewellery. And last, but definitely not the least, a gift from one of Bahrin's elderly relatives: a huge chiming fluorescent wall clock embossed around the edges with Koranic inscriptions and surrounding a picture of a large sailing ship made entirely from nuts and bolts with the digital clock face set into the vessel's bow.

It was amazing how that clock just slipped out of my hands and crashed to the floor shortly after it was unwrapped.

Twenty-seven

It is incredibly strange to live in a world where time is marked by an ancient call to prayer and the days on the calendar evaporate unnoticed. So it was for me in Terengganu. I was suspended in a time limbo where the real world existed only on the outside, in far-off Australia and other countries, where the seasons changed and the years were marked by Christmases and holidays.

My days were not calculated and no anniversaries were kept. In many ways, I did not age at all from the eighteen-year-old I was when I started married life there; in others, I became a wise old woman, with the mask of naivety torn from my face.

The first order of business was for me to become fluent in classical or 'High' Malay; that is, the form of the Malay language with all its antiquated terminologies that is peculiar to royal circles. Bahrin decreed that I was to speak only Malay to him and the rest of the family. He reasoned that by isolating me from my own native tongue by way of language immersion I would be forced to become fluent in record time. He was right. I had no choice but to force myself to comprehend Malay and, in eight weeks, I was able to carry on fairly complex conversations.

The next task on the agenda was my re-education

on details of manners and decorum. Being a member of the immediate royal family had its hazards in the etiquette stakes. Ordinary Malay people had similar things expected of them with regard to the social niceties, but for them, especially if they resided in the capital city of Kuala Lumpur, their code of conduct was far less rigid and more easygoing than what society expected of me. I was expected to walk, talk, sit, stand, dress and eat according to an unwritten code of protocol. Only occasionally, when I was alone with Tengku Zaleha and Auntie Zainah, could these rules be relaxed a smidgen. Other than a few exceptions where I was pre-warned on the socially acceptable way to behave, it was a case of the royal family allowing me to blunder along and learn by a form of osmosis. When I truly did slip up, the senior royal ladies would pull me quickly into line with a lecture on how big the steps I took should be, or how to point delicately without using the index finger. Worse still would be when Bahrin himself caught me in an un-royal gaffe – then I would have to sit for aeons listening to him lecture me on my new postion and my mistakes. He often appeared to be more an etiquette lecturer than a husband.

How the younger members of the family absorbed all these rules and regulations I will always wonder. There was certainly no time put aside for actual lessons in this area – that would have been considered ill bred and bourgeois. I rather fancy that Bahrin and his cousins all learned the rigid rules of protocol by mimicry, a high threshold for boredom, steely detachment and constant correction by their nannies as they were growing up. Certainly any form of uncalculated response was something reserved solely for the times when the younger royals were on holidays or studying in the USA or England, unburdened briefly from the disdainful looks of courtiers and household staff.

I lost my own spontaneity on the day I saw my first tropical rainstorm. It was late January 1982 and the monsoon season had arrived, bringing with it a slight respite from the punishing humidity and heat. Temperatures dropped to the mid-twenties, and a breeze rippled the fronds of the coconut trees in our garden and penetrated the modest full-length clothing the women wore.

On this particular day, I was busy unpacking the crates containing our personal effects which had finally arrived from Australia after eight weeks. As I was in the privacy of my own home, I had dressed that day in clothes which allowed me more freedom of movement than the long skirts which Bahrin preferred me to wear. My baggy towelling tracksuit with its zippered front was far more functional and sensible for unpacking boxes. As I delved into my long-lost treasures and arranged books on shelves with the help of my maid, Wan Su, I became aware of a pattering on the windows that quickly turned into a thunderous pounding. It was rain. Sweet, pure and tantalisingly refreshing. I had almost forgotten what the sound was until I saw the water cascading over the gutterings and into the garden. Somehow, knowing that there would never be a winter in my new home had almost convinced me subconsciously that heavy rain belonged in Australia or England, not Malaysia.

I felt myself drawn outside onto the covered verandah where I could breathe in the freshness and watch the dust get washed away from the paths and trees. I had never seen such a torrential downpour. It fell with a kind of desperation onto the earth, as though it could quench only through pounding. For minutes I splayed my hand out under the eaves, catching the water and wondering at its warmth. I had expected it to be icy cold, not tepid. Urges overtook my reason and suddenly there I was, laughing and dancing fully dressed in the rain that bucketed down from above. I was exhilarated. It was like standing under a warm waterfall, cleansing and stimulating. I felt no chill, no wrongness, only a freedom and a happiness that I had never experienced before. It was absolutely wonderful – and then it was over, brought to a halt by a hand on the scruff of my neck dragging me backwards, out of the deluge and away from my wet happiness. I could barely hear Bahrin above the pelting of the rain as he yelled admonishments at me and told me I should be ashamed of the spectacle I had made of myself. It was then that I realised that most of the servants and family had come out of their respective houses and were watching me as if I were a mad woman, as if I were truly unhinged.

In all my time in Terengganu, I never did anything spontaneous like that again. It wasn't worth the humiliation or the abuse. I wasn't brave enough to risk it and I wasn't secure enough to thumb my nose at the conventions of behaviour that constricted me.

The price that I ultimately paid to Bahrin for my rain dance was the incineration of my 'Chinese' self. At his behest, I laid out all my treasured possessions, which had just been unpacked from our Australian shipment, for him to survey and pick over. He insisted I add to this pile of memories the small antique figure of Buddha that I usually wore around my neck; it had been bequeathed to me by my father who had worn it until his death. The Buddha was the closest link I had to Father; it had no religious significance for me, nor did the red quilt embroidered with dragons and phoenixes, nor the two Chinese silk-scroll paintings, but Bahrin chose to consign the lot to the fire he had laid in the rear of the house, accompanied by some of my clothing that he deemed unsuitable and un-Islamic. Ironically, some of the blouses and mid-calf-length skirts and evening dresses he now considered too risqué to be stored in our home were the very same items of clothing which he had complimented me on during our courtship.

As the smoke from the fire billowed across our garden, Bahrin explained that the 'spring cleaning' of my life was for my own good – I would no longer be contaminated by the uncleanliness of either Western culture or my Chinese family. I would now be free to become immersed in my new religion and society. I could say nothing, I could think of nothing to say, I just stood with my arms wrapped tightly around myself, watching the only tangible connections I had with my father turn to ash.

Although illegal and considered pornography in Malaysia, Bahrin's collection of *Playboy* magazines remained 'uncleansed', safely stored in the bottom of his office sideboard beneath his copies of the Koran and Islamic law books. He had not baulked at bribing Malaysian officials to let him import them, offering each official three magazines to look the other way. My desensitising to Bahrin's double standards had begun.

One of the first things I had to try to come to terms with about Malaysian life was the lack of privacy inherent in their culture. Even in our own home, our life was governed by the rules and regulations of Islam, the royal family's expectations and the natural and almost histrionic complexities of their familial 'need to know'.

Tengku Zaleha, my mother-in-law, lived next door to us. Our bedroom window overlooked her terraced sitting area, where she, her sisters and their servants would spend the afternoons chatting and sipping tea. The close proximity meant that nothing could happen in my house that she didn't know about. Very early on, she and one of her friends, Che Gu Gayah, a religious teacher who spoke a little English, sat me down to lecture me on the fundamental doctrines of an Islamic marriage, with special attention paid to hygiene.

My duty, they told me, was to please my husband in all ways possible. If he said the moon was green with purple spots, I must agree. If he wanted a foot massage at two o'clock in the morning, I should comply with a cheerful smile. I must never withhold sex from him for any reason other than my menstrual cycle which, under Islam, was considered unclean; not only that, but a husband's 'contamination' by the menstrual flow was said to lead to undue influence and control upon his morals and mind by his wife. I must be a good wife, always cheerful, ready with meals and delicacies to tempt his palate. And, foremost, I should hurry up and get pregnant as quickly as possible to prove my worth. And I must not talk too much; it was preferable to men that women not chatter unless bidden.

Where hygiene was concerned 'everyone' must know that I was a clean woman. After sexual intercourse, they informed me, I must cleanse myself with water from the last hair on my head to the tips of my toes. Bahrin was expected to do the same. My mother-in-law knew, she told me, that I was not washing my genitals with water each time I used the toilet. This was unacceptable in Malay society, she said with a smile on her face. She had stood outside our bathroom window to check on my habits and had not heard running water from the hose attached to the wall in the bathroom before I flushed the toilet. It was a very dirty habit, she said, something that they were willing to excuse because of my barbaric Western upbringing, but from now on I must stop using toilet tissue as it stood in the way of my becoming closer to Allah.

All of these pearls of wisdom were related to me in conspiratorial tones, as though the two women were doing me a great favour by putting me on the path to marital success. Tengku Zaleha, or Mak, as I had begun to call her, assured me that she would do no less for her own flesh-and-blood daughter, had she been lucky enough to have one. She professed that, at first, she had been very dubious about Bahrin and me marrying, but now was determined to give me her total support to make our marriage a success and to help me fit into her world. What else could I do except express my gratitude at her concern and caring, and promise to live by their rules?

Bahrin's mother had hired a live-in servant named Wan Su for us at a salary of one hundred and eighty Malaysian ringgit, or about thirty-five pounds sterling, a month, with one half-day off per week. Wan Su's duties, Mak informed me, were to cook and clean. Another woman, Zah, would take care of all the laundry. My duties, I was told, were to keep her son happy, get pregnant and not bother too much about household work – leaving me free to focus all my attention on Bahrin and keeping myself attractive. Women in my new family, she explained, did not become bogged down in menial chores; that would definitely make the husband disenchanted and look to greener pastures. 'Leave the menial chores to the servants and just focus on your husband's contentment,' she lectured me. 'Besides Bahrin doesn't like your cooking, he needs proper Malay food to keep him strong.'

When I broached the subjects of domestic help and my cooking with Bahrin, he actually agreed with his mother, adding that I should stick to making cakes and desserts and the occasional spaghetti dish. When I told him how much I disliked having a servant and how wrong I thought it was for Wan Su to have to sleep on a thin foam mattress on the living-room floor, he chided me for being too soft-hearted, adding that she probably thought it the height of luxury to sleep under a ceiling fan.

The only way I had left to rebel was to buy Wan Su a folding bed and insist she use it, and to give her two days off a week instead of the half-day usual for servants of the royals. My 'Australian labour terms', as they were dubbed by the aunties, did not make me too popular with my neighbouring in-laws, who told me that it was dangerous to give my servant extra time off and a bed as she would be sure to gossip to their servants and soon all the help employed by the family would expect the same conditions. Over the years, I would find myself continually at odds with relatives over the *mat salleh*, 'white man', employment terms I set. It always amazed me that they could justify in their own minds the dismissal of the needs and feelings of their servants with an *orang kampung sahaja*, 'only village people', throwaway line.

Twenty-eight

I fought to keep calm as another pain made me groan and gasp for breath. After thirty hours of this, all my resolutions to remain stoic were looking decidedly idealistic. I had spent the past twenty hours sitting cross-legged and bolt upright on a narrow examination table in a dimly lit operating theatre clad in a batik sarong and gingham blouse. My only visual distraction was a wall clock with a picture of the holy city of Mecca.

My first contraction had struck around dusk the previous day, Valentine's Day. I can distinctly recall feeling very smug at the way I kept my composure and handled what had really only amounted to an uncomfortable twinge – obviously, I thought, the pain of labour was something I was going to be able to cope with brilliantly. In fact, I was sure that I was going to pop the baby out in between chapters of the new book I was reading.

Twenty-eight hours and a couple of hundred contractions later, I was ready to tell anyone who would listen that it was all a mistake, that I'd decided to give birth another day and that I had a pressing engagement elsewhere.

Being alone in a labour room for hours gives you a lot of time to think and reflect on your life with a kind of fuzzy and agony-ridden perspective akin to an out-of-focus roll of film.

* * *

My pregnancy had been confirmed on the morning of my nineteenth birthday. I had waited months to be able to tell Bahrin that we were having a child and had gone to the doctor with a mixture of trepidation and expectation. From the moment I knew that I was definitely pregnant, I was overwhelmed with elation and wonder at the idea of a tiny life growing inside me. Bahrin's reaction was one of pride and self-congratulation and, from the moment I told him, he became adamant that I was carrying a son. My hope was that this baby would cement our cracking marriage and give us a common interest, so bewilderingly lacking in our relationship. But, most of all, I wanted this child with all my heart and soul. I was determined to protect and care for him or her, and shower him or her with all the love and security that had been lacking in my own childhood. My focus and priorities changed from the moment I knew I was expecting and, early on, I began to prepare Bahrin and his family for my hands-on, 'Australian-style' approach to parenting.

I made it very clear from day one that I would not be employing a nanny to look after our baby, that I would be breastfeeding – this was virtually unheard of among the affluent royals – and that I would not be following all the traditional hocus-pocus attendant to a royal pregnancy. To say that they were not pleased would be an understatement; however, it was more palatable for them to put my new determination down to the vagaries of a pregnant woman than to see it as open rebellion.

Over the months preceding the confirmation of my pregnancy, Bahrin had begun to treat me with the indifference he usually reserved for his servants. He had begun work as an architect at JKR, the state public works department, shortly after our *Bersanding*. This twelve-month job was to serve as a sort of internship in architecture before he opened his own practice. Whilst Bahrin served his apprenticeship at JKR, I served my own, catching up on all the refinements in which I was found lacking by the standards set for the women of Bahrin's family.

Twice or three times a week the royal family's religious tutor, Che Gu Ali, would arrive at our house to teach me to pray according to the tenets of Islam and to instruct me in Koranic law and Arabic. Ali was a balding, rotund little man who prided himself on the fecundity of his wife and the many sons that she had produced. Always dressed in white *baju melayu* shirt, checkered sarong, slip-on sandals and a white crocheted skullcap, he would chuckle loudly as I attempted to get my tongue around the difficult Arabic phrases set out in the day's lessons. His sense of moral propriety dictated that we always be strictly chaperoned whenever we were together; this meant ensuring all the doors and windows were left open in the living-room where we sat for classes or that one of my servants also was also present in the room.

As I learned more about the teachings of Islam and heard more of Ali's interpretations of the Koran, I realised that this chaperoning was not to protect my chastity but to protect him from the conniving and sexual slackness that he was exposed to by being in my presence. He taught me that under Islamic beliefs, women were not only the weaker sex, they were also the gender more likely to seduce the other, through sheer weakness of morals and inferior intelligence. In one of the lessons, held in the presence of Mak, he explained that women were inherently evil and had to be educated away from their natural inclinations to sin and corruption. Allah, he went on to explain, had put women on earth to serve and service the higher male species;

we had a duty to God to learn to curb our inbuilt contrariness and hide our bodies with the shame and humility they warranted.

In other words, women were mindless walking sex beacons ready to entrap any male with their genetically conniving and wicked natures, a necessary blight put on the earth for man to use for procreation of his line and to facilitate his comfort. A glimpse of a feminine knee was able to addle a man's brain, a tendril of hair could cause an instant erection, and a whiff of illicit perfume had the ability to trigger the downfall of Islamic society. Allah only knows what a well-rounded shoulder exposed by a female could do.

What astounded me was that Che Gu Ali, the son of a peasant farmer, barely literate in anything except the Koran and religious Arabic script, was considered a scholar and arbiter of most living things. He had studied at the religious university in Cairo, Egypt, where entry prerequisites did not generally demand either intellectual prowess or the ability to understand debate. To the best of my knowledge, and as described by Ali, courses there did not involve intellectual dissection of Islamic doctrine, supposition or questioning. Rather, the men who attended the school from all over the world – and it was only men who were eligible to enrol – had to be conversant with the entire Koran and have an unswerving commitment not to pose questions or relate to modern times. To question or debate or even dare to attempt reinterpretation of the Koran to make it more relevant to the twentieth century was considered blasphemous. Islam, as taught in Malaysia within the Malaysian royal family, brooked no enquiring minds; passages and phrases were learnt by rote, not reason.

Che Gu Ali himself did not understand the Arabic words he was teaching me and my place as a pupil and a woman precluded me from asking him the reasoning behind most edicts. In any case, I doubt that he himself would have been brave enough to query his own teachings as he very firmly believed in hell for the disbeliever.

As the weeks went by, however, I came to learn many things about the practices of Islam and its laws. Put simply, a system of merit and demerit points could summarise one's life at the time of death. Merit points could be collected by good deeds: fasting, prayer, modesty, humility (feigned or real), charitable works and self-denial. These points were referred to as *parlar* and would be the deciding factor on your entry, or not, to heaven. Demerit points were earned by sin: greed, wearing a wig, speaking ill of another, dabbling in black magic, fornication, lying, cheating and a whole host of other actions. These were referred to as *dosar*. Strictly speaking, *parlar* could cancel out *dosar*, or vice versa. Looking around me, I would often observe people in the royal family trying to stock up on *parlar* points against the day when their *dosar* points would have to be accounted for.

Heaven, I was told, was a garden of delights filled with doe-eyed *houries*, described as scantily clad sex angels, to fulfil the every whim of the male inhabitants who had been fortunate enough to make it there. However, I never heard of the equivalent incentive being offered to pious women. Hell, on the other hand, encompassed all of mankind's ill deeds magnified one thousand times over and inflicted upon the damned in a never-ending cycle of tortures.

My mother-in-law also had her own personal list of incidental demerit indicators which could damn the hapless forever. These were: Muslim men wearing any form of gold or silver jewellery on their person; being the possessor, male or female, of a first name which is not mentioned in either the Koran or other Islamic teachings; having an unclean anus when praying; and, most particularly for men, wearing any form of jewellery around the neck – this, Mak told me, would lead to the offender being dragged by the necklet down into the fires of hell. Mak's well-known piety seemed to be born more of fear than the desire to be philanthropic.

Admittance to heaven also seemed to have a great deal to do with genetic lineage. Both Bahrin and Che Gu Ali were adamant that the Jewish race had no hope of redemption and was rightfully destined to burn in hell for the millennium. Bahrin was so maniacally anti-Semitic that he once destroyed several of my books written by Jewish authors; however, he conveniently forgot that my maternal grandmother, although a practising Catholic, was of Jewish blood and therefore, under Jewish law, so was I. Coward that I was then, after I received a backhander across the face for disagreeing with him about the impurity of the Jewish race, I chose not to point my antecedents out to him. Even though I had always felt a sense of outrage at the persecution of my great-grandmother's people, my sense of self-preservation overrode my pride.

The more settled Bahrin became in his own importance and the more secure he became in his identity as a Malay Muslim residing in an Islamic state, the more his racism against Jews, Chinese and Indians became evident. He hailed the Holocaust as brilliant social cleansing and lamented that it did not go further and wipe out the American Jews, or puppeteers, as he called them. He applauded and actively supported the terrorist branch of the PLO, he referred to Indian Malaysians as *kelings*, a derogatory term referring to their history as imported slaves to the rubber plantations; and he labelled Chinese Malaysians as filthy dogs, the Jews of Asia.

Bahrin tried to instil in me many other lessons he

had learned growing up as a Malaysian royal; most important of these, he assured me, was not to 'lose face'. He drilled into me that never, ever should you let your worst enemy know of your dislike for him; if that enemy came to your home, he must be treated as an honoured guest. The secret, he told me, was to bide one's time to exact revenge for any slights. Even if it took fifty years, a poker-face demeanour and bonhomie were imperative until your enemy's destruction. It went the same, Bahrin said, for Indians and Chinese: his motto was to use wherever useful and then discard.

I often wondered how useful I was to him and when I too would become dispensable.

My contractions were now much closer together, gripping my back and stomach every four minutes. The doctor had ruptured my waters hours earlier to try to speed things up but to no avail; my baby seemed to prefer the slow and steady course rather than the express way.

As I submitted to another poking and probing by the midwife, I let my mind drift away from the labour room and back over the months to the first time I knew that I was trapped in this country where my child was about to enter the world, and had realised also that my worth to Bahrin had been in my face, my lack of familial ties and the malleability of my youth.

It had been a stinking hot day about a month before I discovered I was pregnant. Raja Ahmad, Bahrin's father, had come to visit and I had organised a special luncheon which included chilli crab, his favourite. Abah, or Father, as he had asked me to call him, and Bahrin were due home from Friday prayers at the mosque around 1 p.m. The food was set out under *tudum saji*, woven rattan insect protectors, and ice had been added to the pitchers of rosehip syrup and condensed milk that the two men preferred. By 3 p.m. they hadn't arrived. By 4.30 p.m. the crab had begun to smell in the heat, and by 5.30 p.m. I was not only anxious about Bahrin but wondering where the hell they were. By 6 p.m. the lunch and desserts I had prepared were no longer edible. I decided to walk around the garden – and it was then that I noticed Bahrin's BMW parked in the far corner of his Auntie Zainah's garden, two houses down from ours.

That's when I began to see red, Western-style. I stormed over to that house across the way in high dudgeon, only to find both of them reclining on couches, fast asleep, replete with a sumptuous meal, the remnants of which were strewn over the dining-table nearby. I shoved Bahrin awake. I told him how thoughtless and selfish he and his father were when they both knew that I had prepared lunch for them at home. As Bahrin leapt to his feet and followed me out to his aunt's courtyard, I told him what a shit I thought he was for not even telephoning, as he knew I was bound by his customs not to eat until the men of the household had partaken of their food. I yelled at him that he and his father were both thoughtless bastards for not coming home to the meal of crabs which they had both been adamant they wanted. It was then that he swung his right fist at me, knocking me backwards onto the concrete floor. He caught me with a backhand slap as I struggled to my feet and grabbed a fistful of hair with his left hand. I was so stupid; I should never have spoken to him like that. Everything that I had avoided doing so as not to provoke his rage was obliterated by my show of candid anger. And I forgot to duck.

Bahrin dragged me by my hair, screaming and struggling, through his aunt's garden, across the private road which divided the homes and into our house. He punched my arms, stomach and back and kicked my legs from under me each time I tried to stand or attempted to break free. Once inside our bedroom he tossed me onto the floor, locked the door, pocketed the key and drew the curtains tightly shut.

I began to beg him to send me home to Australia, to divorce me, to let me go home where I belonged. But he kept repeating that I belonged to him, that Malaysia was now my home and that, as long as he owned me, he would never let me leave. As he began to warm to his subject he called me every foul name he could think of. He told me that I was a useless slut and accused me of purposely not getting pregnant to thwart him. He told me that I was worthless, that I was entirely incapable of surviving anywhere without him, that I was mad and that people would know it if I tried to tell them he had hurt me. He went on and on for what seemed like hours. I sobbed and begged to return home. Finally, with one more jab of his foot and the comment 'I haven't finished with you yet', he left me alone, locking me in the dark bedroom.

I didn't dare switch on the light for fear of his return. It was then that I realised that the entire royal compound must have heard my screams and been aware of our fight but that no one had come to investigate or help me. I knew then that no matter what happened his family stood behind him – I was just the outsider with the womb.

I had no plan or idea of where I could go. I tentatively opened the bedroom window and waited. I had no money, no passport, no refuge and no one to talk to about Bahrin. And, if I tried, who would believe me? In any case, according to Islamic law, Bahrin had every right to beat me, as long as he didn't leave a mark on my face. Uppermost in my mind was to get away for the night, to escape what I was sure would be his renewed rage when he saw me again. Hoisting myself up onto the window ledge, I wriggled my body and twisted myself around until my legs dangled outside. I silently blessed the fact that Bahrin, unlike many of his family, loathed steel security bars on windows. Holding my breath, I dropped quietly to the ground below, narrowly missing the open drain which ran parallel to the house, and tried to blend into the shadows.

I decided to get as far away from the house as I could. Leaving our own compound meant being illuminated by the streetlights that ringed all the royal houses, so I chose to head for the antique house at the bottom of our garden against the perimeter fence. It took me about ten minutes to zigzag my way from tree to tree and arrive at the steps of the old building. A car driving into a neighbouring house forced me further into the shadows under the house, where I decided to remain. I felt safe in the darkness hidden in the shadows cast by the two-foot-thick supports of the structure. I didn't come out until dawn. Spending the night huddled in the grass with the mosquitoes buzzing around was preferable to submitting to more abuse from my husband. Once, around 10.30 p.m., as Bahrin made a perfunctory sweep of the compound with a torch, he came perilously close to discovering my hiding place. I managed to avoid the torch's beam, which was probably just as well, as his voice was still tinged with the hoarseness of rage.

When I finally did emerge, Bahrin had decided to try another tack to curb my will. He refused to talk to me for over a week and moved into another bedroom to sleep. His father had returned to Kuala Lumpur before I resurfaced. About two weeks after his son had beaten me, Raja Ahmad suffered an attack of angina which resulted in his hospitalisation. Bahrin blamed me for his father's chest pains and sent me to nurse him as punishment for my deeds. It was strange, but during the ten days I cared for my father-in-law in Kuala Lumpur, we seemed to reach a mutual, unspoken liking which stayed long after his recuperative period. Abah confided to me that he didn't really like Bahrin very much and blamed the late Sultan, his father-in-law, for his son's priggish behaviour. Silently I agreed, but I didn't dare verbalise criticism of my husband for fear that his father was merely drawing me out so as to report back to Bahrin.

The door to the labour room swung open to reveal the Dowager Tengku Ampuan. 'Omar', as she was nicknamed, swept into the room on her high heels and came to stand at the head of my trolley, just as another strong contraction took hold. As I panted my way through the pain, I couldn't help thinking what an incongruous sight she looked, standing in a delivery room decked out in pearls and silk. She was certainly an original though. As soon as she was widowed she had thumbed her nose at many of the royal constraints, developing a much-gossiped-about friendship with a jovial female lawyer. I rather admired and envied her. Free from the stranglehold of an arranged marriage to a very old man, and independently wealthy, Omar answered to no one and kept herself well divorced from the intrigues of her bickering stepfamily.

She patted my knee brusquely as I drew in a sharp breath and winced as the next pain hit me. I think Omar realised then that this was not the ideal time to drop in for a chat. So, with a few words and supportive clucks, she departed as quickly as she had arrived, leaving a whiff of French perfume and a line of curtseying nurses in her wake. By this stage, I was beginning to wish that she had invited me to leave with her.

I leaned back against the pillows and thought about

the strangeness of Omar's visit. I began to wonder what changes in my life motherhood would bring. During my pregnancy, my hobbies had been curtailed to suit the family's superstitions and fears, my every move monitored by someone to ensure that I was kept contented and well fed. I felt more like a valuable brood mare than a woman with a new life growing inside her.

Superstitions about pregnancy abound in Malaysian culture, from the dietary requirements of the expectant mother to the causes of infant deformity; each restriction or edict on my pregnancy espoused by Bahrin's family reeked of ignorance and primitive belief.

Prior to conceiving, I had taken to surreptitiously visiting the royal stables, housed in the grounds of the Crown Prince's (at that time) unoccupied palace. Here the family polo ponies were kept a stone's throw from the beach. A couple of times, with the complicity of the stable-hands and a few well-placed banknotes, I had experienced the exhilaration of taking one of the smaller horses for an early-morning canter along the sand at the water's edge. Unfortunately, nothing stayed secret for long and it wasn't more than a matter of days before I was berated by both Bahrin and his mother for indecorous behaviour and for risking my chances of conception by straddling a horse. Groping around for a defence, I attempted to point out that Princess Anne was an Olympic eventer who had also successfully brought forth two children and that Queen Elizabeth was an accomplished horsewoman, but to no avail. My time in the saddle was over for good; in their opinion, my womb (not me) must be protected at all costs.

Up until I announced that I was having a baby, I had begun to fill a little of my spare time with visits to a home for disabled children on the outskirts of town. I had discovered the existence of the institution by accident and hoped that I could do something to help the sad collection of children incarcerated there. The building where the children, ranging in age from a few months old to late teens, were housed had been a detention centre for wayward girls, unmarried mothers and delinquents. When the girls had been moved out, the children had been moved in from all over Malaysia.

They were the discarded ones, abandoned at bus stops or dumped at hospitals in the hope that someone would care for them; in Malaysia, any form of physical deformity or mental handicap was a reason for shame and rejection by their families. Here in the Terengganu institution, the children's ailments ranged from mild cerebral palsy or physical disability to Down's syndrome and blindness, but they were all lumped together.

When I first entered the hostel, I was shocked to find the children lying on heavy sheets of red rubber overlayed with batik sarongs amidst pools of their own urine. Others crawled along the red concrete floor, rocked back and forth against the walls or pulled against the bars on the windows as a single ceiling fan in each ward turned half-heartedly, barely creating a breeze. There were no toys, no brightly painted wall murals, nothing in those rooms that could be remotely described as visually stimulating. No attempt to educate the children was made and physiotherapy was unheard of. The place was staffed by mostly untrained workers who slapped and railed at any of the inmates if they made a mess.

I was astounded to find that there was actually a board of directors made up of various socialites and one female member of the royal family. This committee did virtually nothing to improve the quality of the lives of these kids, they simply collected the *parlar* points by lending their names to the institution; none of them would have ever contemplated rolling up their sleeves and adopting a hands-on approach to their charges. It was far more palatable for them to make regular inspection tours of the building. Decked out in silk and perfectly coiffured, the board would cluck their concern and distress at the disabilities of their charges, drawing their skirts aside hurriedly if one of the children stretched a hand out towards them, silently blessing the fact that their own children at home were perfect and whole.

When I told Bahrin and his mother that I was interested in becoming involved with the institution, they had no hesitation in allowing me to do so provided that I only went there during Bahrin's office hours. I think that at first they assumed that I wanted to become involved with the board of directors, and did not envisage what I really had in mind.

I began visiting the children, taking an old cassette player with me to play music for some of them. The thing that overwhelmed me was their longing just to touch me. Denied physical affection for most of their lives, hugging was a new concept for them but one they caught on to very quickly. There was one little girl in particular whom I named Mina. She was about five or six years old and had huge dark eyes and short hair that was a mass of curls. Mina would grin whenever she saw me and hold out her arms to he picked up. Being with the children, I didn't have to worry about any of the stiff protocol or rules which bound me everywhere else in Terengganu. I could just be myself – that's all the kids wanted and that's all they got.

All that changed, though, the day I told Bahrin that I was pregnant. One of the very first things that he forbade me to do – and in this he had the full and unequivocal support of his entire family – was to visit the children's institution. When I tried to protest, I was overruled. When I tried to reason with them, no one would listen. When I threatened to keep going anyway,

Bahrin said that he would lock me up until I gave birth. The family did, however, patiently explain to me why I had been forbidden to go there any more. They firmly believed that all outside influences affect the unborn child *in utero*. According to their beliefs, if I were to be exposed to any child who was less than perfect, I ran the risk of producing a retarded or handicapped child myself. They called this syndrome *kenang*, a form of infectious transference of deformity. No matter how many medical or pregnancy books I showed them, they refused to be swayed. The family even cited an example to me: the youngest son of Bahrin's uncle, Tengku Ibrahim, had been born with a slightly deformed arm. This, they sagely pronounced, was because his mother, Auntie Rosita, had kicked a cat and injured it whilst she was pregnant. As a result, Zainol had been *kenang*.

Nothing I could say or do could dissuade the family from their primitive and superstitious beliefs. I was sternly warned not to touch or look at dolls, particularly ones with opening and closing eyes, as this would result in my own child being born deaf, blind or dumb. Mak pointed to my washing woman, Zah, as an example of this. Zah's last son had been born blind and deaf, apparently because she had handled a doll.

When I questioned Zah closely on her family tragedy and went through each month of her pregnancy, I was pretty certain that there had been an outbreak of rubella or German measles in her village during her first trimester which had resulted in her child being born blind. Vaccination against rubella was virtually unheard of in Terengganu. Most devout Muslims believe that it is the will of Allah that people become ill and that vaccination against any disease is extremely rare.

In the seventh month of my pregnancy, Mak insisted that I go through a traditional bathing ceremony to ensure an easy labour and to keep evil spirits from interfering with the birth. An old village midwife was brought to my house to examine the shape of my protruding belly. After much poking and prodding and meaningful 'hmms', to which I submitted myself much against my better judgement, she announced that she would have to reposition the baby as it was lying the wrong way. This I categorically refused to let her do, no matter how much my mother-in-law and her sisters insisted. I would not risk a ruptured placenta or harm to my baby just to fit in with royal practice and tradition.

As a result of my refusal I was not that popular, but they continued on with the rest of the ceremony, which I considered harmless. A holy woman and the midwife prayed and blew into a bucket of water, adding to it fresh limes cut into quarters. I was stripped down to only a batik sarong and asked to stand in the bathroom. They then proceeded to douse me with the blessed water from head to toe whilst I was instructed to repeat verses from the Koran. When they had completed my bathing ritual, Mak distributed alms to the poor to further ensure a healthy baby and easy labour for me.

It was difficult trying to keep my own perspective on what was happening to my body during pregnancy. I tried to stay as well informed as possible and 'did' most of my pregnancy by books which I had managed to obtain from Australia and England. Penelope Leach's books from the United Kingdom were an invaluable source of information, as was a birthing video I managed to obtain from the USA. There were no antenatal classes in Terengganu and the doctors, as well as female relatives, were entirely unforthcoming when I posed questions about the birth process. So I followed the antenatal and pelvic-floor exercises from my books and decided what type of labour I was aiming for.

* * *

I felt very alone in the labour room. The nurses came and went on their shifts and the doctor would occasionally enter to check on me but I was left pretty much to my own thoughts. I don't think the medical staff were very pleased with me, as I kept rejecting their offers of pethidine – which I knew would cross the placenta barrier and affect the baby's suckling ability, a thing I wanted to avoid – and the oxytocin with which they wanted to speed up labour. A couple of nurses in particular kept insisting that I lie down through my contractions instead of sitting up. I had found that being upright made me more able to cope with the pain, and it was also the most comfortable position. But these two nurses refused to listen to my reasoning and repeatedly pushed me down flat onto the bed, which would make me vomit with the intensity of the contraction and I'd have to struggle to sit up again. I began to understand how a beached whale felt writhing on the sand. Frighteningly, I really did bear more than a passing resemblance to a whale, weighing in two days before I went into labour at a massive twelve stone, which was an awful lot of bulk to be carrying around on a five-foot-three-inch frame, especially when my normal weight was less than eight stone three.

I had hit the thirty-hour mark by now and had begun to fantasise about jogging or trampolining to speed things up. I knew that the baby was maintaining a healthy heartbeat and that there was no sign of foetal distress, but this was getting a little ridiculous. I had just about reached the extent of my endurance and the offer by the nurse of some nitrous oxide and oxygen to take the edge off the pain was starting to sound tempting. I promised myself that I would give the baby another half-hour and then I would resort to gas. In the meantime, I forced my mind to drift away again back over the last months.

* * *

One of the things I had never realised about life in Malaysia was just how isolated I would be from people outside Bahrin's immediate family circle. Normal friendships were just not possible due to a number of factors. Bahrin ruled that I must not leave the house without his permission other than to visit his aunts or mother; in any case, I had no idea how to make the sort of friendships that I needed with people in Terengganu. Their value system was so different from mine; none of them read books – there wasn't even a bookshop in the whole town, unless you counted the religious bookstore – and a conversation on ballet or music was unheard of. Bahrin also read all my mail from Australia and usually insisted that he read my replies to my nanna, so that avenue of reflection was closed to me as well.

Very occasionally, Bahrin and I would attend a non-royal wedding of a business acquaintance or a social function where Bahrin's old schoolmates and their wives would be present. These functions usually proved excruciating for me, as he and I would never be treated as ordinary guests and would be accorded blatantly deferential treatment. It made me feel so set apart from the other women of my own age, particularly when many of the wives saw this as an opportunity to corner me and ask probing and intrusive questions about the lives and habits of the royal family. Inane questions like did the badminton hall at the palace really double for a movie theatre, how many nights did the Sultan spend with each of his wives or how much did one of my in-laws pay for that new necklace which was photographed in a magazine. Another favourite comment from this gaggle of chattering women was how lucky and fortunate I was to have married a royal, how I was set for life financially and how clever I was to have trapped him. I longed to tell them that they were welcome to my lonely life, that I hadn't realised how much better off I'd been in my own country. But I didn't dare tell them the truth, instead becoming adept at playing the role they expected from me and deflecting their invasive probings with an icy smile and silence or feigned incomprehension.

I did find solace in one of the most unexpected quarters, though. The Sultan's consort, Tengku Ampuan Bariah, became my confidante, trusted friend and ally. 'Endah' as I called her, proved to be the one person to whom I could turn. I can't remember how we came to realise that we had a lot in common, but somewhere along the way I began to be invited to afternoon tea at the palace every few days. Thankfully no one, not even Bahrin, could refuse me permission to escape to the cool and peaceful haven Endah had made for herself in her private apartments at Istana Badariah. When Endah had her lady-in-waiting telephone her invitations through to the house, Bahrin had at first insisted on drilling me over and over again in the right forms of protocol I must use and reminding me to be on my best behaviour. He really had no idea at all what his aunt was like; very few people ever did, and certainly few were ever allowed to know about the sadness and humiliation she endured every day of her life as a queen without an heir.

As Endah and I became closer, she did away with much of the formal protocol which usually governed her contact with other people. She was a petite woman with beautiful fair skin as soft as silk and a softly spoken voice. Endah always smelled of Joy perfume and preferred to dress very simply in her private life, favouring silky fabrics made into flowing kaftans and red kid slippers when indoors. A keen badminton player and cook, she cultivated roses of all varieties and had the gentlest smile I have ever seen. We would sit for hours poring over magazines and discussing cake recipes or clothes. I had told her a little about Bahrin's tempers and as a result she offered herself as an excuse for me to find refuge at the palace whenever necessary.

Endah would sometimes tell me about her early married life when she became a Crown Princess to the court of Terengganu. She had been barely sixteen when she married Bahrin's uncle and she told me with some amusement that the day before her wedding she was still wearing her Girl Guides uniform. A daughter of the Sultan of Selangor and sister to a great many siblings, she had grown up in a fairly progressive family by Muslim standards, partly due to the influence of the British colonisation of Selangor. She had not met Ayah Mud, Uncle Mahmud, before the wedding but had been shown a photograph of her twenty-year-old fiancé so she knew what he looked like. Immediately after their wedding, the new husband and wife were shipped off to England to study, he at military college and she to do a diploma in home economics. They settled in a small cottage in picturesque Surrey, in an England still subject to rationing. A faraway look would come into Endah's eyes and her voice would become wistful as she told me how she and Ayah Mud played house together, undisturbed by servants or royal protocol, for the first years of married life. Ayah Mud rode a bicycle through the country laneways and they would often walk hand in hand to the local picture theatre or to the village shops, she wearing seamed stockings and Western clothing, he in country tweeds. But when they eventually returned to Malaysia, their idyllic relationship changed dramatically. Gone were the moments of intimacy and quiet fellowship; instead their lives were dominated by social obligation, royal protocol and their positions as Crown Prince and Princess of Terengganu – and the all-consuming need for an heir.

Despite many years of hope, prayers and operations,

Endah was unable to produce the son and heir they both longed for. So, one day, Ayah Mud found himself another wife, a Singaporean girl named Sharifah Nong, to continue his line. As this new wife produced baby after baby, so she gained ascendancy in the then Crown Prince's affection until Endah was virtually relegated to ceremonial occasions and the royal portraits in office buildings. By the time Ayah Mud became Sultan, the courtiers of Terengganu had very definitely become members of Sharifah Nong's camp, the mother of the Crown Prince, or had cast their loyalties behind Endah. Many of them, however, paid only lip service to Endah's rank and took every opportunity to pay sycophantic homage to Sharifah Nong as de facto consort. The Sultan's brothers and sisters played both sides of the fence in this honey-sweet game of Machiavellian manipulation. Everyone was afraid of Sharifah Nong; her spite was legendary for its calculated sharpness, affected under the guise of ingenuousness and bonhomie. But we all knew never to trust her: the results could be devastating. Courtiers and family alike were always careful to present a gift of the same value, or even more expensive, to Sharifah Nong if they had also sent something to Endah.

Ayah Mud adhered to the strictest of schedules so my time at the palace was normally when he was residing with Sharifah Nong. He kept to a timetable of two days with Endah, two days with his other wife. Overseas vacations or trips abroad were divided between the two women, but more often than not the mother of his heir would accompany him away on all trips which did not include official duties. When Endah accompanied him to Europe or England she would always return laden with thoughtful gifts for me. A stylish handbag, a length of fabric or ornate hair pins. On one occasion she brought home a pile of coffee-table books on the Princess of Wales with the thought that I could adapt some of Diana's clothes to suit Malaysian sensibilities. Endah knew that I chafed against the dress restrictions of my adopted country and the conformity of design I must adhere to, so she told a few of her sisters-in-law that she saw no reason why I shouldn't wear vaguely Western-style clothes as long as they maintained a decent level of modesty in hem, neck and sleeve line. Endah understood how, at nineteen, the prospect of wearing the exact same design of dress for the rest of my life was depressing.

It was a very cunning move on her part as the Malaysian royals seemed to have a fascination with Princess Diana and approved all she wore or did. Endah and I had great fun tweaking Diana's clothing into designs suitable to our court sensibilities. Sometimes it would be the adding of a skirt to a pretty short dress or the lengthening of one of Diana's skirts, maintaining the ruffled collar and nipped-in waist from the original photograph. Later, as I grew more confident, Endah encouraged me to be more daring and adopt my own dress style. It wasn't long before I was adding dolman-style sleeves and shoulder pads to my formal *baju kurungs* and tempting providence with a V-shaped neckline or slightly lowered back. Anything I could think of to break the monotony of my strict Islamic dress, whilst still preserving the edicts of modesty and a close interpretation of traditional ensembles, I would instruct my favourite tailor to create for me. I knew that I had broken through a fashion barrier when my clothing began to be copied, first by other royal ladies. Later, due to the detailed coverage in the media of all royal events, the general public began to imitate a lot of my wardrobe as well.

Bahrin's reaction to my evolving wardrobe was rather mixed. On the one hand he enjoyed the fact that I was constantly being singled out in television coverage and magazines, but on the other he disliked my nonconformity. For him, I suspect, it was confusing. Praise for the good looks and fashion style of his wife translated into kudos for himself and vidicated his choice of me as a spouse. Conversely, my gentle and seemingly innocent rebellion in terms of dress lessened his control on me and, with the backing of his aunt the Tengku Ampuan, made it impossible fo him to chastise me on the level he felt I warranted. He settled instead for making his disapproval felt by never once in four years complimenting me on my dress or appearance.

Endah was my one true confidante and ally in Terengganu. She burst into tears the day I told her I was having a baby. I made sure that I shared as much of my pregnancy with her as I could. We spent hours sitting together in the arbour of her rose garden overlooking the South China Sea as I embroidered the baby's singlets and layette. Flanked by her large aviary of tropical birds, we would chat or simply sit in silence as the breeze from the ocean wafted around us. On other days I found refuge from the heat in a suite of rooms she put aside for my use in the old wing of the palace. There, ensconced with my sewing machine, I would make curtains, nursery hangings and baby clothes as Endah popped in and out of the room to check on me. On a couple of occasions, Endah made the unprecedented move of calling in at my house to check on the progress of the nursery, but we soon discovered that this wasn't the ideal thing for her to do. As she never visited any other members of her husband's family, they reacted jealously as a result.

Even though Endah had not been able to have her own biological children, she had fostered many, bringing them to the palace to live. Later, when they were old enough, she educated several of them overseas and allowed them to make lives for themselves in the United States. She was also raising one of the Sultan's natural children, Tengku Baharuddin, or 'Adik', as he was nicknamed. Adik was the Sultan's youngest child by a village girl to whom he had taken a fancy and married for a short time. After the girl had given birth he placed the baby boy in Endah's care to mother as her own.

For the most part I got through my pregnancy relatively unscathed by Bahrin's temper. The one exception was the day during my fifth month when I found proof of his infidelity. He had been spending a considerable time away from Terengganu on business. I was unpacking his overnight bag as his mother sat chatting to me when I came across a large bowl of scented dusting powder and a pair of women's knickers pushed into the corner of the bag. As I sat in a heap on the floor reeling in shock, Mak repeated over and over as she shook her head 'just like his father, just like his father'. I felt as if I had been kicked in the stomach. The girl involved obviously wanted me to find out about their relationship, but I doubted that Bahrin had planned it this way. He had returned from his trip in quite high spirits and had given me hope that he still had some fondness for me by the interest he took in my blooming tummy. I realised at that moment that the interest he had exhibited had been more in the proof of his masculinity growing inside me than the result of any tenderness he felt for me.

Mak immediately said that she would have extra prayers said for our marriage and that she would arrange for some talismans to be made for me to entice Bahrin back to my side. I listened to her ramblings as my head pounded with fury and hurt. I could still hear her muttering about the downfall of the world's morals as she made her way across the garden to her house next door. I resolved to demand the truth from Bahrin as soon as he came home for lunch. Not wanting the servants to overhear my humiliation, I despatched Zah home early and sent Wan Su on an errand. This was my first mistake.

I met Bahrin at the front door as soon as I heard the car door slam and followed him through the house as he made his way to the bedroom. As he reached out to turn the handle of the door I held out the offending item of underwear to him and demanded an explanation. At first he tried to tell me that they were in fact mine, a statement which he and I both knew was a blatant lie. He then told me that they must have fallen into his bag somehow and that he didn't know how or to whom they belonged. When I spat back at him that I didn't believe his weak explanations and that his mother had told me that his behaviour mirrored his father's, his demeanour changed from haughty and derisive to aggressive. Bahrin moved towards me so fast that I wasn't able to anticipate the shove that sent me flying through the open hallway door behind me and down the six or seven terrazzo steps leading down to the concreted courtyard area. I landed with a dull thud. My legs sprawled over the stairs and my head crashed onto the concrete below with the vertebrae of my lower spine and my elbows taking the most impact.

By the look on Bahrin's face, I think he was as shocked by the fall as I was. He rushed to help me up, asking over and over again if the baby was all right. I was as concerned as he was that our baby might have been hurt, but I could feel it kicking and moving as normal. It was me who was bruised and battered; I had instinctively done all I could to protect my stomach as I fell. I was crying by now and Bahrin helped me into our room and eased me onto the bed. Telling me to lie still, he left the room and a moment or two later I could hear him talking on the telephone. I made out the words 'tripped', 'one step', 'clumsy' and 'just thought I should check', before I heard him hang the phone up and re-enter the bedroom.

Standing by the edge of the bed, Bahrin reached over and took my wrist in his hand. Clenching it tightly, he told me he had telephoned the doctor and told him what had happened. When I retorted that I bet he hadn't told the truth, Bahrin replied that he had told the *keling* doctor all he needed to know and that he didn't want me contradicting him. He told me that if I let anyone know what had really transpired, he would take the baby away from me the moment it was born and send me back to Australia alone. Bahrin knew that he had played his trump card and he knew that I believed it was no idle threat; I was well aware that precedents had already been set for this sort of punishment. I nodded stiffly that I understood and told him to leave me alone.

I lay alone on our big bed, my whole body throbbing. I could feel my back beginning to stiffen and prayed that the baby was unhurt. There was no way on earth that I would risk losing my child, either by further violence or by disobeying Bahrin. The only thing that mattered was the baby. I lay and sobbed for hours on the bed. I sobbed for our baby and the type of life I was bringing it into, and I sobbed for the husband whom I still believed I loved.

Bahrin subsequently let it be known to his family that I had carelessly tripped and fallen down the courtyard steps and that he had warned me to be more careful for the sake of our child. Mak was very concerned that I had been injured in the fall and also seemed a little sceptical at the explanation Bahrin had given for my bruises, but she, like the rest of the women in the royal family, had been raised by the code which forbade them to question any male family member's word, so she asked nothing.

Instead she called in an elderly village woman named Mok Soong to examine me and treat my aching muscles. Mok Soong was a diminutive octogenarian whose wizened face resembled a smiling walnut and whose hands and feet were gnarled with age. She had a cackling, jolly laugh and an absolute fascination with television. A *tukang urut*, or masseuse, Mok Soong began to visit me once a week at my mother-in-law's instigation to massage my back and ensure that all was well with the baby. Mak and Auntie Zainah would sit and chat in my bedroom as I lay on a foam mattress on the floor and submitted to the ministrations of the masseuse, whose small size belied her strength. The going rate, Mak informed me, for a two-hour massage was ten Malaysian ringgit or about three pounds fifty. This was so little money for so much work that I always slipped her more cash, which caused great chagrin to my mother-in-law and her sister, who complained that I was inflating the prices for everyone else.

Mok Soong's massages were the only physical contact I really had with any other person during my pregnancy. Bahrin had long since given up the sexual side of our relationship. If he ever happened to catch sight of me undressed, he would take great satisfaction in telling me that I was the most grotesque thing he had ever seen. Even before I had become pregnant, he relished telling me at every opportunity that I should be grateful that he had made me a Muslim as I had the ugliest legs he had ever seen. He would also say that he had 'seen better legs on a table' and that 'it's fortunate that Muslim women have to cover up'. I began to feel so self-conscious about my body that I would be at pains to cover myself completely whenever he was around.

During this time I managed to gain permission from Bahrin to maintain a friendship with an expatriate American woman named Fiona. Fiona's husband, a helicopter pilot, had been seconded by his company to Terengganu to maintain the air links between the mainland and the oil rigs off shore. I met Fiona's Oregon-born husband, Bill, when he drove into the palace compound in error. Summoned by the aunties, who were taken aback at the appearance of a strange white man in their garden, I was prodded to interpret for then. It appeared that Bill was trying to find a house to rent before the arrival of his wife and child from America. After much discussion amongst the aunties, Mak and myself, it was decided that we would assist him in his search for a house. Mak, I think, finally acquiesced to my pleading looks, understanding that I was desperate for some Western companionship. She made me promise, however, that I would let her be the one to break the news to Bahrin. This was a conditon I gladly agreed to.

Bahrin laid down very strict rules about my contact with the *mat sallehs*, as he referred to Fiona and Bill. I was only to speak to Fiona for a total of two hours a week and she was never to casually drop in to our house when Bahrin was at home. Never, he warned me, was I to tell Fiona any of our personal marital details. I must limit our conversations to babies, shopping or America and I must emphasise my 'Malaysian-ness' and take the focus off my Australian nationality when speaking to her. My life with him, and as a royal, was strictly taboo. 'Break any of these rules and your friendship will immediately be terminated,' he decreed. I knew that Bahrin would instruct our servants, as well as the rest of his family, to report my behaviour back to him, so I only dared risk a slight infringement a couple of times. Having an American woman to converse with in English was far too precious a treat to jeopardise by confiding in her about the true state of my marriage. I could see no point; there was no changing my situation. I belonged to Bahrin and my home was with him, for better or for worse.

I always felt that I was keeping myself at arm's length from Fiona and felt quite dishonest making excuses when I knew that she longed to spend more time at my house and was curious about the palace. It was wonderful being able to speak to another woman about the impending birth of my baby. Fiona could fill in all the blanks that the antenatal books didn't cover and I was able to see Terengganu through her eyes. She hated it too. I didn't blame her. Life for a white woman in Terengganu was difficult and lonely. Dressing in Western clothes, no matter how modest, did not protect her from harassment by the young Malay males who roamed the streets and beaches.

One day Fiona came to me in tears. She had been at the beach with her little girl when suddenly they had been surrounded by six or seven youths chanting, 'Charlie's Angels, Charlie's Angels.' The boys then proceeded to masturbate in a circle around her and her daughter before they left, frightened off by the approach of two fishermen. She hadn't been in a swimsuit but was dressed in a long T-shirt and cotton trousers, her blonde hair tied back into a ponytail. I had to try to explain to her that many Malay men from villages had a stereotypical image of blonde Western women as something akin to prostitutes. Through their own warped mentality, they behaved disgustingly towards any white woman they came across. I don't think that she ever quite recovered from her shock and she certainly avoided going to the beach again without her husband.

When I related the story to Bahrin, he really shocked me by saying that she had probably deserved it for sitting on the beach alone. I argued that she had been with her small child and that the boys' behaviour warranted summoning the police. He then began to rail that only sluts went to the beach and that decent women stayed at home and covered up. I should have known that to try to have a discussion with him about Fiona's experience would be impossible; after all, he had forbidden me ever to swim in the ocean. I had even tried to persuade him to allow me to paddle in a swimsuit with a long kaftan over the top, but Bahrin pronounced that even that was too risqué when wet. How quickly he had forgotten our idyllic week in Kuantan when he had me pose on the beach in my swimsuit, my hair blowing free. I lived not five hundred yards from the azure blue South China Sea, but I couldn't ever swim in it.

Stoicism finally gave way to realism as I turned to the nurse and demanded some of the much-lauded gas to take the edge off the pain. Once I finally got the hang of inhaling the oxygen and nitrous oxide and began to feel its effects, the whole situation in the labour room began to take on a humorous perspective. At least that's what I thought – after all, they don't call it 'laughing gas' for nothing.

However, the comedic novelty of lying on a bed in excruciating pain trying to pass what seemed like an immense basketball quickly lost its hilarity as I entered 'transition'. Transition sounds more like a yoga pose done at a railway station than a description of the moment before you become a mother, but it was anything but peaceful. It was as if someone had suddenly yelled 'battle stations' in the delivery room. Trays of equipment rattled as they were pushed into position. There were precise multiple snaps as the attendants thrust their hands into rubber gloves. And, at an alarmingly high speed, my bed for the past thirty-two hours was converted into a structure more akin to a chicken rotisserie. I was rudely pushed onto my back and my legs jerked upwards as the nurses tied my ankles to the stirrups, disregarding completely my very loud protestations to the contrary. Wriggle or contort as I might, I found it absolutely impossible to disengage my legs from their undignified position akimbo and pant and push at the same time.

Mind, body, intellect, modesty. I couldn't have told you what those words meant at that moment: they were entirely meaningless. For those few, extraordinary minutes, instinct had no name or reason – it just was. Instinct birthed my son, not a doctor. It was the sanest, most logical and pure thing that I had ever done – I gave birth to life.

He cried as the doctors suctioned his airways but stopped the moment they laid him in my arms. And as I looked down into his tiny, perplexed face, I knew what true, unequivocal, soul-tearing love was for the very first time in my life.

Twenty-nine

Occasionally, during moments of uncertainty, I wonder if I should have done things differently after Iddin's birth. But to have denied my instincts and quashed my feelings for my child would have cheated our son as much as it would have been lying to myself. So I presented a shiny veneer of compliance and cooperation to the world at large whilst privately resolving that I would 'mother' my son myself.

To the world I had, on 15 February 1983, delivered Raja Muhamad Baharuddin Ismail Shah bin Raja Kamarul Bahrin Shah. His name had been decided upon many months before he arrived. How could anyone saddle such a small and defenceless being with such an imposing and cumbersome name? I couldn't. Looking down at him, I knew he should be called by the abbreviation of Baharuddin, Iddin – pronounced 'Eden' – and fortunately Bahrin's family agreed.

Raja was his hereditary title, as was the Shah on the end. Muhamad, the name of the Muslim prophet, was the name chosen by his grandmother to ensure his entrance to heaven. Baharuddin, his grandfather's middle name, joined the list. This was followed by Ismail in honour of the late Sultan, Bahrin's grandfather. Raja Kamarul Bahrin Shah, Bahrin's forenames, doubled as a type of surname following traditional practice. All this for a tiny baby weighing seven pounds, two and a half ounces.

After over twelve months spent living in Terengganu, consternation became my middle name. That was what I continually seemed to evoke in Bahrin's family. Consternation because I insisted on breastfeeding and consternation because I refused point-blank to keep the *pantan*, a type of strictly enforced dietary and behaviour code adhered to by new mothers in the forty to one hundred days following the birth of a baby. The confinement period is considered by Malaysian Muslims a time of uncleanliness and recuperation and a time when physical contact, even sharing the same bed with your husband, is forbidden. The *pantan* covers a broad cross-section of everyday life and dictates that a new mother must not consume foods which are considered 'cold': fruit of any type, vegetables, ice, cold water or chilled beverages. The fear is that her vagina will remain too slack and become undesirable to her husband. Plain, dry food is prescribed for the woman in confinement and usually consists of a bland diet of grilled fish, boiled rice and fresh ground black pepper; sometimes this is varied with chicken and ginger strips fried in sesame oil. These foods are considered to add to the body's natural heat and aid the regeneration of the uterus. Heat is supposedly a major factor in regaining the elasticity of the vagina after giving birth. Young women are exhorted to wear woolly socks and sweaters regardless of the intense tropical heat, and it is judged very dangerous to take large steps in the *pantan* period in case one's uterus plops out and dangles somewhere around the knee region. What an odd picture that conjured up in my mind when Mak and the various aunties solemnly explained the consequences of my rebellion.

They were absolutely horrified when I demanded iced water an hour or so after giving birth. I'm sure that I caught a number of the female relatives shooting surreptitious glances at me and waiting with bated breath for my uterus to prolapse before their very eyes.

Absolute joy in my baby son – and the relative equilibrium his arrival seemed to bring to my relationship with Bahrin – was interspersed with anxiety and worry for his health during the first six months of his life. Iddin developed bleeding from the bowel, each episode of which would be heralded by his inconsolable screams and obvious pain. When he was thirty days old, Iddin was admitted to Kuala Lumpur's General Hospital for observation and treatment. Iddin's doctor in Terengganu had suspected 'intersusseption', a condition in which part of the intestine telescopes into itself. The condition can prove fatal if surgery is not performed quickly. I insisted that I remain at the hospital with him, as I was breastfeeding. This resulted in the hospital authorities assigning a whole ward for our use. It seemed quite ludicrous really, being alone with my baby in a massive room usually accommodating twenty patients, but the royal family insisted that I couldn't possibly sleep surrounded by 'ordinary people'.

Kuala Lumpur General Hospital was absolutely filthy – potholed floors of red concrete, mosquito-ridden and surrounded by unhygienic open drains. The bathroom attached to the ward where we stayed was crawling with cockroaches, its toilets were the squat, hole-in-the floor type, encrusted with the evidence of many misses, the showers were unusable. One morning I awoke to discover that Iddin and I had been marooned in the middle of the room, surrounded by a lake of faeces two inches deep – the toilets in the ward had backed up during the night. In order to alert the nurses to our predicament, I had to pick my way through the stinking mess in open-toed sandals, alternately gagging and dry retching as I held Iddin as high above the filth as I could.

At the General Hospital, Iddin was shunted from doctor to doctor, examination to examination, ranging from X-rays to blood tests to pokings and probings and, finally, having a drip inserted into his forehead, all without a definite diagnosis. Eventually, when the bleeding episodes had finally ceased, I insisted that they allow us to return to Terengganu, where we managed to settle down in a close approximation of a family for a few undisturbed months. Bahrin's attitude towards Iddin's illness was concern and worry but he was infuriatingly unquestioning of doctors in general and really vexed me with his *qué será será* attitude.

Fate, what will be will be, was the reasoning behind many frustrating decisions and opinions espoused by the circle of people in which I now lived. Couched in different terms, the phrase '*nasib Tuhan*', or 'the will of God', seemed to cover tragedies and triumphs alike. It was and is one of the most difficult of attitudes to come to terms with. It is, I believe, such a negatively fatalistic approach to life that the comment '*nasib Tuhan*' always left me grinding my teeth and wanting to rail against such apathy and shoulder shrugging. I longed to point out the difference, and occasionally did, between allowing a snake to bite you and moving out of the snake's path.

One example of this was what happened when a child with a cleft palate was born within hours of Iddin at the same clinic. The tiny girl's mouth was so grossly deformed that she was unable to suckle from either a bottle or the breast.

At night I could near the baby crying in the nursery next door as the nurses tried, with little success, to dribble milk into her mouth off a teaspoon. I feared that the baby would die from lack of nourishment so, early one morning, I snatched an opportune moment to speak to the baby's mother in private.

When I questioned her gently, she told me that she and her husband were from an outlying village and that this was their first child. The couple had saved all their money to cover the costs of the birth at the private clinic, opting, as I had, to avoid the Terengganu General Hospital because of the high incidence of maternal and infant mortality. After some generalised talk between us about our new babies and our concerns for them, I explained to her that it was often possible for doctors to repair a cleft palate and that in countries such as Australia, the USA and England this type of operation was both common and successful. I told her that I could arrange for her and the baby to fly to Kuala Lumpur to meet with a surgeon and promised that I would cover all the baby's expenses. But my gung-ho Australian approach was not what she wanted to hear. Looking me straight in the eye, and in a voice that almost had a pitying tone, she said, 'Nasib Tuhan,' and shrugged. The will of Allah was what she believed had caused her baby daughter's deformity; it was preordained, meant to be; whatever Allah wished for her child would happen. It was not for mere mortals to tamper with God's higher wisdom, she patiently explained to me as if I were some impetuous girl. Her baby's cleft palate had to be accepted without rancour and Allah's will obeyed.

No matter how I tried to reason with her, she remained unmoved. I pointed out that as Allah had made it possible for doctors to make new scientific discoveries, to operate and to repair, then surely Allah meant for us to use their skills. God, I said, had given human beings a brain to use and the ability to develop knowledge that was unheard of when the Koran was written hundreds of years ago. But I argued to no avail. I quoted Koranic teachings and tried to reason with her that even God did not forbid us to move out of the path of a bus if it would save our lives, but she looked at me as if I were talking blasphemously and asking her to join a league of Satanists. She was appalled by my reasoning and, ironically, I realised that she pitied my inability just to accept what she saw as the inevitable. Our conversation ended abruptly when her husband arrived to take her home. I watched them from the upstairs window as they climbed aboard a motor scooter for the long journey. She held her baby close to her chest with one arm and her husband's waist with the other. As they turned the corner and disappeared from sight, I was left with the urge to scream and scream and scream until the populace of Terengganu snapped out of their apathy and entered the twentieth century. I felt as if that one tiny baby summed up my inability to truly belong in my husband's country – a place where human life was not only cheap, it was not worth fighting for. Ten days later, I heard that the baby girl with the cleft palate was dead.

Outsiders never see what the real Malaysia is like. They stay in the rarefied bubble that their status as tourists provides. They enjoy the beaches, tropical weather and food, they accept the hospitality of the locals and comment amongst themselves about how generous, warm and civilised their hosts have been or how quaint the local customs are. What they aren't aware of, and couldn't comprehend even if they were, is the vast difference between being treated as an honoured guest or cultivated as a prospective business partner and actually living permanently in Malaysia as a Malay Muslim woman.

For me, as a woman, that difference had hit me like a thunderbolt, pinning me in its path and paralysing my will and obliterating my independence and self-esteem. How can one explain that as the years and months of my marriage rolled on, the expectations of my husband grew? Bahrin's expectations encompassed the very way

I thought, moved and spoke. To him, the longer I spent in Malaysia, the more he expected me to become subservient and mindless. It was as if a tiny pocket of my true self were locked away and only surfaced when I was alone with Iddin. Then I could laugh, sing and nurture to my heart's content, follow my instincts and feel that I was still a human being. But it seemed that the longer Bahrin and I were married, the less he respected and loved me.

I was a constant source of exasperation to him. I was ill-equipped to cope with all the official duties expected of me as I had never been taken aside and coached on what exactly, in ceremonial terms, was the right 'form'. I didn't have the foggiest idea how to organise a royal wake and mourning ceremony, something that should have been scheduled and implemented with the correct incantations and menus on a regular basis for the late Sultan, Bahrin's grandfather, to ensure his soul's peace. How to book the holy Imams and order goats for slaughter and largesse to the local population – was it done by weight or currency value? My husband would often spring these occasions on me at short notice and be angry when I looked at him blankly and stammered that I would ask Mak for advice. I could feel myself plummeting further in his estimation and being dismissed as moronic.

The more formal expectations of ceremony weren't quite as stressful; I could hide behind perfectly coordinated shoes, handbag and jewellery, not a hair out of place and make-up perfect. Taking part in the interminably long investiture events or the opening of schools, I would often accompany Endah in her official party, following her lead and catching a slight but encouraging inclination of her head when I was in doubt as to protocol. These public displays and private royal events were pretty nightmarish for me. I always felt gauche and uneasy, although they were far preferable to Bahrin's scrutiny and derision.

After the birth of Iddin, our intimate relations became more and more violent and degrading. Sex had never been a driving force in our relationship, and certainly for Bahrin once a week was quite enough, but now the tenor of our intimacy changed – Bahrin began to use me with no equanimity whatsoever. I began to fear sex with him because of its increasing violence. He would take pleasure in pinning me down and using me like some sort of masturbatory tool. He'd slap and jeer and curse me not to move, not to respond in any way at all. If I dared to move, he would hiss into my ear that only Western whores did that; that I was his wife and not some paid slut. When it was over – and it was always finished quickly – he would throw himself off me and immediately shower himself from head to foot. Sometimes he would force me to bathe too, citing the *parlar* points obtainable by doing so; other times I would curl up into a ball on the bed and weep as I listened to the water running in the bathroom as he washed.

It was much worse if Bahrin was angry with me for some minor or major indiscretion or disobedience. Then he would use my hair as a weapon. Immobilising me by snatching my long hair in his fist, he would wind the length around his wrist, making me unable to struggle. I didn't dare hit him back; he frightened me so very much that I feared how he would retaliate.

What made things worse is that he would do these despicable things in front of Iddin, who shared our room as I was still breastfeeding. Once Bahrin became completely infuriated with me because I had forgotten to switch off the electric water heater. Screaming at me that I was a useless, careless wife and filthy *mat salleh* slut, he began pushing me and slapping me around the face, swiping my cosmetics off the dressing-table and sending the basket of baby toys flying through the air. This woke Iddin with a start and he began to cry. He stood up in his crib and jiggled against the railings, but Bahrin refused to let me go to him and comfort him. Instead he screamed at Iddin to be quiet and lunged for me, grabbing a fistful of my hair and yelling to me that he was going to teach me a lesson once and for all. He ripped my nightgown from me and began to bash my head against the wall near the bathroom door. Then, swinging me around so that my face pressed hard into the door frame, he jerked my head around sideways so he could speak into my ear. 'Remember this next time you waste my money,' I heard him say as, with one swift action that made me feel as if I were being ripped open, he began to sodomise me. I was crying out with the pain and begging him to stop but he ignored my pleas. All the while I could hear Iddin whimpering behind us in fright. I hated Bahrin so much at that moment that I wished I could kill him.

When he had finally taught me my 'lesson', he pushed open the bathroom door and flung me onto the tiles telling me, 'Clean yourself up, you filthy *kaffir* bitch.'

I have heard stories about small children, inmates of overcrowded orphanages, abandoned by the dozen in countries like Romania; these children fail to thrive for the simple reason that they have been denied any physical love and affection. I truly understand why. I know what it is like to feel as if your heart is shattering, to physically ache for a hug or a gentle embrace, to long to just sleep close to another human being and feel their body warming yours or to catch your breath expectantly in the hope of a loving kiss.

This was what it was like for me living as Bahrin's wife. Always I would feel that it was my fault that he seemed unable to love me the way I needed to be loved. He would use physical affection like a weapon to bring me to heel. I would have to wait for verbal permission before sleeping close to him at night and he would ration me to a perfunctory squeeze of the hand at moments when I was bursting with happiness.

At times I knew that he felt angry with himself for even needing me as a sexual release, but still I hoped that I could ultimately win his approval. My life revolved around gaining his approval and staving off his tempers. At home I would refrain from speaking unless spoken to, precisely as he ordered. I'd serve his food first, always ensuring that I adhered strictly to the royal protocol he had drummed into me, and I would sit for hours cross-legged on the floor massaging his legs when he demanded – all in the hope of receiving an approving smile. His control over me was such that I lived in continual fear of rejection and a belief in my own worthlessness. I was completely isolated from the normal attitudes and amenities of a Western country. The respite that contact with like-thinking people would have brought me was entirely non-existent; my isolation within my own home meant that I was left without a sane point of reference. There was little hope of succour from the royal family of Terengganu; their dictums and implacable attitudes had all but engulfed me.

I hadn't realised how Australian I was until I lived in Malaysia. My treat to myself, and my only link with the far-off world that had been my true home, became my subscriptions to an Australian women's magazine and *Vanity Fair*, both of which arrived six weeks after publication. I pored over their pages and tried to absorb Australia and the happenings of the outside world through the print. It was as if part of me were trapped within the pages and part of me were reading about some far-off and distant alien culture. I was Jacqueline through the looking glass, able to see but not touch, understand cerebrally but never experience physically.

It was as if my very essence had been frozen over and shards of fire had thawed only enough of me to function as an automaton. After a long while, and for the most part, I learned to quash most of my emotions and retreat behind the hollow shell of being Yasmin, wife of Raja Bahrin and member of the royal family. As far as Bahrin was concerned I was his creation, his property and his bargain-basement purchase, albeit badly chosen. If he thought that he had caged me, he was right; I had nowhere to go and nothing to do. But sometimes his caged trophy could be a very pesky bird indeed.

The 1980s was the decade of aerobics, and leg warmers, leotards and headbands became essential items in many people's wardrobes. American actress and exercise queen Jane Fonda coined the catchphrase 'Go for the burn', which echoed around the world like some sort of sweat-induced call to arms. By the mid-1980s the word 'aerobics' finally reached Terengganu, filtering in via foreign video tapes, magazines and the occasional television programme.

During a visit to the United States, Endah discovered the existence of Fonda's workouts and brought the aerobics 'bible' back for me. As we sat together one afternoon in her sitting room, poring over the book, Endah and I began to hatch a plan which we both considered daring in the extreme: a Jane Fonda-type aerobics class for Endah and her badminton team. The team was made up primarily of middle-aged and overweight ladies, the wives of courtiers and 'knights of the realm' who, over the years, had met socially to play and gossip. Endah decided that I would be the instructor, as I was the only woman with any experience in physical exercise, and that her badminton players would participate in classes held in the badminton hall attached to the palace (whether they liked it or not). Although I tried to point out that ballet was hardly the same thing as aerobics, I didn't argue for very long and gladly jumped at a chance to move to music and break the monotony of my life. Endah promised to arrange permission from Bahrin and Mak so that I could teach twice weekly. It was quite delicious realising that Bahrin could hardly forbid me to instruct the Tengku Ampuan of Terengganu, his aunt and consort of the Sultan. For once someone outranked him and could make his life uncomfortable if he disagreed.

In preparation I managed to obtain a pirate copy of the workout video so I could see the exercises in motion and the techniques used. I had plenty of reservations about the level of flexibility required and the nagging suspicion that many of the ladies who were to participate in the classes would faint if they knew what would be expected of them. I developed a hybrid form of workout, much gentler than the Fonda one but incorporating some of the same movements and using pre-taped loud and energetic dance music.

The day of our first class dawned. I arrived at the palace and made my way to the badminton annexe which, in the days before videos, also doubled as a private cinema. Inside I found Endah surrounded by a group of twenty large and chattering women dressed in an odd assortment of kaftans and men's Adidas tracksuits. All of the full-length windows in the hall had been covered with blackout curtains and, after I entered, the doors were locked to ensure no prying male eyes. Endah had thought of everything: sound system, mats and a nanny to care for Iddin while I took the class. All that was left was to get started. An audible gasp rippled around the room when I stripped off to reveal my leotard and tights, luckily salvaged from my dancing days, old but still serviceable; from the ladies' reaction, I might have been standing there naked.

They settled down fairly quickly and were eager to

begin. As I went through the first series of exercises, I ran from lady to lady, correcting posture and trying to get them to keep some sort of rhythm. To'puan Farah, one of the more flamboyant characters of the group, voiced the opinion that, according to her pirated copy of the Jane Fonda workout video, what I was teaching was not difficult enough; she wanted to 'go for the burn'. And there was very little I could do to stop them doing just that. Some of those ladies threw themselves so hard into the exercises that the room began to resemble a steambath. No matter how I tried to impress on them that it was very unwise to embark upon this sort of violent physical exertion suddenly, none of them showed the least indication that they believed me. Watching them all, I had an intuitive feeling that many of the group would be feeling more than 'the burn' the next day after their muscles had had time to stiffen up in protest at the unaccustomed punishment.

After a ten-minute cool-down session on the floor, which I insisted everyone take part in, I was surprised and bewildered to hear Endah summon the staff to serve refreshments. On entering the hall, the uniformed footmen swiftly whisked away the snowy white covers from a line of trestle tables, which until then I hadn't noticed, to reveal surfaces groaning with cream cakes, pastries and sweetmeats as well as bright pink syrupy milk drinks and tea and coffee in silver pots. I was completely flabbergasted. Every single calorie that they had just burned off was being replaced threefold before my very eyes. What had started off as a fitness session had now turned into a gourmand's tea party!

I heard during the course of the next day that many of the men in the upper echelons of Terengganu society were very perplexed at their wives' sudden inability to walk, sit or move around the house without extreme pain. And as for praying, I received several telephone reports from members of the new aerobics class telling me that a sudden stiffness had struck, leaving them unable to kneel or perform the necessary body stances for prayer rituals. I have to admit that I couldn't resist an 'I told you so' attitude as these tales began to filter through to me. But all in all, our aerobics sessions were declared a success by Endah and her ladies and were to continue for many months, incorporating a routine of energetic exercise and hearty post-workout gorging.

Thirty

Iddin's illness inexplicably reappeared when he was six months old, inducing in me a state of panic and a deep mistrust of the Malaysian medical system. This time I held my ground against Bahrin and insisted that I be permittted to take Iddin home to Melbourne for specialist treatment. Bahrin railed at me for insisting on an Australian doctor's opinion. He told me that I would have to stop expecting to find Western medicine in Malaysia and he accused me of overreacting. I refused to be swayed and was backed up my mother-in-law, who also agreed that the cause of Iddin's bleeding had to be ascertained as quickly and as concisely as possible, preferably in Australia. I was not going to have my baby poked and prodded unnecessarily by the same doctors in Kuala Lumpur.

Eventually Bahrin gave in, citing the free medical care available to all Australians under the Australian health service. He positively crowed with delight that it wouldn't cost him a penny for Iddin's care. Following Iddin's birth, Bahrin and I had decided to register him as an Australian citizen. Bahrin was keen for our son to be educated in Melbourne, as he himself had been, and we had also discussed the possibility of one day returning to live there. So Iddin had been issued a birth certificate by the Australian High Commission in Kuala

Lumpur after we had filed a joint application witnessed by the private secretary to the Sultan. Bahrin's self-congratulatory stance made me feel quite ill. We had more than enough money to pay for competent medical care and, in any case, my husband spent more on his wardrobe than what I estimated the entire bill would have amounted to.

Coincidentally, Iddin and I were able to accompany the Sultan and his family aboard a Singapore Airlines flight to Australia, where they were enrolling Ima and Anna, the two younger daughters, in boarding school. Once there, however, I was on my own. I spent several days sleeping on a chair next to Iddin's bed in Melbourne's Royal Children's Hospital. I refused to leave him alone at the hospital as I was still breastfeeding and, in any case, he would cry whenever I moved out of his line of vision. After five days, during which the bleeding again ceased, and an endless series of tests and examinations, the specialist declared that Iddin had most probably been passing polyps from his bowel. I was instructed by the surgeon to watch Iddin's diet carefully to ensure that he did not ever become constipated and to continue breastfeeding for as long as possible to avoid any allergies that might be caused by cow's milk. I left the hospital much relieved and thankful that at last I felt confident about a diagnosis of Iddin's condition. Then I headed off straight away to show off my baby to his great-grandmother, my nanna.

Nanna was overjoyed to meet Iddin for the first time and spent every possible moment of our stay with us. Bahrin joined Iddin and me in Melbourne for a brief holiday and, for a wonderful ten days, the Bahrin I had met and fallen in love with resurfaced. It was as if he had suddenly woken up from a long sleep. We walked hand in hand along the street with Bahrin proudly pushing Iddin's pram and spent hours chatting as we ate in restaurants and shopped together for clothes for Iddin.

Before I had left Terengganu, Endah had presented me with a commission to shop on her behalf. Armed with a large sum of cash and a broad brief, I proceeded to acquire a selection of items for her: designer shoes in gold lace brocade from Manolo Blahnik, silk pumps in black from Salvatore Ferragamo and two small evening bags – one in white satin with intricate beadwork and the other a gold metal purse from Dior. Bahrin had no objection to my shopping for Endah as long as I didn't hamper his own orgy of spending at his favourite stores. For a few short days I revelled in striding out with big steps clad in jeans and sweaters, feeling like an ordinary person and eating pizza until I was almost ill. All too soon, though, it was time to return to Terengganu and the stifling life I led there. It was absolutely heartbreaking leaving my nanna behind and knowing that she would miss so very much of Iddin's growing up. And it was also frightening how the instant we stepped off the plane in Kuala Lumpur, Bahrin reverted to his Malaysian self and the coldness that I had come to expect from him.

The time which passed between my first and second pregnancies seemed to be spent in the quest to gain my husband's approval. I would have done anything to have Bahrin acknowledge that he and I shared more than just the same address and a son. Looking back, I seemed to have spent every moment I was in Bahrin's presence scurrying around nervously, trying to penetrate his consciousness and elicit something other than annoyance or contempt. But more than anything, I wanted him to tell me that he was happy. Happy with our marriage, happy with his life, happy with our son and, most of all, happy with me. Sometimes, with an aching of expectation and loneliness caused by his emotional dissociation, I would ask him if he was happy. Holding my breath, I would wait for his answer, praying that he would turn to me smiling, sweep me into his arms and declare emphatically, 'Yes!' But it never happened. Instead he'd answer, 'I'm content, that's enough,' with such a look of resignation on his face that I felt doubly wounded by his indifference and his lack of passion.

Nothing I could do or say elicited any further expansion on his pronouncement or evoked any deeper reaction or verve for life. Bahrin's resignation and acceptance of just being 'content' stung me more than a slap across the face and stripped away my layers of hope. 'Content' was such a lukewarm word, with no elasticity and no promise. It was as if Bahrin were telling me that he had no reason to expect anything more from our marriage and that his stoicism in the face of a life stretching before him with nothing more than lukewarm contentment was commendable.

Bahrin's contentment did not loosen his rein on me. If anything, it tightened his feeling of ownership over me. Simple things like a bank account of my own were out of the question and 'totally inappropriate', according to Bahrin, as I earned no money. In his opinion, he was the master of the house and I could not be trusted with access even to our household account: the chequebook was solely his domain. Every month he would present me with a wad of cash for the household expenses and staff wages. I would have to apply to him for any extra money I needed for unexpected bills or home maintenance. When, because of the rust contamination in our drinking-water supply, we had to install a new water tank outside, he stormed and railed, saying that it was my fault; that I had engineered the necessity for a new tank because I was a lazy Australian and had an obsession with new things.

Finally, when the new tank had been erected and plumbed in, he suddenly refused to give me the money to pay for it. He closed all discussions and went interstate 'on business'. Mak and I were left with the question of how to pay for the newly installed tank. We both knew that once Bahrin had made an assertion like that he would never alter his decision. With his mother muttering comments to the effect that Bahrin had always been *kedukut*, or stingy, even as a child, she and I proceeded to investigate a way of coming up with seven hundred Malaysian ringgit. All of my money from the *Hantar Belanjar* had been spent long ago on a new electric stove, a refrigerator and furnishings. The only alternative left open to me was to try to sell some of my jewellery to cover the bill. This was arranged by Mak through a middleman, ensuring that my identity as the seller was protected. It was a measure to which I would have to resort many times over the years when, due to a fit of pique, Bahrin would withhold my housekeeping money or refuse to pay the electricity or telephone bills, citing my mismanagement or wastefulness as justification. Yet if the evening's dinner menu was not up to his high standards, due to the lack of money for shopping, I would receive not only a lecture on slovenly housekeeping standards from Bahrin, but also a beating.

Fathoming the system of market shopping in Terengganu was something that I was never able to do. For starters, the markets didn't in any way resemble the clean food halls and refrigerated butcher stalls of Melbourne or other parts of the Western world. I was dumbfounded that their food markets were so incredibly filthy, with open drains and fly-infested rubbish troughs standing cheek by jowl with fish stalls. It was not uncommon to see cane baskets full of offal and fruit peel rocking from side to side as the rats fought each other over the choicest titbits. There was no refrigeration for the meat and fish and not a stainless steel bench in sight. Beef was an unheard-of commodity in Terengganu and steak, imported from Australia or the United States and flown in from Kuala Lumpur, was obtainable only at the tourist hotels.

Fresh vegetables and meat were the most expensive items on our shopping list and something of an extravagance for ordinary people. The red meat available to the populace at large, including the royal family, was buffalo meat, which was as tough as old boots and quite suspect as to its freshness. In fact, one couldn't actually buy a cut of meat such as sirloin, T-bone, rump or blade: buffalo was sold by the slab, a nondescript lump of filleted flesh from an unidentifiable area of the beast. Chicken was very expensive and slaughtered and plucked on the spot for the purchaser. We didn't eat very much chicken. I didn't like to buy it because of the suspiciously uniform plumpness caused by the uncontrolled and scientifically unsupervised injection of antibiotics and steroids common in Malaysia to enhance size. These injections pumped the chicken up to such an extent that upon closer inspection of the filleted carcass, an oozing yellowish substance would be clearly visible between the skin and the flesh. Fish was the staple of most Malay diets, varying from dried anchovies to steaks of tuna, or *ikan tendiri*.

In the main produce hall of the market, a dank and unhygienic place, buffalo and fish, prawns and chicken carcasses and the occasional side of goat were laid out uncovered on stone slab benches next to open gutters running with blood, water and fish innards. Fruit, vegetables, nuts, rice and precooked delicacies, along with the seasonal treats like turtle eggs and durian fruit, were sold in the open-air square abutting the produce hall. Here, wizened old ladies squatted beside their baskets of food touting for business, their feet shoved into open-toed plastic slippers, their teeth stained black by years of betel nut chewing. I was actively discouraged from frequenting the marketplace by the women of the family, none of whom would have been caught dead anywhere near the place, all their grocery shopping being done by their cooks or drivers. I must admit that after a few forays into the market accompanied by a servant as chaperone, I too was more inclined to leave the shopping to our cook, and on the whole I did. There would often be some confusion as to quantities and orders as very few of the domestic help working for the royal family were literate.

Tengku Zaleha, my mother-in-law, insisted that our servants cook in the *dapur*, or kitchen outhouse, a shack not really fit for habitation, let alone the preparation of food. She loathed the smell of cooking and also preferred the servants to cook on kerosene stoves in the *dapur* instead of by gas. In her Western-style kitchen in her house proper, she kept her refrigerator and double burner electric hotplate for reheating food and preparing her cats' food. During my life in Malaysia we had either one or two cooks depending on Mak's current frame of mind. Mak effectively felt it her domain to hire and fire my cooks as well as her own and, often unreasonably, her servants would fall from favour and be replaced by others in the course of twenty-four hours.

Although she showed nothing but kindness and support for me during my marriage to Bahrin, living with one's mother-in-law is not the easiest thing to do. Mak would come and go from my house to hers with no compunction whatsoever and she expected me to do the same. On the rare occasions Bahrin would allow Iddin and me to accompany him to Kuala Lumpur, I would always come home to find that Mak had taken it upon herself to completely reorganise my cupboards or my furniture. Even my underwear wasn't safe. She would change its location too, sometimes sorting through my wardrobes and donating to charity clothes she felt I no longer wore. I was constrained by the etiquette of my situation from complaining to her or forbidding her to do these annoying things. On the one occasion that I did so, she refused to speak to me for several weeks and would pass messages to me through her sisters or servants. I had to be more than tactful: I had to be mute.

I learned early on in my new life that to lose the support of my mother-in-law in this unfamiliar society was to make myself a pariah to the family at large and risk through this withdrawal of support the inevitable suggestion that the current daughter-in-law be traded in for a newer and more congenial model. One of my main redeeming features, in the eyes of the royal family, was the total acceptance as a daughter-in-law that Tengku Zaleha gave me even though I was a foreigner. That, and my relationship with Endah. With these two champions behind me, very few people had the temerity to snub me.

Mak chain-smoked and had an almost compulsive attitude to bathing which led her to spend two or three hours a day in the bathroom. She was a woman who had never cooked a meal, done her own washing or read a book other than the Koran and holy Islamic writings. She had an abiding passion for cats and had a ragtag collection of fifteen felines, all of which could do no wrong. Subservience to male 'superiority' was deeply ingrained in her, colouring her perspective on all facets of daily life and undervaluing her self-worth. Tengku Zaleha was the progeny of the Sultan of Terengganu, the late King of Malaysia, who had had a total of four wives and ten children. She had been brought up on a staple diet of palace and familial intrigue where sibling rivalry ran rife. Her late father, a manipulative and authoritarian man, had controlled every last aspect of his children's and grandchildren's lives with little thought to their prospects of going it alone once he was gone. The girls of the family were particularly affected by their social status and upbringing, passing from the influence of their father to their husband via arranged marriages.

Mak had no idea about the domestic side of life and found the concept of housework a novel idea rather than a menial chore. One afternoon she decided that it would be rather fun to wash her own clothes and proceeded to empty a whole box of detergent into a tiny plastic basin full to the brim with water, into which she immersed one of her silk garments. Her sister Zainah, myself and the servants looked on in amusement as she squatted on the edge of her outdoor terrace, scrubbing, splashing and giggling with delight at the normality of her actions.

Faced with the arrival of her first grandchild, she and Auntie Zainah threw themselves into a frenzy of high cluck. I had to carefully watch them both when Iddin was tiny, as they had very little idea about basic hygiene or how to hold a small baby correctly. Neither of the women had ever cared for their own babies. A battery of servants and nannies, supplied by the Sultan, had taken care of their offspring, changing nappies, bottle feeding and generally leaving them free to loll.

There was one comic scene that took place shortly after Iddin's birth that I don't think I will ever forget. I was quite busy baking biscuits and cakes for the Hari Raya festival, the end of the Muslim fasting month, so Mak and Auntie Zainah offered to help out by changing Iddin. As I used only disposable nappies, with no pins involved, I couldn't see that this simple operation would cause them too many problems. I handed Iddin over to his eager admirers. When over forty-five minutes had elapsed and the trio had still not emerged from the bedroom, I went to investigate. I found Mak and Auntie

Zainah convulsed in nervous giggles and red-faced with embarrassment, a whole box of discarded and useless disposable nappies on the floor and Iddin lying bare-bottomed on the changing table. It seems that between the two of them, these middle-aged ladies were unable to successfully insert a baby boy into a disposable nappy without managing to get slippery castor oil cream all over the adhesive tabs, thereby rendering nappy after nappy unusable.

The unfortunate thing about Mak was her tendency towards hypochondria and her fascination with prescription drugs, which she used as a panacea for the boredom and unhappiness in her life. I know from talking to her that she greatly regretted that she hardly knew her son, Bahrin. The only problem was she had no idea about how to forge a bond with him at the age of twenty-eight.

Bahrin's attitude towards his mother, when alone with me, indicated nothing but contempt. He told me on many occasions that he regarded any attention he paid her or conversation he had with her as obligatory filial piety as set down in the Koran. It was very sad that his moral obligation did not extend to sincere intellectual respect or regard for Mak, for although he was careful to couch his contempt for her in the strictest of courtesies and in the handing over of cash, she was still conscious of his lack of feelings for her and often lamented that she wished she had cared for him as a baby the same way I was caring for her grandson Iddin. But royal protocols and an all-pervading fear of the late Sultan had precluded any such contact.

Mak did her best to try to keep Bahrin and me together the only way she and her family knew how. With every new sign of Bahrin's varied and numerous infidelities, she would drag me off to see the most fashionable *bomoh*, the equivalent of a witch-doctor with a spiritual bent, currently in vogue with the women of her family. No matter how much I protested my disbelief in these strange hocus-pocus practices, she was insistent that I comply with her wishes. For my own part, I eventually resigned myself to traipsing after her to remote villages to meet a collection of con men and women who sold themselves as healers of broken hearts. These *bomohs* practised a deeply rooted traditional Malay mysticism which was frowned upon by the tenets of Islam. So, to make their potions and charms more acceptable to their God-fearing clients, they muttered verses from the Koran as they wrote on scraps of fabric, burned photographs or 'blessed' holy water – all in the name of Allah – and collected a sizeable cash remuneration for their troubles.

The more I got to know about the mysticism practised in Malaysia, the more bewildered I was by the apparent acceptance and use of *bomohs* by the population at large. They were a superstitious people, and even the most sophisticated of doctors I met did not baulk at the alleged existence of *gins*, or genies. Genies, I was told by Che Gu Ali, my religious tutor, inhabited the earth and caused untold mischief and harm if offended. Allegedly citing passages of Islamic text, he said that *gins* could be called upon by prayers and incantations to either protect a house or destroy the peace and sanity of the inhabitants. This was one of the reasons that Koranic verses were placed above entrance doors: to guard against evil. Mind you, Che Gu Ali also believed that the first moon walk, by the crew of Apollo 11, was nothing more than a Hollywood movie stunt. He believed that Neil Armstrong walked across a cleverly built film set and not across the lunar surface. This, he solemnly pronounced, was 'another bit of treacherous American propaganda' and something that no true Muslim should swallow.

Thirty-one

Iddin grew at an amazing pace, developing into an intelligent and beautiful child. He had the most enchanting grin and a rumbling chuckle broke out whenever he was tickled. We used to spend hours together curled up on my big bed as I read him stories and sang children's songs to him. He especially enjoyed playing 'this little piggy went to market' – except that I had to be careful not to use the word 'piggy' around Bahrin because the Muslim prohibition on pork extended even to nursery rhymes. I worried that because of the beliefs and restrictions placed on him, Iddin was missing out on the sort of play and stimulation that Australian and European toddlers take for granted, simple things like getting dirty in a sandpit, and water play. It caused a furore when I insisted that I was going to let Iddin play under my supervision in the shade outside. At almost two years old, and with a little baby brother or sister on the way, I was determined that he develop into a confident and sturdy little boy which, as far as I was concerned, meant enjoying his childhood – dirt and all. Playing with the garden hose became one of Iddin's favourite pastimes, along with watching my pet goats, Noneng and his mother Susu.

I acquired Susu and Noneng shortly after Iddin's birth. As I was forbidden by custom and religion to keep a dog, the next best thing, I decided, was a goat. Susu was a white, short-haired nanny goat who was getting on in years and only narrowly avoided the slaughterer's knife by my timely purchase of her and her baby. Noneng was a mischievous and lively animal, full of life and very affectionate, with a pelt of rich tan edged with touches of black. I managed to semi-housetrain him and allowed him inside occasionally when Bahrin was at the office. Unfortunately Noneng didn't understand that entrance to the house was by invitation only and would wander into the living-room and prop himself up on the couch, where he would bleat loudly, refusing to budge until I scratched him behind the ear. I had a goat pen built in the garden to accommodate the animals and a chicken house set up for the free-range hens I later added to the menagerie. My growing number of pets were a source of bewilderment to the neighbouring relatives, who shook their heads at my actions and labelled me eccentric.

I had been wrong to think that the arrival of Iddin would do anything to thaw the ice between Bahrin and me. I was very much a sole parent, with Bahrin's major contribution to the life of our son being an occasional 'family' drive in the afternoons, during which he and I sat, barely conversing, in the front seat with Iddin chortling away in the back. The times he spent playing with Iddin were few and far between. Bahrin refused to understand that a small child could not be simply switched on and off. This caused difficulty, as Bahrin didn't play with Iddin for sustained periods of time. A quick rough-house or tickle, a piggyback once around the garden and then nothing. He would suddenly walk away from Iddin, leaving our toddler confused and wanting more. Bahrin shut himself away from his son as completely as he excised me from his heart. It was quite hard to cope with Iddin when this happened as he would invariably burst into tears. Not understanding, as I did, that for his father, the novelty of anything new quickly wore off.

At the end of 1984 I realised that I was pregnant again. I knew exactly when this baby was due as I could pinpoint the time of conception to the hour, so few and far between were the occasions when this could have happened. This time when I told Bahrin that I was expecting, he showed little enthusiasm, only a polite interest in the due date. This pregnancy took a lot more out of me than Iddin's, sapping my energy and making it hard to keep up with an energetic toddler. I was still breastfeeding Iddin at bedtimes as per the recommendation of the Melbourne doctors and as prescribed in the Koran, which ruled that two years was the minimum time expected for a Muslim mother to breastfeed, although Iddin was on solid food and drank juice from a cup. The other reason I opted to continue feeding Iddin myself was that fresh milk was an unobtainable commodity in Malaysia and the powdered formulas available in Terengganu were milk products dumped by large multinational companies on Third World countries with the 'use by' date long expired. My plan was to have Iddin weaned by the fourth or fifth month of my pregnancy so as to make way for the new baby. I wanted to try to develop a strong sense of bonding between Iddin and his new baby brother or sister and avoid sibling rivalry as much as I could. I hoped that Iddin would be secure enough in my love for him to accept 'his' new baby, as he called him or her, without too many problems.

Before I had children, my day revolved around Bahrin. After Iddin was born, and as far as Bahrin was concerned, it still did.

I would get up quite early to ensure breakfast was

ready for him. Bahrin would perhaps say his dawn prayers, depending on his mood and how pious he was feeling that morning. He was never particularly diligent about praying, except when there was an audience to witness his supplications to Allah; then his holiness would be for public consumption and he would go through his prayer ablutions with great gusto, donning his sarong and unfurling his prayer mat. After three years of marriage, I was used to his public persona, the cultivated humility which he described to me as being royal enough and clever enough to make people think that he regarded them as his equals. This, Bahrin proudly told me, he had learned at an early age at school and he found it a useful tool. Religion and humility, he lectured me, were the necessary keys to his business and political future. Playing the soccer-mad, religious and humble prince suited his purposes and he was very skilled at it. Sometimes I would watch bemused as he made civil servants grovel and business clients glow with his calculated disarming of them. I wondered to myself if they ever had an inkling that they were merely watching a polished performer at work, a man who hid himself behind a façade and created an illusion, always with a polictical agenda in mind.

It was only after Bahrin had departed for the office that I was able to give my full attention to Iddin. His morning baths and playtime were the best parts of my day; he was a real water baby and loved to splash. I think if I had allowed it, Iddin would have spent most of his time out of his clothes and in the bath. Mak would arrive as soon as Bahrin had left for work. She seldom ventured near our house when Bahrin was home – she was afraid of his sullen moods and his temper, which she described as *bekeng*, or fierce. Together we would sit and play with Iddin and, during his morning nap, Mak would recite the Koran whilst I laboriously read the Malay and English newspapers. That was more out of habit, as I knew that the three pages of 'news' were heavily censored by the government and nothing ever appeared in the press without being thoroughly vetted first. I would scan each page for a mention of Australia; there was not usually much else of concern except the Malaysian royal family news, most of which I had already heard on the ever-present and efficient grapevine.

Bahrin, who by this time had opened his own architectural practice, arrived home at lunchtime for a full four-course midday meal, returning to work following an afternoon nap. To fill the emptiness of my afternoon hours I read and reread copious numbers of books. This was not a place where soap operas reigned supreme; television ran only from 4 p.m. and even then it was heavily censored, to the extent that kissing scenes, including very tame ones, were cut from all films. With no bookstores other than religious ones in Terengganu, I was forced to import books by the boxload from Singapore and Kuala Lumpur and sometimes as far afield as London.

But even my reading was closely monitored by Bahrin, who would use this small pleasure against me, often forbidding me to read for days on end as punishment for some real or imagined misdemeanour. He knew full well that books were my one form of escape, my window on the outside world and a pastime that I relished. At the height of his anger he would frequently curse me and scream that I shouldn't read, that I was virtually the only woman in his family who did, and that I chose to read as an affront to him. He would accuse me of trying to be different and of being arrogant, of poisoning my mind with 'filthy *mat salleh* publications'. Bahrin increasingly used these types of rebukes for everything and anything, from a book by

Charles Dickens to the way I sat. I did my utmost to absorb or ignore his insults and anger. I had learned that to do otherwise would be to inflame his ire further and, besides, I still wanted to please my husband.

Pleasing Bahrin was not a simple thing to do. He was fastidious and pedantic about so many things that I lived in terror of not coming up to scratch. His clothes and the way in which they were cared for were a constant anxiety to me. Our dressing-room contained all of his clothes; mine were stored in wardrobes in the service portion of the house as there wasn't enough room for both. Bahrin's shoes were kept on a tiered rack outside the dressing-room, immaculately polished English loafers, tasselled and slip-on style, in size six. I can still recall the sound of Bahrin choosing his shoes each day from their rack and dropping them onto the terrazzo floor in front of his feet, ready to be put on. As they hit the ground they made a hollow yet resonating 'plop' that echoed throughout the house and signalled his imminent departure.

I'm sure that Bahrin mimicked his late grandfather with his obsession with his wardrobe. His grandfather, too, had always been immaculately turned out and his clothing so carefully kept that part of the palace was still set aside for his things – just the way he had left them, his dress uniforms laid out and his shoes highly polished and stored in dust bags. Bahrin's detailed household laws about his clothing were very specific, right down to the last thread. Zah, as the servant in charge of washing and ironing, lived in mortal fear of attracting Bahrin's displeasure and spent hours maintaining his apparel. All shirts had to be placed on plastic-coated hangers, buttoned on the second button and facing to the left. They then had to be hung in colour-coded blocks, pink with pink, white with white, striped with striped and yellow with yellow; all sleeve lengths were also grouped together, short-sleeved pink with short-sleeved pink and so on. Each shirt was freshly starched and hung without crushing the other next to it; they would have to be re-ironed if so much as a minor crease appeared after a month on the clothes rack. As a precaution, I numbered all of Bahrin's shirts with an indelible laundry pen from '1' to '169'. I did this because I had received several slaps and kicks when he could not find a particular shirt and so I wanted to keep track of what shirt went where. I was sure that some shirts went missing during his business trips to Kuala Lumpur. I wasn't certain if he left them in hotel rooms or at his father's house and this was the only way I could think of to help me keep count.

Trousers had a different set of rules. Every pair had to be hung on its own individual heavy wooden hanger; this was to minimise the slight creases which appear midway down a trouser leg when hung on the narrow wire type. Colour blocking was again enforced, as was an exact way of hanging, waistbands on the left of the hanger, legs on the right. Bahrin had an unnerving habit of calling snap inspections of his closet during which I had to stand in the room as he surveyed each shirt and ran his hand beneath his trousers to check that they were hung exactly even on either side. To forestall his displeasure I usually checked on the condition of his closet every day.

In the fourth month of my pregnancy, I developed blinding migraines which put me in bed for several days at a time. It was a struggle just to manage Iddin, let alone supervise every minute detail of the house. One morning, as I lay on our bed with the curtains drawn to shut out the sunlight, an ice pack on my head and the air-conditioning running full blast in the hope that the drop in temperature might alleviate the pressure I felt behind my eyes, Bahrin came bursting into the room.

He lunged towards the bed and dragged me roughly into the dressing-room, growling, 'Look at this, just look at this!' I didn't know what he was talking about. I could hardly see, as the room was spinning, and I was doing my best not to vomit as I stood swaying with dizziness.

'What's wrong, darling?' I said, trying to focus my eyes.

'This, this!' bellowed Bahrin, gesticulating wildly towards his rows of trousers. 'You useless, lazy Australian slut. You can't even keep my clothes properly! They're not even, they're not right! I wanted to wear these but now I can't because they have a crease right across the knee.' He screeched at me, each word enunciated staccato fashion and with absolute hatred, as he thrust a pair of blue linen trousers under my nose.

'But it was an accident. I didn't do it, please listen to me. Zah hung the trousers after she ironed them, I didn't.'

'I don't care. It's your responsibility to supervise the servants. You're just a fucking bitch, a fucking useless *mat salleh* bitch.'

I didn't see the wooden coathanger coming towards me, but I certainly felt the impact as it cracked into my nose and caught me below the left eye. I doubled over as my nose began to bleed, instinctively hunching in case he decided to aim a kick at me, the uppermost thing on my mind being to protect the baby. I begged him not to hit me any more, to think of the baby. I swore that I would never let it happen again and that I would re-iron all his clothes myself. His reply was to grab a fistful of my hair, using it like a handle to drag me back into the bedroom, where he flung me back onto the floor and screamed yet more abuse. I remained hunched over on the floor, terrified at what he might do next, making a futile attempt to staunch the flow of blood from my nose with my dress as I listened to him continue on about my uselessness and stupidity. Finally he told me that he was confining me to my room and that I was to remain there and not to make a fuss as he would make me regret it. And so saying, he threw himself out of the room, locking the door behind him.

I don't remember much about the days that followed the trouser episode, only that I was a prisoner in my own house and that Iddin was brought to me at regular intervals. Everyone was told by Bahrin that I had carelessly slipped and fallen in the bathroom, smashing my face on the washbasin, and that I was still suffering from a migraine. Mak asked no questions of me and avoided looking me directly in the face. I didn't need Bahrin to spell out what he would do to me if I tried to tell anyone what had really happened to my nose and, in any case, he was my husband and I had displeased him – I could expect little better. A woman was powerless to protest and no man I turned to would have supported a theory that gave a woman the right to castigate her husband about his disciplinary actions.

I had no strength to leave him, no resources to call upon. It was as if he had broken all my confidence in myself. I was convinced that I was worth nothing; that I was ugly and a failure for not being able to sustain a happy marriage. And, ironically, I still hoped that one day those sporadic glimpses of his 'Western' persona, which surfaced briefly at the most unexpected moments, would somehow return permanently and magically bring back the man with whom I had fallen in love all that time ago during a Melbourne spring.

As my pregnancy continued and I felt the baby moving inside me with the promise of new life, my marriage seemed to stagger along like some mortally wounded beast as I struggled to blind myself to its demise. I took refuge in my role as Iddin's mother and spent an increasing amount of time with Endah at the palace, safe in my special room overlooking the South China Sea or sitting in the rose garden watching Iddin play in the shaded bower. My health had rapidly declined since the trouser episode; I had developed tachycardia, a condition that made my heart race at over triple its normal rate, and I truly feared for my baby. I found it difficult to keep food down and failed to put on the weight necessary for the development of the child. Bahrin now spent only one or two nights at home; he was either working, attending dinners or travelling to Kuala Lumpur or Singapore on business. And when he was home I attempted to win him back, in a kind of desperation to create a family life for our children, which invariably left me humiliated and him disdainful.

Mak continued to suggest the assistance of *bomohs* to help me bring her son back to my side and she dragged me off to meet old women who offered me concoctions to infuse into Bahrin's food to assure his faithfulness. My mother-in-law would gratefully accept these potions and carry them back home with her as if they were the Holy Grail, mixing them into Bahrin's coffee herself when I refused to do so and justifying her actions in the name of her grandchildren. If I were really desperate, Mak told me, assuming the tones of one who is about to commit a mortal sin, she knew of a new *bomoh* from the northern state of Kelantan who worked from the remnants of the wife's soiled sanitary pads, burning and grinding them to powder and blessing them through prayer, which made a potent ingredient to be added to the husband's diet, unbeknownst to him. She said that although she knew this sort of magic to be a grave sin, she was willing to risk it for me and the children. I told her that I was very grateful for her love and support but pointed out that, as I was pregnant, I was without the correct ingredients and that I really didn't agree with that practice. So, instead, she set off on a whirlwind of alternatives, from sewing talismans made from Bahrin's underwear and Koranic verses into his pillow to ensure he would dream of me, to having a *bomoh* bless the house and cast out evil influences. I didn't stop her harmless exercises; I was too worried about my future and that of my son and unborn child.

Bahrin began to remind me with increasing frequency that I held no official residency status in Malaysia and that my visa was solely dependent upon his goodwill. He would point out that he could take Iddin away from me and have me deported from his country with the tilt of his little finger if he so wished. He would accuse me of always being different, of not thinking the same way as other women.

Sometimes Bahrin would screech at me to grow up when I confronted him with the evidence of his infidelities and tell me that I was insane and useless as a wife. To him, my young age at the time we married had been the added attraction; he saw youth as equating with malleability – but somehow that attraction faded when he realised that, as I grew older, I would unfortunately develop my own opinions, brought about sooner by my early motherhood. I lived on a seesaw of emotions that tilted from the desperation of keeping my husband and repairing our marriage to the utter terror of incurring more of his abuse and violence.

I began to understand more and more why the women of the royal family hoarded jewellery in amounts that made the average European jewellery collection pale into insignificance. Jewellery was their only form of security; few women operated bank accounts in the circles I moved in and hardly any of them had a means of supporting themselves. As if the sword of Damocles were hanging over their heads, they lived in constant fear, often well founded, that their husbands would trade them in for a newer model and they would be relegated to the 'back room' with all that that entailed, including the financial precariousness that being an older multiple wife brought. I had always, up until this point, been unable to comprehend why these women seemed to think I was stupid when I spent my allowance on furnishing our home and buying plants for the garden rather than following their lead and purchasing gold and jewellery for a rainy day. My female in-laws held afternoon teas rather like the Tupperware parties English and American women held – except that at these parties the sales revolved around jewellery set with diamonds, rubies and emeralds. I went to one of these gatherings once and watched in fascination as the salesman spilled pouches of gold, pearls and unset precious stones across the coffee tables. Trays of diamond rings, full necklace sets and ropes of natural pearls were handed around with as much casual interest as might be shown in the cosmetics at an Avon meeting. Jewels were the currency of security, a justifiable and necessary expense easily explained to a husband and just as easily converted into cash if the need arose. It was sad to realise that all of the women I knew in Terengganu viewed their marriages so pragmatically and so fatalistically that they planned for the day when they were no longer loved.

Thirty-two

Life in a royal court is full of contradictions, obscure occurrences and opulence. Much of it has no semblance of sanity or logic. The immediate royal family lived a rarefied existence so unattainable to the average member of the populace as to be obscene. The foreign cars in the garages were painted a vulgar but mandatory royal yellow: Rolls-Royces, Corniche and convertible models, stretch Cadillacs and Mercedes limousines. These were the ceremonial vehicles. Then there were the toys of the younger members: Ferraris, Porsches and BMWs. Range Rovers were only beginning to become popular after it was discovered that the British royals were driving them as recreational vehicles. All of us had special single-digit number plates on our cars, ensuring that everyone but the ignorant would be aware of who was the owner and possibly the driver. This was the way the police force avoided pulling over any speeding royal and facing the unsavoury consequences of their ill-advised actions.

Vintage cars were another favourite, although primarily with the older generation; these were kept in mint condition and seldom driven. From the classic red Alfa Romeo Spider which Bahrin's father drove to the convertible Mercedes Sport and the 1920s Rolls-Royce, only the best would do. As no import duty was paid by royals, the collections of our family and other relatives in neighbouring royal houses were comprehensive and expanding constantly. Bahrin and his cousin Ihsan had possession of a hand-built and custom-upholstered sports car, stored in the royal mews. The boys were not yet teenagers when they became the proud owners of the best in British motor-car design. Built in Britain in the 1960s, it had been presented to them as a gift during their grandfather's (then the King of Malaysia) state visit to Iran. The Shah and Empress Farah Diba were long-time friends of Bahrin's family and their photographs remained in pride of place on the sideboard in the entrance foyer to Istana Badariah long after the revolution and the advent of the Ayatollah Khomeini. Omar, Bahrin's step-grandmother, still made regular visits to the former Empress Farah Diba in the USA, where she maintained a select but still active court in exile.

The contradictions presented themselves with little pattern, reason or predictability. Whilst piety and Islam were espoused, the raw truth was often so much further from the religious doctrine than anyone outside the collected families of Malaysian royalty would ever allege or admit, now or then. A complicity of silence existed, binding each family to the other, each cousin to the next, in a rancid façade of moral superiority.

All the ruling houses of Malaysia are related, often through first-cousin marriages. Normal circumstances brought the relatives from different states together both socially and ceremonially. So it wasn't unusual for me to hear about a weekend away at a popular resort being organised by the young single males of a number of courts. Suffice it to say, however, that a gross act of barbarism occurred that particular weekend at the lush tropical resort. It was not the first instance of abuse of power I was to witness or hear about during my time in Malaysia.

Droit de seigneur left anyone who was not of royal

blood or connection vulnerable to the whims and rages of any of my extended family. Ima, the Sultan's daughter and the tomboy of the clan, had been secretly arranging trysts with a young village boy with whom she had begun a friendship when sneaking out of the palace to play soccer. Unfortunately for the boy, the last rendezvous was organised in one of the many deserted rooms of the Istana Pantai where she resided with her mother, Sharifah Nong. Ordinarily, Ayah Mud's routine was as regular as clockwork. However, for some reason that never became apparent, His Royal Highness arrived unannounced at his second wife's home and immediately made his way to the room where Ima and her boyfriend were playing cards – fully dressed and on different sides of a table. An explosion of rage from Ayah Mud resulted in him drawing a gun and pistol-whipping the boy from the house and into unconsciousness. All this was related to me in hushed but titillated tones by my aunts-in-law, the Sultan's sisters, after Sharifah Nong, never discreet at the best of times, had poured out her problems to the family. 'Thank Allah,' said Auntie Zainah, 'it would have been very tricky if he had pulled the trigger and killed the boy.'

As reported in the London *Times*, the Malaysian royal families have a history with firearms, often resulting in dire consequences when the weapons come into the hands of the more volatile members. One Sultan (whilst still a Crown Prince), ruler of a southern state, took umbrage with a businessman of Chinese origin who had inadvertently overtaken his unmarked car on a major highway. Giving chase at high speed, the Sultan caught up with the bewildered motorist, dragged him from his car and put a bullet through his head. This incident made international headlines, especially when the then Crown Prince was pardoned for his actions.

Obscure occurrences could sometimes have a direct

effect on me. It had been necessary for me to fight tooth and nail to be allowed to breastfeed Iddin. This was not considered seemly, and it took the sourcing of well-researched quotes from the Koran and protestations on my part for Bahrin and his family to agree. I calculated that I was the first member of the family to breastfeed since the turn of the century. The Princess of Wales's decision to nurse Prince William was also a great help, but it wasn't until Queen Noor and King Hussein of Jordan made a state visit to Malaysia that the question was settled once and for all. Queen Noor (formerly Lisa Halaby, an American woman) had refused to leave her new baby at home as she was breastfeeding too. The Agung's (Malaysian King) staff, our families and the courtiers were agog and initally at a loss as to how to accommodate a breastfeeding queen and her child, but somehow they managed. I will always be grateful for Her Majesty Queen Noor's stance and the support affored to her by His Majesty, her husband, as it allowed me the vindication I needed, with an Islamic queen holding her ground on such an important issue.

Joining such exalted company as Queen Noor and the Princess of Wales quickly became fashionable, and by the time I was pregnant again, a number of other royals had begun to try breasfeeding and would often ask me about techniques. The irony was not the choice, rather the reason.

The day of my twenty-second birthday was anything but happy. The anxieties of the impending birth of our second child had prompted me to appeal to Bahrin for a full and joint effort by both of us to try to salvage our marriage. I feared for the future, I feared for our new baby and I feared for Iddin and the effect his father's increasingly violent tempers would have on him in the long term, as he had often witnessed my beatings.

I had rehearsed my plea to Bahrin and was very careful to maintain my composure whilst I spoke. Unfortunately this seemed to infuriate Bahrin more than tears and he flew into a rage, screaming that I was a worthless slut and that he had done me a great favour in marrying me, a stinking *kaffir* bitch.

I could only react with the despair I felt welling up inside me, a lump of misery that seemed to be magnified by the movements of the baby. As Bahrin cast a loathing look at me, turned on his heel and left me sitting on the verandah in the hot night air, I began to sob – great pain-wracked tremors that tightened my chest and made me feel as if my air were being cut off and my world careering down a cliff.

Sometime before dawn that same night, I was woken by Bahrin shaking me and asking me to talk to him. He told me to follow him into the dressing-room, where he had spent the night, and he sat down next to me on the floor. Leaning there against the closet door he appeared agitated, as if he didn't know what to say now I was actually in his presence. As for me, I was wary, not knowing whether I was in for another beating or if some tragedy had struck and this was what he wanted to relate to me.

What came out of his mouth shocked and confused me.

'Yasmin,' he said, 'I do want things to be all right between us, I'm so sorry for everything. I only wish that I could make you happy.'

He seemed to become more distressed as he went on and began to wrap and rewrap his arms around his knees, which were drawn up to his chest.

'Sometimes I just don't know what I'm doing. Something in my brain just snaps and I can't stop my anger. I wanted so much to have a normal life with you when we married, I just don't know how.'

And then he began to cry, sobbing as he rocked back and forth in front of me, just as I had done hours earlier.

What he said next has stayed with me for years, haunting my memory of him and summing up his inability to ever have a 'normal' relationship in Western terms.

'I do want you to be happy. I'm sorry for all the times I've hit you. I'm really sorry. I want to make you happy but I know that I can't. I can't give you what you need and deserve, what you want. You need a man who will make you happy, who can make you laugh and give you all the attention and love that you need, someone who can hold you and kiss you all the time and be your friend. I wish that I could find you that man and give you to him to make you happy. But if I did, I would still be your husband and you'd still belong to me. He would just be to make you happy and give you what you need.'

I said nothing, I was too shocked to take it all in. By this time we were both crying, sitting on the floor side by side with the moon's reflection through the open window casting eerie shadows on the floor. I reached out for Bahrin. He was in so much pain, and I couldn't bear to see him like that. I drew him against my chest and felt him rest against the swell of our baby. What would happen to us from here? Was this a sign that Bahrin had had some sort of cathartic experience and was now returning to his senses? I could not comprehend this turnaround in his attitude, or even begin to understand what sort of relationship we would have now. As I held him to me, I wanted so much to believe that he was sorry for the way he had treated me but I couldn't understand the full meaning of his last statement. I was tired and exhausted, heavily pregnant, with the baby well overdue. Was he playing some cruel trick on me? Was he saying that I was his chattel to give away to someone else? I simply didn't know, and I was so tired of riding on a roller-coaster of fear and uncertainty. We fell asleep together, lying on the spare bed, a forced optimism and also a great weariness the last things I remember before I finally found sleep.

Our daughter, Shah, was born less than forty-eight hours later on 7 July 1985. A delicate silk-skinned bundle with dark hair that grew in soft tendrils against her scalp, she had arrived after an induced labour of thirteen hours and a distressing delivery.

I had been left alone in the labour room; the doctor had calculated that I wouldn't deliver for many hours and he had returned home for a round of golf and a meal. But, as usual, the best laid plans often don't fall into place that simply, and I began to have the definite feeling that the birth was imminent. Summoning the nurse, I told her so. Her reply was to scoff and tell me that I was wrong – but she fell into a flat panic when she looked and saw that I was indeed right.

The senior nurse summoned two attendants, both of whom were untrained village girls dressed in white sarongs. She instructed them in an agitated voice to hold me down flat and keep my knees together so I was unable to push while she contacted the doctor. I pleaded with her to deliver the baby herself, as she was a qualified midwife, but she replied that it was not worth her job to intervene in a royal birth, as I was required to deliver in the presence of a doctor.

The two girls pinned me flat as the labour spasms took hold, one of them across my chest and the other with her full weight immobilising my legs and keeping them firmly together. I couldn't quash the instinct to push as my body jack-knifed in protest at the pain and the forced delay. It was if my whole body were being torn apart as the baby fought to be born against their protestations and efforts. Within minutes the doctor arrived, took one look at me and managed to insert his hands into rubber gloves in time to catch Shahirah as I gave one almighty push and bellow and felt my daughter slither out.

She didn't cry straight away. I noticed that the cord was around her neck two or three times and her whole body was an ashen grey. I held my breath as I waited to hear a sound from her and prayed that she would make a noise to let me know she was all right. After what seemed like a frozen moment when the world caught its breath, Shahirah let out a wail that made the tears roll down my cheeks with joy. I held out my arms to her and laid her on my breast, cradling her close as she latched on strongly and began to take my milk. I marvelled at her fragility. She was so thin, much smaller than Iddin had been at birth, and she felt very cold. I knew then and there as she opened one exhausted eye and looked with great concentration at my face that I was hers for ever – I was a mother again.

Bahrin entered the labour room a few minutes later to see our new daughter. I held my hand out to him as he advanced towards the bed and, smiling, tilted Shahirah slightly so he could see her better. But instead of holding my hand he placed it firmly back onto the covers and patted it brusquely, peering at our baby as he did so.

'I love you,' I murmured just loud enough for him to hear as I looked hopefully up into his face.

'I know,' he replied flatly, patting my knee and starting to leave. At the door he paused and turned, said 'I'll see you later,' and pushing his way through the swinging doors, was gone.

Iddin was brought to see me an hour after Shah's birth. I had prearranged this with Mak as I wanted to ensure the bonding process between the new baby and

Iddin began as soon as possible. He bounced into my room happily and was just about to throw his arms around me when his eyes suddenly opened as big as saucers and he stopped dead in his tracks, staring at his little sister. I stooped to kiss and hug him tightly and introduced him to his sister as he stood on his toes to get a better look. My mother-in-law and Auntie Zainah were horrified when I told Iddin to scramble up onto the bed with me, gasping with concern at my supposed delicacy. I ignored them and instead helped Iddin to wriggle into a comfortable position and placed a pillow across his lap. He was absolutely enthralled as I laid his baby sister in his arms. He stared at her intently and was mesmerised when she made a sound, slowly opening her eyes and gazing up at him. As she grasped his finger he raised his beaming face to me and said, 'This is my sister, I'll be very gentle,' and went back to smiling at her.

Later that night, I took Shahirah from her crib beside my bed. She was numb with cold as there were no humidicribs in the clinic to keep her warm, so I slipped her inside my nightgown and piled blankets on top of us both to generate more heat for her. She spent the whole night like that, nestled against my body, feeding from my breast and dozing in between drinks.

'Raja Shahirah Aishah,' I whispered to her as I kissed her brow, 'what have I done bringing you into a life like this?'

Thirty-three

Despite Bahrin's revelations before I gave birth to Shahirah, he resumed his withdrawn disposition as soon as I came home from the clinic with the baby, disappearing for a couple of weeks to Kuala Lumpur and ignoring the gossip that his behaviour roused amongst the family.

During the first few weeks of Shahirah's life, I became entangled in a battle of wits with my mother-in-law. Mak announced that she was making arrangements for Shahirah's *sunnat* to take place before she reached forty days of age. I was horrified at Mak's nonchalant pronouncement about her only granddaughter. *Sunnat* for girls is circumcision, also known as clitoridectomy, a procedure carried out by a village midwife without sterilisation or benefit of anaesthesia during which a girl's clitoris is excised. I argued with Mak and her sister Zainah for days, voicing my opposition and my objection to the mutilation of my tiny daughter. During these sometimes heated discussions, I discovered that members of the royal family were usually only a few days old when the clitoridectomy was performed and that both my mother-in-law and her sisters had been mutilated in this way. At last I understood their attitude to sex. I had been told by them on numerous occasions to simply submit myself to Bahrin's 'needs' and lie still until it was over. That is what they had done all their married lives. They expected no pleasure from sex, only pregnancy, so I surmised from this that they had probably never experienced an orgasm – not that I was an expert in that area. Amongst these eye-opening revelations came their realisation that I had not been circumcised and was therefore walking around in an unclean state, a fact which they found quite shocking but about which they were powerless to take action.

There was no way on earth that I would submit my child to the barbaric practice of clitoridectomy, a tribal custom imported to Malaysia from Arabia and thought to control a woman's temperament and passion. As it was described to me, a small gathering of close female relatives would be called, during which the women would dine on specially prepared food and laugh and gossip in a party atmosphere. The baby would then be brought forward and its genitalia exposed for the midwife who would apply a block of ice, in lieu of a proper anaesthetic, and then cut away the clitoris and surrounding area with a razor blade.

Trying to veto this operation required a delicate balance of diplomacy and chess. When I mentioned my opposition to Bahrin, he replied that as the baby's father he would receive *parlar* for his consent to the operation and thought it would not be too bad if it quietened her down and kept her from being like me when she grew up. Realising I must find another way of preventing the procedure from going ahead, I cast around desperately, finally turning to my newly acquired knowledge of the Koran. After much debate with Che Gu Ali, I managed to prove to them all that *sunnat* for girls under Islamic law is not a compulsory action, but only a recommended practice – and one which did not appear in the Koran but found popularity through its use by a certain Muslim prophet long ago. I won that round, but I couldn't help worrying that the moment I turned my back someone would step in and irreparably mutilate my baby.

Bahrin exacted his own revenge for my opposition to Shahirah's *sunnat*. He flew in long enough from Kuala Lumpur to attend her forty-day celebration, which incorporated a remembrance *talil* for his grandfather. Traditionally, the father of the newborn entertained a large number of religious men for dinner, during which they said prayers for the well-being of the infant and also for members of the baby's family who had passed away. A huge amount of food was provided to the guests, curries, rice, pickles and sweetmeats, all laid out on pristine white tablecloths on the floor, around which the all-male guests would sit. Excess food from the feast was normally sent to relatives and the poor in the area.

The day before Shahirah's *talil* I was relaxing in my sitting-room and playing with Iddin and the baby when I heard the terror-stricken bleats of a goat. Immediately realising that it was Noneng, my pet goat, I rushed outside to find a scene that still haunts me. Noneng was hanging upside down, roped around his hind legs and dangling from one of the support beams of the antique house in the garden. He was surrounded by turbaned men, a few of whom I recognised, and Bahrin, standing a little to the side.

'What are you doing to Noneng?' I screamed as one of them tightened the ropes and hoisted my pet higher.

'I'm providing fresh meat for the *talil* tomorrow night,' laughed Bahrin in reply.

'No! You can't! No!' I shrieked, and made to run towards the group. I was stopped by the restraining hand of my mother-in-law, who tried to get me to leave and would not let me advance.

It was too late anyway, for at that moment I saw the flash of a blade as it slashed into my beloved pet's throat and heard his tortured scream – and then silence.

'I hate you, I hate you!' I spat at Bahrin as I sank to the ground and began to weep. Surrounded by the servants and Mak, I was taken back inside the house, where I vomited for what seemed like hours, the image of Noneng's torture replaying over and over again in my mind.

The next evening, after all the guests had departed, Bahrin entered our bedroom carrying a tray of food for me. Looking at me coldly, he commanded me to eat. As he knew I would, I refused the curry that was sitting on the plate. It was made from my goat, an animal that I had hand-reared.

My refusal seemed to satisfy Bahrin in a perverse way. It gave him an excuse to bring me to heel. He grabbed me by the hair and pushed me backwards on the floor, straddling my body and pinning my arms to my sides.

'You will eat this good and nutritious food. You will do as you are told.'

'No!'

'Then I'll have to make you, won't I, Yasmin? Why do you always have to make everything so difficult?' he questioned as he grabbed a chunk of the meat and dangled it above my face. 'This goat cost me a lot of money to feed and keep, so now I've saved some money by cooking him up.'

I began to gag as he tried to thrust the chunk between my teeth. I spat and bucked and tried to get him off me but with little success. Finally he prised my mouth open and forced the meat inside my mouth, firmly covering my lips with his hand to keep me from spitting it out in his face.

'Chew you bitch, chew!'

I shook my head. He then began to bash my skull against the marble floor hissing 'Chew!' at each impact. Finally I had to give in. The look in his eyes was terrifyingly determined. I thought at that moment that he might continue banging my head against the floor until he killed me if I didn't comply.

'Now swallow,' he ordered, smiling. 'Good girl,' he praised mockingly as I did as I was told while trying not to gag. Then, getting up off me, he left me alone in the room and I heard him start his new car and drive off.

Within two or three weeks of this event, our marriage continued on its downward spiral. Many parts of a puzzle began to fall into place: credit card receipts in Bahrin's pockets for jewellery worth £10,000, tighter restrictions on my movements around Terengganu, telephone calls that would be mysteriously terminated if I walked into a room, missing items of clothing and a sudden edict that I was forbidden to leave the house unless I telephoned him first. Even my visits to the hairdresser at the Pantai Hotel were forbidden, until I felt more trapped and isolated than I ever had before. And then the final piece of the puzzle snapped into place with a phone call from the wife of one of Bahrin's former school friends, Kasim, someone I knew only in passing.

Kasim's wife asked me to come to her house as she had something important to tell me. My curiosity was piqued at the strangeness of the invitation so I obtained permission from Bahrin to visit her and arrived that afternoon with my children in tow. She watched my face carefully as she placed a photograph on the coffee table before me. It was of a woman named Elmi Salleh, a less-than-successful nightclub singer from Singapore. As I raised a quizzical eyebrow at Kasim's wife, she began to explain why she had brought the photo, which was from a promotional blurb, to my attention. Elmi, she told me, had been imported to Terengganu from Singapore by Bahrin, who had obtained an extended contract for her to sing at the Pantai Hotel. She had been performing there for several months now and had only recently departed for Singapore. This woman, she told me, was having an affair with Bahrin. It was a fairly public liaison and I was almost the last one to know. She felt, she said, that I should know what was going on before it was too late.

I felt unadulterated hatred for Bahrin at that moment as I sat staring at the image of his lover before me. Clad in lycra pants and strapless bikini top and with cropped hair like a boy, she was the exact opposite of me, his wife. Me with my long flowing gowns and totally covered limbs as per my husband's instructions, me with the waist-length hair that Bahrin forbade me to cut, me forbidden now even to attend aerobics classes at the palace, me who lived in mortal fear of my husband lest I should offend his Islamic sensibilities, and for what? So he could sleep with another woman, a tawdry lounge singer with an eight-year-old child? So my husband could beat me and humiliate me and treat me like scum? Or so he could keep the Australian girl as a type of experiment in conversion to Islam whilst he shook his boogie with a Malay slut who'd latched on to him because it was fashionable in her circles to acquire the money and backing of a royal? And here I was learning all of this from a relative stranger whose motives were not exactly clear. Had I been informed so she could discuss my reaction with her friends? Was she simply concerned and sorry for the treatment I was receiving from Bahrin? Or was it because she felt ashamed that one of her countrymen had duped his foreign wife and played her for a fool? I didn't know and I didn't really care. I just knew I had to get home, confront Bahrin and put a stop to this whole sickening situation.

I cornered him by locking us into the bedroom together. I had lost all of my composure. I wanted to hear the truth from him no matter what. At first he denied it, telling me that Kasim's wife was being malicious. Then he told me that I was quite insane and imagining everything, that the £10,000 worth of jewellery had been a bribe to a politician and that I was going to be locked up in a mental home if I didn't stop these delusions. But I refused to back down this time and became quite hysterical, so hysterical and bereft of all pride that I ranted and raved. I threatened and screamed at him. I felt as if I were fighting for my children's lives and for their futures.

And then, like an electric shock, I remembered something that until then had been inexplicable. A recent trip to the gynaecologist had revealed I had somehow contracted an infection, which was treated with penicillin. At the time, I had pressed Bahrin for answers as my doctor had refused to give me a precise diagnosis, instead telephoning my husband for a chat. Now I knew what it was and where it had come from and I felt violated and ill at the contamination. I had to reach out and steady myself against the door frame.

I asked him how he could manipulate me all these years, insisting that I convert to Islam and follow the tenets of his religion faithfully, when he was screwing around with a Malay woman more outrageously Western in behaviour than I was. Picking up my dressmaking scissors, which were sitting on my bureau, I told him to stay exactly where he was as I shrieked more abuse at him. Before I really knew what I was doing, I gathered my hair into two random bunches on either side of my head and sliced them off with two quick movements of the blades, throwing two-foot lengths of hair at his face. All I could think of at the time was how he had always insisted that I did not cut my hair short and how he always managed to turn my own hair into a weapon against me. 'Well, not any more!' I screamed at him. 'Not any more!' If he could choose a short-haired slut over me, then he was never going to tell me how to keep my hair again.

I wept, I pleaded, I threatened to consult his uncle, the Sultan, about his behaviour. I reminded him about his holy oaths on the Koran and told him I would expose him for the bastard he was in front of the congregation at the main mosque. This time he didn't frighten me, this time I was not going to give in.

Finally his mother arrived, banging on the door and demanding to be admitted. When she entered the room I babbled out the whole sordid story, which she listened to in horror. She then began to berate her son. Bahrin hung his head in shame; whether sincere or not, at least he was not trying to deny it any more. Mak warned him that as far as she was concerned I was the only woman she would ever accept as her daughter-in-law. She reminded him of his holy oaths on the Koran not to take another wife and of the responsibility he bore me as he had taken me at such a young age from my own country and brought me to Malaysia as his wife.

Bahrin fidgeted and shifted from foot to foot like some recalcitrant schoolboy caught raiding the refrigerator at midnight. He picked up the Koran which was kept in the bedroom, pledging as his mother bade him, promising that he would sever all connections with the singer and all the other women he had had affairs with and that he would resume a normal life with me and the children. When he had done this to Mak's satisfaction, she dismissed him and gathered me up into her arms as I began to weep uncontrollably for the loss of my hair and my self-respect.

Thirty-four

Bahrin and I kept a truce of neutral indifference, politeness dripping from every word we said to each other. He was also totally indifferent to Shahirah and barely acknowledged her existence, to the point where I had to plead with him to have his photograph taken with the two children. I didn't want our daughter to grow up feeling as if her father had not taken any interest in her at all. I wanted her to be able to look at pictures and identify with him. As for me, I immersed myself in the children, reading stories to Iddin and wheeling Shahirah round and round the garden dozens of times a day, as I was still virtually housebound.

Endah was shocked when I saw her for the first time after I had cut off all my hair. I looked more like a bony scarecrow than a woman who had just decided to change her hairstyle on a whim. She tactfully asked few questions of me, sensing that I had come to her for the tranquillity I so desperately needed in my life. She would sit quietly by me on one of the palace's open verandahs with the children at our feet, or potter in the flower garden while I stared blankly at the horizon and the sea.

In late September, Bahrin announced that he was leaving on a business trip to the Philippines and Indonesia and would be gone for about ten days. He would be driving his new Mercedes Benz to Kuala Lumpur and leaving it there for servicing before flying overseas. I tried very hard to regain a flicker of approval from him before he left, offering to pack his bags and preparing his favourite foods, but all along I felt as if I were sitting naked in the eye of a storm, waiting for the next deluge to break over me.

And it did, ten days later, on 19 October 1985.

Bahrin had arrived home at midnight the night before and had immediately taken me to bed with a ferociousness and roughness that barely made an impact on my mind. He bruised and used me like a thing, not a person. In the morning he left for work, bidding me goodbye in a polite but frigid manner. As I watched his car turn out of the driveway the telephone began to ring. Hurrying inside I answered it and heard the voice of Kasim's wife on the other end. Once again she asked me to come to her house and once again I agreed. Leaving Iddin with his grandmother, I drove to the other side of town with Shahirah in her baby seat in the rear of the car. When I arrived, Kasim's wife asked me to sit down. She was not alone; her mother-in-law and her sister-in-law were also present. I could feel the tension in the air as they made stilted small talk and waited for me to broach the reason why they had brought me to their home. But I couldn't bring myself to ask.

Finally, sensing my reluctance, Kasim's wife glanced furtively from one woman to another and brought out a newspaper. Laying it open on the table before me, she pointed to a large article and photograph. My world began to spin and my body went cold as I picked up the paper and tried to read the Malay text. But the headline and the photograph were all I really needed.

It hit me between the eyes: 'Elmi quietly marries a young Malaysian royal.' The picture showed a smiling Elmi dressed in formal *baju kurung*, sitting with her pudgy eight-year-old son and holding a wedding album. The text of the article said that Elmi had met a young Malaysian businessman from Kuala Lumpur aboard an aeroplane and had begun a romance with him after he recognised her as the famous nightclub singer that she was. It went on to explain that she wished for nothing more than to keep house for her new husband and would continue her singing career when given the opportunity. According to the quotes, her new royal husband was very shy and was not interviewed for the story.

I knew, even though there had been no mention of Elmi's new husband's name, that it was Bahrin. Blinding white rage began to well up inside me as I reread the article. It was quite obvious that this newspaper story was meant as a message and announcement to me; the very fact that she had been careful not to make mention of her husband's identity, nor add that she was only his legal concubine and not a first wife, was telling indeed.

Gathering up Shahirah in her carry cot, I threw myself from that house without a further word and into my car. My heart was pounding so hard I thought it would burst. My one thought was to get to Bahrin's office and find out the full truth. I can't remember which route I drove along to his office; I only remember the shocked look on his secretary's face as I strode into the office carrying Shahirah in her car seat and bellowing Bahrin's name. My husband was not there, Miss Lim informed me as I placed Shahirah safely on her desk and pushed past her into Bahrin's private room. There I began to ransack his drawers and cupboards, searching for the truth. When I finally found it I felt as if I had been kicked in the stomach. Inside my Lancel overnight bag under his desk I discovered many things, including a new marriage certificate dated a week earlier and stating that he was a bachelor at the time of his marriage to Elmi and wedding photos of the happy couple. The antique *songket* fabric which I had given him as a present at our wedding was clearly visible in the pictures as his costume for this wedding. There were hotel receipts and more photographs which showed the location of their honeymoon and wedding ceremony: the Kuantan Hyatt Hotel, where he and I had spent that idyllic week before we were engaged. In fact, he had posed Elmi in exactly the same positions on the beach where I had been photographed so long ago.

I was overwhelmed by a sense of outrage so great that I threw myself into a frenzy of destruction in his office. Catching sight of his architectural diploma on the wall I snatched it down, smashing the glass on his desk and tearing the paper to shreds – I had helped him get his honours degree, sitting on the floor of our Melbourne house typing his thesis night after night. One by one I smashed the delicate Persian paintings that I had carefully framed for his office and then I tried to rip and tear his bag full of honeymoon clothing. When I had finally had enough, I strode from his room defiantly furious and began to upbraid his staff, many of whom had accepted my hospitality with alacrity over the years and, according to the evidence in my hands, had obviously been a party to my deception. Wheeling on his secretary, I ordered her to tell Bahrin to meet me at home, picked up my daughter and left, banging the door behind me. Miss Lim was later to tell people that I had taken my baby into Bahrin's office and placed her in danger as I smashed glass picture after glass picture around her head.

Tears were streaming down my face as I sobbed uncontrollably. Fastening Shahirah into her safety harness, I pushed the car into high gear and sped home as if my life depended on it. I made straight for Mak's house to collect Iddin. She had obviously been alerted to what had happened as she was not alone. Present were Che Gu Ali, Auntie Zainah and sundry others to whom I poured out my grief and outrage. Then with a screech of brakes and a slam of doors, Bahrin arrived. He strode into the house and made directly for me, throwing a punch at my chest which sent me reeling across the room. The others tried to restrain him but he only made to attack me further, screaming abuse and telling me that I was an uncouth Western slut with no idea of decorum.

It was little consolation when he told his mother that he had not known that his new wife was going to call a press conference to inform the public about their marriage, and that he was very angry with her. He had not intended to tell me of his new marriage at all; he was merely going to keep two households in two different cities.

Made braver by my rage and the presence of others, I started to scream at him, calling him every name under the sun and telling the others how he had sworn on the Koran never to take another wife. Bahrin shouted back at me that his marriage was none of my business, and that I was to keep my nose out of things that didn't concern me.

Didn't concern me indeed, I screamed back. He had lied on the wedding application, stating that he was a bachelor with no children, slinking away to another state to marry when he knew that in Terengganu he needed the written consent of his first wife to take a second. He followed his dick around like some oversexed bull and didn't care where he put it. He was a coward and a shit, I told him.

We were standing in the middle of Mak's dining-room when he grabbed my throat and thrust me against the wall beneath the light switches.

'Be careful what you say,' he warned. 'I'll divorce you and take away the children. If I divorce you, you'll be thrown out of Malaysia and never see your children again. I mean it, you'll never see the children again. I've been very patient with you, Yasmin, but don't push me too far or you'll regret it.'

All I could see was my future flashing before my eyes: the misery of being an unwanted wife in a strange country, the probability that I would lose my children to another woman, and the despair of being totally and surgically excised from life as I knew it. I knew that Bahrin's threats were not idle – it had happened many times before in the royal family, the unwanted woman cast out from her home and her children given over to another fresher and favoured wife to raise. Auntie Rosita and Tengku Ibrahim were one example of this: Auntie Rosita had raised his children by another woman and ruled them with an iron fist. I had seen the humiliation of Endah and watched for myself the degradation of the older wife being pregnant at the same time as the younger one, and the vicious competition that was rife in those sorts of households.

In utter desolation and despair, I went to the kitchen and tried to slash my wrists before the knife was wrested away from me by Che Gu Ali. I just wanted to get the pain over and done with; I couldn't go through years of this sort of humiliation and abuse any more. I heard Bahrin's voice in the background before I passed out, rebuking Ali for taking the knife away from me and saying that it would make things simpler for him if I were dead.

I came to later in my own bedroom when they brought Shahirah to me to feed. Iddin, I was informed, had been taken back to Auntie Zainah's to give me a chance to calm myself. Mak sat on the bed at my side, holding my hand and muttering about how there was little she could do now to help the situation. She told me proudly that she would refuse to meet with the nightclub singer and that she would speak to her brother, the Sultan, and have Elmi barred from entering the State of Terengganu. She would not be received at the palace or anywhere else in the circle of socially prominent people in which we moved. Her words bounced off me; I was too shattered to mutter the expected words of gratitude, too dead inside to care.

The following days passed in a haze broken only by the times the children were brought to me. One after the other, the women of the royal family came to me in my room, entering as though I were some sort of corpse awaiting burial and they were paying their last respects. They propped themselves on the edge of the bed and muttered their sympathies and proffered unsolicited advice, most of which seemed to favour turning a blind eye to my husband's new marriage. I was advised so many times to 'pretend that you don't know, pretend that he is just away for the night on business and then welcome him home with joy, comfort and a warm bed when he returns from spending the night with her'. Others took an even more pragmatic view of things, volunteering that I should not worry too much as I was still the senior wife and the only one allowed to attend palace ceremonies. Another volunteered the opinion that as long as I still received my full housekeeping, clothing and jewellery allowances, I should carry on as if nothing had changed. And so this surrealistic procession continued to trundle past my bed, shaking their heads and silently thanking Allah that it was not them lying in my place.

It was many days before I was allowed to leave the confines of my house. Bahrin had ordered that I be kept locked inside my bedroom until I 'came to my senses' so I would cause him no further embarrassment. My punishment was to be strict, my food rationed to one meal on alternate days and my contact with the children

kept to a minimum. Mak had to seek special permission
from Bahrin for me to visit Endah and even then he
only acquiesced because he said that she might be able
to teach me how to accept my new situation.

Endah did nothing of the sort, but she did know the
right thing to do. She put her arms around me when I
sat at her feet and laid my head in her lap as I cried
and cried and cried. She coaxed me to eat, reasoning
that I would lose my milk and be unable to feed Shah
if I didn't.

Before I left the palace that day I managed to get to
a telephone and call the Australian High Commission
in Kuala Lumpur. I told the consular official to whom
I spoke about my situation, adding that both of the
children were Australian as well. I asked him if I could
seek refuge in the High Commission as I feared what
my husband would do next. His reply made it very clear
that I was well and truly on my own.

'Madam, Mrs Raja Bahrin, you are very welcome to
come to the High Commission if you feel that you are
in danger, but I must advise you that if a request was
made to us for your children, we would comply. I'm
sorry, but we cannot risk a diplomatic incident.'

I tried to argue with him, reminding him that the
three of us were Australian, but to no avail. My
embassy's position was made very clear: they would help
me but not risk incurring the wrath of the Malaysians
by protecting my Australian children. I automatically
thanked him and terminated the conversation, leaving
the palace and getting into the back of the car Endah
had sent for me.

I was beaten. I had nowhere to turn now.

Thirty-five

During the first days of November 1985, I received word that Nanna had suffered a severe stroke and had fallen down a flight of concrete stairs at the block of flats where she lived. I was beside myself with worry over her condition, which I was told on the phone was not good. She was in intensive care at the Alfred Hospital in Melbourne with a broken arm and a dislocated hip as well as being paralysed down the left side of her body and suffering concussion.

By this time, Bahrin was inflicting physical and emotional abuse upon me on a daily basis. Entering the bedroom, he would begin to berate me, telling me that I had brought it all on myself and slapping my face when I attempted to ignore him. He would tell me that he was going to kick me out of the country and take the children away from me.

I begged him for a divorce so many times but he refused, telling me that I belonged to him and that he would decide the fate of our marriage, not me. It was like my daily torture. I would hold my breath at the times when the children were meant to be brought to me, worrying that they wouldn't come, worrying that he had already carried out his threat. As I watched my weight fall and my face become lined and grey, I battled hard to keep my milk supply up for Shahirah.

When the news about Nanna arrived, I pleaded with Bahrin to let me return to Australia to see her. At first he refused outright to contemplate it, telling me that he hoped she died quickly and alone. Later he began to taunt me, saying that he would consider letting me go but that I must choose which baby would accompany me. At other times he would decree that I must go home by myself and stay there, and that the children would be given to his new wife to raise.

These emotionally destructive games continued until the Sultan criticised Bahrin for mistreating me and recommended that I be allowed to return to Australia with both children. It was an edict that Bahrin could not ignore and continue to live in Terengganu, so he grudgingly said that I could go.

And so the procession of matrons began again, each one advising me to go to Australia, see my grandmother and spend lots of money to make myself feel better. They said it would be wise to take some time away from Terengganu and all its recent pressures. Some of the aunties even gave me money to spend on myself whilst I was there, thinking that it would ease my pain.

The three days prior to my departure were nightmarish. Anxiety about Nanna, coupled with sheer despair at the state of my life, left me in a continual state of tears. As well, there was the added spying that Bahrin had ordered the servants to do on his behalf. Every item I packed in my bag was inspected and checked, and formal evening garments were added to my suitcase on Bahrin's instructions.

He and I, he decreed, would, on the evening of my return from Australia, be attending the wedding of his cousin in Kuala Lumpur. It was a declaration I considered surreal, given the situation – I did not relish the prospect of parading my utter humiliation for public consumption. Nevertheless, from sheer habit I knew I would comply with his orders, not daring to demur.

The jewellery I packed in preparation for the forthcoming nuptials was minimal. That was my rebellion. None of my large jewels went into my luggage; I left the majority in the palace vault, nestling in their yellow and red boxes embossed with the royal crest and sealed with red wax and tape, having first been stamped by a staff member and affixed with a security tag. I stored only a small set of diamonds and the pieces I considered my 'everyday bits' – rings, gold chains and one short string of pearls – in my hand luggage. I was sick of looking like a Christmas tree in pieces of cold-stoned finery not chosen by myself. Even though I must, Bahrin ordered, be prepared to shine and smile at the wedding as if nothing had happened, I had no intention of play-acting. How could I show a face shining with domestic bliss? How could he honestly expect me to do so? In complete contradiction he would be back hours later, standing over me as I sat nursing Shahirah, telling me that he was going to send me and the baby back to Australia permanently. He kept me in a state of emotional flux. I didn't know what would happen at the hour of my departure; I could only wait and pray that I would not lose my children.

I was summoned to the palace by Endah to say goodbye. We met in her private apartments, sat on the bed together and played with Iddin and Shahirah. She aksed me to take a photograph of herself and the children and held Shahirah close and kissed her cheek repeatedly. Later she took my hands in hers and told me that she wanted me to be happy, that she didn't want to see me live the sort of life that she had. Then she removed a thick wad of English money from her pocket and placed it into my hands, saying, 'This is for your grandmother in case she needs anything in hospital and

it is for you and the children to use as you think best.'
I protested at the amount and told her that I would use
it to buy her something special in Melbourne and bring
the change back to her. She only smiled and shook her
head, again saying, 'Use the money for yourself, Yasmin,
and for the children.' She reiterated with great intensity,
'You must use the money as you think best.' Then she
rose and embraced me close, kissing me gently on my
cheek. She placed her hand against my cheek and looked
at me with tears in her eyes, and then she turned and
walked from the room without a backward glance.

Bahrin enjoyed playing mind games with me. He
continually took Iddin away from me for hours on end,
telling me to say goodbye to my son because I would
never see him again. The night before we were due to
leave, he burst into the room and picked up Iddin, who
had been sleeping in the bed with me, and threw him
over his shoulder. When I begged to know what he was
doing, he replied that I might or might not see Iddin
again.

Bahrin kept him for over twelve hours, returning him
to me only one hour ahead of the flight to Kuala Lumpur.
I clung to my son in relief when he ran to me, kissing
his head and feeling his arms wrap around my neck.
For those long, agonising hours I had sat bolt upright
in my rocking chair watching the dawn break, fearing
that I would have both children snatched away and that
I would be bundled onto the plane alone.

Finally a knock on the door indicated that the cars
had arrived – it was time for us to leave for the airport.
Bahrin stood in the living-room, one hand on his hip,
his face wearing an impenetrable look. I bade the few
assembled family members goodbye as the servants
looked on. The atmosphere was instensely guarded. I
dared not meet Bahrin's eye as he extended his hand for

me to kiss. Instead I curtseyed deeply, his hand resting limply in mine, and touched my lips to the back of his wrist. Then, joining Shahirah and Iddin in the back of the waiting Mercedes, we departed, headed by a police escort travelling at speed.

As the cars pulled up at the airport, my stomach heaved with apprehension as I realised that Bahrin's car had followed us to the terminal. Having already paid my respects to him and taken my leave, I could only believe that he meant to take our children from my arms at the last moment. Even as he drew me aside on the pretence of saying goodbye and whispered the words, 'I don't want you, you're a useless Australian whore, don't hurry back, just fuck off,' I didn't trust the veracity of our departure. And then, without a further utterance, he suddenly turned on his heel and stalked out of the airport.

I stumbled aboard the Fokker Friendship aircraft with only minutes to spare, Shahirah safe in a baby pouch secured to my chest and Iddin clasped firmly by the hand. As I took my seat, the one thought I had on my mind was that I had to get away to think; if I didn't, I would surely suffocate and die.

I waited for a number of hours in the Kuala Lumpur airport hotel, starting nervously whenever anyone knocked on the door or the telephone rang. Iddin sat on the floor playing with his collection of Matchbox cars, oblivious to what was going on around him. More royal relatives, including Auntie Zainah, descended upon us at the hotel, pressing money on me and exhorting me to spend the time in Melbourne coming to terms with my new marital situation. I took little notice of this puerile advice, fearing that at any moment Bahrin would burst into the room and take my children away. When the Sultan's equerry, Major Shaf'ie, who was in Kuala Lumpur on business, telephoned from the lobby, I was ready to fly with both my little ones straight out of the window if it would help me get away. Thank goodness the Major only wanted to enquire if he could be of any assistance.

When I finally staggered onto my Melbourne-bound plane, I didn't allow myself to believe that we were truly on our way until the aircraft had cleared Malaysian airspace. I was fearful right up until then that somehow Bahrin would manage to throw me out of his country without Iddin and Shahirah. When I finally knew that this was not going to happen, I burst into tears and sat there crying until I realised that I was drawing attention to myself. In answer to the concerned questioning of the cabin attendants, I blurted out the words 'My husband just died' and asked to be left alone.

In fact it wasn't my husband who had just died; it was every hope and dream that I had ever had.

Thirty-six

My arrival home was vastly different from my earlier visits to Melbourne. Then the aircraft had been met by officials from the Australian Department of Foreign Affairs; there had been no customs checks, no immigration scrutiny, just a car waiting outside the airport to whisk us away to the hotel. There was no VIP treatment this time as I trundled with the children through the arrivals hall and queued behind the rest of the disembarking passengers. It was quite a juggling act, Shahirah asleep in a baby pouch on my chest and Iddin sitting tired and weary in a stroller as I shoved and slid our suitcases before me across the breadth of the terminal.

Once through the formalities, I managed to get us all into a cab and made my way to my grandmother's flat. I cried all the way there, much to the consternation of the taxi driver, who was too polite to ask me any questions. Dropping the bags off at the empty apartment, I made straight for the hospital to see Nanna. It was quite a shock to see her lying there in a narrow, impersonal hospital bed – she looked so small and fragile, her bruised face swollen almost beyond recognition and her arm encased in plaster. I sat beside Nanna's bed holding her hand in mine whilst Iddin pottered on the floor and Shahirah squirmed in my arms.

Now more than ever I wished that I could just lay my head in my grandmother's lap as I had done when I was a child. Selfishly I longed to wake her and blurt out the circumstances of how my life had degenerated into an utter shambles and feel that unwavering security return as her strong hands wielded a brush deftly through my hair, untangling the knots and restoring for a short while my peace of mind. But that was impossible. Nanna was not yet conscious and wouldn't be strong enough for my problems for a long time; so I stayed only a short time and then left, trying to keep the children as quiet as possible as we navigated the hospital corridors and emerged into the grey Melbourne day.

Later that afternoon when I entered Nanna's tiny flat with the children, all that I had been through finally hit me and I began to cry uncontrollably. I still can't recall how the children and I got through the next three days. I know that we lived off toast and milk and that somehow I still managed to feed Shahirah, but for the most part I was so emotionally devastated that I could do nothing more than lie there and weep. So unsure was I of what the future held for the three of us that I felt it preferable to put off facing the reality of our situation until I had exhausted my tears – it was much safer to hold the world at bay and stay in the safety of Nanna's flat.

I eventually surfaced days later, hollow-eyed and empty-hearted. I resolved that I must do my best for Iddin and Shahirah. I knew that my decisions now had to be made for the children and only for the children. Iddin and Shahirah had to have hope in their lives and I had to make sure that I did my best for them.

One of the first things I did was contact my old friend Peter Wallace and pour out my heart to him. Peter suggested that I seek legal advice to find out where I stood and he helped me to obtain the names of some law firms. In the meantime he stocked Nanna's refrigerator for me and filled the cupboards with food; I was still too shell-shocked to attempt a trip to the supermarket and it took all my remaining energy to care for the children's most basic needs. My weight had plummeted to below seven and a half stone and my thoughts came in odd jolts of pain, despair and fear. I felt that I would never know happiness or joy ever again and that the best I could hope for was to provide for my children's happiness and normality.

My first appointment with the law firm of Stedman, Cameron, Meares and Hall, who were based in an unobtrusive grey office building in the conservative heart of the city, engendered in me more confidence than I had felt in a very long time. I liked Lillian Webb, the solicitor assigned to handle my initial enquiry, immediately: down to earth and very astute, she was a petite and attractive dark-haired woman in her mid-thirties with a deep, rich voice and throaty laugh. She listened with great concentration as I related my situation to her, her eyes narrowing as she scribbled notes and fired no-nonsense questions at me which demanded concise answers. And, just as importantly, she adapted well to the necessary presence of Shahirah and Iddin in her office, an occurrence that strayed very far from normal circumstances of a legal briefing. Finally, after outlining the basic chain of events which she anticipated would take place if I chose to set the legal wheels in motion, Lillian took a deep breath and said that she believed I had a good chance not only of gaining custody of the children but also of being able to stay in Australia and not return to Terengganu, if that was what I wanted to do.

It was a big decision to make so I returned to Nanna's flat to weigh up the pros and cons overnight. I had no idea if I could make it on my own as a single mother; I had never had to cope without the extra support of domestic staff and in-laws. But I knew for certain that I did not want my children to grow up in an atmosphere of violence and abuse, nor did I want to run the risk that Bahrin would carry out his threat and take both of them away from me. I was determined to be with Iddin and Shahirah, to watch them grow up and give them all the love and security that I had not had as a child. I wanted them to become independent-thinking people, to develop tolerance and self-respect; and I wanted Shahirah to grow up as a first-class human being and not be treated as anything less simply because she was female. I also knew that I would not survive if I returned to Malaysia and that I would be of no use to my children if I were dead. In the morning I telephoned Lillian Webb and told her to go ahead with all the necessary legal work – the children and I were home to stay.

On 20 November, I telephoned Bahrin with the hope that I could convince him to come to Melbourne and discuss a reconciliation, but it was a wasted call. Bahrin, I was told by Mak, had left Terengganu to be with Elmi. Was I forgetting all my troubles and having a fun time in Melbourne? my mother-in-law asked.

My course was now set. I had to do all I could to ensure the children's lives were secure. On 27 November 1985, I obtained sole interim *ex parte* custody of Iddin and Shahirah and the right to stay in my own country with them. I could only be glad for Bahrin's insistence that both children become Australians from birth and that they held Australian birth certificates. My barrister, Noel Ackman, laughingly called me 'princess' as we walked from the court, a term that made me cringe at the reality of what that title meant. Noel and Lillian had been a marvellous team, giving me the confidence to feel that what I was doing was right and buoying me up during the tense moments in court. Noel, with his sense of humour and his steady eyes, allowed me to hold my head up and remain resolute that day. If I am entirely honest with myself, I have to admit that in the back of my mind I did harbour a minuscule hope that Bahrin and I might, by some miracle, be able to reconcile our differences and live a normal life in Australia with the children, and that some magical thing would happen to bring him to his senses, but intellectually I knew that was a terribly naive last-ditch clutch at a dead marriage.

On 4 December 1985, I telegrammed my mother-in-law to inform her that I would not be arriving back in Malaysia as planned and to let her know both the children and I were safe. I felt it wiser not to embroil her in my decision any more than was absolutely necessary, so I kept the details brief and non-specific.

As soon as Bahrin knew that I had changed my mind and wasn't coming back to Malaysia as per the original plans, I realised that we would have to go into hiding for a while in case he came to Australia to find us. Even though he'd been vehement in his dismissal of me at the airport, I could well imagine his furious reaction to the realisation that I'd decided to take him at his word and the vengeance he would exact if he were able to corner me alone. So I left Nanna's flat and moved in with an old friend for a couple of weeks as I hunted for an apartment of our own.

Establishing the children in a secure environment became my main priority. Peace and stability were things that Iddin had never really known and I was determined to make sure that he would never have to watch his mother being beaten up again. Rather idealistically, I had a vision of my life ten years down the track which was to sustain me for a long time whenever I felt despondent. I wanted little more than to live with the children quietly in the suburbs and be a 'scout mum' who drove a station wagon and took part in all the children's school activities. I had no desire then to remarry or stand out from the crowd, only an overwhelming wish to blend in with normal people and give my children the opportunity to do the same.

Taking one step at a time was the way I lived when we first came home. Readjusting to a normal society was the hardest thing to do. It took me a very considerable amount of time to believe that I could move freely from one place to the other without obtaining permission from Bahrin to do so, and to accept that I was in charge of my own life. Clothes were another major revelation. I had brought only Muslim dresses with me from Malaysia and only enough for the week or so I had planned to spend in Melbourne, so eventually I had to purchase more. I chose a sedate and longish skirt, a short-sleeved shirt to match and a pair of baggy jeans. The first time I wore these garments outside the house I felt positively naked and was sure that the whole world was looking at me aghast. It took several days to feel comfortable again in Western dress and not feel as if I were being immodest. After years in ground-sweeping skirts, baring my legs was very daring indeed.

Iddin coped extremely well with his new environment. The single-parent situation was not a break from his normal circumstances; at two years and eight months he didn't notice the absence of his father, probably because Bahrin had seldom been at home in Terengganu. Gradually I could see my small son becoming more sure of himself, and the worried look on his face that had so often been present in Malaysia was appearing less and less. After a couple of weeks had gone by, I began to notice that he had ceased to flinch at sudden noises, that the colour had heightened in his cheeks and that he had begun to attack life with the zest and enthusiasm a toddler should have. Iddin certainly revelled in his new-found physical freedom, running in the wide open spaces of the local park and getting down in the dirt and making mud pies, an activity that had been forbidden to him by royal etiquette. I would watch him running towards me from the other side of the playground clutching some treasured discovery in his hand to show both me and his baby sister and feel peace wash over me; the ordinary activities which children usually take for granted had, until we arrived home, been incomprehensible adventures for him.

After much searching, the children and I at last found a comfortable home in South Oakleigh with a small garden for them to play in. I furnished our first home with an odd assortment of donated and purchased things, a couple of bright rugs and some cheap prints that I found at the market. I bought the basic necessities of life such as warm clothes for the children, blankets, towels, sheets and a washing machine with the emergency funds released to me by the initial trial judge as urgent maintenance. This money had come from the sale of our house in Carlton which Bahrin had insisted on keeping in an Australian bank as a tax dodge and to expedite our return to Melbourne at some stage.

I was entirely accountable for all the money spent and kept a detailed record of every penny that I used on the children and myself. If anything, I regret that I was frugal to the extent of being 'penny wise, pound foolish', as I couldn't quite bring myself to spend the money on a proper lounge suite and settled for a cheap foam divan. This couch was almost entirely useless for sitting on unless one was two years old. Any larger and heavier than that and the whole thing had a disconcerting habit of folding around you like a squashy banana and threatening you with suffocation or the permanent displacement of the hip joints.

When I finally plucked up the courage to telephone Bahrin on 16 December, I was told by Mak that he still hadn't returned home and that she didn't know where he was. I gave her my new telephone number in Melbourne, left a message for Bahrin to call me and quickly cut our conversation short. Later that same day, Bahrin telephoned Lillian demanding to know what had happened to the money from the ANZ bank account we held in Melbourne. He had apparently decided to withdraw our nest egg and had been notified by the bank of my solicitor's name. Not once did he ask her about the children or me, only about the money.

Later that same night, he rang me. When I picked up the receiver, my 'hello' was met by a torrent of abuse and threats. At first he ordered me to return to Malaysia immediately, telling me that I was ill-equipped to cope with life on my own with two small children. He said that I would never make it alone and that I was totally useless and too stupid to fight him on this matter. When I told him that I had no intention of complying with his demands, he changed tack, telling me that he loved me and missed me very much. My answer to him was that I was willing to consider a reconciliation but that he had to come to Australia for the discussion and it would include his divorcing Elmi and moving back to Australia. He remained silent at this suggestion and then suddenly exploded, screaming down the phone that he would kill my grandmother if I didn't return straight away, that he would kill me, but first he would teach me a lesson for being disobedient. I hung up the phone, trembling all over and feeling as if I would vomit. Even when thousands of miles away, Bahrin still had the capacity to terrify me and make me doubt my faith in myself. I went to bed that night agonising about my own capabilities and the rightness of my stance.

Halfway through the night, Shahirah woke for a feed

and I brought her into my bed and held her tiny body close as she suckled. Minutes later Iddin wandered into my bedroom and clambered under the covers with us, falling back to sleep with barely a murmur. I lay awake most of the night watching the moonlight play on my children's profiles as they slept beside me and listening to their deep, untroubled breathing and tiny grunts as dreams flickered across their faces. I was frightened of what Bahrin's next move would be and I prayed that the children and I would make it through the times ahead intact and together.

Following his tirade, I thought that it was wise to warn Nanna that there might be trouble. She was alternately defiant and apprehensive when I told her the truth about my failed marriage and Bahrin's threats and decided that she would stay with friends until things had settled down. Nanna continued to improve slowly, regaining the use of her left side and her sense of humour. Her speech remained a little slurred but she persevered doggedly with therapy. The joy and relief on her face when I told her that the children and I were home for good was immense and I'm sure this news made her more determined to get her strength back.

The children and I had our first real Christmas together in our tiny flat; it was wonderful to hear carols on the radio and shop for presents for Iddin and Shahirah. Christmas had been one of the hardest times for me in Malaysia, a day when the most gut-wrenching homesickness would strike me, brought home by the added complication that Bahrin had forbidden me even to mark the day with an exchange of gifts or the playing of Christmas music. During all those years in Terengganu, the only time that my precious Christmas tree had been taken from its storage box had been when Bahrin had lent it to his Filipino employees for their private Christian celebration. But Christmas 1985 was totally the opposite. Iddin and I chose a real pine tree for the living-room, albeit one that was a little bit crooked, and decorated it with ornaments inherited from Nanna and bought at the local supermarket; we sang 'Rudolf the Red-Nosed Reindeer' loudly as we drove along in the ancient car I had purchased for £600; and Iddin hung stockings for himself and Shahirah from the chimney piece for Santa Claus to fill.

However, this was only the lull before the storm. In the back of my mind I knew that Bahrin would never allow us to live in peace without exacting revenge.

Thirty-seven

Legally, it was mandatory that Bahrin be served with notification of my action for custody of the children in the Family Court of Australia and of his right to contest this action. As he refused to take delivery of the documentation from the Singaporean lawyer I had retained for that purpose and who'd travelled to Kuala Terengganu to do so, it became necessary for us to serve the documents and full facts of the case to Bahrin by way of an advertisement in the Malaysian English daily newspaper, the *New Straits Times*, on 24 December 1985. I really didn't want my humiliation more publicly known than it already was but I was left with little choice. So it became public knowledge that I had returned to Australia with my children and that I had been thrown over for a nightclub singer. The dubious honour of being the first woman in the Malaysian royal family to leave the family with her own children in her arms following the demise of a marriage was now mine.

I knew that Bahrin would never forgive me for allowing the public to be privy to the private doings of his family, or for the fact that my actions were in complete contradiction to the story that he had told his second wife's brother: that I had been living in Australia for more than two years and that we had already been in the process of divorce. Elmi's brother had supposedly been shocked to learn that I was still actually living in our marital home at the time of his sister's marriage to Bahrin, and that I had just given birth to Shahirah, but that did not seem to lessen his resolution that an alliance with a member of the royal family was too valuable to be complicated by the mere fact of a concurrent wife and two children.

The year 1986 arrived, bringing with it both hope and fear for me. Any moment I expected Bahrin to break down my front door and beat me to a pulp, carrying the children away when he was done. I felt sure that he would not simply let me and the children go. Thirteen days into January 1986 brought another telephone call from Bahrin, this time telling me that he was coming to Australia and wanted a reconciliation – but that he wouldn't divorce his nightclub singer.

Bahrin arrived in Melbourne on 19 January and immediately retained lawyers at one of the city's largest law firms. He took his normal tack: obtain the best that money could buy, and for whatever money could not buy, lies would suffice.

It was interesting and sickening to observe how the legal fraternity of my own home town aligned itself to one faction or the other – comments flew around the corridors of the Family Court as to the merits of my case. A couple of barristers were heard to say that I 'had made my bed and should lie in it'. Others seemed to be in awe of any hint of royal blood or patronage and professed to hold the throne of any country higher than the rights of a lowly Australian woman and her children. Others indicated, around the watering holes which the legal fraternity frequent, that I had done the unspeakable, the disloyal, by marrying outside my own countrymen to a foreigner and a Muslim, therefore disenfranchising myself of any succour in my own nation. And so, whilst the Family Court of Australia has no system of jury summation, I found myself tried in the corridors of its precincts by a minority of people who looked upon the whole exercise as an intellectual debate and not one that held the lives of my children in the balance.

I was summoned to the Family Court of Australia at 570 Bourke Street, Melbourne, on 29 January 1986 by an action from Bahrin's lawyers. The battle had begun.

Noel Ackman, retained in another matter, was unable to represent me again, so it became necessary for us to brief a new barrister, John Udorovic. To say that John was a little disconcerted at our first meeting is probably putting it mildly. Our appointment was for 8.30 a.m. in his office on 29 January. As Lillian anticipated our being in court for most of the day, I had no choice but to bring Shahirah with me. After depositing Iddin with my close friends Sue and Rob MacArthur, my intention was to leave Shah in the crèche provided by the court so I could be nearby to breastfeed her during the day. But the childcare centre did not open until after 9 a.m. and so Shahirah and I, out of sheer necessity, arrived together for my first meeting with the new barrister. I think that it was probably the first time that a client had arrived in John's chambers complete with briefcase, baby, pram and nappy bag but I suspect that Lillian had already warned him that I was not the sort of client who expected the lawyers to do all the work on their own. As I listened to him giving his views on the case and questioning me closely on what I wanted for the children and for myself, I tried to fathom how much trust I could put in this tall, dark-haired man with a shock of thick hair and black moustache. At first I thought that he was too aloof for me to communicate with and that I was not welcome in his office with my baby – but that was until I saw his eyes soften and his whole demeanour change as he inspected Shahirah in her pram. I knew then that he would do his best for us.

Bahrin's lawyer's first tactic in court was to attack, accusing me of kidnapping the children and arguing that Australia was not the forum to discuss our marital difficulties. He also alleged that Iddin was in line to the throne of Terengganu and that his absence from Malaysia had jeopardised the succession. Allegations were also put forward that I had forged Bahrin's signature on Iddin's application for an Australian birth certificate, although these were withdrawn as soon as Bahrin's solicitors had sighted the application with Bahrin's signature on it and his written request for the same.

I sat on the opposite side of the room to Bahrin, willing myself not to look in his direction and trying to keep myself in check as more and more blatant nonsense about Iddin's royal prospects was put forward. Even at a distance of twenty feet I could feel Bahrin's rage towards me. It was a palpable vibration and one I knew was restrained only by the fact that we were not alone.

Then he played what he thought would be his trump card: an Islamic court order, made just days earlier in Terengganu. This Khadi court order did not mention that I, the defendant, was in fact residing in Australia, having been sent there by my husband. It seemed to lead the Muslim judge to believe that the children and I were merely elsewhere in Terengganu and that I was refusing to sleep with Bahrin. This Islamic document charged me with being a disobedient wife and ordered me to resume cohabitation with my husband, restore his conjugal rights and return myself and the children to his sphere of influence. In practice, what Bahrin's side were demanding from an Australian judge was my immediate deportation from my own country to Malaysia on the grounds of my being a recalcitrant wife. An application was also made for my current address and telephone number. Thankfully it was deemed sufficient to release only our telephone number, which, in any case, Bahrin already had.

Faced with all this new material, the judge, Mr Justice Brian Treyvaud, called an adjournment for the following week as it was quite obvious that the case was becoming far more complicated than had been anticipated. Questions of jurisdiction and royal succession had now been thrown in to further complicate matters and cloud the important issue at hand – the simple right for the children and me to live undisturbed in Australia.

Bahrin then applied for access to Iddin during the intervening adjournment, only adding a request for Shahirah when offered by the judge. It was finally ruled that Bahrin was to be allowed supervised access in a public place that Sunday.

Walking out of that courtroom with Lillian and John, I felt physically sick and weak with panic at the proposal that I resume living with Bahrin under an Islamic court order. When walking past Bahrin in the corridor, I had the sensation that I was about to buckle at the knees and vaguely remember Lillian hissing at me under her breath to 'keep walking'.

Over the ensuing days, weeks and months, it was the children and Lillian who did keep me walking. Whenever I faltered, whenever I felt that I couldn't go on throwing myself against the seemingly insurmountable wall of Bahrin's wealth, lies, power, white-cold rage and determination to destroy me, I turned silently to look at my children and their growing happiness. I knew that I could not give them a mother they could not respect, nor allow them to live lives that left them devoid of the normal values of humanity. Every time that my will to fight wavered and I longed to curl up in a ball in a corner beneath a blanket of numbness, Lillian would ask me if I still had the same reasons for wanting to stay in my own country that I had voiced to her that day in November 1985, and always I would answer 'yes'. She, more than anyone, stood beside me and fought hard for my rights, often at a cost to her own personal life and to the detriment of her health. We worked as a team, devising the wording of answering affidavits, researching precedents and wading through the quicksand of Islamic and Malaysian constitutional law to rebut all of the outrageous claims which Bahrin tried to make in court.

But it was far from an easy thing to do. Proving, for example, that Bahrin's uncle, the Sultan of Terengganu, appointed the Islamic judges in his own state and influenced their very livelihood was tremendously difficult. I spent several late evenings at the homes of Malaysian law students who were doing postgraduate studies at Monash University, trying to persuade them to commit their true opinions to affidavits for presentation to the Australian courts. Two of the young men initially agreed to swear affidavits as to the influence and legal sway that a Sultan held in Malaysia and the probable prejudice this would cause in any case against me, but at the last moment both of them sat in Lillian's office and stated that on second thoughts it was not worth the total ruin of their careers or that of their families to go against the Terengganu ruler. What should have been simple matters of research often presented huge difficulties and we found ourselves blocked from obtaining the most mundane pieces of information on the Malaysian civil laws. I will always be grateful to Jennifer Took, an Australian lawyer seconded by her firm to Singapore, who, without having met either Lillian or myself, sourced precedents and researched much-needed facts for us.

I was able to show the court that Iddin was

approximately seventieth in line to the throne of Terengganu, and even then that was doubtful as his Terengganu blood came only through his grandmother, who, being a woman, herself had no valid claim. I showed too that he was double or triple that many times removed from the Perak throne as well.

It seemed that, once again, Bahrin had wrenched the children and me away from any shred of normality. The next few weeks were spent in and out of court as Bahrin tried one manoeuvre after another to delay the Australian courts from hearing our custody dispute. My nights passed in a blur as I went over Bahrin's sworn affidavits with a fine-tooth comb, marking down any discrepancies for Lillian and John's attention. Lillian and I begged and borrowed textbooks on Malaysian constitutional law to look for arguments. We sifted for contradictions and ambiguous meanings in every word that was put into Bahrin's sworn material to give John more ammunition to use when he was putting my case. And all through this I tried to reassure Iddin and to maintain my milk supply for Shahirah. I lived in a daze of nappies, babies and legal documents, every moment wondering if we would ever have any peace and fearful that I would lose my children if the judge didn't understand my arguments.

The pattern for us in the mornings on the days I was expected in court was to drive to the MacArthurs' house and leave Iddin in Sue's care. Luckily their house soon became Iddin's favourite place to visit as he would play all day with their son Ben, who was the same age. Then Shahirah and I would drive into the city in peak-hour traffic and leave my old wreck of a car at a car park not too far from the courts. The manager, Tony, was a tremendous help each day, helping me unpack Shahirah, the box of documents, the briefcase, the nappy bag and the pram. Tony would then help me juggle all this from the fourth-floor level (where he had given me a reduced parking rate) to the ground floor and assist me in balancing my load on top of Shah's pram ready for my walk to Lillian's office.

Once there, as Lillian and I went over all the facts necessary for the day's litigation, I would breastfeed Shah, swear affidavits and telephone John to let him know that we would meet him at the court shortly. Lillian would have started work at 6.30 a.m. to allow her to maintain her other clients' cases. From her office, Lillian would then help me push Shahirah, and all the documents, two blocks to the court, usually managing two bulging briefcases and an armful of files and books herself. After settling Shahirah in the court's crèche I would be ready to join Lillian and John in the courtroom for the day's proceedings. Shahirah's growth rate and happy burblings were equalled only by the rapidly mounting legal papers, and I had pangs of guilt that I couldn't simply stop everything with a snap of my fingers and just revel in my baby's progress and smiles.

Arguments would go on for hours, but at least by this stage Bahrin had had to withdraw his allegations of kidnap. I had proven that I had come to Australia at Bahrin's bidding and that he had married Elmi although he was still married to me. I had no full-blown intention of staying in Australia when I came home; I hadn't known what I would do when I had arrived in Melbourne. Now the argument was one of jurisdiction and the importance of Bahrin's royalty.

My respite from all this was to escape during recesses to feed Shahirah. She'd hold up her arms to me when I entered the room and cry until I picked her up and put her to my breast. I'd sit in one of the stiff-backed chairs in the crèche and agonise about our future as I watched her small face nestle trustingly against me, one hand playing with my shirt or mouth as she fed. To me it seemed as if we had been blown loose like three leaves in a gale with no resting place in sight, tossed sideways, to and fro and upside down, no control over our direction.

And then Bahrin's telephone calls began when I was at my lowest ebb, late at night and in the early morning, wearing me down, leaving me feeling trapped like a possum in the glare of a searchlight. He would confuse me, sometimes asking for a reconciliation, sometimes demanding my capitulation, but always reminding me of my uselessness, my idiocy and my total helplessness in the face of his violent will should he choose to exercise it. In some strange, terrible way, these calls were mesmerising. If I was alone with the children, they held me fixed, too petrified, mostly, to hang up the phone on this man who had been my lord and master in all senses of the words.

Eventually, he demanded a meeting at his lawyer's office early one morning. 'I'm willing to divorce Elmi,' he announced proudly, as if I should offer congratulations. 'Yasmin, you have to understand. I was *kenang* by her, and I'm already going to a *bomoh* for treatment.'

'Bahrin, I don't want to meet with you, and I don't want to hear about *bomohs* and things. Please just leave me and the children alone,' I replied. But he continued to threaten and cajole. 'For the sake of the children,' he kept on saying, knowing that they were my weakest point. Wearily I gave in.

Once I had arrived at the squat, bluestone building that housed his law firm, I was ushered upstairs to a small conference room where Bahrin and a solicitor were waiting. As I took the empty chair that was waiting for me on the other side of the table, it was as if I were a schoolgirl who had arrived late for class. And this was to remain the tone of the meeting. Bahrin and his lawyer launched into an outline of the terms of a reconciliation that would see me reside in Malaysia and in which I would return to exactly the same life I had been leading before. In turn, all Bahrin promised was to forgive me for my ridiculous stance in Australia and to take me back.

Rather than feeling outraged at his magnanimous attitude, I felt myself illogically trying to explain to his female lawyer how unacceptable this was and the reasons why my return to Malaysia was so impossible. I tried to make her understand what my life had been like there and what sort of life I could expect for my children if we returned, hoping that she would perhaps reason with her client and convince him to leave us in peace. But she only stared at me condescendingly as I tried to describe to her the alien existence we had there, the isolation, the violence and the barbaric superstitions that dictated our everyday lives. In hindsight I can see how futile it was to try to tell her of these things, to try to show her the true side of Bahrin's reality, when before her stood Bahrin in his 'Western' persona: polite, immaculately cultivated and displayed, speaking in a carefully moderated voice – just as he had been with me in the days of our courtship. I could almost feel the unspoken messages passing between them as my voice trailed off in defeat. The silence was clear; Bahrin had portrayed me to his legal representatives as unstable, rabid almost, a woman who spoke of a man who didn't resemble their urbane royal client, an embittered and thrown-over wife.

I realised then that the meeting had been a great mistake and moved to leave, but not before Bahrin asked for a private moment alone with me, to which his lawyer immediately agreed. Once we were by ourselves, he sat down at right angles to me on the other dark-coloured chair.

'Yasmin, I want you to come back. I love you,' he said, and then, digging swiftly into his right-hand pocket, he produced a small red velvet box, which he opened to display a diamond ring. 'See, I do love you. I bought you this,' he said as he placed the open box in my lap. 'Everything will be all right now if you just come back.'

I felt my stomach twist with anger as I looked down into my lap at the diamond nestled in its box and glinting as it caught the light from the fluorescent globes overhead.

'Did you really think that after all you've done to me, after every bruise you've given me, the humiliation, the loneliness, the threats to take the children and to hurt my nanna, that one diamond ring would be enough to get me to come back to you? And you haven't even mentioned that slut you married! Does she know that you're asking me to come back?'

'My wife doesn't concern you,' Bahrin stated flatly. 'That's none of your business.'

'You really are a shit, Bahrin. You don't care about anyone but yourself; you don't care about Iddin and Shah and you don't care about me. I will never, ever live in Terengganu again. Shah and Iddin deserve a better life than with you.'

'Listen, you little bitch,' he said in quiet tones that no one could overhear, 'I have this, and don't think I won't use it when I get you back home.' He waved a piece of paper under my nose. I immediately recognised it as a document from the Terengganu religious authorities with the royal crest above the writing and was able to make out my name scrawled in Arabic across the top. 'I will get you back to Terengganu, you fucking little bitch. You know that, don't you? Your shit-for-brains Australian judge doesn't want to cause a diplomatic fight; he's going to give you back to me; you are going to regret ever causing me so much trouble.

They're going to use the *rotan* on you, six times, and you're going to rot in the Balai Police for as long as I want. Remember, Kasim is the inspector of the Special Branch.'

All this he spat out as the force of his bulging eyes locked me to my seat. I didn't doubt that what he said was true and that he meant every word. I managed to stand and push my way past him towards the exit and, as I did, the ring in its box fell to the carpet. I stumbled out, sobbing, into the summer sunshine and somehow made it to Lillian's office. When I told her what had happened, she was furious with me for going to a meeting with Bahrin alone and angry that his solicitors had encouraged it without her knowledge. But to me that was the least of my worries. It was as if my real life had suddenly appeared again and I had been fooling myself to hope that I could ever get away from Bahrin. It took Lillian a long time to calm me down and convince me that Bahrin hadn't won yet; when I finally left her office to pick up the children, I was still badly shaken.

No part of the courtroom battle was simple. Bahrin had even flown out from Malaysia, at great expense, a Malaysian advocate to give evidence to the Australian court on the dealings of Islamic law. Our side, unfortunately, couldn't have found an expert witness from Malaysia willing to come to our aid even if we had had the money to fly him or her over.

But Bahrin hadn't finished propositioning me yet. On Tuesday, 4 February, he rang me with one last disgusting proposal: he wanted to buy Iddin from me. Assuring me that I would live as a wealthy woman for the rest of my life, he wanted to split the children, leaving Shahirah and me in Australia. He browbeat, cajoled, abused and screamed at me, threatening never to rest until he had destroyed me and taken both children, telling me that I would never have a life away from him. I listened to all this, unable to hang up the phone, then slid down the living-room wall, sobbing and dizzy with fear and utter despair. It was as if Bahrin still controlled my every breath. I was terrorised by a voice coming to me over the telephone lines.

I recall very little of the next few hours. I remember Iddin standing in front of me, crying. I remember holding Shahirah and him to my chest and rocking back and forth. I found myself on the phone to Lillian but I don't know exactly what I said to her. I do know that I teetered on the abyss of utter desolation that day and longed to close my eyes and never wake up. But I didn't. Somewhere in the fog that had taken over my brain, I realised that my children still needed me.

Thirty-eight

I left Sue and Rob MacArthur's house at 8 a.m. on 11 February 1986, kissing Iddin goodbye as if for the last time. I even had Rob take a photograph of Iddin and me sitting together on their front verandah moments before I drove away. I was steeling myself for the worst that day, preparing myself to have my small son taken away from me by the police and bundled onto a plane for Malaysia at 4 p.m. if the judgement went against us. I knew that I could expect some respite before they took Shahirah: as she was being breastfed, I was her sole food supplier; I knew also that Bahrin was not really interested in his daughter and therefore wouldn't press for her. I took one brief look over my shoulder as I carried Shahirah out through the green garden gate and I saw Iddin standing on the top of the steps waving his Paddington Bear's paw in goodbye, grinning cheekily. I swallowed the lump in my throat, blowing one last kiss to him and unlocking the car door.

Lillian, her assistant Sue Stephenson and Noel Ackman sat on the left-hand side of the courtroom with me a little behind, boxes of files, legal books, pens and papers covering the table in front of them. John Udorovic arrived halfway through the proceedings and sat behind Lillian. On the right-hand side of the room was Bahrin's force of legal heavyweights: a Queen's Counsel, a barrister, two or three solicitors and his Malaysian 'expert'. We all waited for the judge to enter and my mind flashed over the points that had to be covered by him. The kidnapping allegations put forward by Bahrin's side had been dismissed by the judge long ago as having no merit; after much questioning, Bahrin had admitted that I hadn't kidnapped the children and that he himself had sent me home. The judge was satisfied that my course of action had not been premeditated. What now had to be addressed was the petition by the other side to have the whole matter dismissed from the current jurisdiction and fought out in Malaysia instead. There was no motion for custody brought by Bahrin for the children, only his application that the children and I be deported from our own country back to Malaysia.

In the event of the judge ruling that way, we had requested a dozen or more safeguards to be built into any orders he might make. This included a personal guarantee from the Malaysian Internal Affairs Minister that if Bahrin gained custody of the children and subsequently divorced me, I be allowed to remain in Malaysia to be near them. This was one of the major concerns I carried, as he had always threatened to have me deported and, if he divorced me, I had no legal residency status there and no means to obtain a resident visa. We also demanded that Bahrin obtain, from the same minister's office, written assurances that I would be immune from prosecution and imprisonment under Malaysia's Internal Security Act, which allows any person residing in Malaysia to be held in prison indefinitely with no charges being laid. We were worried that this would be my fate as I had made allegations in open court about the high level of corruption and double dealing which went on in the corridors of Malaysian politics and the government. Sworn guarantees were also requested from Bahrin to undertake to drop all proceedings in the Islamic courts of Malaysia and to litigate solely in the civil courts, which more or less followed the old English civil code. This was important, as we had been able to prove that the Islamic courts would be prejudiced against me in any matters opposing the royal family. There were also other matters which covered financial support of the children and myself should I have to return to Malaysia, provision of an apartment in Kuala Lumpur, the capital city, not Terengganu, and a lump sum of money from Bahrin to be held in trust to cover my legal costs in Malaysia.

Finally Justice Treyvaud entered the courtroom and, as we all rose to our feet, Bahrin shot me a look of smug confidence that shook me to the core. In essence, His Honour ruled that the children and I should return to Malaysia to litigate the matter of custody in the civil courts of that country, that Bahrin must fulfil all of my demands for the forms of security I had requested, that all proceedings and judgements in the Islamic Court of Terengganu be dismissed at Bahrin's request and that he must also, on oath, promise not to take any further action against me in the Islamic courts and confine all legal action to the civil courts of Malaysia.

Lillian and John instantly turned around in their seats to grasp my hands. In a low voice, John said, 'We'll appeal, simple as that, we'll appeal, everyone knows that.' Noel shrugged in his relaxed way and simply said, 'We'll appeal.' Lillian, catching sight of the tears welling up in my eyes and hearing the groan that had started in my throat, squeezed my hand fiercely. 'Don't you dare cry, don't you dare give up,' she hissed sternly, giving my hand one last tight squeeze before turning back to listen to His Honour's summation.

I dared take one look towards Bahrin's side of the courtroom, where it was plain to see no one was happy with the judgement either. Bahrin glowered and his lawyers shook their heads in disgust; it was obvious that they had expected everything on their terms. I turned back, satisfied that Bahrin wasn't pleased to be told by an Australian judge that he couldn't use the Islamic courts against me. When the mutterings and quick conferences had finished on both sides of the courtroom, Noel rose to his feet and calmly told Justice Treyvaud we would appeal. He was quickly followed by Bahrin's Queen's Counsel, who indicated the same thing. The judge himself didn't seem at all surprised that both sides were determined to appeal against his decision and adjourned any further action for several days.

I left that courtroom feeling as if I were now living on borrowed time. I didn't really understand what the whole process of appeal entailed and I felt as if I should be breathing in deeply and quickly in an effort to inhale as much of Australia as I could before I was forced to leave. But at least I had the comfort of knowing that Shahirah, Iddin and I would all be together on Iddin's third birthday that Saturday.

As we made our way from the building together in a tight formation, 'my team', as I had begun to think of them, tossed legal jargon around in the air, talking of precedents, time frames and appeal books, very little of which I understood. All I cared about as I loaded the pram full of files and bags and held Shahirah close to me and she gurgled in my ear and tugged at my dress was that I had the children for at least a few more days and that I didn't have to say goodbye to them – yet.

Bahrin departed Australia on 13 February, leaving his lawyers to represent him in court and without asking to see the children. For the children and me nothing was certain, no real plans could be made; our futures remained unresolved and our lives were about to be placed in the hands of the appeal courts.

Over the next weeks I struggled to bring normality back into the children's lives. Shahirah was now crawling and Iddin had begun to paint wildly colourful pictures and to ask for a puppy. I began to make friends and to draw unstinting support and love from Sue and Rob MacArthur and their two sons, Nicholas and Ben, who were Iddin's very special friends and who doted on Shahirah. But no matter how much I wanted to pretend that we were now home to stay, the reality of the complicated legal conferences I attended and the endless study and research sessions I had with Lillian kept me aware of just how fragile our existence in Australia was and how much of a fight it would be to obtain a life for us there.

Lillian assembled a formidable team to present the appeal: Sue Stephenson, E.W. (Bill) Gillard QC, a very tall, slim and dapper gentleman with bushy eyebrows and dark, intelligent eyes, and barrister John Cantwell, quiet and steady with the concentration of a chess player. These were the people who worked day and night to prepare the appeal books in the record time of ten days and the ones who flew to the city of Adelaide in South Australia, to appear before the Full Bench (three judges sitting at once) of the Family Court on 13 March and fight the case. It was totally unfeasible for me to go to Adelaide, and unneccessary, as the appeal would not be calling witnesses to give evidence. The whole matter would be decided on written material and the submissions and arguments of the Queen's Counsels on either side.

I personally felt that the speed at which the appeal was set had quite a bit to do with government pressure and the fact that Australia did not want to find itself embroiled in another diplomatic ruckus with Malaysia. At the time, two Australians, Barlow and Chambers, were facing the death penalty in Malaysia for drug trafficking and there was quite a bit of ill feeling between the two nations. Usually appeal cases took anything from six months to a year before appearances before the Full Court were made, and they normally took place in the originating city, i.e. Melbourne.

I had no other choice but to wait at Sue and Rob's house for Lillian to telephone me with progress reports. It was terrible being so far removed from the fight in Adelaide. I tried to go about life over the next two days as usual, feeding the children, bathing them and reading stories to Iddin, Shahirah, Ben and Nicholas to pass the time, but I still couldn't stop myself from jumping every time the phone rang and I slept very little at night. The appeal hearing took place in Adelaide on 13 and 14 March, during which time my legal team set many new precedents in appeal law, including being allowed to submit new and faxed evidence. Ultimately, two days was not enough time for both sides to argue the case and the matter was adjourned back to Melbourne for a continuation of the hearing on the 3 and 4 April 1986. So it was more waiting. I wasn't sure whether to be glad of the prolongment or to wish for some final decision about our lives as quickly as possible. But I did cherish every day that I spent with Iddin and Shah in case it was my last.

By the time May arrived there was still no word of when the judgement on the appeal would be handed down. As it could be months before we heard anything, I decided to take the next step towards a permanent life in Australia and moved us into a house owned by my friend Peter's father in the leafy suburb of East Malvern. As Shah had become a fast-speed crawler and Iddin more and more active, it had become apparent that the flat and its tiny garden would soon be too small to house two rampaging and growing children. Uncle Eric, Peter's father, offered the old house to me at a fraction of the normal rent in the comfortable middle-class suburb. It had an enormous garden with fruit trees and plenty of space for children's adventures. Uncle Eric lived next door on his own in a large, rambling old house with a tennis court in the back which Iddin could use to ride his tricycle around. The whole arrangement would be absolutely wonderful for the children. There was one catch, though: the house hadn't been lived in for over five years, nor ever renovated in its seventy-year life span, and much of it was uninhabitable. I was absolutely determined that I wanted this house for Iddin and Shahirah and that small details such as no floor in the bathroom, mildewed walls or the lack of a stove would not keep them from it – so I became a renovator.

As I stepped backwards to survey my handiwork, I suddenly wondered what the royal ladies of Terengganu would say if they could see me now. There I stood, clad in filthy overalls, a scarf wrapped around my hair to keep the flying dirt out, with wellington boots on my feet and Shahirah strapped to my back in a baby sling. Iddin was even dirtier than I was, if that was possible, but seemed to revel in his role as assistant, running around the house and collecting the scraps of wallpaper we had stripped from the walls, then filling the wheelbarrow with them for Uncle Eric to dispose of later. It was early June 1986 and getting colder every night as winter came on, but I finally began to see the progress that I had made since we had moved in. I had stripped all the faded and water-marked wallpaper from the walls, steaming, scraping and sometimes picking it off until I had no fingernails left. This occupation was something Iddin enjoyed, ripping great lengths of it off at his height and saving me from having to crawl around on my knees to do it.

As soon as I had washed down the walls with solvent,

I planned to polyfill the cracks and crevices, sand it back and then paint everything in warm apricot tones. I had already laid a new tile floor in the bathroom and, with Peter's help, installed a second-hand washbasin and regrouted all the tiles in the shower and bath recess. The children and I now didn't have to go next door to Uncle Eric's to use the bathroom, which was a great plus. The new stove I had bought at a 'seconds' sale had been installed and was now working properly, and that weekend Peter had helped me to lay a new cement floor in the laundry outside and it was almost dry. The only trouble was that in attempting to allow for water drainage we had put too much of a slope in it and therefore the washing machine was probably going to have to balance on a hill. Some other friends had arrived two or three days before to help me rip up the old and dirty carpets in some of the rooms. I intended to hire a floor sander and polish and seal the bare boards myself, as new carpet was far too expensive to consider. The children's room was the only really comfortable and finished room in the house; however, the rest was coming together slowly but surely.

So much for being 'useless, stupid and unable to cope' on my own with the children, I thought, as I stripped off my headscarf and released Shahirah from her baby sling on my back, bringing her around and putting her on my breast as I sat back on the kitchen chair. I had learned to look after myself and the children – and I could use a saw and a hammer and an electric drill. I only prayed that we would now be allowed to live in this home we had created. Looking out of the window, I saw Iddin playing in the back garden, jumping onto a huge pile of red and gold autumn leaves, his face beaming with delight as he squealed and tossed handfuls up in the air.

Until now I had always followed the law, coming

back home and registering my presence with the courts, submitting myself to their jurisdiction and not running off to hide where Bahrin couldn't find me. But now, as one day merged into another and still no judgement was forthcoming from the appeal, I began to wonder, after eight months at home, what I would do if the ruling ultimately went against me.

In my mind I began to go over the options: I could follow whatever the court ordered; I could appeal again, this time to the High Court of Australia, if I were ordered back to Malaysia; or I could simply disappear with the children. As a knee-jerk reaction, the last course seemed the most attractive, but as I thought more deeply about what that would mean to the children – uprooting them, pulling Iddin out of kindergarten and maybe living on the run, pretending to be different people – I realised that I would be stripping away every bit of security and normality I had so painstakingly tried to build up for them over the preceding months. I therefore ruled it out.

I would, I concluded, exhaust every legal avenue to protect our life together and keep meticulous records along the way to answer any questions the children might have when they were older about my reasoning and my actions.

I clambered down from the ladder as swiftly as I could, taking care not to drop the brush or slosh the tray of paint I had been using to finish the living-room ceiling, and leapt to snatch up the telephone before its ringing woke Shahirah from her nap. Just as I reached the telephone the door bell chimed, waking the baby and making her cry. Breathlessly I shouted in the direction of the front door that I was coming and panted 'hello' into the mouthpiece.

'We've won, we've won!' Lillian screamed down the phone line. 'You and the kids can stay!'

'When? How?' I managed to blurt out.

'Hang on a minute. I'll read you a summary.' I could hear Lillian fumbling with papers and then her voice came back on the line. 'Twenty-seventh June 1986, blah, blah, blah. Orders of the Full Court and Judgement. (i) That the wife's appeal be allowed, blah blah blah. (ii) That the wife have sole custody of the children. (iii) That the husband be restrained from removing the children out of the State of Victoria and out of the Commonwealth of Australia. (iv) That the husband's cross appeals be dismissed. Congratulations, welcome home!'

I scarcely remember putting down the receiver but I do remember somehow retrieving Shahirah from her cot and opening the door to my friend Susan, who'd been left to stand outside all that time in the rain on my unprotected verandah, waiting patiently for me to open the door.

Worried that something terrible had happened, Susan gripped my arm concernedly until I managed to gurgle out a hoarse 'We've won!' to her. I was numb all over, but strangely not elated or jumping around with excitement as I had fantasised I would when I had imagined this moment as I lay in bed at night. When I had filled Susan in on the details as I knew them, I handed her Shah and I went into my bedroom, flinging open my wardrobe and pulling out the *baju kurung* that I had often been forced to wear in court due to my shortage of clothes. Flinging the coathanger on the bed, I bundled the dress up in a ball and returned to the living-room where Susan sat with Shahirah. Pulling aside the heavy black firescreen, I tossed the hated *baju kurung* into the fire and watched the flames as they caught hold of the silk.

'Now we're home for good,' I said, as Susan watched me open-mouthed, and I promptly burst into tears.

Thirty-nine

The children and I grew up a lot in the four years that followed my appeal win. Building a new life wasn't easy and I found it ironically amusing that I had more or less gone from palace to pension in one fell swoop. But I had no regrets. I had neither the time nor the inclination to long for the hollow life I had led in Malaysia; the decisions I had made had been the right ones both for the children and for myself. Ruminating on the past would have kept me anchored there, trapped by my own self-pity, exactly where Bahrin hoped I would stay; instead I allowed myself only to look forward and never spoke in depth about Terengganu, even with my closest friends. The future was all I was interested in and the only thing that was possible to consider, alone with two small children.

I returned to the workforce as soon as I was able, at one stage holding down three jobs to make ends meet. I found that with Shah still being partially breastfed, this was a more convenient way to juggle the children's needs with the financial ones. I did typing for students, babysat, took part in market research surveys and baked cakes for a small deli. Later on I worked part-time as a waitress, covering the lunch hour in a busy city bistro. This meant I was only away from Shah and Iddin for a short while each day and the job fitted in well with

Iddin's kindergarten times and the offer of babysitting help from my friend Susan.

But, most of all, the first four years at home were a time for me to heal, to find out that I wasn't such a useless person and to rediscover my self-respect and confidence. The last two took an awfully long time to find again. It's funny that self-respect is so intangible, and its absence so hard to recognise when it has been eroded over a long period. I didn't miss my self-respect until it was gone and I had lost an essential part of myself. I didn't believe that I deserved any better. I found it difficult to disagree with anyone in an outright manner and I had a continual battle within myself not to leap like a well-trained puppy dog trying to please its master and win approval whenever I was around other adults. Bahrin had done his programming well; I felt soiled and a failure, and that is a big pit to crawl out of. As for my heart, that was so battle-scarred and bruised that I doubted whether I would ever have room in it for anyone other than Iddin and Shah.

I had spent four long years in Malaysia, four years of not knowing what music was popular on the radio or what films had been screened, four years of having very little knowledge of the world outside Terengganu and of virtual ignorance about the political situation in Australia and around the world. Reagan and Thatcher were merely captions beneath photographs of ill-defined characters in the newspaper and the bulls and bears of the stockmarket sounded as if they needed an animal trainer. New electronic banking machines on street corners left me fazed and bewildered at the leaps made in technology, while my experiences in Malaysia made me feel weary and wiser than so many of my contemporaries. For a long while I felt as if I only partially existed in relation to the everyday world. I felt out of step, alienated and far older than my packaging, but at the same time I struggled to be the mother that Iddin and Shah needed. Suddenly being transplanted back into my own country had made me realise how much of my youth Bahrin had taken from me, or, rather, how much I had allowed him to take.

In mid-1986 I wrote to the Chief Imam of Terengganu requesting a divorce from Bahrin and assuring the Imam that I had no objections to Bahrin performing the traditional divorce decree. I chose this course of action as the simplest and most expedient way of obtaining my freedom, and it was also the cheapest – there was no way I could afford another legal battle. I purposely asked for no property settlement, no money, nothing, nor did I expect anything or want anything more than my freedom and my children. The family could keep the trinkets, the art, the jewellery and the gowns; as long as my battered old car could get me from A to B there was no need to fret about the loss of my BMW or the lack of a Rolls-Royce in my life. What would I have done in my new life with Waterford Crystal wine glasses and silver cutlery? For the sake of expediency, all my dishes now had one benchmark – dishwasher-proof. My library of books was the one thing I did lament the loss of. They had been my true friends and a source of solace and education, and to think of them ending up on a bonfire of Bahrin's making made me very sad. Elmi could wear my diamonds around her neck and my rings on her fingers – they would always be my hand-me-downs. I had no desire to cling to a dead thing and no wish to remain 'number one wife' in the distasteful *ménage à trois* Bahrin had created from his perverseness. I didn't want to belong to anyone any more; I just wanted a chance to find out how much of me still existed.

Bahrin arrived back in Australia on 6 September 1986 expecting instant access to the children and with total disregard for the convenience or the day-to-day lives of anyone but himself. Bahrin being Bahrin, he sent the court system into a frenzy by demanding a totally unnecessary 'urgent hearing' to obtain access to the children. He seemed to have absolutely no concept that the world did not revolve around his instant whims and desires and expected his royal rank to carry the same weight in Australia that it did in his own country. I had never indicated that I had any objections to the children seeing their father; in fact, I had done everything I could to make it easy for him to speak to them over the telephone, but he seldom made the effort.

I believe that the trumped-up reasons he gave for hauling everyone back into court were a ruse so he could demand my new address in East Malvern. I didn't mind his having my telephone number so he could speak to the children, but I had very strong reservations and fears that once he had our address the children and I would lose our security and privacy. In the witness box I told the judge that I believed I had been followed a number of times by a private investigator hired by Bahrin and that I feared his motives and wished to keep our new address private. Under cross-examination by John Udorovic, Bahrin finally admitted that he had had me photographed by a private detective but denied that he had employed him to follow me. I had to choke back my exasperation with the legal system when the judge ruled that Bahrin be given our full address immediately. I wanted to demand that the judge recognise the threat to our safety but I held my tongue and bit back the words, realising the futility of fighting the system and understanding that the court would need real proof that Bahrin intended to cause me harm.

The second day in court, John and Lillian decided to spring a few surprises on Bahrin since he had dragged us all into court on bogus grounds. We decided that whilst he was in Australia we should take the opportunity to try to get an order from the court directing that Bahrin return all my possessions which I had left in Malaysia and an order for maintenance payments. Always one for outward appearances, Bahrin came prepared for this likelihood, crying impoverishment from the moment he landed in Melbourne. He dispensed with his high-powered and expensive legal representatives in court, saying that he could no longer afford to pay them, and checked in to the cheapest hotel the city had to offer. He also made an application for Australian taxpayer-funded legal aid. I was very sceptical that he would ever attempt to go into court without legal advice and was not surprised when he was spotted using the back door to visit the chambers of his 'former' barrister as soon as the hearing was finished.

John handled the news of Bahrin's sudden descent to the breadline magnificently. Before the day's court session began he walked casually over to Bahrin, shook his hand and complimented him on his new Ferrari watch. Then he marched into court and proceeded to demolish Bahrin's protestations that he couldn't afford to send any money for the children's upkeep, delivering the *coup de grâce* by drawing the judge's attention to Bahrin's new and very expensive watch (estimated value well over a thousand pounds) displayed ostentatiously on his right wrist.

Finally, the judge ordered that Bahrin pay monthly maintenance and swear on the Koran that he would undertake to forward all of my possessions – clothing, photographs, books, linen, crockery – and the children's toys and books to us in Melbourne. I didn't hold my breath in expectation. I expected neither the maintenance to arrive nor for Bahrin to keep his word; it was simply the principle of the matter. It was ten months before any of my things were eventually sent to me by

Bahrin, and even then he still didn't keep his oath made on the Koran in front of the judge. The two boxes I received contained Muslim maternity dresses, torn towels that looked as if they had been shredded in a tremendous rage, some of my Balinese dancing costumes and my *songket* wedding dress – not exactly the essentials of a Western woman's life. None of the children's clothes or toys were included. It was also ordered that Bahrin notify me in writing one month before any intended visit to Australia to see Iddin and Shahirah so that I could ensure that his plans did not clash with any other arrangements I might have made for the children and myself. This condition was made at my suggestion to help ease the difficult situation and so that Bahrin would be sure of seeing the children when he wished. No permanent access arrangements were ordered by the court and none were requested by Bahrin for the future.

Bahrin did, however, use the opportunity of the September court appearance to play his 'wronged royal' persona to the hilt. Standing in the witness box, he turned to face the judge and passionately declared that he intended to consider it his own personal *jihad*, or Muslim holy war, to retrieve his son Iddin from Australia. I don't think that anyone in that courtroom except me understood the significance of Bahrin's statement. His Honour certainly didn't seem to comprehend the fury or the passion behind that short, foreign word. (This was, of course, well before the 11 September terrorist attacks.) Its connotations, wrapped in over a thousand years of misinterpretation and self-interest, screamed to me silently just how much Bahrin hated me and what he would be prepared to do to seek his revenge. It sickened me that he would couch his threat in terms of the Islamic religion. A *jihad* was not something brave men waged against women and children; a *jihad* was a violent battle to the death in the name of Allah in the defence of the Islamic religion. Under Islamic teachings, the warrior who lost his life in a battle to defend his religion and the Muslim way of life was considered a glorious martyr whose unhindered and immediate entrance to heaven was assured. I tried to laugh off his avowal as his way of trying to intimidate the judge and me, but, try as I might, and even listening to the rational witticisms made by Lillian and John after the hearing, Bahrin's mention of a *jihad* had planted a tiny stone of icy fear in the back of my brain that rattled around in my head whenever the doorbell rang unexpectedly or I heard noises outside the house in the middle of the night.

The only good thing that Bahrin's week-long visit brought was our divorce decree from Terengganu, signed, sealed and official. Since 3 September 1986, I had belonged to myself and I hadn't even known it.

Our lives flowed on once I got my bearings and the passage of time was marked by Shahirah's first tentative steps, guided by her big brother, by holidays spent at the beach, by birthday parties with loud games and chocolate cakes, and by the Christmas tree which stood in the corner of the living-room. When I close my eyes, all those times flash past like snippets of film, happy and noisy, snatched phrases and giggles, tears and whispers, all there inside my head. A teddy bears' picnic in the park, children and friends sitting on a blanket in the sun; skiing attempts during which the children excelled and I failed abysmally; quiet times curled up with a book, Iddin on one knee and Shah on the other as I read to them; the three of us singing along to *Sesame Street* and *Play School* tapes as we drove along in the car; Iddin's love of the Beach Boys song 'Kokomo', which he hummed slightly off key. They are all there in my head as though they happened yesterday. There, too, are the times when single parenting wasn't so easy or so rosy, the times when I wished I had been more patient or when I shouldn't have been so quick to yell, days when I felt so lonely that I switched on the television to hear an adult voice or floundered when I realised I didn't know how to teach Iddin to urinate standing up. That we managed to get through those times, good and bad, intact as a family, is more a credit to the children's patience with their mother and their wonderful and unique personalities than to me.

Iddin's kindergarten years turned me from a mother into a taxi driver. His popularity with the boys and girls in his class meant his social life became more active than mine, and I was kept busy picking him up or ferrying other children around East Malvern. He developed a liking for drawing and a passion for the Knights of the Round Table and Robin Hood and spent countless hours with his friends building hideouts in the garden and 'riding horses' around the old apricot tree that spread across the lawn and offered low-slung, sturdy branches as worthy mounts for the 'Indians, cowboys, Knights or Merry Men' of the East Malvern Forest. Even at a young age Iddin was always eager to take on responsibilities, offering to collect the kindling for the fire, unload the dishwasher or help me put away the clean clothes. I worried about this serious side of his nature; I didn't want him to feel that he had to step into the gap created by having only one parent at home. Maintaining a balance between teaching Iddin responsibility and not allowing him to be caught up in a prematurely adult world was something I had to keep in mind constantly. As Iddin got older he would sometimes listen with great concentration to the news bulletins and then offer me his opinion on the latest world happenings. He had no time for unfairness, as he called it, and in his simplistic way couldn't understand why people had to starve when the shops displayed so much food. Come to think of it, nor could I.

Shahirah was nearly always included in Iddin's games with his friends; she became a sort of mascot to the older children, well able to hold her own in her brother's games and equally capable of protesting loudly if she felt that she was being taken advantage of. Her nickname evolved into 'Me too', an indicator that she was never backward in coming forward. She was the grubbier of my two, able to attract dirt like a magnet; our family joke was that if I dressed Shah in a white dress and sat her in a white room, she would still manage to come out covered in grime. Gregarious by nature, Shahirah loved everything to excess, whether it be the colours in the rainbows she drew or the loudness with which she sang; Shah had no half measures and few inhibitions – as far as life and people were concerned, she wanted to open her arms and hug them all.

Our lives were made complete by the good and trusted circle of friends that had become closer than family. We spent our summer holidays at the beach with Sue and Rob MacArthur and their sons Nicholas and Ben, who were like Iddin and Shahirah's cousins, and rainy winter evenings with Uncle Eric. Special times would always see our same close friends gathered together: the MacArthurs, Susan and her children Josette, Mason and Spencer, the McMenamins and their children Natalie and Lewis, and the Jenner-Baker family. We sat through school Christmas pageants together and hid Easter eggs for each other's children, and every year our families spent Christmas Eve together at our home, drinking egg nog, exchanging small gifts and watching the traditional 'Carols by Candlelight' performance on television.

Nanna was always a very honoured guest at these

celebrations, holding court in a comfortable chair and happily accepting attention from all the children and adults alike. She took great delight in teaching her great-grandchildren how to Charleston and waltz and in opening her ample arms for hugs and cuddles on her comfortable lap. The children took no notice of Nanna's lapses of memory or the fact that she repeated some of her stories time and time again. Iddin would sit with her on the couch, patiently listening to her relate a story and gently prompting if she lost her place in the tale.

I myself discovered a subtle change in the balance of my relationship with Nanna. Where once I had been the cosseted grandchild, whose hair she would brush for hours on end and over whom she would fuss and fidget, I had now graduated to the position of fellow woman. I was taken aback by her frank revelations on sexuality and the course her life had taken, the evaluations of her daughter – my mother – and the sadness with which she spoke of a stillborn son. Over a glass of port one evening, I realised that she viewed her life as a failure, incomplete and unresolved. She made some sort of vague remark about having had so few choices in her life and wondering about what it would have been like to grow old with my grandfather by her side; she said that she had nothing to show for her life at all – except me. Within the strict parameters of Nanna's life, family milestones, wedding anniversaries and a greying husband by her side were the measure of success; even a weekly visit to a weatherbeaten gravestone would have been preferable to her status as a woman in marital limbo. 'But things are different now,' she added quickly. 'You have choices and opportunities and no one to point the finger at you.'

If only she knew. I felt just as constrained by the expectations of the nuclear family as she had been by the moralistic 'depression years'. Deep down inside, of

course, I wanted to play happy families. I wanted the
grind of supporting two children to be shared with
someone I truly trusted and loved, and I wanted to share
my life with another adult who accepted me exactly as
I was, a package deal. However, what we want and
what we get are often two completely different things.
For a few years after my divorce I had a couple of
desultory stabs at developing a relationship with another
man, but I was never satisfied with the outcome.
Sometimes, quite irrationally, I felt a sense of gratitude
for the mere fact that they wanted to go out with me,
a mother of two, and I infuriated myself by feeling that
way. One person I saw on and off for a while even
insisted that whenever we went out with the children
the restaurant bill be divided in four – with me paying
three-quarters of the total to cover the children's meals.
Shah was eighteen months old at the time and Iddin
four, not exactly a strain on the pocket to feed. I tried
dining out once with a tall, blond Adonis. This proved
to be a mind-numbing experience and, I can confidently
conclude, he achieved more pleasure kissing himself
goodnight in the mirror than he did me. Others simply
exasperated me by their lack of maturity and sensitivity;
but, mostly, I wound up loathing myself for just settling
for someone to avoid the loneliness. And, besides, I was
damned if I would continually make excuses for my
children's existence. They were well-behaved, intelligent
and loving little people who obviously deserved better
than being treated like awkward and unwanted
appendages by any would-be suitors.

Soon after our return to Australia became accepted as
a permanent arrangement by Bahrin's family, I began a
fairly regular correspondence with some of them. My
most loyal and understanding friend remained the
Tengku Ampuan, Endah, who took every opportunity

to keep me up to date with all her news and the family machinations. We spoke on the telephone frequently and exchanged photographs; Endah also sent me some of my personal photo albums and my fur coat, which I had left with her for safekeeping. She managed this on one of her chance visits to Perth in Western Australia, when she accompanied the Sultan on an inspection of the mansion he had built there. We were both bitterly disappointed when her husband vetoed any suggestion that she should make a side trip to Melbourne, but felt that it was wiser not to push the issue with him as Endah did not want to bear the brunt of his unpredictable temper.

Raja Ahmad, Bahrin's father, also dropped us the occasional line, enclosing photographs of his newborn son by his third wife; it did seem odd that my children's father had a brother younger than they were. My father-in-law's notes and cards were not laced with recriminations or criticisms; they only mentioned that he missed the children. I replied that he was welcome to come and visit them any time he wished, a point I reiterated whenever I wrote back to any of the family in Terengganu.

Bahrin's other aunts also wrote to me; Auntie Rosita was especially supportive and understanding in her letters, congratulating me on finally being free of Bahrin and expressing the hope that I find someone else and settle down. This was a turn of attitude that I had least expected, but I guessed that this was caused by the fact that Bahrin's arrogance and disdain of his uncle's choice of a Chinese wife had not after all gone unnoticed by her. Auntie Zainah kept me up to date on the latest gossip as only she knew how, sending me news of the latest scandals and liaisons and passing on messages from Mak to the children and me. I was also grateful for the Malaysian recipes she included in some of the letters, which I used to try to recreate the dishes that I had never been allowed or encouraged to cook when I had lived there. Zainah's daughter, Diana, wrote only sporadically; her new job and first pregnancy ensured that she was kept busy. I always got the impression from Diana's notes that she preferred to keep as far away from the Terengganu royals as possible, hence the decision to work in the capital city, Kuala Lumpur. But she still managed to write as one young mum to another, and after her daughter was born I sent instructions to my mother-in-law that all of Iddin and Shah's baby equipment and toys should be passed on to Diana's daughter, my new cousin.

For Mak, corresponding was not an easy thing. Her familiar child-like scrawl painstakingly etched across the page saddened me; her stilted and basic sentences were an indicator of her lack of literacy, of an education that had been focused solely on the religious and the decorative, leaving her inadequately equipped to act as her own advocate, orally or in writing.

It was easy for me to picture the women of the family gathering at Mak's house around sweet cakes and rosehip syrup, lying on the pillows with one or two servants massaging the aunties' feet or shoulders and reading my letters out loud. I had watched them come together like this hundreds of times as they twittered with excitement at a glimpse of themselves (or sometimes me, because of my rebellious fashions) on the television, attending some official reception or ribbon cutting. All life existed inside their insular bubble of royalness – or so they thought. Now they were faced with the reality that one did not cease to exist if the bubble was stretched and breached, or even burst.

None of these letters I received from the female members of the family ever bore the signs of anger or ostracism – if anything, I was continually assured of their love and in some I picked up an undercurrent of envy, perhaps because I was in possession of the freedom that these women only dreamed about.

Bahrin, however, was not one for communicating, either by telephone or by letter. Months would sometimes go by between his phone calls to the children. I even tried offering him unlimited telephone access but this achieved no enthusiastic response at all. The lines of communication with the children were left very open to him but he obviously didn't feel it was worth the effort. Sometimes I would try to interest him in Iddin's schooling, requesting that he make joint decisions with me about private school choices, but I got little or no response to my overtures.

I had thought that encouraging Bahrin's participation in Iddin and Shahirah's lives would be a way of creating a relationship between him and the children. I had hoped that it would be a way of helping him to accept that the children and I had new lives and that the inclusion of his views and opinions would go a long way in helping him come to terms with the reality of the situation. It proved to be a futile expenditure of effort, though, for Bahrin's attitude towards our children resembled the dregs of his behaviour I had come to know during our marriage – non-comprehension, petulance and erratic disinterest. The only time he ever sent either of the children anything was his yearly birthday present and card to Iddin; Shahirah's birthday went entirely unmarked by her father until her sixth, when he sent her a present and a card for the very first time in her life.

For the most part, Bahrin remained a shadowy figure in the background, his visits to Melbourne sporadic and designed to cause the maximum chaos in our lives. Thirteen or fourteen months would usually pass before he descended upon us for his much-lauded annual visit, and when he did fly in to Australia he only saw the children for five or six days at the most, fitted in around his scheduled appointments and business meetings. Those visits were not happy ones for either of the children and would usually precipitate Iddin coming home complaining that Shahirah was not being looked after properly by Bahrin. Following one overnight stay with their father I collected both children to find that Shahirah had been left overnight in a putrid nappy full of faeces. Iddin explained to me that he had argued with Bahrin as best he could about his father's treatment of Shahirah but had not been capable of pushing the issue further. He went on to tell me that Shahirah was made to sleep on the floor on a blanket, whilst he and Bahrin shared the double bed, and that his father had refused to provide a cot for Shahirah. I felt that this blatant differentiating between the children by Bahrin was an extremely callous thing to throw in to the perfectly healthy and equal relationship that Iddin and Shah had. How do you explain to a caring and loving boy that his father doesn't think that his little sister warrants presents or treats because she's a girl? This, unfortunately, was to be the pattern of Bahrin's visits for a number of years. I tried many different ways to get him to treat the children equally: personal pleas, polite conversations and, finally, legal letters, but all to no avail.

I think that Bahrin's complete lack of childcare capabilities became apparent when I received a late-afternoon telephone call from a woman telling me that she had found Iddin and Shahirah stuck inside an elevator at the Victoria Hotel. The woman, a tourist from Taiwan, explained that Iddin had told her that his father had locked his sister and him inside their hotel room and gone shopping. Luckily, Iddin knew our telephone number at home and asked the tourist to help him call me. When I finally spoke to him he was distraught, saying that they had become frightened after being left to their own devices and had decided that they wanted to come home. I was just about to throw myself into the car to set off to collect them when Bahrin arrived back at the hotel. By his own admission, he had spent the afternoon shopping at the exclusive department store, Georges, which was to Melbourne what Harvey Nichols was to London or Barneys was to New York. I was furious with him for leaving our two young children by themselves in a seedy hotel room, but he refused to admit that there was anything wrong with what he had done. Our children were six and four respectively; how could he have been so irresponsible?

I'm afraid that his off-hand manner made me lose my temper – the one thing I had studiously tried to avoid during the preceding years. My tongue took over as a huge boulder of indignation and resentment expanded in my chest. 'It doesn't take much intelligence to be a father – any brainless stud bull with a test tube can be one – but it takes a real man to be a daddy,' I spat into the phone before I slammed the receiver down.

Forty

I began to make tentative moves towards getting some sort of career on track for myself when three-year-old Shahirah commenced kindergarten. I wanted to provide for the children's future and be able to ensure that they wanted for nothing. I contemplated studying law. Being twenty-five, I was eligible for entrance to university without the normal requirements of a high school diploma, and I even got as far as making applications for admission before I had to face the reality of my situation. Adding up childcare fees, textbooks and the expenses of raising two children over the years it would take me to earn my degree, the costs were too prohibitive. I also didn't believe that I could achieve what I wanted without Iddin and Shahirah paying too high a price for their mother's aspirations, and I didn't want to miss their growing up.

After working for several months on a part-time basis for a television station, I began work for a number of temporary employment agencies as a relieving personal assistant or, when necessary, a receptionist. The agencies would send me out on assignments lasting anywhere between one day and a month. The flexibility of working for an agency allowed me to pick and choose jobs and to tailor the work around the children's hours. I was lucky. I could do the work assigned with my eyes closed and I was earning quite decent money, paid by the hour. I specialised in stepping in to fill the gap at advertising agencies and public relations firms, finding my confidence grew from job to job as many of my temporary employers asked me to stay on full-time. Finally, after one long stint at an advertising/graphic design studio, I accepted their offer to take up a job with them on a permanent basis. The agency had a broad client base and I was assured that I would not be tied to administrative work indefinitely but, with the firm's upcoming expansion, would be given the opportunity to move back into public relations and the creative side of the business. The company's attitude was supportive towards my being a working mother and they gave me the option of taking any unfinished work home with me rather than putting in overtime.

Once committed to the forty-hour week, I was hit by the reality of what that entailed. In exchange for a weekly salary I had the onerous task of juggling babysitters and after-school care programmes along with every other working parent. What a nightmare! Waking up at 6.30 a.m., hassling the children to get up and dressed at 6.45 a.m. and rushing them through their breakfast as I alternately pleaded with them to hurry up or to eat, all the while wielding a bread knife in one hand, laden with peanut butter as I cut the lunches, and a make-up brush in the other, as I applied lopsided eyeliner to my harried face over the kitchen sink. Out the door no later than 7.30 a.m. to deliver Shahirah and Iddin to the before-school sitter and then fighting my way through peak-hour traffic to be at the office by 8.30 a.m. Evenings were just as hectic: rushing from the office to arrive at Shahirah's babysitter's prior to 5.45 p.m. and practically flying on to the school to collect Iddin before 6 p.m.; getting an evening meal started as I listened to Iddin's reading and caught up on their news; bathing them and washing and drying Shahirah's hair; then sitting down at the dinner table before bundling them both off to bed so I could have the privilege of doing it all again the next day. I stuck it out for nine months, just long enough to earn the money that I needed to buy a second-hand car, then I quit. I missed the children too much and I knew that I could never replace all the lost hours of their lives that I was paying other people to share with them. I had begun to hate the sound of my own voice telling the children to hurry up.

Returning to temping did not prove as lucrative as it had been earlier, for the recession had by this time taken hold of business in general. I supplemented our income by landing a stint as a freelance PR consultant, later opening a small business of my own, and I also began to teach dance part-time at the National Theatre Ballet School.

John Savage walked into my life in March 1989, bringing back my lost self-esteem with a vengeance. We were together for six months and it was a relationship that was to change the way I viewed myself for ever. A well-respected film and stage actor in America, John had arrived in Melbourne to star in an Australian film, *Hunting*. Raised in Vermont and New York State in the strict Dutch Reform Church, John had rebelled, marrying young, launching a career in acting and juggling the demands of new fatherhood with difficulty. The pressures and temptations of Hollywood contributed to the demise of his marriage and set him off on a quest to 'find himself'. When we were introduced by mutual friends, I had no idea of his professional reputation or of his career in films, which included *Hair*, *The Deerhunter*, for which he received an Oscar nomination, and, most recently, one of the *Godfather* trilogy; all I did know was that the attraction was mutual. With his piercing light-blue eyes, wide open smile and unruly blond hair, his ability to turn his stage presence on and off at the blink of an eye fascinated me, as did his way of sitting back on the periphery of a room, simply absorbing the occupants' mannerisms like the ultimate chameleon he was.

John taught me to expect far more from a relationship than I ever had before and he convinced me to look into the mirror and truly like what I saw. He developed a separate friendship with Iddin and Shahirah without missing a beat and included them in horseriding adventures, restaurant dinners and, with seemingly effortless grace, conversations. Most especially, though, he talked with them, not at them, and listened to what they had to say with the attentiveness normally reserved for in-depth discussions on life choices. With John, life was one exciting new door opening after another, and his thoughtfulness and often extravagant nature sometimes left me panic-stricken when he'd arrive weighed down with gifts for the three of us. Even Nanna fell victim to his charms when John lavished a spectacular Mother's Day lunch on her, complete with penthouse view provided by his hotel suite, champagne, four-course meal, a corsage and handmade chocolates. Sometimes I used to wonder who he was trying to woo.

We discussed marriage – we even examined the sticky subject of pre-nuptial agreements – but even though I did love John there were tiny pieces of the puzzle missing and the sort of love I had for him just wasn't enough. Something almost inexplicable seemed to stop me from saying 'yes'. I knew from our long talks that John viewed the children and me as his key to normality and that he bitterly regretted not being a hands-on parent to his teenage children Jennifer and Lachlan, but I found myself unable to provide his escape clause from

Hollywood, Broadway and all the demons that kept him tethered there.

When John finally left Australia, at first he continued to telephone me daily and ask me to change my mind. He travelled to South Africa and became increasingly involved with the activities of the World Vision charity and then got caught up in other film projects in Europe, always somewhat rootless and always battling to avoid temptation. We maintained our friendship, keeping in contact by phone or occasional letter-writing, but mostly our contact consisted of messages from the strangest locations around the world which he would leave on my answering machine at the oddest hours of the day or night, sending love to me and special messages to the 'wombats', as he called Iddin and Shahirah.

John was, and still is, a sort of champion for the children; when faced with my ex-husband's autocratic behaviour during one of his fleeting forays into fatherhood, John made it very clear to Bahrin that it was totally unacceptable for Shahirah to be expected to bed down on the hotel floor. Just seconds before we delivered the children to Bahrin's hotel room for an overnight stay, John whispered in my ear that he would handle Shah's sleeping arrangements with her father. I barely had time to open my mouth as, with a wink and a quizzically raised eyebrow, John knocked confidently on the door. Bahrin was quite taken aback at the materialisation of me, the two children and a strange American man of whom Iddin and Shah were obviously fond. What further threw him off balance was John's physical appearance: four days' beard growth for the film, muddy boots and a weatherbeaten stockman's coat. With an 'I'm just a slow American cowboy' look on his face, John proceeded to meander around Bahrin's cramped room and ask innocently where the children's beds were. Embarrassed and defensive, Bahrin hastily explained that Shahirah's cot had not yet arrived. John was ready for that and pointed out that at four years old she was far, far too large for a cot and a bed would do much better. Just as hastily as he opened his mouth to protest, Bahrin shut it again, having caught sight of John's steely-eyed stare and fixed smile.

I was entirely transfixed; I had never seen Bahrin back down that quickly before. I kissed the children goodbye quickly above their protestations that they wanted to leave with John and me and went out through the door – but not before I heard John's voice pointedly telling Shahirah, 'Tomorrow I want you to tell me what a lovely comfortable sleep you had in the nice bed Abah is organising for you.' It was necessary for me to stuff my fist in my mouth to stifle my laughter as John pushed me into the elevator and hurried me out of the building.

We will always have a friendship that endures. We speak to each other whenever something major happens in each other's lives and keep up to date on news about our respective families. So it was in March 1990, when I spent three days trying to track John down somewhere on location in Italy, where he was filming the final *Godfather* movie, to tell him that I was getting married.

Life is full of possibilities and coincidences, missed opportunities and chance encounters. One such encounter on a bright and clear summer day brought Iain and me together. After John left Australia, I made a half-hearted attempt at seeing other people, with abysmal results. I had come to realise I could no longer settle for second or third best in a relationship, so I resolved to swear off men entirely except as friends. I suppose that's like waving a red flag under a bull's nose; it's just tempting life to prove you wrong – which is what happened on 2 December 1989, the day I arrived to collect my friend Viv from a vague address that I had been given. The front door was opened by a handsome-looking man with auburn hair and moustache who smiled and invited the children and me inside. He introduced himself as Iain Gillespie and ushered us into his living-room, where my friend was waiting.

We spent a really relaxed and happy morning chatting, oblivious to my friend's hints that we should leave. Those three hours flew by. We discussed music and films and I mentioned that I had seen a very moving documentary the night before, entitled 'Suzi's Story'. I went on to describe the film, about a Sydney family stricken with the AIDS virus, and was mid-sentence when I caught the pained look on Viv's face and hesitated.

'Thank you, I'm glad you liked the film,' said Iain as his hazel eyes darted from my stricken face to Viv's with amusement. Seeing my confusion, he explained that he worked as a documentary film maker and television journalist and had written, produced and directed the documentary I had been praising. I did feel terribly gauche, but my lack of knowledge was tactfully and quickly forgotten. To cover my discomfort, Iain began to play his guitar, charming the children with his nonsensical lyrics and jaunty tunes. They were captivated by his warmth, as was their mother. In fact, I have to admit that I found myself singing along with his music and enjoying myself as much as Iddin and Shahirah, so much so that I was disappointed when it became clear that it was well past the time to leave. Inwardly I held my breath and mentally prayed that he would ask me for my telephone number. I knew I wanted to see this man again; I only hoped that he felt the same. When we finally stood up to go, he did ask me for my number, scrawling it on the side of an empty tissue box. I found out later that he had held Viv back as we were departing and hurriedly asked her if she thought I would go out with him if he asked. She answered in the affirmative and that was that.

When he rang twenty-four hours later, I let out a sigh of relief. In the intervening hours I had imagined the old tissue box being consigned to the rubbish by an overly efficient housekeeper and, as a result, never discovering if the attraction I had felt towards Iain was reciprocated. When, in a tentative yet flippant voice, he suggested dinner that night, I quickly accepted, hoping that I would be able to arrange a babysitter for the children at such short notice and keeping my fingers crossed that he would still seem as interesting in the rarefied atmosphere of a first date as he had chatting in his own living-room.

The doorbell was echoed by the barking of our dog and the squeals of the children as we all hurtled towards the front door. Suddenly there he was, standing on my threshold, staring at me as though he had expected someone else to open the door.

'Jacqueline?' he said, with a bewildered half grin, as I quieted both the children and Buffy the dog.

'Hello, Iain, welcome to my madhouse. I'm ready to go if you are.'

'Terrific, I've booked the restaurant for eight.'

With a last admonishment to Iddin and Shahirah to be good for Karen, the sitter, and kisses and hugs goodnight, we escaped down my garden path and out to his car. As he opened the door and settled me comfortably into his old Mark II Jaguar, I received the distinct impression that he was glancing at me sideways, but I couldn't quite fathom why.

Over dinner at a small French restaurant with an Italian name, Tolarno's, he was intelligent and witty, with an open smile that lit up his entire face and left his eyes warm, happy and approachable. Dinner with Iain was not a disappointment and I found him even more interesting than I had recalled, although I did have to be firm with him when his journalistic instincts turned the conversation into a borderline interrogation about the hints he had gathered from Viv regarding my former marital alliance in Malaysia. That was a topic I deemed firmly out of bounds to all but my closest friends. I found myself laughing continually throughout the meal and enjoyed his extravagant tales and the insane character voices he delivered with great gusto – it was like having the entire Goons ensemble at the table.

On the drive back to my home his old car began to splutter and cough until finally, at the top of my street, it wheezed, heaved a little and refused to budge any further. So much for travelling in style. If this was a ploy on his part to stay overnight he was about to get a very rude awakening. I reminded Iain that his car breaking down wasn't terribly original, but he laughed and assured me earnestly that he was always having trouble with his old Jag and had only driven it that night to impress me. As we walked the remaining hundred yards or so back to my house, the mystery of his earlier sidelong glances was resolved.

'When you opened the front door tonight . . .'

'Yes?'

'Well, I didn't recognise you. You looked so different. I mean, it didn't look like you.'

'You mean I was dressed up, had my make-up on and looked halfway presentable?' I teased.

'Yes, er, I mean no, well, yes. I don't know, you looked different to how I remembered you,' he stated, trying desperately to get himself out of the tangle from which I took great delight in offering no escape. 'You just looked so beautiful,' he continued. 'I didn't realise you were beautiful until I saw you again tonight.'

'Then why exactly did you ask me out tonight?' I

asked, holding my breath and hoping for the ideal answer.

'Because I really liked you and enjoyed talking to you and I thought you were very interesting. But I had no idea you were attractive, er, I mean . . .'

'I know what you mean,' I interrupted, taking pity on him. 'I had no make-up on, one bloodshot eye because of an accident with my contact lenses that morning, and I was dressed to help Viv move house. But you still rang,' I smiled up at him.

'Yes, I did. And it was an extremely wise move on my part.'

'Yes, it was,' I replied. 'It certainly was.'

We went out every night that week and spent every spare hour during the day together. Time was limited as Iain was due to leave for China that coming Friday and although he would only be away for ten days the prospect of our separating so soon after meeting contributed to the sense of urgency we both felt. Ludicrously he rang me twice a day from Beijing, running up a telephone bill of hundreds of pounds as we spoke for hours at a time, reassuring me that the speed at which we were hurtling towards some form of relationship was neither ridiculous nor insane, even for a cynical and jaded old journalist like him, as he kept referring to himself.

Finally, there he was, striding out through the airport doors and smiling at me a little uncertainly. Watching how his face lit up when he saw me banished from my mind all the reservations I had about what we were both getting into. He was home and we would take things from there.

Our children hit it off immediately. Iain had three children from previous marriages: Skye, eleven, Tyson, seventeen, and Drew, fifteen. Frighteningly, it was the three youngest of our children who first broached the subject of marriage. After huddling together in Skye's bedroom, they emerged to announce: 'When we are all married, we'll need a bigger house.' They had also worked out how we would not only merge two families but blend our menagerie of pets as well. Iain always maintains that I asked him to marry me, but I maintain that we asked each other and both said 'yes'.

We were married five months later in a beautiful church ceremony, surrounded by our children and friends. Uncle Eric gave me away and Skye, Shahirah and my friend Wai Lin acted as my bridesmaids, with Susan Cole organising a sedate bridal shower. Susan refused to stand as bridesmaid on the grounds that she was six foot two, I was a good foot shorter and the photographs would look ridiculous. I wore an ivory silk and lace dress with elbow-length sleeves and a low scalloped neckline. My veil was a length of simple lace held in place by a band of pearls. I carried a bouquet of gardenias, tuberoses and yellow roses; the girls wore dresses of ivory lace, with Skye and Shahirah wearing Iain's clan tartan over one shoulder. Instead of bouquets they had wrist corsages. Iain wore a full kilt in deference to his Scottish heritage with Iddin insisting on wearing one as well. Acting as best men were Iain's sons, Tyson and Drew.

After Iain and I had made our wedding vows to each other it was the children's turn. They had organised amongst themselves to say their own vows, taking each other as brothers and sisters. They had been adamant about us all becoming a united family and this was reflected in no uncertain terms by this very public statement. The church ceremony was followed by a relaxed and informal party at our new home with our respective grandmothers, friends and a Scottish piper complete with kilt. It was, and still remains, one of the happiest days of my entire life, full of laughter, tears, dancing and excited and glowing faces. It also held the promise that it was only the beginning, as Iain was continually reminding me.

We settled down to our new life together in a lovely old Victorian home in Hawthorn. It had taken a lot of time and legwork to find a house big enough to accommodate all seven of us. I had been quite adamant that it wasn't fair to cram everyone together in a small space and expect the kids to become an instant family. This way there was plenty of room and everyone from the biggest to the smallest had a space of their own.

I found that I had to learn rapidly to be very organised with so many people to look after. Cooking meals for between seven and sixteen people took a bit of getting used to but I soon got the knack. I tailored my working day around the drop-off and pick-up times of the children's schools and would drive between Shah's kindergarten, Iddin's school and Skye's college at five-minute intervals. In the first few months I was always confused about where I was supposed to be and for what school function – right day, wrong school, or right school, wrong day.

Iddin insisted on using the surname Gillespie when he transferred to Canterbury Primary and Shahirah followed suit. Iain and I were somewhat wary about this notion but Iddin put up such a strong argument about how we were all one family now that we let him decide, emphasising, however, that Bahrin was and always would be his real father.

Our new life rolled on, full of children, family and each other. Weekends and holidays we spent at Iain's fifty-acre farm property in South Gippsland. His mother and stepfather lived there full-time and when our family stayed overnight we used the converted barn, which was only moderately comfortable but which the children loved. They said it was like camping; at least there was running water and a flushing toilet, even though the existence of hot water was dependent on my stoking the wood-burning boiler. The days at the farm were spent swimming in the dam, bushwalking and relaxing. To get around we used small motorbikes. It is an idyllic spot, set high on a hill overlooking the Westernport Bay. A mob of kangaroos has free run of the land and giant goannas (lizards about three feet long) inhabit the trees. A small creek with a bed of white clay winds its way through the lower portion and occasionally there are gemstones to be found in the water.

Iain worked at the Ten Televison Network as an investigative reporter and producer as well as making documentaries. I still taught part-time at the National Theatre Ballet School and kept my hand in with the occasional public relations job and working with Iain.

I seemed to have at last found happiness with a man who was intent on making me laugh almost constantly. Every single day I woke with a smile and looked forward to what the day would bring. Shah and Iddin were growing quickly, contented and well adjusted. They both formed their own special relationships with Iain and opted to call him 'Daddy' of their own volition. Luckily, Skye and I built a really special friendship which developed into her decision to call me 'Mum'. It took a lot of work to find a balance in allowing the relationship to find its own level, but it was worth it. Tyson and Drew lived with us on weekends and holidays and became Iddin's idols. With an age difference of only eight years, Tyson and I became friends as well as family and I consider myself extraordinarily fortunate that our relationship is so good.

Evenings we often spent listening to Iain play his guitar and singing funny songs. Shah and Iain in particular developed their routines to performance perfect. Iain would play and sing 'Mr Froggy went a-courting' and Shah would dance and sing along. Both girls began ballet class at the National Theatre and Iddin joined the cub scouts. He was so keen to become a cub that I had to agree to become a deputy Akela for the pack to make up the supervisory numbers!

At Christmas, birthdays and other milestones, our friends congregated at our home, overflowing from room to room and filling the house with laughter. I enjoyed entertaining and relished any excuse to invite people over. Open house was our traditional Christmas Eve bash for the adults and the children. I would make a wicked egg nog with a kick and the tables would groan under the weight of the food stacked on top. Our first Christmas together as a family saw me volunteer to cook the traditional turkey dinner for eighteen. I learned to be less eager to volunteer after that experience. Dealing with a clan of Scottish in-laws all intent on scoring a turkey leg was more than I could cope with and made me wish for a roasted centipede instead of a two-legged fowl.

In the finer weather we began to cycle in a convoy of bicycles; 20 miles a week we rode, accompanied by the dog, Muckle. Iain made sure that Shah had a special seat on his bike as she was too small to keep up with our pace and none too steady on her own two-wheeler. I can visualise Iddin now as he cycles on ahead a little, turns and shrieks with pleasure as the wind blows his jacket back and the dog runs to keep up. We would carry drinks and snacks to munch along the way as we covered our favourite Melbourne cycling tracks: along the Yarra river to the old Studley Park Boathouse, where we would dismount and hire a rowing boat for an interlude on the river and water fights. Often we were joined by John Udorovic and his children, Nadine and Joshua. We would row our boats until we chose a spot to moor then, withdrawing our water pistols, we'd chase each other through the woods, seeing who would end up the wettest.

I suppose the only thing that in any way marred our perfect life together was the four miscarriages I suffered and the problem of endometriosis. Conceiving wasn't an issue, but I had difficulty bringing a pregnancy to term. I tried to stay optimistic, especially after all the bits and pieces of surgery and the tests, but it was painful coping with the loss, especially as the grieving process was difficult for anyone else to comprehend. Iddin, Shah and Skye were always disappointed when I miscarried, as they all wanted a baby in the family; but until that happened, we would be blissfully content.

Forty-one

I often wonder how many other people in this world can pinpoint the exact moment that their lives were changed irrevocably: smashed, redefined, uncategorised and for ever divorced from the normal comprehension of their peers.

I had known, even before I steeled myself to walk into that hotel at the appointed hour, that its doorway was more than the entrance to a nondescript building – it was the gateway to hell. I caught my reflection in the mirrors that lined the lobby and noted with detached satisfaction that my face appeared calm and gave no indication of the turmoil I was mastering beneath its shell as I walked to the phones and dialled Bahrin's room. No answer, but then I knew that there wouldn't be. They were gone.

If I try to recreate the chronology of events and the feelings of general disquiet leading up to July 1992, I have to remember the telephone call that came from Bahrin in February. His unexpected contact with the children around Iddin's birthday was not what triggered the uneasy sense that all was not as it seemed; rather it was something about the nature of the call itself that had me pondering its origin for hours afterwards. In the rush of receiving what I assumed to be an expensive international call, I had hurried the children to the telephone. It was only later that I realised that the normal international 'pips' had not sounded when I picked up the receiver. I had instead heard the distinctive 'beep, beep, beep' signalling connection of a long-distance call within Australia. When I mentioned this strange anomaly to Iain and a couple of friends they assured me that I must have been mistaken or had confused the international call sign with the Australian one. I wasn't entirely convinced, but I opted to go with the general consensus as it was the easiest course to take and the least likely to prompt raised eyebrows and insinuations about overprotectiveness or jokes about paranoia.

To write this portion of my story is to verbalise the scenes, nightmares and ineptitudes that have coloured my life for the interminable months gone by. 'If only I had . . .' is the phrase that I scourge myself with throughout every waking and sleeping moment that I draw breath. If only I had what? If only I had listened to my gut instincts, if only I hadn't listened to other people, if only I hadn't wanted to behave like a mature adult, if only I had listened to Iddin and Shah and taken heed of their wishes. But I didn't, and hindsight and 'what ifs' won't change any of our lives now.

Recuperating following yet another miscarriage, this time of twins, I had resumed work at the television network and at the radio station but the effort left me drained and depressed. I had vowed that July would be the month for everything to return to normal, starting with our traditional birthday bashes for Shahirah's seventh birthday and my own. After the forthcoming term break I would surprise Iddin with the saxophone lessons he'd been hankering after and Shah and I would begin the construction of a prefabricated doll's house I had ordered. All the children in the family would be back in school and life would settle down to its regular schedule of parents' committees, ballet classes and long bike rides.

Bahrin telephoned after a silence of several months to confirm the details for his impending visit the following week. It did strike me as strange that he telephoned during the school day to speak ostensibly with Iddin when he knew that both children would be at school. But, as his tone was more than conciliatory and his voice devoid of its usual belligerence, I did my best to be friendly. He was so charming, in fact, that I wondered why. When I reminded him that the children were never home at that time he settled down to have a long chat with me, commiserating over the recent loss of our babies, hoping that I was keeping well and politely enquiring after the health of my nanna. It was only later that I realised that I had never told him about any of my recent pregnancies or miscarriages. Then he began to do an astounding backflip in attitude, one that I had always hoped for but never expected to hear.

'Look, Yasmin – sorry, Jacqueline – this time when I come to see the children, I'd like it if things could be more friendly between the two of us. For the sake of the children we should let bygones be bygones and concentrate on making them happy. What do you think?'

I was stunned. Not only could I not equate the cordial voice I was hearing with Bahrin, I was too dumbfounded at first to mumble more than assenting sounds.

'That's all I ever wanted, Bahrin,' I replied. 'I just want to make things easy for Iddin and Shah, and so does Iain.'

'Fine, then, I'll see you next week. Please send my best to Iain and your nanna. Bye,' and the line went dead.

That left me sitting bemused and off balance, staring at the receiver I still held in my hand and wondering if, after all those years of backbiting, threats and abuse, Bahrin had finally grown up.

To try to make sense of this turn of events, I rang Iain at his office and Lillian at hers and repeated verbatim what had just passed. Iain was very pleased, telling me to take it as a sign that Bahrin had finally accepted what was best for the children and was behaving rationally and maturely for once. Lillian's reaction was identical to Iain's and she dismissed my 'what's his angle?' question with an impatient groan. For some intangible reason, the hairs on my neck were standing on end and my stomach felt queer long after I had replaced the telephone onto its cradle. But at that point in time it was the least of my worries: I had a seventh birthday party to organise and fifteen children to transport to the Plaster Fun House, where Shah had decided to hold her celebration. Her present from Iain and me was a much-wanted Minnie Mouse doll that she had not so discreetly angled for over a number of months; just seeing her face as she opened her present that morning confirmed that we couldn't have chosen anything better. Long after that day had passed I could remember with relief that I was able to give Shah the type of party that she wanted and could be thankful that I had encouraged Iddin to bring along his two closest friends to be his companions.

Sunday, 5 July 1992 was a good day, a happy day, a day when all of our closest friends and family descended on our house for my birthday. They stayed until the evening, laughing and joking, as hordes of unruly and excited children played hide-and-seek and chase through the house and around the garden as the sun went down. At this new milestone I was finally happy, safe and looking forward to many more birthdays like this one: children and friends everywhere, a blossoming career, a caring husband and the hope of a new baby at some stage to anchor us all even more firmly together. The only thing that marred the thought of the following day was the impending arrival of Bahrin and the fact that Iddin and Shah would be spending the night with him at his hotel.

Monday dawned bleak and rainy, the children protesting that they didn't want to go to a hotel and that they'd rather spend their school holiday at the farm with Iain's parents and Skye. Iain lectured Iddin on the positive sides of the impending access period and also forbade him to write our telephone number on his leg in felt pen as he had secretly been doing for a couple of years. Iain told him that it wasn't necessary, that there was no danger from Bahrin and that it was going to be a wonderful treat for Shah and him to stay with their father at the hotel. Iddin's face showed how dubious he was about this advice.

Their father arrived in the middle of the afternoon to collect them. Studiously cordial and polite, he turned down Iain's offer of coffee and requested the use of a telephone to book a taxi for the return trip to his hotel. Shahirah began to complain in a loud voice that she didn't want to go with Abah, and Iddin echoed her sentiments as Bahrin stood poised by the kitchen bench with the telephone receiver clenched in one hand. I noticed the whiteness of his knuckles and the stiffness of his neck, a sure sign of his displeasure and of the undercurrent of tension that ran beneath his blank face. I put his reactions down to the fact that our dog, Muckle, was sniffing around his ankles, having earlier greeted him with growls and furious barking. Bahrin loathed dogs and had always been intimidated by their presence at close proximity. I took secret delight at his discomfort and hoped that he noted our children's love of their pet and their nonchalance when around her. To me it illustrated just how different from him, how normal and natural, they were. Animals had always figured in our family life – cows, rabbits, dogs, cats, horses and kangaroos – and neither of them could ever abide a 'sook' around the creatures they loved. Looking back now, I truly think that Muckle had the measure of the situation and kick myself for restraining her when she nuzzled in the general direction of Bahrin's crotch. I wish she had taken a piece out of him then and there or had leapt straight at his jugular. Instead, I ordered her to sit and drop on her belly at my feet, where she continued to eye my ex-husband balefully and follow his slightest movement with great intensity.

In the new spirit of cooperation that both Bahrin and I were exuding, I persuaded him to let me drive them back into the city, citing the inconvenience of taxis and the rain, but not daring to voice the opinion that the children's transition from one environment to another might be eased by this show of unity and harmony. So I found myself shepherding Bahrin, Skye, Drew, Iddin and Shah into Arnold, our sturdy red four-wheel drive, for the trip into town. Bahrin and Iain shook hands at our front door and the children kissed him goodbye with Shah, as usual, throwing her arms around his neck and saying in a loud voice, 'Daddy, I love you.' Iddin and Shah were less than enthusiastic about this overnight stay with Bahrin and made no bones about letting their father know it. Shah also insisted on taking Whitey, her white fluffy goat, which had been Iain's first Christmas present, to keep her company at night.

The conversation between Bahrin and me was painfully polite throughout the drive and I found myself groping desperately for some topic or common ground. I had tried the children, their schooling and hobbies, but this subject seemed to hold minimal interest for him so I turned to architecture, pointing out one particular building I thought would interest Bahrin – a beautifully renovated and deconsecrated church which now accommodated a successful advertising agency. His reply, with its venomous contempt, stunned me.

'That's disgusting, only *mat sallehs* would use a holy place as an office.'

I heard my own voice begin to try to justify the restoration, not demolition, of a gracious building, but, realising the futility of this, my comments trailed off and we lapsed into silence, all attempts at conversation abandoned. Mercifully we soon arrived at the hotel and as the rain was pouring down there was a mad scramble of half-mouthed protests from Iddin and Shah, goodbye hugs and kisses and shouted messages between Skye and the children as Bahrin, with an audible sigh of relief, carefully opened his door and alighted. I told the children firmly that they had to stay with Abah and that I would see them again on Wednesday, reminding them that Bahrin and I had agreed that they were allowed to telephone whenever they wanted and to say goodnight. This reminder mollified them somewhat and I quickly jumped back into the car with a wave and kiss blown into the air, leaving them on the footpath beside Bahrin, their father who was little more than a stranger to them.

The front gate clanged shut, announcing Iddin and Shah's homecoming to the accompaniment of frantic barking from Muckle and the ringing of the doorbell. As I swung the heavy white door open, I could hear Shah on the other side crying.

'Mummy, he wouldn't let me bring Whitey home. I can't get to sleep without him,' she sobbed as I took her into my arms. I looked enquiringly over her head at Iddin.

'Abah wouldn't let us bring anything home with us,

he even made us leave our toothbrushes. He said it didn't matter,' Iddin explained.

Quickly I looked towards the gate and saw Bahrin lift his hand in greeting to me as he slid into the back of the waiting taxi. 'Wait,' I yelled in time to catch the car before it drove away.

Leaving the children standing on the verandah, I ran to the gate.

'Why didn't you let her bring her goat home? She can't get to sleep without him.'

'She doesn't need it.'

'But I told you about her, how . . .'

Before I could go on he interrupted me, clearly trying hard to control his anger. 'Look, I don't care, Yasmin, it doesn't matter. She can get it when I take them back to the hotel tomorrow.' And with that he slammed the taxi door, effectively cutting off the conversation, and the taxi drove away.

How I wished I could simply cancel the access arrangements then and there, but I didn't dare risk another court battle. At least the children would not be with Bahrin for longer than two nights. And I mentally thanked my foresight for the stipulation that as Iddin and Shahirah were not that familiar with their father, his access was to be broken up throughout the week.

After we went inside, Shah threw herself on her bed sobbing for Whitey and I sat on its edge stroking her hair and trying to convince her that Whitey would be all right for one night alone at the hotel. I told her that we were all having dinner with some of her favourite friends that evening: Rob, Jo and their son Nicholas, who was her own age. Nothing made a difference; she was still sobbing as I closed her bedroom door and went to talk with Iddin. I felt so utterly infuriated with Bahrin: why was he so callous and uncaring? What was so difficult about packing up two small overnight bags and a fluffy goat?

Dinner that night was alternately relaxing and tense. Jo and Rob went out of their way to make this an enjoyable interlude in the midst of a difficult time, but the evening was punctuated with Iddin and Shah using any excuse to tell anyone who would listen that they didn't want to go back to the hotel and Abah. Around 8.30 p.m., just as we were sitting down to port and coffees, Shah announced that she felt tired and wanted to have a lie down until we were ready to go home. Minutes after she had snuggled down in Jo and Rob's bed she began to cry for Whitey. She begged me to drive to the hotel and collect him; she said that she never wanted to go back there and she asked Iain and me not to send her back with her father the next day. She kept crying until her nose was running and her shoulders heaved with sobs as I rocked her in my lap. Iddin edged into the room with Nicholas, who was carrying a small white teddy. 'Here, Shah,' said Nicholas, 'this is my favourite teddy. Maybe he'll make you feel better.' He pressed the small bear into Shah's hands.

'Thank you,' she said, her bottom lip wobbling as she struggled to catch her breath.

During the drive home that night, Shah dozed next to her brother in the back seat as Iain and I talked in quiet tones about the children and Bahrin.

'Don't worry,' Iain told me. 'He'll be gone by next week and it will all be over until next year.'

'But I don't want to go back tomorrow,' came Iddin's voice from the rear of the car. We had assumed that he, like his sister, was asleep until his comment came from behind. 'It's so boring there and he doesn't understand anything about anything and there's nothing to do there. He's trying to suck up to us with presents and toys and stuff. I want to be with Skye at Nanna's land for the holidays.'

'Look,' Iain told him, 'it's only for a few more days. Just try to have a good time and we'll go down to the land next weekend to see Nanna. It's not like these are the only holidays you're going to have to go and visit Nanna and Grandad.'

Forty-two

Thursday, 9 July 1992

After the phone call came at 5.10 a.m. telling me that Kelvin was dead, I lay beside Iain and watched the night change into a grey day. It hadn't felt real hearing that Kelvin was gone; after all, the children and I had been to see him only the day before. Shah had drawn him a picture of a unicorn and brought it with her; she had kissed him gently on the forehead as she laid it on his bed and walked quietly from the room. Iddin and Shah had both known that Kelvin was dying from AIDS and that he was getting weaker by the hour but they had insisted on following me upstairs when I went to check on him. I myself had kissed him goodbye as he slept, tiptoeing from the room not knowing that it would be the last time I would see him. I was glad that he had died in his own home, surrounded and cared for by a roster of his close friends and visited by a constant stream of former students, colleagues and ballet partners. He had his dignity and he had love; those were the most important things to him.

Kelvin Coe was a former principal dancer with the Australian Ballet and an internationally respected artist and ballet master. We'd been nothing more than casual acquaintances during my ballet years; Kelvin was a virtuoso performer, a much more senior dancer than I was, and someone whom I'd worshipped from afar for many years when I was growing up. Even when we were teaching at the same school and sharing the same friends, I was too much in awe to do anyting more than take his direction in pas de deux class and mumble affirmative replies. More recently, though, I had become very close to both Kelvin and his partner Stuart when I had profiled their relationship in a special television report. I had joined Kel's care team and ferried casseroles and chocolate cakes from my kitchen to theirs; so when the phone rang again some time after 7 a.m. I knew what it would be. I was being called into work to put together his obituary for the evening news, just as I had promised him all those months ago. It was rare for me to work flat out when the children were on holiday. My job with the radio programme and the special reports I did for television were tailored around the children's school hours and allowed me the flexibility of being able to drop them off and collect them from school every day, which was just as important to Iddin, Shah and Skye as it was to me. This one time would be an exception and I knew they would accept it as the right thing for me to do.

I was already up and dressed when the children arrived at the breakfast table. They took the news of Kelvin's death with sadness and understanding and Iddin's comment was particularly insightful: 'At least he won't be so sick and hurting any more. He didn't look happy for a long time, Mum.' I kissed his head in agreement and gave him a hug.

The film crew arrived at the house to collect me at 11.30 a.m. amidst the children's protests about the second instalment of access time with their father. I remember being very firm with them both and explaining in no uncertain terms that they did have to go and that I would be speaking to them by telephone throughout the day and to say goodnight before they went to sleep. After kissing and hugging everyone goodbye, I turned to Iain, promising to ring home during the day to see how everything was going. Iain would be staying home to be with Iddin and Shah and to effect the official handover when Bahrin arrived at 5 p.m. that afternoon. We always covered each other; our work usually enabled one of us to be home for the children and we juggled our respective schedules to accommodate the hiccups of family life. 'It'll be all right, Jack,' he told me reassuringly, with a concerned smile. 'The kids and I will have some fun together and Elizabeth [our housekeeper] and I will get their bags ready and packed for when he comes.'

Turning to wave one last time before I drove off with the crew, I saw my family standing on the front verandah blowing kisses and clowning around for my benefit by pulling funny faces. And then I gave full attention to the questions I would ask at my first interview that day.

I checked in with the children around 4 p.m. and told them that I loved them 'billions, trillions and infinities' and that I would speak to them later that night at the hotel. I will always remember that Iddin asked me one last time for a reprieve from the impending visit with his father and that I, in the midst of editing problems and the rush to have my story on Kelvin completed for the five o'clock news, cut him short with a definite 'no'.

'All right, Mum,' Iddin dragged out in a resigned tone and with a heavy sigh. 'I love you. Here's Shah.'

'Hello, Mummy, I love you, love you, love you. Bye bye, bye bye,' she sang down the phone.

That was the last time I spoke to my children.

* * *

I arrived home quite late that evening, thoroughly depressed and exhausted. Iain had organised dinner for us both and reiterated that the children had been collected exactly on time by their father. I missed the children's presence that night; somehow their happy voices and sticky fingers would have helped to reaffirm the positive sides of life after having dealt with death and bereavement all day. I suppose most of all I wanted to tell them how much I loved them. So it was with this thought in mind that I reached for the telephone and dialled the number of the Victoria Hotel, where Bahrin and the children were staying.

For the next seventy-two hours I tried at regular intervals to contact Iddin and Shah by telephone. The first call I made was answered by Bahrin at his hotel. He refused to allow me to speak to either of the children, telling me firmly that both were asleep and that they would call me in the morning. I waited all of Friday for their call but it never came. I tried to turn my mind to the weekend radio show I was meant to be preparing but I couldn't seem to keep a focused train of thought. By evening I began to telephone their room at hourly intervals, comforting myself by rationalising the situation, telling myself that they were off on a day trip to the zoo or somewhere and that they would be back in their room soon – but with little conviction and all the while driven by this strange and prickly sense of urgency. I left message after message at the hotel reception until the operator there began to recognise my voice.

Saturday was worse. Iain and I had to complete all the pre-production work for the weekly radio programme but I found that I was unable to focus on the tasks at hand. I found it even harder to refrain from charging straight over to the hotel and sitting there until Bahrin and the children returned. If I intruded on the scheduled access time that I had voluntarily agreed upon, I risked sanctioning from the Family Court of Australia and a resumption of the hostilities between Bahrin and me. I also knew that it would be ludicrous to seek the assistance of the Australian Federal Police (the equivalent of the US Marshals' Department and the FBI, but vastly understaffed and grossly under-resourced) until there was tangible evidence that something was amiss. By 5 p.m. my hand gravitated towards the telephone and I was again ringing on the hour, leaving what had degenerated into perfunctory messages with the hotel telephonist. Each time she heard my voice she would kindly assure me that none of the staff had seen Iddin and Shahirah enter or leave since my last call but that she would pass on my message when she did.

My stomach was a ball of knots, my rib cage constricted my lungs like an iron corset and all I could do was pray that the worst possible scenario, the one that kept running through my mind, was an overreaction. Iain tried hard to calm my fears and reminded me that Bahrin and the children were probably out somewhere having a terrific time; but his reassurances did little to convince me or quell my uneasiness.

'Everything's OK, everything will be OK,' I stressed to myself over and over again to stem the rising panic I felt. 'He couldn't have done it, not after all this time, he couldn't have,' I reasoned. Kidnap after seven years was ridiculous, insane, far-fetched – but deep down inside, in the very core of my being, I knew that was exactly what Bahrin had done, even though I refused to verbalise what I knew was true.

By 8 p.m. I began to wonder if my behaviour was becoming irrational. I put myself on a strict quota of one phone call to the hotel every half-hour. I only hoped that the staff there wouldn't become exasperated with this frequency and cut off my only tangible pinpoint on the children's location. Nine o'clock arrived without any indication that my messages had been received. Every fibre in my body told me that something was seriously wrong. I couldn't wait for the access period to expire at 12.30 p.m. the next day, I had to do something, so I rang the Family Law Squad of the Australian Federal Police. The officer I spoke to understood my distress and agreed that the situation as it stood did point to something suspicious but his explanation about procedures and the need for tangible evidence of the children's disappearance was nothing more than I had expected. There was little more I could do but wait until the official expiry of the agreed deadline for Iddin and Shah's return. Prior to that, all the officer could do was make an unofficial note of my call and concerns and hope for the best.

Minutes ticked by like hours and by the time the clock showed 11 p.m. I knew that I had to try to enlist the help of the hotel staff. The duty manager understood immediately the seriousness of the situation and told me to wait by the phone; he would call me back after checking with his staff. In fact, he did more than that – when his call finally came he painted an ominous picture that left me climbing the walls in despair. The adjoining rooms shared by Bahrin and the children had not been slept in for two nights, nor had any of his staff seen them come or go since Thursday night. Only the luggage and toys that peppered the rooms made me clutch at the hope that it was all a huge misunderstanding and that Bahrin was merely attempting to twist the knife. I thanked the hotel manager profusely for his help and put down the phone, steeling myself for the longest wait of my life: thirteen and a half hours before I would know the truth. My emotional control was almost non-existent by this stage;

it was everything I could do not to lash out at Iain when he continually assured me that I would see the children the next day and that I was getting far too overwrought about the whole thing. But I knew. It was as if Iddin and Shah had a pulse beat within my body that I had never recognised before and that pulse was weakening, leaving me with a dull ache and a feeling that my soul was teetering on the brink of a precipice.

Sunday, 12 July 1992
Somehow I got through the radio programme the next day, glancing at the clock continually, willing its hands to reach 12 noon and signal my release. Iain and I then drove directly to the Victoria Hotel to collect the children. We were fifteen minutes early, so Iain insisted that we wait in the car until the designated time. We were playing this game of Bahrin's strictly by the book. As we sat together outside the hotel, rain began to drizzle down the car windows, falling in murky puddles on the street. Laughing people strolled beneath hastily unfurled umbrellas and the aroma of freshly made coffee filtered through the car from the Italian café nearby. Finally 12.30 p.m. came round, signalling it was time for me to confront my greatest fear. Iain squeezed my hand reassuringly before I swung open the hotel's door and placed one foot in front of the other to get me to the bank of house phones at the reception desk. Before lifting the receiver, I mumbled a tangle of words. I prayed that I was wrong or that I would spin around and catch sight of Iddin and Shah running towards me across the foyer: anything but my worst fear.

I dialled. No reply. I tried again in case I had misdialled, even though I knew I hadn't – anything to avoid the inevitable. Careful to keep my tone even and squashing the hysterical note that broke through my voice, I turned away from the phones and made a request to see the duty manager. She immediately swung into action, leading me towards the elevators and speaking rapidly about security, privacy and legalities. Her words tangled in my mind. I found myself nodding dumbly in acknowledgement of whatever she had just said. At this point I would have colluded with the devil just to get some information about Iddin and Shah. Eventually, after scurrying down a dimly lit corridor, we stood before the door that held my children's future behind it.

'Remember, you have to agree not to touch anything, Mrs Gillespie,' she admonished as the key was inserted in the lock and the door swung open. Behind her the room was deserted but the scene presented something more haunting and terrifying to me than any scene from a horror film. I looked down, only dimly aware that I was treading on more than a dozen messages from me that had been slipped beneath the door during the preceding twenty-four hours. The first room was obviously Bahrin's. A suitcase lay open on the floor to the right, its contents spilling out. The bed hadn't been slept in – a bad sign. Continuing through the communicating door to the adjoining room, I noticed that Bahrin had finally given Shah her own bed, except that that too was empty, as was Iddin's. In this room I could almost imagine that the echoes of the children's voices still hung in the air. Balloons and streamers hung from the central light fixture, a piece of glossy gift-wrap paper was affixed to the wall and a giant birthday card hung crookedly beside it.

My gut twisted as I realised that the room had been left by Bahrin for me to find, its messages clear only to me. Atop Shah's bed sat Whitey and Minnie Mouse, silent witnesses to what had transpired there. Near the foot of the bed lay Shah's red cloche hat, the one that we had chosen together weeks earlier to match her new winter coat, but it was what Bahrin had done to the hat that made my stomach heave and the room begin to rock: the small, bright object had been crushed and twisted in such a rage of vindictiveness that it was irreparably destroyed. Iddin's pride and joy, his oversized Reebok sports shoes, the ones that he had nagged me for months and months to buy, stood pigeon-toed and discarded by the bureau, his baseball cap flung on the bed as if he had just tossed it there. Time stood still in this cheap hotel room. It was a vacuum created by a twisted mind bent on the ultimate revenge. The scene brought to mind the ghost ship *Marie Celeste*, deserted mid-ocean, meals half-eaten and the radio on full blast. Only this was not the Bermuda Triangle and this was no unexplained mystery to titillate the tabloid press: it involved my babies and they were gone.

I stumbled from the room and managed to rejoin Iain in the lobby. I blurted out what I had seen upstairs, holding back the sobs that were rising in the back of my throat and fighting to keep control so I could summon the only help that was available, the only chance that my children had.

There followed a whirlwind of fear and anxiety. The next minutes, hours and days flashed by in a jumble of despair, anger, rage, hopelessness and battle that suffocated me in their intensity and remained with me in every millisecond of my existence. A frantic phone call to the Federal Police from the lobby of the hotel, a barely coherent conversation with Lillian Webb and garbled messages left for John Udorovic alerting him to what had happened, and a hastily arranged formal interview at Federal Police Headquarters.

Questions, questions and more questions. The officers from the Family Law Squad were kind and to the point as I struggled to remain coherent against the catch in my throat that rose every time I spoke Iddin and Shah's names. Details were requested and given:

ages, birthdates, clothing, possible destinations. I spewed forth all these answers with machine-like rapidity. Anything, anything to raise the chances that my children would be found. Although I volunteered much, no one asked me about their weight and height. And then came the request that brought the reality of the situation home to me, that made me realise that this whole experience was indeed real and not some disjointed dream from which I would soon wake: one of the officers asked if I had a recent photograph of Iddin and Shahirah to put out on the police alert computer and all points of exit from Australia. I groped for my handbag and rifled through its contents, searching for my wallet. Only days before I had inserted Iddin, Shah and Skye's new school photographs into the plastic window reserved for maternal pride. Only the day before I had flipped my purse open to proudly display how much the three children had grown, and now I was fumbling as I withdrew their faces and handed my babies over to the policewoman, a stranger. From just a single frozen moment in time, how could a stranger comprehend that these children were living, breathing human beings? 'These are my babies,' I wanted to scream. 'Please find them, help them, bring them home.'

I fought the urge to grab the officer's sleeve and demand that she listen to me. I wanted to tell her about the children, about their personalities, their likes and dislikes, about how terrified they'd be feeling in the midst of all this mess; but I correctly gauged that the officers weren't interested in my histrionics and that I had to keep myself under control. When the tears did come I quickly curbed my desire to dissolve into a blissful sobbing escape. I knew that there would be many more questions I would need to answer coherently and I knew that I had to keep myself together for the children's sake. They were counting on me; they would know that I would move heaven and earth to find them. I couldn't let them down; I had to hold on. I had to try to stay one step ahead of Bahrin's thinking.

When finally I had exhausted all the answers I could give the police, Iain led me from the building and out into the cold, grey Melbourne street just as my stomach began to heave. I lurched towards a marble pillar and began to dry retch, wave after wave of nausea engulfing me until I felt as if my stomach had been turned inside out, until my body began to shake uncontrollably. Iain half-dragged, half-carried me to our car and bundled me into the front seat for the journey home to an empty house.

It took ages to locate John Udorovic that Sunday. It seemed as if I spent hours by the phone, my fingers dialling and redialling his numbers until one of my messages found him and he telephoned our home. A line of action was quickly decided upon once he contacted us. We needed to obtain a warrant for Bahrin's arrest and the return of Iddin and Shah and, more importantly, it was urgent that I receive formal permission from the Australian Family Court to publicise the children's kidnap in the hope that someone somewhere had a vital clue about their whereabouts and would come forward with the information. Under the privacy provisions of the Family Court of Australia, no parties to an action or details of a case may be disclosed in the media without a publication order under section 121 of the Family Law Act.

Rick Willis, our former business partner, arrived sometime mid-evening. He had answered Iain's call and had come to help. Between them, John, Rick and Iain planned a three-pronged attack to try to prevent Bahrin leaving the country. John contacted the registrar of the Family Court to organise an immediate hearing before a judge as a matter of urgency. This was eventually obtained during an 'in-chambers' session late that night, conducted in the Family Court building in the presence of the registrar, with the judge at home several miles away making orders via speaker phone.

The first set of warrants obtained were very specific in wording: they ordered that officers of Australian Federal Police and all police forces of Australia search for Iddin and Shah, and that they search all vessels, ships and planes for the children and to use force, if required, to take custody of the children and return them to me, their legal custodian.

I waited at home with John's two teenage children, Nadine and Joshua, watching over me with great intensity and care. It was an agonising time. I kept glancing at the telephone, willing it to ring, hoping that at any moment the children's voices would come down the line and into my ear. I did nonsensical things to fill the oppressive silence in the house; I prayed that the whole thing was a misunderstanding. I couldn't sit still, I couldn't cry either. I tried to fill the hours by cooking one of the Iddin and Shah's favourite meals of fruit and veal curry. I made two huge steaming pots of it. I tried to believe that we would all be sitting down together as a family the next evening and laughing about this ridiculous kerfuffle as we ate our meal. This meal was later eaten by the scores of police, helpers and journalists who filled the house the next day. I cleaned the bathroom and walked the dog up and down the hallway, but none of it really helped; nothing could erase the growing reality of what was happening to our lives.

At 10.30 p.m., finally armed with the necessary court documents allowing publication and identification of myself and the children in the media, Iain and Rick burst into the two major newspaper offices in the city and laid before the respective news chiefs our private life stripped bare. It was hoped that all the attendant publicity would aid in the search. I, in turn, telephoned the acting news director of my own television network to beg for help and to let him know what would be splashed across the daily papers the next morning. I raised him at home, dragging him from his comfortable bed; when I told him that Iddin and Shah had been kidnapped by their biological father, he laughed at me. Obviously interpreting what I had blurted out as a joke, he said, 'Yeah, yeah, sure, Jack,' and put down the phone.

Associated Press were notified as well, flashing the news by telex across the nation in order to cover the broadest possible area. I knew that we had to get the children's faces and names plastered across every paper, television screen and radio wave possible – that would be our only chance of finding them before Bahrin managed to spirit them out of Australia. I prayed with every fibre in my body that we weren't too late.

Joshua and Nadine had fallen asleep on the couch by the time I had finished my phone calls. For one brief split second I would have given anything for their sleeping forms to be replaced by the compact ones of Iddin and Shah, praying: 'Dear God, where are they, what are they thinking, are they safe?' But no answer came. My close friend Deb arrived within minutes of my call. She was to hover and help for many hours that night as I alternately retched or rocked.

The sobbing noise came to me from the direction of the family room at the back of the house. Raw, ragged and barely controlled, I opened the door slowly to find Iain leaning on Deb's shoulder, crying and whispering hoarsely to her. 'She'll never be the same after this, she'll change, Deb. What am I going to do for her? She'll turn hard and bitter and she won't be the Jack that I love so much, I . . .' Iain hurriedly pushed Deb away as he became aware of my presence behind him. He rose from the sofa, threw himself towards the bathroom and closed the door, avoiding all eye contact with me as he did so. I looked to Deb for some explanation but all she did was hug me and say, 'He blames himself and now he's overwrought with worry for you and the children.'

Sliding back the bathroom door, I joined Iain in the room where only days ago I had bundled four squirming children, Iddin, Shah and their cousins Allison and Kira, into the bath, soaking and scraping off the remnants of birthday cake, paint and glue, evidence of a happy day spent partying as a family. I struggled to bring my eyes back to Iain. I murmured something like, 'Tell me it'll be all right,' and moved a step closer to him. As I did so Iain turned and grabbed me by the shoulders, talking determinedly all the while. He could have been talking to a stranger for all the recognition of my identity I saw in his eyes.

'I'll show you what I'll do if I get my hands on him. I'll shake him till his head snaps off.'

'Stop it, darling, you're hurting me. Iain!' I gasped as my head was thrown back and forth like a rag doll's. Releasing me immediately with a curse of recognition, he spun rapidly and punched the left wall of the bathroom and then the right, leaving two gaping holes in the plasterboard which were like mouths open in a silent scream. Then he began to apologise, rocking me in his arms – but I couldn't banish the image of a triumphant and smirking Bahrin from my mind as I pressed my head into Iain's chest.

We lay in our bed that night for an hour, barely touching, two shell-shocked people too afraid to say anything else lest we fall into the pit of despair that we both teetered on.

I was numb all over on the outside and terribly cold, the type of cold that cuts through your bones and makes them ache. Every few minutes I ran to the bathroom to retch up the bile left in my stomach. All food had long since been disposed of either by this non-stop vomiting or the diarrhoea that had gripped my stomach with monotonous regularity. The world had changed, nothing balanced any more, and somewhere out there Iddin and Shah were terrified of what tomorrow would bring. What would Bahrin do when Shah demanded her Whitey goat? Would Iddin manage to get to a telephone? Had they eaten? Who was comforting them when they cried for me, or were they being hit to make them stop crying? Were they warm enough? Shah had a bad rash that needed cream – had Bahrin even cared or remembered? Where, oh God, where were they? The questions went on and on in my head, as did my fears for them. I curled myself up into a foetal position and imagined every angle of their faces, every smile, every hair, how it grew around their hairlines and how good their arms felt around my neck. When would I feel them again? When could I tell them that it was all over and that nothing and nobody would hurt them again? But, most of all, when would I be able to rock them in my arms and tell them how very much I loved them? When?

Monday, 13 July 1992

I was strangely relieved when the telephone rang at 5.30 a.m. Sleep had eluded me entirely during the hour I had spent in bed. I'd lain rigid, willing my mind to fathom Bahrin's next move and tormented by fears for the children. The ringing of the phone gave me an excuse to get up. Anything was preferable to remaining inert and sick with worry. The call was from the media with a request for an interview, the first one of the thousands that were to engulf us for the next days, weeks and months. News of what had happened to our family was plastered on the front page of the Monday morning newspapers. HUNT FOR PRINCE, CHILDREN; KIDNAP AUSSIE KIDS and POLICE TOLD TO FIND CHILDREN were the headlines, accompanied by copies of Iddin and Shah's school photographs. I had never before allowed Iddin and Shahirah to be identified publicly as members of the Malaysian royal family; I had always shielded them from the media and never used their titles openly. Privacy was a very precious element in their lives and one which I felt was intrinsic to their being able to grow up as normal children with a good set of values, undisturbed by media intrusion. However, now all that was about to go out of the window, our anonymity would be no more and my children's heritage would make them objects of curiosity. It all seemed so surreal to me. It was other people's children who disappeared, people with whom I commiserated from afar and for whom I felt concern – not mine. Within twelve hours I had gone from reporting the news to being the news and it was a side of the camera that I did not relish at all.

I steeled myself the best I could before the first television crew arrived at 7 a.m., dragging cables, lights, monitors and microphones into our home and setting up a large broadcast van on the street outside, topped by a satellite dish and television logo. Nausea still controlled my stomach, leaving me no choice but to continually run to the bathroom. I fought very hard to halt the shaking that had gripped my hands since reality had hit me; my right hand was the worst, jiggling so much that I was unable to hold a glass without guiding it to my mouth with the support of my left. I was a mess, but it was a luxury I could ill afford. Self-pity and a complete collapse weren't going to help me get my children back. I needed to fight, I told myself. I had no choice other than dissolving into a puddle of tears and giving up then and there. So I did the only thing that my soggy brain could think of: I resolved to pretend as much as was practical that the media barrage I was about to face was part of my job, that it was work and that my 'job' was to get a message out there about my children, to reach people I had never known before and to ask strangers for help. I think my attitude initially threw the various media off balance. Here was a 'victim', but the victim was known to them already; she worked in the industry and she knew how to fasten her own microphone to her collar and was comfortable in front of a camera. But I had neither the time nor the inclination to bother about how my demeanour affected their perception of me during a time of personal crisis. Iddin and Shah were my only priority and it was imperative that I do my best for them.

I did thirty-six interviews that first day: eight television interviews, radio from all around the country and newspapers as well. The strangest part of it all was the scenario that unfolded that first morning as the TV crews began to trail into the house. Many of the cameramen and their assistants knew me either socially or because I had worked with them in the past. Some of them gave me an encouraging hug or pat before the interviews began. That personal contact, and the sight of familiar faces, made me feel less vulnerable as the questioning started. Over and over again I explained the same details to the various journalists, patiently outlining the history of the case and spelling and respelling my babies' names. I refused to weep on camera and repeatedly begged the viewers, who would eventually watch the reports during their comfortable evening meal, to contact the Federal Police if they had any information about where Iddin and Shahirah could be.

As a result of the kidnap I got to see the uglier side of journalism as well: the cold calculation to come up with a fresh angle, the drive to bring back the emotion-charged picture that would label the story as tragic, and the outright manipulation that one journalist was willing to perpetrate to snatch 'vision' of me weeping uncontrollably in Iain's arms. The man in question used every trick in the book to trigger my tears, phrasing questions in the most dramatic fashion and asking the same thing over and over with a slight variation each time. 'How will you feel if you never see your children again, Jacqueline? Do you blame yourself for not being careful enough? How much do you love your children?' Eventually he had me so distraught that I could feel myself losing control as my throat began to close and a terrible pain overwhelmed my body, a mixture of howling grief and utter despair. I could feel myself drowning in it, unable to go on with the interview. I requested that they switch their camera off, saying that I needed a respite and some privacy, and I was assured earnestly by the journalist that the camera was no longer filming. I succumbed to tears, sobbing wildly as Iain comforted me, blaming myself for listening to others and rambling about how I had forced the children on the access visit and now they were gone. Needless to say, and regardless of the assurances that I had been given, excerpts of that private grief-stricken moment were broadcast nationally that night, laying me open and naked for increased ratings points.

Friends. Friends are what kept me semi-sane throughout this entire nightmare; I will never be able to repay them for their support and understanding, their protectiveness and selflessness. It is amazing, too, how quickly it is that one discovers who one's true friends are. From the moment that they heard the news our real friends were there to support us in every way imaginable. At 8.30 a.m., in the middle of the first press conference, our doorbell rang announcing the arrival of Rob and Sue MacArthur, George Craig accompanied by his daughter Amber, Jo Pearson, Heather Brown and Rob Gell in quick succession. This team of amazing people swept in and took over the phones and the door, made endless cups of coffee, cleaned, cooked, comforted me and stayed with us in what were to become twenty-hour shifts of endurance over the next fourteen days. And they were truly needed. A control centre eventually evolved in our living-room, with four incoming telephone lines, two borrowed mobile phones and a fax machine which whirred and shrieked every few minutes. At the height of the media frenzy surrounding us, one or other of the telephones rang every ninety seconds. It got to the stage where two people were answering the telephones non-stop in shifts of two hours on, two hours off, vetting all incoming calls and taking time-coded messages in detail from all over Australia and the world as the story spread farther and farther. The telephone would begin ringing at 5 a.m. every morning with requests for updates from the late-edition morning papers, radio stations and, depending on the events during the preceding night, live broadcasts from our home for one television network or other during the day. It was utter madness and remained that way until the last phone call came in around midnight. Our stoic group of helpers kept my telephone contact with the media to a minimum, leaving me free for the endless legal conferences and conversations that punctuated each day at unscheduled moments. George cancelled all his work commitments to spend every day for two weeks with us, and when he finally did return to work, his evenings were spent at our home. Sue and Rob forwent their holidays to remain with us and help; Jo spent her mornings answering our phones, cleaning our house, washing floors, providing tureens of soup to feed our swollen establishment and then rushing to the studio in time to read the evening news for Network Ten. Without the support of our true friends I would have turned up my toes and crumbled.

It was also bewildering and sad to discover the phalanx of 'fair-weather' friends and curiosity seekers who purported to be friends but merely arrived to probe voyeuristically. Some of these people we had considered close and intimate friends and it will always remain a point of some distress to me that at a time of great need and emotional turmoil they either disappeared from sight or used the friendship as a means to an end, a meal ticket they could dine off for months, using the details garnered from us direct to pepper their conversations over drinks and hors d'oeuvres.

That first day I didn't eat a thing, drinking only orange juice when it was placed in my hand by someone. I wasn't able to cope with the thought of eating; I could only think about the children. I was desperate for news, anything to ease the total silence that surrounded their whereabouts. I prayed that Bahrin hadn't managed to get them out of Australia and that he was lying low somewhere waiting for his opportunity to flee. Throughout the years that he had come to Melbourne to exercise his right of access to the children, I had remained cautious and distrustful of his motives. I had never forgotten the dramatic oath that he had made about a *jihad* and therefore had always taken the precaution of insisting that he surrender his passport, airline tickets, credit cards and travellers' cheques to my solicitor before seeing the children. This time, however, the routine was varied somewhat at his insistence. My solicitors had been approached in October 1991 by Bahrin's lawyers, suggesting that their client wished to sign over full custody of Iddin and Shahirah to me. This would settle, once and for all, the uncertainties of future litigation and ratify the status quo as it had stood for the past seven years. All he asked in return was two weeks' access per annum, of which I knew he would never avail himself, and a relaxation of the conditions I had placed upon his access to his credit cards and documents. At the time it had seemed like an offer too good to be true, but whenever I voiced my reservations to either Lillian or Iain, I received reprimands such as 'Can't the two of you grow up and work things out?' or 'Don't rock the boat, you're getting nearly everything you want anyway'. I was accused by Bahrin's lawyers of being too severe, too extreme, paranoid and neurotic. For the sake of harmony and balance, I ceased to question and caved in to his demands.

On 1 November 1991, Bahrin signed full custody of the children over to me in the Family Court of Australia by way of court orders made by consent. It was stipulated in the orders that the children be able to telephone me a minimum of once a day during the time they were with their father and that Bahrin's passport be held, not by my solicitor, as in the past, but by his. There had been absolutely no request by Bahrin for anything else to be included in the terms and conditions of access. It had all sounded too good to be true, and it was.

The knock at the door came at 11.55 p.m. on the first day of the kidnap. It caused everyone in the house to freeze in mid-motion, to hold their breath and will the children to be on the other side of that door. Hurling myself at the front door, ignoring all admonishments from Iain to let him answer it, I flung it open wide, only to find a man and a woman brandishing police identifications. They introduced themselves as Sergeant Graham Downs and Constable Fiona Pedersen of the Family Law Squad of the Federal Police. They told me they were the officers assigned to our case and that they needed to run through some details. Upon entering our living-room, which was crowded with concerned friends who had arrived after finishing work, the officers indicated that they wished to speak to us in private and requested that everyone else leave the room. Then, with little preamble, they presented me with a list of phone numbers that Bahrin had dialled from his hotel, along with duplicates of faxes which he had had transmitted from there. I was asked to identify any numbers which appeared familiar to me and to provide further information about Bahrin's Australian friends or business acquaintances. I did the best I could on the sketchy information I had gathered over the years, but they had to remember, I told them, I hadn't been his wife for seven years, so any information I could give them would be woefully outdated. But I told them what I could, mentioning that the Sultan of Terengganu owned a mansion in an exclusive suburb of Perth in the state of Western Australia and that certain members of the family had access to both light aircraft and boats. Having told them this I then asked them if Coastwatch had been alerted to the search. The Sergeant assured me that they had.

Some of the telephone numbers called by Bahrin belonged to various interstate bus companies and country hotels scattered across the state of Victoria. The police viewed these numbers as an attempt by Bahrin to throw them off the scent, to make them think that he had merely decided to extend his holiday with the children in defiance of standing court arrangements. A photocopy of another fax was also shown to me: it was the text of a handwritten letter which was faxed by Bahrin to his solicitors advising them in emotional terms that he intended to take matters into his own hands and would be holidaying with the children until he decided he had had enough. This fax was dated and sent Thursday evening but his firm of solicitors maintained that they didn't receive it until he had already kidnapped the children. I was later to learn from the Attorney General's Department that this was not the case.

The conversation then turned to information volunteered by the public. The police officers assured me that, as a direct result of the media coverage, a valuable public response was still flooding in. I questioned how valuable and asked them if they had any idea where my children were. In reply to my query, Downs and Pedersen adopted a conspiratorial demeanour and spent a number of minutes warning us of the dire consequences should we divulge any of the information they were about to 'share' with us. They stated that they usually worked with victims on a 'need to know' basis and that ordinarily this type of information would not be related to someone like me – the 'victim'. Both Iain and I had to swear to keep what they were about to tell us in inviolate confidence or it was likely that we would never see the children again, they warned. Neither of us had any intention of hindering the police in the search for Iddin and Shah; we both would have done anything to ensure their safety. Finally convinced, and after remonstrating once again that we could tell no one, neither friends nor family, they gave us something to cling to.

I was told that there had been two definite sightings of the children and Bahrin: the first at 8.30 a.m. on the Shepparton Benalla Highway, a major country thoroughfare, where a fellow motorist stopped to give assistance with a flat tyre. The witness told police that the children had been in the back of the car and that they were also accompanied by a six-foot-tall, red-headed man. This man had been aggressive in behaviour and had told the concerned motorist to leave, that they didn't need any help. The second 'positive' sighting was in a toy store in the township of Griffith in the neighbouring state of New South Wales. There, they told me, the children had been hurried from the store and into a car. My hopes rose, of course, and I hugged the possibility that the children hadn't left Australia like a life buoy in a choppy ocean. Nothing would get me to break that confidence.

When I made enquiries about the abandoned hotel room and the children's possessions, the officers told me that the room had been sealed and had been thoroughly looked at by members of the force. With that, and a promise that they would be staying in close contact, the Federal Police officers departed, leaving me with a faint glimmer of hope to nurture.

John Udorovic and his children Joshua and Nadine had arrived earlier in the evening to go over legal details that would need to be put in place for when the children were located. The presence of Josh and Nadine, along with Amber, was a welcome respite for Skye, who had arrived home that afternoon from her grandmother's farm. She was quietly worried about her missing brother and sister and I was concerned that I had nothing much left inside me to give her as comfort; it was all I could do to stop myself screaming and breaking windows as the hours ticked by. I paced and retched and paced and retched. Sleep held no appeal for me and every sound grated on my nerves like fingernails down a blackboard. During the first twenty-four hours of the kidnap I had been offered Valium and various other tranquillisers to calm me down but I had adamantly refused all. I had no desire to go through this nightmare in a drug-induced stupor that would only leave me to deal with the realities and the horrors at another time. I needed to be as clear-headed as possible and as in charge of my faculties as the trauma allowed. I owed that to Shah and Iddin – they were counting on me to bring them home. So I spent another night lying rigidly in bed on the pretence that I was actually attempting to get some sleep.

Eventually I gave up even that and crept down to Iddin's bedroom, collecting Muckle on the way down the hall. I didn't reach for the light switch as there was a direct shaft of moonlight coming through the open drapes. It bounced off the white marble fireplace and spread itself across the foot of Iddin's bed like a splash of fluorescent paint. I huddled on Iddin's quilt with the dog, burrowing my head against Iddin's pillow to catch the scent of him there. I inhaled it deeply and with such longing that I thought my heart would break. I conjured up fleeting images of them both and heard snatches of conversations long gone. Until they came home, this was all that I had and it would have to do.

Tuesday, 14 July 1992

I woke up cold and stiff in Iddin's bed the next morning, my whole body primed to relax from a very bad nightmare. Instead the realisation that this was my new reality gripped me and offered nothing but shaking and the now familiar onset of diarrhoea and retching. As I showered and dressed I was careful to avoid looking at myself in the mirror. Automatically I brushed my hair and cleaned my teeth; the only topic on my mind was what the children were doing at this precise moment. I was just scraping my hair into an elastic band as Iain entered the bathroom behind me. Peering over my shoulder at my reflection in the mirror, he appeared to examine me minutely. 'Put some make-up on, Jack,' he said. 'The public is more supportive of pretty women and more sympathetic.'

'I can't. What does it matter?' I replied, as another wave of nausea began it's ascent from the pit of my stomach.

'It does, trust me, I've been in the media game long enough to know what's needed, and right now pretty is better than plain,' Iain pronounced with such certainty that I didn't dare equivocate. But at every stroke of the make-up brush and every sweep of powder, I was disgusted and numbed – this felt as if it were a secret betrayal of the children. And I railed at the shallowness of a world which apparently demanded victims appear spruced up and photogenically ready in order to garner public support and network coverage.

The day limped into the pattern of phone calls, questions, television crews, photographers and journalists. I dealt with the finite details and answered all media enquiries with the utmost patience; this was our one thread of hope in finding the children.

I jumped when a call from Federal Police came in but it was merely a formality, a courtesy to let us know they were on the job. Our early-morning shift of friends arrived, but I could tell them nothing new. Thank God for friends; their hugs, their silence, their actions were my lifeline. I spent that whole day either giving interviews, answering legal questions or crying, crying until there were no tears left. The waiting was endless and hollow.

At some stage I talked with Tim Watson-Munro, a close friend and forensic psychologist, whose daughter Jessica was Shah's best friend. He tried his best to comfort me but he knew as well as I did the psychological implications something like this has for children and also that the normal platitudes would do nothing to still my fears. Iddin's best friends from school, Mark Maddern and Jack Brown, telephoned to ask if they could help. I didn't know what to say to these young children; I wanted to say something to help them get through the shock and pain they felt for their lost friend but I had very little to offer them.

The telephone didn't stop at all; it seemed as if all the world were clamouring to find a way to help, but it felt as if my two children had suddenly become nothing more than two very small needles in an extremely large haystack. I managed to keep Cadbury Roast Almond chocolate down, and a small orange juice: that was all I could eat. Somehow I remembered to telephone Nanna's nursing home and warned them to keep the news from her until we knew something further and concrete. Why wasn't there any news? I couldn't understand why no one else had seen Iddin and Shahirah or, at the very least, Bahrin. That evening passed the same as the night before. Friends came over to sit with us but it seemed as if we were all infected by the same jumpiness, all waiting for the doorbell to sound or the next telephone call to come in. The telephone eventually ceased ringing at 11 p.m., but I was far too wound up to sleep. Instead, I sat in front of the television until just before dawn, staring blankly at the screen, rerunning my last conversation with Iddin and Shah over and over again in my head.

Wednesday, 15 July 1992

Still no definite news arrived. No one seemed to know with any certainty where the three of them were; I merely went through the motions of existing, hoping and praying that if I continued to talk to the media someone in the general public would remember a small detail that could take us to the children. The lead in Griffith was the one that the police were counting on, but why did the trail end there? Phone calls kept pouring in, sightings, information; so many people were absolutely sure that they'd seen the children or Bahrin. That was what kept all of us going, but how to choose or even begin to sift through such a myriad of detail? With something like ten sightings in the one day in three different states, where did the authorities hope to begin to unravel the tangle? Some of the calls were passed on to me via the television networks, rather than being forwarded on to the police, and I couldn't restrain myself from checking out the more likely ones in person. One man told a television journalist that he had spotted the children at an air show ninety miles from Melbourne, and that they were boarding an aircraft. Another caller phoned to tell the authorities that she had seen the 'prince' travelling in a convoy of BMW cars in the direction of Melbourne International Airport. The children, she said, were dressed in private school uniforms complete with gloves, ties and hats. This one made me laugh at least, particularly at the immediate assumptions some people make when they hear the word 'royalty'. I had to find it funny that people's imaginations are capable of putting a crown on the head of a pauper if they're told he has blue blood. One friend contacted me wanting me to speak to a clairvoyant she knew; at that stage I was not yet desperate enough to do so, but I didn't rule it out entirely.

We were still on every front page around the country; I saw it as our only hope that someone, somewhere would turn Bahrin in. The Federal Police rang to tell me that they were certain that Bahrin and the children hadn't left the country. They were so positive that I believed them without question.

So many things flashed through my mind as I sat inside what had once been our happy family home. Would it ever be again, I asked myself repeatedly. Would Iddin and Shahirah ever bounce through the family room on the way to a refrigerator foray, and would any of us ever recover enough to return to normality?

I decided to telephone Endah, the Sultan's consort, in Terengganu and appeal to her for help.

I replaced the receiver in its cradle with an overwhelming mixture of despair and dread. If Endah, a woman to whom Bahrin owed fealty and respect, knew nothing, what was I to do? What I had heard in her voice was the incredible shock and dismay at Bahrin's very public actions. 'How could he possibly subject the family to this type of publicity with no thought for his uncle's heart condition?' she ruminated aloud. She promised to do what she could but, as she reminded me, she was virtually powerless unless she had the Sultan's support.

Thursday, 16 July 1992

I seemed trapped in what had become my morning routine: arise, vomit, retch, run to the toilet yet again with another bout of diarrhoea, be reminded to put on lipstick, give interviews. The children were so much in my mind that I was incapable of focusing on anything else. Everyone wasted a lot of energy trying to coax me to eat but I simply had no appetite. Friends never stopped ringing and I was far too nervous and jittery to allow anyone to switch on the answering machine, even at night, just in case somehow Iddin or Shahirah managed to contact us. I knew I was irritating Iain by leaping for the phone whenever it rang but I was unable to restrain myself. Every time I heard the phone I'd hold my breath and pray for news of the children before I lifted the receiver. I felt a frantic dependency on the lines of communication into the house and, as irrational as it was, I felt that if I wasn't the one to answer the phone, the children wouldn't ring.

Iain shared my anxieties and deep anger over Bahrin's actions but I had no sage words to comfort him. Perhaps, in all honesty, I had to fight back a desire to say the futile words to Iain: 'I told you so.' This would have served none of us in any way. Iain felt betrayed by Bahrin. Two days before the kidnap, Iain had tried to offer Bahrin the olive branch, commiserating with him about being a non-custodial father and offering him any support to make things easier on the children and him.

There was even a suggestion in the conversation that Bahrin stay with us next time he came to town so that he could understand the children's lives and interact with them on their home ground. Bahrin complained to Iain about the restrictions that were placed on him and about the access period and generally tried to enrol Iain into the males against females club. Afterwards I remember warning Iain not to believe any of the sentiments my ex-husband expressed to him and that he had no idea how truly manipulative Bahrin was. Now he knew.

I wished that I could simply freeze time until the children came home. I hated the sunset that eventually turned into night; it marked off another day not knowing where they were and told me I'd have to go through all this again tomorrow.

At midnight, as I surveyed the city skyline from the living-room window, I looked up and caught the stars in my peripheral vision. I was so furious and depressed at the same time that I didn't know whether to open the front door and run out into the night smashing windows or curl up into a ball and will myself to disintegrate. I found it difficult to comprehend that the Federal Police of the Commonwealth of Australia were really bumbling incompetents. Constable Pedersen had rung earlier that afternoon to inform me that the staff at the Victoria Hotel had packed up Iddin and Shah's belongings. She requested that I go to the hotel to pick them up. But it was something I shied away from; it seemed so final, as though a chapter had been closed tightly, never to be opened again. I asked Tim Watson-Munro to collect them for me.

Tim arrived at our home at 11 p.m. carrying four green plastic garbage bags into which had been bundled everything that had been left at the hotel by Shah and Iddin. I couldn't stop crying as I emptied the contents of the bags onto the floor; it was just Tim and me alone in an empty room with the remnants of my children scattered across the floor. Suddenly I had a flash of understanding that stopped my breath and shredded my optimism: Bahrin wanted to obliterate anything that could remind the children of home. Every single item of clothing, socks and underwear, even their shoes, had been discarded by their father when they left. It explained why Whitey had been left behind, along with the things that the children treasured most. As far as Bahrin was concerned, they had had no other life before he kidnapped them. He intended to reshape their personalities, their very selves, into what he desired, like clay dolls without minds or feelings. Iddin and Shah he considered his possessions, his belongings, 'things' he owned and had lost once but was now determined to reinvent to suit his ego and his desire for revenge on me.

Digging further through Iddin's overnight bag, which had been stuffed into a garbage bag for the journey home, I found evidence that Iddin was worried about what was happening around him before the kidnap. As I emptied all the contents I discovered that Iddin had secreted swing tags and receipts from the new clothes that Bahrin had dressed them in beneath the hardboard lining in the base of the bag; these bits of paper were computerised till receipts from the David Jones department store; they itemised and described the purchases in minute detail. It meant that we finally had an accurate idea of what the children were now wearing. I felt so proud of Iddin at that moment. He was so clever, so quick-witted and resourceful to think of leaving behind some clues.

Further into the things I found a pair of Iddin's dirty socks balled up. When I rolled the socks out I found a strand of reddish-brown hair that tallied with one of the sightings of an accomplice the police had mentioned. As Iddin loathed wearing shoes inside, the only way that sock could have picked up that hair was if the man had been in the hotel room. There were also several glossy books across which I could see large adult-size fingerprints. These I also laid to one side. The sheet of birthday paper I had seen stuck to the wall in the abandoned room had been folded and included amongst the children's things; it also had large fingerprints on it. All of this the Australian Federal Police should have found; there was no excuse for this omission. Even the hotel staff had rifled through the children's possessions – how much forensic evidence had been discarded as rubbish by their untrained minds?

The AFP sounded very sheepish when I rang to tell them about my discoveries. It was so obvious that they had given the hotel room nothing more than a perfunctory look. A forensic officer would be around to collect the various items in the morning, the voice on the phone told me; in the meantime they asked me to be very careful not to damage the forensic evidence in any way. I assured them that I had already placed all the items in separate plastic bags and had scrupulously avoided touching anything more than necessary. I told the AFP officer that I had learned that from a detective novel and asked if they used the same book in their training. I hope he understood my sarcasm.

Some time around 3 a.m. I recall that I wanted to sleep, but I think I'd forgotten how.

Friday, 17 July 1992
Eventually I did sleep for about two hours that night but I wished I hadn't. Nightmares held me fast in terror. In the dream I could hear Shah and Iddin crying for me but I was blind, I couldn't help them, I couldn't even see them – all I could hear was them asking me to come to them over and over again. I woke up crying out their names.

My morning routine still held little variation: the phones started at 5 a.m., then came the interviews and cameras accompanied by what had by now become the standard symptoms of nausea and diarrhoea. Scanning the headlines of the morning, I read about Iddin and Shahirah's kidnap with as much detachment as I could: CLASSMATES SHARE GILLESPIE ANGUISH; PRINCE IN HIDING IN AUSTRALIA; TOYS, BUT NO CHILDREN COME HOME.

Taking it upon themselves to offer us some form of support, the parents from Canterbury Primary, Iddin and Shah's school, began to drop in casseroles and prepared food. I was very grateful for this kindness because although I had a house full of people to feed, I found it impossible to cook. Children from the school also started to deliver letters to us and drop posies of flowers at our front gate with small notes and drawings attached; their juvenile handwriting and misspelt words reminded me how small my own children were and how trusting, kind and vulnerable these little people were. How would they ever cope, without the support of everyone who cared for them?

I'd never realised before the kidnap how loved by their friends Iddin and Shahirah were and how much a part of our local community they had become. It came out in all the letters we received, which I folded away and filed carefully for future reference. I planned to show the children these notes of love and support when they came home, thinking that it would be good for them to know how many people had cared about their disappearance. I tried to focus on the positive and ignore the negative as much as possible, but it was a huge internal battle to do so.

A cold-blooded and rhetorical commentary in the *Age* newspaper did very little to help my frame of mind. I can summarise this twelve-inch column in a few words: a sacrifice of two small Australian children on the altar of international trade is worth it for the export dollars. It called for compromise. Perhaps the writer saw it in simplistic terms such as slicing the children into pieces or, better still, rescinding their legal Australian citizenship? After all, the trade dollar must be gathered at all costs.

An official from the Ministry of Foreign Affairs placed a courtesy call to me. He was polite, if noncommittal, but it was quite obvious that they were expecting the worst. With the AFP still assuring me that the children hadn't left the country, I really found it hard to keep a perspective on what was real and what was useless, but I resolved to keep fighting.

My reluctance to eat and my inability to keep food down even when I did try triggered an influx of friends bearing Cadbury's Roast Almond chocolate. News had travelled fast that it was the only food I managed to keep down. Inwardly, though, I wished that everybody would stop trying to feed me. I couldn't eat – especially when I had no way of knowing what the children were going through.

Muckle insisted on following me everywhere; she refused to let me out of her sight. Dogs have a way of offering comfort just by their presence and it also seemed to make her pine less if I allowed her to stay at my heels.

I believed intensely that it was all my fault that the children were going through this ordeal. I felt that I should never have trusted anyone else's opinion when my instincts were screaming no. I had promised Shahirah and Iddin that everything would be all right, that Bahrin would never try to take them away. Now they knew I had lied.

There was, by this time, an almost hysterical drive within me to ensure that I said exactly the right things to the media. If the children were still in Australia, this continuing pressure and attention would, I prayed, flush Bahrin out. All the journalists kept requesting new 'vision' – after so many days the story had begun to go a little stale. They wanted to photograph Iddin and Shah's rooms but I refused; the children would have little enough privacy left when all this was over and I was not about to let people poke around their belongings unless it was absolutely necessary. In the course of the huge media interest, several women's magazines began leaving messages every hour on the hour. They all wanted to do stories on the kidnap but I wasn't interested. The children, I promised myself, would be home by the time any of the magazines were published and a feature in them wouldn't help locate Iddin and Shah. We needed the type of immediacy that only the daily press, TV and radio gave, I decided with Iain's backing.

That dismal afternoon I reluctantly agreed to speak to a nightly current affairs programme – anything to bring the children home. The outside broadcast unit arrived to set up their satellite dish as I was finishing my eighth trip to the toilet that day. I was coming close to deciding that it was much simpler not to eat anything at all in an effort to control at least one of my bodily functions. I felt so ill that I didn't know how I was going to get through the interview with any semblance of intelligence or dignity. I was, by now, so physically and emotionally run-down that I was unable to control the shaking of my right hand and continually teetered on the brink of passing out.

It had been agreed in the pre-interview negotiations that before I spoke to the host of the programme I would first view an interview conducted earlier in the day via satellite with Bahrin's uncle, Tengku Ibrahim. It was further agreed by the producers that I would not be put into an adversarial position against the uncle, but would be free to comment on his statements. What in fact happened was that without warning I was hooked up to a three-way exchange via satellite between the host, the uncle and myself. I was devastated and absolutely furious by the time the pre-record was over: I had had to sit through Tengku Ibrahim's callous comments about female circumcision, during which he admitted that if Shah did end up in Malaysia with her father then of course she would be circumcised. 'What's the big deal?' he said. 'We all go through it. Millions of girls go through circumcision and it's no big deal. It's a minor operation.'

This particular operation, where the clitoris is cut away from the genitals of female children, is generally considered worldwide as sexual mutilation and is recognised in civilised societies as a total invasion of human rights. The concept of this form of mutilation being inflicted on my daughter completely snapped whatever reserves I had left and caused me to lose control. I began to sob openly as I leant against Iain's shoulder for support. It wasn't for several seconds that I realised that I was doing so in the full hearing of Tengku Ibrahim, who was still on the line and not, as the producers of the programme had promised, disconnected. The television movers and shakers got what they wanted: increased pathos that without doubt upped their ratings points. Far be it from me to point out that their little stunt may have jeopardised both my children's safety and any future contact for me with the royal family.

Talking to Tim helped immensely. He took to dropping in once or twice a day to check if he could do anything. I wished Iain would talk to him as well. Iain and I circled each other, afraid that our individual pain would explode if we collided; we weren't talking very much by this stage, except about Iddin and Shah, and we lay in bed at night together trying to exchange silent comfort – words just hurt too much. Once again it was our friends who kept us going. I felt so guilty that I didn't have the energy left to do more than smile at them or cry when they said something comforting.

Saturday, 18 July 1992

Nine days had passed since I'd last held Shah and Iddin in my arms and I still had no definitive lead on their whereabouts. The newspaper headlines still carried the story and screamed across their pages: MALAYSIAN KIDNAP MUM TELLS; GILLESPIE KIDNAP. One journalist even managed to dredge up a story that was three years old and included quotes from John Savage about our past relationship. To be fair, there was nothing wrong with the article, but I failed to see what my relationship with an American actor and the fact that we had both worked on a film together had to do with my children.

In any case, I had rung John only days prior to this article going into print. Somehow I tracked him down in Prague to let him know about the 'wombats'. He immediately said he would set about organising some diplomatic assistance through his American contacts in case they were ultimately needed. I told him that I refused to believe that the children were out of Australia until I saw irrefutable proof with my own eyes.

Everything in the house seemed frozen in time, even the inhabitants, and no matter where I looked, I was reminded that our normal lives had perhaps been destroyed for ever. The family bikes were in their usual places, lined up along the hallway. I tried to avert my eyes whenever I passed them – it hurt too much. They conjured up vivid images of Saturdays long past, days when we cycled twelve miles in a family convoy, laughing and singing as the dog ran to catch up. Would we ever do that again?

Small things now had the ability to make me furious. The feeling that the children were being mauled over and were having their humanity chipped away tormented me more than anything, so when I noticed that the two photographs of them which sat on the mantelpiece were being ruined and smudged with journalists' fingerprints, I couldn't cope. It forced me to venture outside the house for the first time in seven days to buy proper silver frames for my babies' images. Rationally or irrationally, it became a burning compulsion, almost symbolically so, to protect anything associated with them. This spur-of-the-moment shopping trip was a real disaster. I refused to have anyone come with me; this was a mother's duty. It was horrible being recognised on the street, everyone pointing, whispering and staring. This was something I hadn't been used to, and it was hardly flattering to become recognisable via something as terrible as the loss of my children. When the shop assistant held my hand and squeezed it, telling me that she was praying for us, I broke down and left as fast as possible.

Jeff Goldstein, the owner of the local video rental shop, arrived on our front doorstep that same afternoon bearing bags full of tapes. He said he thought that we needed something to take our minds off things. Jeff was right – except where do you start when your body feels as if it's been slit open and your heart and soul have been ripped out?

Sunday, 19 July 1992
One week exactly had now passed since we plummeted into this abyss, although it felt more like an eternity. When I tried to sleep, I was racked by terrifying nightmares, waking Iain with my thrashing and then finding that the leftover anxiety would prompt me to leave our bed to be ill yet again.

Every morning I would scan the newspaper headlines,

trying to pinpoint anything that would bring the children closer and to double check that I was doing the best job I could. Iain kept my body and soul together, especially during those first tumultuous days when there was absolutely no constant in my life except his presence. He was like a raft, keeping me afloat this side of sanity.

Indications had begun to appear in the newspapers that the Malaysian royals were beginning to rally around Bahrin to present a publicly united front. With headlines such as ABDUCTION OR RESCUE? A QUESTION OF RELIGION I realised that many avenues of potential information were about to close to me. This particular article exasperated me. It quoted the royals as saying that Bahrin hadn't known that the children had been christened in an Anglican church; this was quite untrue. Bahrin knew that the children attended normal kindergartens and schools in Australia and he also knew that they took part in Christmas pageants and all the other things that are part and parcel of Aussie life. Furthermore, he was formally notified that the children had been christened nine months before he offered to sign permanent custody of the children over to me. He was never denied the right to have a say in the children's upbringing, he just never concerned himself with it. If he hadn't been happy with the way Iain and I were raising the children, he should have said so in court, not kidnapped them.

What made me very angry about this article was that the journalist, Di Webster, used, I believe, every means available to cultivate me, giving me assurances that, given the opportunity, she would try to find out anything she could about the children for me. This was not just another story; this was a story that involved two innocent children, my children. I wished I'd never given Ms Webster the information she was after, let alone the protocol and etiquette procedures for dealing with

Terengganu royalty. I felt misled in the worst possible way, and it made me physically ill to find that my children became caught up in what I viewed as a journalist's self-interest, furthering her income and securing her an exclusive story.

My diary entry for that day reads: 'I love Iddin and Shah so much. They've never spent this long away from me since the day they were born. I feel like I am functioning minus a limb, or both limbs. Where are they?'

It was a question no one could answer for me.

Friday, 24 July 1992

Despite our situation, or because of it, the Australian Government of the day was less than forthcoming in its support of our family. Indications came out of Canberra that they would be very pleased if the children were indeed found to be in Malaysia, especially if I could be backed into a situation whereby I agreed to fight for Shah and Iddin in the courts there. The government hardly seemed perturbed that Australian federal law had been flouted by a member of the Malaysian royal family. This attitude appeared to be the malaise which attacked the Keating government whenever any touchy issue came up between the two nations, especially in the sphere of human rights. It's called placate at all costs and sacrifice the lambs. They would rather back down over moral issues than risk offence. The then Foreign Minister, Senator Gareth Evans, continually insisted in the media that my children's kidnap was a private domestic matter, nothing to do with governments. My only question was: if the breaking of a major federal law wasn't an intrinsic government issue, what was?

As a result of the less-than-supportive stance which my own government took, a friend, Micky, began a public petition urging the Foreign Minister to take action to effect the return of the children and the apprehension of Bahrin and his accomplices. Thousands of people signed the petition and I have been told by journalist friends in other states that similar documents started to circulate in their cities as well. The idea seemed to snowball. I hoped that, with other people behind us demanding definitive action, the government would fight for Iddin and Shah. Without them standing firm and insisting that the children were Australians, we were lost.

The second week of the kidnap was far worse than the first. As the hours went by, my hopes that we'd find the children in Australia faded. No matter how many times I was reassured by the Federal Police, my confidence in them began to ebb away – particularly when they admitted to me that they had not checked on the Sultan's house in Perth and that they had neglected to search a departing cargo vessel, the *Bunga Delima*, when it had steamed out of Perth only a few days earlier. There was no centralised taskforce searching for the children; the Federal Police considered their abduction a purely domestic spat. With very few avenues left open to me, and because ultimately I realised that, by their own admission, the AFP didn't have the manpower or the resources to follow up the most basic leads, I began to jump up and down in the media.

Some sixth sense also prompted me that day to personally contact the owner of the Griffith toy store. As this was the sighting that the Federal Police continued to work on as the only lead, I was desperate to know more. It was like clutching at straws, but I had to know. The bottom fell away from the basis of all my hopes when the proprietor began to apologise profusely, telling me that he had been mistaken, that the children he had seen in his store were new arrivals to the community and not Iddin and Shah. He also went on to add that when he had realised his mistake he had left a message for the Federal Police which had never been returned; furthermore, he had never been interviewed by the Federal Police, nor had he been asked to identify the children from photographs.

As a result of my criticism of the AFP in the media, Assistant Commissioner Walter Williams returned my call. He assured me that every possible resource had been applied to the search. I asked him if Coastwatch had definitely been alerted and he reiterated that they had been. It was easy to tell that Assistant Commissioner Williams didn't like me; I can only assume he'd taken offence at my telling the truth in the newspapers about the AFP's incompetence. I didn't give a damn – I was now convinced that if I sat around smiling and witless twenty-four hours a day, I might please the media and the government but I wouldn't be helping the children. If they didn't like what I had to say, they could bloody well handle the situation properly. I was determined to do whatever I had to do to protect Iddin and Shah; everyone else could go to hell. My children's lives were at stake and no one was going to tell me to sit on my hands.

Now that it was drawing near to the close of the second week, a number of Australian journalists travelled to Terengganu to cover the story. None of them had any doubts that the children were either on their way to Malaysia or in hiding in that country. One TV crew from my own network was arrested by Malaysian police for coming a bit too close to the royal family; fortunately they were released unharmed several hours later. The only consolation I could now draw on was the fact that with journalists I personally knew and trusted covering the story, the truth would be told to me with brutal honesty.

It still came as a rude shock when the uglier side of our profession reared its head. It was 11 p.m. when I answered the phone to be greeted by a strident male voice announcing that he was a journalist from a major broadsheet newspaper. Without drawing breath, he proceeded to bluntly tell me that the children were definitely in Malaysia and did I have any comment. I burst into tears. Iain wrested the phone from my grasp to find out who I was speaking to, but before he could say anything else the man demanded a full case history and analysis of the kidnapping. When Iain refused to comply and pointed out that not only was the reporter's statement about the children unfounded, it was also unprofessional to telephone a crime victim at midnight demanding answers and background on a current front-page story without first doing background research, the man became abusive and started using foul language before slamming down the phone. Iain took the journalist's behaviour up with his editor the following morning and we received an apology, but this incident taught me that even though I was ostensibly still a part of the media, some sections had started to conclude that, victim or not, fellow journalist or not, I had shown myself ready to fight doggedly for my children, therefore I didn't hurt. How wrong they were. I hurt like hell, my soul had been ripped out – but, yes, I was still capable of fighting. There simply wasn't any other option.

Tunnel vision was just about the only thing that enabled me to go on functioning. I operated on automatic, blocking out anything peripheral or distracting. Although Iain, George and Deb tried to tempt my appetite and did their best to convince me to relax for a couple of hours, my mind had convinced me that any time spent on sustaining my body was a second lost to Iddin and Shah. Besides, following two weeks of out-and-out battling, I was incapable of remembering what those words meant.

Forty-three

11.15 p.m., Saturday, 25 July 1992
This was the moment when my soul was amputated from my existence and I was left both afraid and fatalistic that it would never return. The only way I am able to tell you this part of the story is by including my diary entries from those days:

I haven't tried to sleep now for more than forty-two hours. My stomach is riddled with knots and my brain is screaming for respite, my hands shake uncontrollably and I've just noticed that my hair is beginning to fall out in clumps when I brush it. God, I'd sell my soul to the highest bidder if it would mean the children were safe in my arms. Iain looks like death as he dozes from exhaustion in the armchair. All around me I see our friends sitting or leaning dejectedly against doors and furniture – none of them have slept in the past thirty-six hours, all of them have been fighting for the children. John has just departed, Nadine and Joshua in tow but barely conscious. Lillian left an hour ago; she'll be back in the morning. Until then all I have to do is make some sense of what has transpired in the last twenty-four hours.

At 11.15 p.m. last night, David Rutter of the

Foreign Affairs Department telephoned Lillian at home to notify her that the children are 'in Indonesia travelling towards Malaysia'. He refused to say anything further. Lillian immediately contacted Jobn and told him to meet her at our house. When they arrived without warning close to midnight, I knew that the news was bad. David Abraham, the managing partner of my legal firm, also knocked on the door. One look at their faces was all I needed and from there it's been one long turmoil of anxiety, fear and absolute rage.

I spoke to David Rutter around midnight. He refused to elaborate on what he had already told Lillian and kept repeating that the children are 'in Indonesia travelling towards Malaysia'. I asked who had sighted them, on what island and what condition were they in, but he maintained his distance, refusing to answer any of my questions. As a result I became furious at the government's unwillingness to give me, Iddin and Shah's mother, the relevant information. I was so distraught by this stage that I told Mr Rutter exactly what I thought of him and his department. How could I fight for Iddin and Shah if my own government refused me the information I needed to do so? David Abraham continued the conversation with Mr Rutter and was told that Senator Gareth Evans, Australia's Foreign Minister, attending an ASEAN conference in Manila, had only hours ago been apprised of the situation and had had a meeting with the Indonesian Foreign Minister, Mr Ali Alatas, about my children. Senator Evans, we were told, was also seeking to meet with Malaysia's Foreign Minister, who was also present at the conference.

On hearing this I leapt to my feet, snatched the phone away from David Abraham and in no uncertain terms told Rutter that under no circumstances was Senator Evans to agree to any deals with the Malaysian Government such as trading one child for the other. I really feared that Bahrin being Bahrin, the value he placed on his son would far outweigh the value he placed on his daughter and that it was likely that he would offer Shahirah in exchange for his own safe passage. 'Don't you dare do any deals without my consent, don't you dare!' I screamed down the phone. 'Please tell me where my babies are.'

After the phone had been replaced in its cradle, we all stood around looking shell-shocked for several minutes before even contemplating what was ahead. That was that. The children were definitely out of the country, despite assurances from the Federal Police that they had not left.

We need to know exactly where in Indonesia they are so that we can try and obtain an Indonesian court order restraining Bahrin from leaving, but I can only do this if I have an idea of their location. Indonesia is a country made up of hundreds of islands. Without my own government's cooperation, it will be like looking for a needle in a haystack. Foreign Affairs obviously know far more than they're telling us and I simply fail to understand why they aren't making a more concerted effort to assist us. Surely the government's first duty is towards its citizens? I'm very proud to be an Australian, but it's got to mean more than carrying a passport with an Australian crest; it should mean that my government will do everything within its power to protect its citizens, especially when the citizens in question are defenceless young children. I really feel that my children and I are being sold down the river for the sake of a trade agreement.

The rest of last night passed in a blur of phone

calls. Rob Gell arrived with another mobile phone close to 1 a.m. and then we began calling all around Australia looking for a way to pressure the government into divulging what they knew about Iddin and Shahirah. As Iain and I woke politicians, unionists, diplomats and journalists across the country, Lillian and John drafted legal documents at the computer with George and Debbie providing the back-up.

I rang Malcolm Fraser, the former Prime Minister of Australia and Chairman of the Australian aid agency CARE Australia, at his country home. Despite the invasion of his privacy in the middle of the night, he listened with concern to events as they'd unfolded and promised to pull strings and do what he could to obtain the information we needed. We tracked down the former chief of the Foreign Affairs Department. He said that he didn't understand the government's stance on the issue and would try to get in the back way and get us information. I rang John Halfpenny, the leader of the trade unions. He was sympathetic and pledged to assist us if possible. I woke the leader of the Senate Opposition, Shadow Foreign Affairs Minister Robert Hill, at his house in Adelaide, South Australia, to apprise him of the situation. He said he would make some calls. None of the Labor politicians I contacted wished to become involved; it seems that I have been too outspoken about the Government's lack of action and so they are steering clear of us. I spoke to the United Nations Human Rights Commissioner, Brian Burdekin. He said that he didn't know what to do but would look into it. We contacted the news directors of the Ten and Seven networks, Neil Miller and David Broadbent, at home. Perhaps media pressure will help.

Phoning, phoning and more phoning. I refuse to give up on my children. I'll bloody well keep phoning and pestering and demanding and begging and calling in favours until I get what I need for Shah and Iddin. What does the Labor government expect me to do? Crawl into a corner in defeat? Iddin and Shah are my babies, my whole life. I love them with all my heart and all my soul. They deserve better than this and I won't give up until this government acknowledges the fact that two tiny Aussies have been kidnapped by a member of a neighbouring country's royal family in flagrant breach of an Australian judicial ruling. I thought that one of the most basic oaths that a sitting government makes is to uphold the laws of Australia. Senator Gareth Evans hasn't seen anything yet; he should know better than to cross a mother whose children are in danger.

One South-East Asian analyst is quoted in the papers today as saying: 'There is no way of resolving it other than through diplomatic negotiations between the two governments. Even if the Malaysian Government does come to an agreement with Australia, it cannot impose its ruling on the royal family because, constitutionally, in Malaysia, rulers are above civil law.' Elmi, the nightclub singer, is quoted in another paper as saying that she hoped 'Jacqueline gets pregnant soon from the new husband and gets children'. I'd say that summarises pretty accurately her comprehension of the bond between child and mother. Besides, I don't know if I can have any more children because of the endometriosis and the fibroids. In any case, children are not some sort of convenient cake mix that one whips up to replace another. Each child is a unique individual, a living and breathing human being, not an inanimate possession that can be replaced at a whim.

And so the day went on: a massed press conference for all the media, questions, flashlights and microphones. Friends, thank God for friends, they are my strength. Rick Willis is doing everything he can to relieve the pressure on us. He has taken over producing the weekly radio programme and is covering for us with the radio station so we can deal with the kidnap. Don't know how to repay him.

Faxed off a plea for help to the United Nations Committee on the Rights of the Child in Geneva. I hope they reply quickly.

Cutting off Bahrin's escape from Indonesia is imperative; it's our last chance to save the children. With Malaysia and Indonesia being so close geographically, time is of the essence. Once he gets them to Malaysia our chances of extricating Iddin and Shah plummet to 1 per cent. I've spread out all the maps and Skye's school atlas on the floor. I don't know what the use is really. I keep staring at the maps of Indonesia and Malaysia, trying to get some sort of telepathic location on the children. On the map, the distance between Indonesia and Malaysia is only three-quarters of an inch – a couple of hundred miles, nothing by plane.

I've spent hours telephoning Indonesia trying to retain a lawyer to act for us there; eventually, through a friend of a friend's cousin, I managed to track down that country's top family lawyer. He had no hesitation in accepting the case but pointed out that he was powerless to file documents or even attempt to mount a case when he did not know where in Indonesia Bahrin and the children were. Even the name of the island – Bali, Java, Sumatra, Sulawesi or any of the hundreds of others – would be enough to start with.

He can't understand how the Australian Government could be so wilfully obtuse in a matter involving two small kids. Left him awaiting further instructions while I try to move heaven and earth to get more information.

Iddin's best friends, Mark and Jack, walked the streets today, targeting shopping centres and supermarkets. They carried with them hundreds of petitions. They're both determined to do something for Iddin and Shah; neither of them can understand the government's attitude and they are very angry. Iain's former wife Gaye, Tyson and Drew's mother, along with her whole family are also collecting signatures for the children. I am so grateful to her for the support. Heard today that the fax machines in Senator Evans's offices in Canberra and Melbourne are being jammed by the thousands of petitions demanding Iddin and Shah's return. Good.

Nick and Ben MacArthur along with Mark and Jack want to talk to the media about Iddin and Shahirah. I said that I'd think about it, but it's really up to their parents.

I feel like we're under seige. The media sense that we are at a crucial point and are continuing to telephone every few minutes. Some of the journalists are becoming quite good friends and follow the story even when they're not working on it, or ring up just to check on how we are.

Dear God, why won't anyone tell us where the children are?

Iain said that I have to try to get some sleep. I don't know how I will – I don't know if I even can any more.

Goodnight, darlings, sweet dreams, God bless. Mummy loves you very much. Just be brave, we'll get you home.

Sunday, 26 July 1992

I imagined what Iddin was thinking. I know what his personality is like: he's very cautious and careful, he avoids taking risks and doesn't like to embark on important ventures without first making sure he'll succeed. I have spent a lot of time trying to encourage his self-confidence, building up his faith in himself. I know that Iddin would have been looking for a way to escape, but that he wouldn't contemplate it unless he could be certain that he could get Shah away as well. Iddin would never risk his sister's safety, of that I'm sure. He would watch and listen and try to get away when the time was right. I can almost hear his voice asking me what to do, if only I could tell him.

I got out of bed as early as I could this morning, accompanied by the usual retching. My pulse is beating so rapidly, I feel as if my chest is going to explode. I'm so worried about the children. Neither of them likes really hot weather and Shah's rash will probably get worse in the Indonesian heat and humidity. When is someone going to tell us exactly where they are? Friends are beginning to arrive early this morning; they all seem to have caught my tense mood. Everyone knows that this will be a crucial day for Iddin and Shah. All I need is a location for them and then the Indonesian lawyer can swing into action.

The house looks like some kind of military command centre: maps, logs, phones and constant activity. I suppose that's what it's turned into – we conduct our battles from here.

CANBERRA MUST CONSIDER RIGHTS OF CHILDREN AS AUSTRALIAN CITIZENS – JUDGE'S PLEA ON KIDNAPPINGS prints the *Sunday Age*, and it goes on to say: 'The Chief Judge of the Family Court, Justice Alastair Nicholson, has called on the federal government to consider a more active stance in cases involving international child abduction. Justice Nicholson said that Australian efforts to retrieve abducted children should not be allowed to lapse at the limit of Australian jurisdiction, emphasising that such children merited full protection of rights accorded to all Australians, at home or abroad. "It is the government's responsibility to consider the rights of the children as Australian citizens," [Justice Nicholson] said. This would mean embassy staff taking an active role, if necessary, to locate and retrieve the abducted children. "It's what they're there for, after all. I think that, at the very least, they would be fulfilling their consular duty."'

So, after all that, are the politicians listening? I hope for Shah and Iddin's sake they are.

Thursday, 30 July 1992

My deepest fear has been realised. Shah and Iddin are in Malaysia. This knowledge has completely devastated me for the last few days; I feel as if my body has been hacked to shreds with a blunt knife. There is an enormous void at the core of my being, so desolate and inconsolable that I know that I will never be whole again. With every pore of my body I long to hold them. Oh God, what will happen to us all? Nothing will ever be the same again.

The first warning we received was a call from the Ministry of Foreign Affairs, just after 1 p.m., informing us that the embassy in Kuala Lumpur had notified them that Bahrin was in Malaysia and had called a press conference at a major hotel for 4 p.m. Melbourne time.

That was the longest three hours of my life as I attempted to balance what was left of my composure and fight to keep a hold of the hysteria that was rising in my throat. I whirled on anyone who irritated me in the slightest, cutting through them with my tongue and silencing them with a look. I paced and retched and shook until Iain insisted that I sit down. I had so many questions. Did the children understand what had happened? What had Bahrin told them? Were they frightened? How were they sleeping? Were they eating? Was Shah's rash hurting her? Were Iddin and Shah separated or together? Most of all, how were we going to get them back without the government's help?

At 4.30 p.m. confirmation came through from journalists that the children were in Kuala Lumpur and presumed to be staying at the Terengganu Palace in the capital. Bahrin announced at the press conference that he had kidnapped the children in the name of Allah. From that moment on, life ceased to hold much value to me.

Many of the hours following the official confirmation are lost to me in a haze of hysteria, anguish and semi-consciousness. I collapsed after hearing the news, my carefully maintained shell disintegrating at last. I was drowning, falling, dying while still alive. When I didn't stop crying, someone rang Michael Jones, my doctor. I had lost the sight in my left eye, which was bulging out of its socket, and my head felt as if it was ready to explode. They put me to bed when I couldn't cease my tears. I remember hearing wailing somewhere, as though an animal was being tortured: long, racked sobs and moans, primitive and lost; I'm told that it was me. Michael gave me an injection of pethidine; it made no difference. This was a pain that no drug could ever hope to alleviate. I was half-carried, half-dragged to the toilet sometime later. I had no vision by this time but I could hear the voices all around me that immediately stopped when I entered the family room. When I asked what was going on, I was told that the house was full to overflowing with the media and lawyers. No one expected me to talk to them, someone whispered in my ear; they understood my distress. I think I eventually passed out. I don't know and I don't really care. Nothing and no one matters except Iddin and Shah.

Friday, 31 July 1992

Iain insisted that I stay in bed and everyone conspired to make sure that I followed the doctor's orders. I was unable to argue as my head ached and I had lost my sight. But Friday, 31 July saw me get up and begin fighting again. I was terrified of what I would have to do; terrified of what the media would ask. As I had not been fighting for the children for the past few days, I was nervous about starting again. Iain, Lillian, John and David Abraham had been covering for me all week but this day it was unavoidable: I had to speak. The press agreed to an 'all in' presser (en masse interview) at the law offices in the city, focusing on the legal issues and the government's response to the situation.

I agreed with some reluctance to an exclusive interview with the highest-circulating magazine in Australia. As I had agreed to discuss, in detail, my former life with the royals in Terengganu, I was extremely nervous and jittery. Previously, I hadn't seen the need to speak to magazines; two reasons now made it necessary: I had to put as much pressure on the government as possible, and we desperately needed money to cover the escalating legal expenses. There would be no fee for the story; instead a donation would be made directly to the 'Gillespie Children's Fighting Fund', set up by friends including former Premier of Victoria Sir Rupert Hamer, Brian Goldsmith, Bruce

McMenamin and Roger Evans of Evans Partners Chartered Accountants. These people would administer the fund, with all money being used to cover legal costs and to go towards the possibility of mounting a legal challenge in Malaysia to rescue Shahirah and Iddin. Any money not able to be used for the children would either be returned to the donor or, in the case of anonymous donations, given to UNICEF's Save the Children Fund.

None of this would have been necessary if the federal government had helped us and become more actively involved. Senator Gareth Evans refused to meet with me or even speak to me, insisting that the kidnap of Iddin and Shah was a purely personal domestic matter and not something for his government to be involved in. He described the children's plight as 'most unfortunate'. I wonder how he would have described the situation if it were his own children in Iddin and Shah's place?

The previous Monday, my legal team, consisting of Lillian, John and David Abraham, were summoned to Canberra to discuss an offer of financial assistance that Senator Gareth Evans had tentatively mentioned to the media. Upon arrival at the meeting they were confronted by the sight of ten public servants from the Foreign Affairs and Attorney General's departments arrayed around a table: not one single minister deemed the matter important enough to attend. An initial offer of $1,000 (around £400) was made, but after three and a half hours of haggling by the bureaucrats and pleadings from my solicitors, this was eventually raised to $2,500 (around £1,000). This didn't even cover the cost of the airfares and accommodation incurred by Lillian, John and David on this farcical trip to Canberra, let alone the cost of mounting a court battle against the royal family of Terengganu. So, with legal expenses now in the tens of thousands, the 'generous' offer was rejected with the contempt it deserved and recognised as the public relations gambit that it was.

Headlines for the past few days were as follows: GILLESPIES MOURN AS HOPE VANISHES; FATHER THANKS ALLAH FOR CHILDREN'S RETURN; PROTEST OF ABDUCTION; CHILDREN IN MALAYSIA; PRINCE, LET'S LAY DOWN THE LAW IN FIGHT FOR 'LOST' YOUNGSTERS; ALLAH BE PRAISED; HOME AWAY FROM HOME; ABDUCTION IS AUSTRALIA'S ACID TEST; PHOTO THAT BROKE A MOTHER'S HEART; CHILDREN TAKEN HOME, NOT STOLEN – PRINCE; MOTHER SHOULD NOT ABANDON HOPE, SAYS JUDGE; MUSLIMS CLAIM MEDIA BIASED IN KIDNAP CASE; CHILDREN'S RIGHTS THE ISSUE, SAYS LAWYER; ESCAPE TO MALAYSIA OVER THE SEA. The headlines went on and on. So too did the public debate and comment about our situation: letters to the papers, talkback radio comment and letters to us that flooded into our mailbox. Letters written personally to me were full of encouragement, love and support, for which I was very grateful. I hoped eventually to answer these kind people, but I didn't know when.

By way of contradiction, the revelation that we were now public property, that our personal traumas were discussed and debated in offices and factories, or as lurid accompaniment to dinner-party chitchat, was anathema to me. It seemed to demean the very existence of Iddin and Shah as individual human beings, and stripped them of their humanity. It was very much a double-edged sword: I needed public pressure for the children, yet I found that total strangers had a proprietorial attitude to us. Then that terrible beast racial prejudice reared its ugly head: comments were made by one Sydney radio personality that I was a 'slitty-eyed whinger' and should be sent back where I belonged. This stance was adopted by some of my fellow Australians, too. I suppose I should have expected this to happen. I guess I'd been too naive, forgetting to look in the mirror and see what some ignorant people judge me by. Radio 3AW broadcaster Margaret Fletcher and Adelaide broadcaster Murray Nicoll, on the other hand, are good friends. They both defended my nationality and my honour; they were unstinting in their support – and in their criticism of Senator Evans.

One journalist rang wanting to do a story on my racial heritage. I told him that my family had been in Australia since 1801, and that they came as administrators and explorers. If I'm honest, I have to admit that the perception that I'm foreign hurts a lot. Are Iddin and Shah less valuable because they are a product of a cross-cultural marriage? Show me the person who says that and I'll scratch their eyes out. How dare anyone evaluate the worth of my children by their racial mix?

Later that day, during the drive to the press conference, something really horrifying occurred. One minute we were driving down one of Melbourne's main streets and the next Iain was being held in a headlock by a screaming man wearing a motorcycle helmet. As the car stopped at traffic lights, a man had suddenly leapt off his motorcycle, which had pulled up beside our car, reached in through Iain's open window and started punching him and screaming unintelligible abuse. Panic-stricken, I tried to prise his arms from around Iain's neck. Susan Duncan, the Features Editor from *The Australian Women's Weekly*, and the photographer, Tony, who were also in the car, looked on in horror. At one stage the man's eyes locked with mine and he screamed, 'You bitch, you deserved to lose your children!' Iain swung a punch at him in return. Unfortunately Iain's knuckles only made contact with the man's helmet before we drove off. We arrived very shaken at the law offices, and with Iain's hand pouring blood from where his knuckles had split on impact with the helmet.

The press conference was a terrible ordeal. I felt dizzy and overwhelmed by the packed room full of people and I kept fighting back the tears. Questions about the children, about the future, about the government, about how I felt now, were fired at me from every direction. I answered them as best I could. I told them that I wanted the children home where they belonged, but that if I couldn't get them back immediately, at the very least I needed to speak to them by telephone. I wanted, and needed, the opportunity to reassure Iddin and Shah and tell them that I loved them. During the press conference I also had the opportunity to deny all the false stories going around the media that I kidnapped the children in the first place. Bahrin had hired a professional public relations firm, purportedly called Damage Control, to handle all his dealings with the media and to disseminate lies about me.

Lillian and David tried unsuccessfully for days to obtain a Malaysian lawyer to act on our behalf. No one in that country wanted to become embroiled in a battle against the wealthy and powerful royal family. I can't say that I blamed them. We made many requests to Bahrin's Melbourne solicitors for a single telephone conversation with the children, but the pleas fell on deaf ears.

How could the government not act when it was revealed by the press that Iddin and Shah were taken out of the country via boat from Queensland, in Australia's far north? The Australian Federal Police had failed to notify Coastwatch, who had since announced that it had heard distress signals from a boat purporting to be an Indonesian fishing vessel, *Pencheroboh*, which had drifted out of control for four days in the Torres Strait, the body of water which separates Australia from Indonesia. Furthermore, Coastwatch had been aware of the boat while it was still in Australian waters and had coordinated a full search and rescue operation from Canberra, the federal capital of Australia. They abandoned it at the very last minute. After monitoring distress calls mentioning that two children were aboard, a Coastwatch aircraft had circled the vessel and a navy boat, HMAS *Dubbo*, had even been dispatched to intercept the drifting craft. It had come within hailing distance when it was suddenly ordered to break off the rescue and return to base because the *Pencheroboh* was refusing assistance from Australian authorities and had requested Indonesian military intervention instead. The radio request, which was monitored and made in English, demanded that a specific Indonesian Army colonel, the Indonesian Military Forces Commander-in-Chief for the territory of Irian Jaya (the Indonesian half of Papua New Guinea), be contacted. The disabled motor cruiser, with the children and Bahrin aboard, was subsequently towed into Merauke, Irian Jaya, by the Indonesian military.

The Federal Police also finally admitted in the media that they had not informed Coastwatch or other similar authorities – it was an oversight, they said. The AFP also failed to follow the terms of the warrants issued by the Family Court; they 'forgot' to formally notify the Queensland Police of the case.

With such blatant Indonesian interference, how could the Australian Government still maintain that Iddin and Shah's kidnap was a 'private matter'?

When I learned about the method used to spirit the children from the country, I could have cheerfully, and without compunction, castrated Bahrin with my bare hands. God only knows what sort of conditions my babies had had to endure adrift in a tiny motor cruiser in the middle of the ocean. Bahrin can't even swim: he's afraid of the water. If there had been an emergency, he would have been totally incapable of saving the children.

Iddin is a fairly capable swimmer – I had made sure of that by spending months taking him to a regular swim class – but Shah was terrified of putting her face in the water and loathed having her hair washed for that reason. Bahrin was willing to put all their lives in danger in his quest to punish me.

Another startling event which the government was trying to ignore had come to light. On 20 or 21 July, the same day that the Indonesian military towed the disabled motor cruiser into the port of Merauke, two plane-loads of Australian government officials were inexplicably detained by same arm of the Indonesian military, placed under house arrest in Merauke, forbidden access to their aircraft and surrounded by armed guards. Coincidence? The Australian Government have declined to elaborate further on the matter.

Other facts were also beginning to surface. Colin Ferguson, a Melbourne helicopter pilot seconded to work in the Indonesian territories abutting the nation of Papua New Guinea, arrived back in Australia. He was shocked to discover that he had travelled on the same small domestic aircraft between the Indonesian territory of Irian Jaya and the island of Sulawesi as Bahrin and the children. At the time, it struck him as strange that two children of Malaysian appearance had been annoying their father by playing word games in a broad Aussie accent. The children were not allowed to leave the aircraft when it landed numerous times on the journey; they were confined individually and not allowed to sit next to each other. Bahrin was accompanied by a bodyguard who was in charge of Iddin and who sat beside him for the entire journey. Shah was placed next to her father in the front seat.

Colin was very kind and took the time to telephone me after news of his experience hit the presses. I took a small amount of comfort in what he told me, as he was very specific about the type of game the children were playing: they were reciting tongue twisters such as 'Round the Ragged Rock' and 'Betty Bought a Bit of Butter' over and over again until their father had become very angry with them. Those tongue twisters held a very significant message for us. Iddin and Shah were copying a game that Iain and I often played when we took long family drives. He and I would compete, reciting those particular rhymes faster and faster as the children egged us on and chose the winner of the game. To me, it was a secret message that Shah and Iddin remembered the game and chose it to annoy Bahrin, knowing that he would never know the significance.

The Chief Commissioner of Malaysia's Police Force announced publicly that he was extending every courtesy to Bahrin along with full twenty-four-hour police protection. It was tantamount to thumbing his nose at Australian laws. Several Malaysian government ministers also held press conferences to show their support for Bahrin's actions. Bahrin was using the children as some sort of staging platform to becoming a national hero; he cunningly turned his self-serving and vile actions into some sort of statement about the Islamic religion and Christianity. Religion was never an issue, and it certainly didn't have anything to do with his kidnapping Iddin and Shah, yet he succeeded in duping the populace of his own country. I suspected too that before long there would be an announcement that he was standing for political office. He had always had aspirations in that area.

The datelines on the newspapers reminded me every day of the passage of time since I'd last held the children and swamped me with memories and wrenching emotions. I wrote in my diary:

I've spent the last hour lying on Iddin's bed holding Whitey to my chest and crying. The children's presence is everywhere, my nostrils drink in their scent and I imagine I catch snippets of voices in the hallway. I remember how I used to kiss them both goodnight, brushing the hair back from their foreheads and settling the quilts beneath their chins. I remember Shah's pleas for one last story and the way that she devoured books just the way I do. I remember hearing her voice singing in Italian at 10.30 p.m. at night and her footsteps as she crept down the hallway towards the living-room door. Sidling in, she announced, 'Mummy, I can't get to sleep.'

'Why not?' I asked.

'Because my brain keeps talking to me.'

'Well, tell it to be quiet,' I replied, trying to keep a straight face.

'I have, but it doesn't listen to me.'

I remember the look of concentration on Iddin's face as we worked together on his most recent school project, on the solar system, and his exasperated comment about what he had learned. 'All I know about Venus is that its atmosphere is made of pneumonia.' I don't know when I'll be able to tell him that that project earned him his very first 'A'. I remember, I remember, I remember – everything. Surely Bahrin can't expect to obliterate any trace of me from their memories. Oh, God, help me get them back.

Nothing is certain any more. The only constant I can count on is the ache that consumes my whole body with longing for them and the nightmares that come at night.

Sunday, 2 August 1992

Television news reported that Bahrin and the children had arrived back in Kuala Terengganu by car.

Apparently Bahrin stopped at mosques several times en route to join in thanksgiving prayers for the children's successful kidnap. Iddin and Shah were surrounded by armed police officers and secreted in my old house behind a ten-foot-high fence that had been specially built. They were treated like caged animals, Bahrin airing them for public showings and photo sessions. One picture released by the Malaysian media had Shahirah brandishing a Malaysian flag while Iddin sat nearby, a detached and pensive expression on his face. Bahrin assured the press that the children were assimilating into Malaysian life with absolutely no problems and no longings for Australia. I wanted to know what happened when they cried for me at night or when they asked to come home. I wanted to know what they were told when they cried for me. Had he told them that I was dead? Had he told them that I had given them away? Did they know how hard I was fighting for them?

Three different child psychiatrists and two forensic psychologists have explained the emotional impact this sort of situation has: the children would be experiencing post-traumatic-stress syndrome, which encompasses insomnia, anxiety and emotional distress, coupled with the Stockholm syndrome, a phenomenon peculiar to kidnapped hostages. With the Stockholm syndrome, the hostage begins to relate to his or her captors as a means of survival. The hostage may even begin to take on the mannerisms and ideals of the captors and, as in the case of kidnapped American heiress Patty Hearst, join in the abductors' activities from sheer necessity. The experts say that it is totally impossible for two children to be kidnapped from the only home and people they've known and transplanted to a foreign country without becoming severely traumatised. How could the government sacrifice two small children in the name of harmonious diplomatic relations? Bahrin told the press that I would not be allowed to speak to the children under any circumstances. What had become of Iddin and Shah's basic human rights?

The headlines kept coming: LOVE-TUG PRINCE SLAPS BAN ON MUM; FEMINIST AND MULTICULTURAL VALUES CLASH. The former was truly ridiculous: 'love' had nothing to do with Bahrin's motivation to kidnap the children. In all his interviews, not once did he say he loved the children. He talked about religion, never well-being or emotional welfare.

There were, however, many letters of support for our family in the newspapers. One in particular, from Heather Brown, really made me chuckle when I imagined Senator Gareth Evans reading it over breakfast. Titled GRATEFUL PRINCE, it went on to read, 'Raja Bahrin Shah has unlimited funds, the full support of the Malaysian Government, the Islamic courts, the Malaysian police, plus, apparently, various powerful Indonesians, including a member of the Indonesian military. He didn't really need the support of Senator Evans and Coastwatch. But no doubt, like Mahathir [Malaysia's Prime Minister], he is truly grateful.'

Australia finally requested that the Malaysian Government allow Australian consular officials access to Iddin and Shah and we waited on tenterhooks for a response. Their reply was ambiguous and noncommittal.

I discussed the feasibility of going to Malaysia to see the children, only to discover that I had been refused a visa to travel there. I was *persona non grata* in Malaysia; not only that, but Bahrin had managed to have me charged with various offences so there was, and still is, a Malaysian warrant out for my arrest. If I attempt to set foot in that country to see my children, I will be arrested on sight. He managed to have court orders backdated to March 1984, the period prior to my return home to Australia and more than eighteen months before our marriage broke up. These orders gave him sole custody of 'both the children of the marriage'. An amazing feat, considering that Shahirah hadn't even been conceived then; perhaps he got custody of my left ovary.

At this time, I began to receive disturbing letters from a man offering to kidnap the children back for me. His letters were full of hints and statements about his prowess with weapons. We found out that he was known to the police and had been on weapons charges. I wouldn't let a person like that within a hundred miles of my children. I wanted them home alive, not dead. His was not the only letter of this kind we received from would-be 'Rambos', who suddenly seemed to be coming out of the woodwork and offering their services – for a fee.

One more thing to rear its ugly head was a private investigator based in Queensland who purported to specialise in re-abducting children. This man was interviewed on national television and intimated to the reporter not only that I was his client but that he had put a foolproof plan to us to get the children back using force and we had rejected it. He also made similar claims in a major women's magazine. I had never spoken to this man in my life; nor would I, considering how he touted for business and lied about me.

Sleep without nightmares eluded me; no matter how hard I tried to make it through the night without one, they proved to be unavoidable. My journal recorded one of the worst:

> Time after time I pound on the glass walls that rise up before me, trapping Iddin and Shah within their confines. The children are separated, incarcerated in perfect bedrooms devoid of windows and doors, surrounded by toys. They both rock backwards and

forwards, crying for me over and over again, their voices strangely out of syncopation with their mouths. I scream that I'm coming, that I love them. I yell over and over that I'm trying but they can't hear me, and all the while I'm beating my fists on the glass. Then the laughing starts, vicious and cruel. I whirl round to find Bahrin watching me, his lips curled back over his teeth, laughing and laughing until I think that I'll go deaf. Its volume fills my ears and muffles the children's crying. I see a flash of steel and feel the intense pain as the blade of his machete hacks off first my left and then my right arm above the elbows. I sink to the floor against the glass wall and pound the bleeding stumps I have left against the glass, desperate to get to the children. I leave trails of blood as I try over and over again to make them hear me, try to let them know I haven't given up, and all the while Bahrin keeps on laughing at me, louder and louder and louder until I can't stand the sound any longer, until it mixes with the wails of the children and I wake, screaming their names again and again.

I wished I could find someone to talk to about the kidnap, someone who had been through it. I felt I was losing my mind. Our friends Tim Watson-Munro and his wife Carla Lechner assured me, in their best professional voices, that I wasn't. The lack of sleep and the weight loss didn't help; my weight plummeted from eight stone five to six stone four. I ceased to care. I couldn't stomach food any more; it wouldn't stay down. I tried to cook but I burst into tears when I went into the kitchen and remembered the pot of curry I had made the night I knew the children were gone. Iain and Skye existed on takeaway food and neighbours' food parcels. My hair was still falling out by the handful in the shower and it began to recede at the front. I wondered what I'd look like bald.

Lillian and John put in incredibly long hours, searching for any legal loophole we could use in any way, shape or form. There was a way to bring criminal charges against Bahrin but the government had to be willing to cooperate and assist us.

On the evening of Wednesday, 5 August 1992, I saw Iddin and Shahirah on television for the first time since they were taken. It was a carefully staged photo opportunity. Iddin looked solemn and angry about being on show and Shah was just Shah – very aware of the photographers and journalists. The children appeared to be fighting but the commentary covered most of the natural sound, making it difficult to decipher. Later, when we boosted the background sound, we were able to hear Iddin telling Shah to behave or they'd get into trouble. To enhance the atmosphere they were surrounded by rabbits, mice and guinea pigs in cages; they both concentrated on the animals and tried to ignore the cameras, except when directed to smile by someone standing out of the shot. Shah's legs were covered in insect bites.

I replayed the videotape dozens of times just to see their images. Iain was upset when he found me resting my head against the television screen and crying against their frozen faces. I couldn't help myself. It was the nearest I could get to holding them.

Goodnight, my darlings, sweet dreams, God bless. Mummy loves you very much and always will.

Friday, 21 August 1992

As time passed, I found it harder and harder to live with the reality of what life was like without Iddin and Shah. I lost my identity just as I lost them. The things that used to be important to me, the ways I defined myself, had been excised from my existence with surgical precision. Our family limped along but the pretence was difficult to maintain; two members were gone, two small individuals around whom we tailored our balance and our optimism. Just to hear their voices would have been an immense joy and relief but those hopes remained futile. Every day I sat beside the telephone and tried any gambit that could give me some form of contact with them. I rang and rang the various phone numbers belonging to Bahrin's family but with no success; they had all changed their numbers. I rang Istana Badariah's switchboard over and over again and begged to speak to Endah in the hope she could give me news of the children. Each time I was either refused point-blank or, if the line was answered by the telephonist Kasim, who was once a friend, I was fed lame excuses. I used a Malaysian accent, and threw in a dialect for good measure, but nothing broke through the barrier. Occasionally I managed to draw Kasim out and extract a promise that he would relay my message verbatim to Endah. 'If she won't or can't speak to me,' I pleaded, 'please tell her I have no intention of causing her any disturbance,' and then I phrased my plea in High Malay, mindful of etiquette and the social niceties:

'With great respect and love I remember Her Royal Highness and hope that she is well. With respect I beg that she will take my children's best interests to heart and for their sake watch over them and protect them. With respect and not with any desire to disturb the harmony of her life, I also humbly beg her to consider whether or not she will tell Their Highnesses Tengku Iddin and Tengku Shahirah that their Mummy loves them very much. For this consideration I do respectfully and humbly thank Her Royal Highness.'

Then I would hang up the phone gasping for breath, sobs escaping as my shoulders heaved and I cried for my babies. I knew that if she had the chance, Endah would watch over them from a distance; it was the best I could hope for, even though I would never receive any indication that she had had my message delivered to her. That door was now closed to me.

On other occasions when I tried the palace, unfamiliar servants answered the phone. They played games with me, tormenting me, adamantly insisting that the entire royal family of Terengganu were residing indefinitely in Singapore, or that none of the family now had a telephone. Sometimes they simply put down the phone for long periods of time, leaving the line open, and I could hear them laughing and planning what sort of verbal games they would play, or arguing about whose turn it was to say something cutting to me about my race before hanging up in my ear. They called me *kaffir* and Satan but I no longer cared; all that mattered was that I tried every avenue to get a message to Iddin and Shahirah. The fight for them was the only thing that kept me going; they must know that I would never give up trying.

We continued, with monotonous regularity, to appear in articles in the media. Our story was fast becoming unnervingly like the Lord Lucan saga: public debate, questioning and opinions flew around us. I became the unwilling rallying point for disgruntled non-custodial fathers and the target for spiteful Malaysian students studying in Australia. Our car tyres were slashed; one night an old man started banging on my car window when I stopped at an intersection.

David Hirschfelder, a good friend who would later be nominated for an Oscar for the musical score for the movie *Shine*, organised other musicians and performers in a public signing of a petition demanding government action and the return of Iddin and Shah. I was incredibly grateful to him and the other signatories.

News reached me by fax that the opposition party would move for a full Senate inquiry into the children's abduction. It wouldn't help Iddin and Shahirah but it would possibly close the inefficiencies still in the system and maybe stop this happening to other families. The call came from Senator Robert Hill, the leader of the opposition in the Senate, and several backbenchers on both sides.

Bahrin began citing a one-off court order made in March 1991 as the reason that he kidnapped the children. He claimed that he was prohibited by the Family Court from taking Iddin and Shahirah to a mosque and he implied to journalists that this was a permanent ban. It made me so angry that he was able to manipulate the facts and make it sound plausible. The circumstances were in fact vastly different; the court order pertained only to one particular Friday, and to no other. Bahrin had arrived in Melbourne unannounced, demanding the royal treatment from the Family Court, using the grounds that he needed an urgent hearing on the Thursday immediately preceding the long Easter weekend. As he had arrived unexpectedly and was demanding access to the children with no consideration that we might have made special plans for the holidays, I insisted that, as the children were already committed to certain activities, he would have to forgo access to them on Good Friday. I did allow him to have access to the children overnight during his four-day visit; I even drove him around Melbourne.

The judge pointed out to him that, yes, Friday was a day of worship for the Islamic community; however, on this occasion, this particular Friday was also a day of religious significance for Christians. And, as he had arrived on an impromptu visit, when plans had long been made for this particular holiday weekend, the children would not be going with him. His Honour also made a point of stating that Bahrin's beliefs and religion were respected by the court and that when the occasion arose and he wished for access to the children on a day of religious significance to the Islamic faith, he would be accorded the same courtesy as had been extended to me. But this was not how the matter was represented in the media.

So many people who didn't know us jumped on the bandwagon, proffering opinions and analysis to the media on the merits of 'cross-cultural' marriages. We became a rhetorical debate on Islam versus Christianity, and I was transformed in one fell swoop from what I am into some kind of born-again, Bible-bashing Christian. These commentators dissected our lives as though they had some inner knowledge of us, projecting their own preconceptions and prejudices onto me and the children. I would become enraged and offended and it was up to friends to constantly remind me that these opinions had no bearing on our case. It was difficult to agree. I felt violated and used. I worried about the public perception. I viewed the people who supported Iddin and Shah's return as important and intrinsic to forcing the government to take action for the children; without this type of backing I couldn't help them.

My chief goal was to force the government into taking criminal action against Bahrin and to file extradition papers with the Malaysians. I felt Australia owed Iddin and Shah at least that much: an acknowledgement of their rights as Australian citizens.

In the meantime, I functioned as best I could, one day at a time, one foot in front of the other.

Forty-four

September 1992

I began to hate leaving the house because it inevitably meant I sacrificed my privacy in the process. Well-meaning people, mostly complete strangers, would approach me on the streets, some of them reaching out to touch me, others hugging me in support of the fight. A section of people merely pointed me out in loud voices or barely veiled whispers as the 'kidnap mum'. If I had to choose, I would have preferred that they come up to me rather than discuss me within earshot as if I were deaf. However, people's kindness kept me going in the really low spots when I felt as if I were beating my head against a brick wall and wanted to just curl up in a ball and never wake up. Stocking up with food supplies was the worst ordeal. It was necessary for me to be accompanied by a friend as the reactions varied enormously. It's unnerving to be whispered about in public, but I can also appreciate the amusing side. I was with Heather when two older women followed me at a distance through the store. They stopped when we stopped, looked at what we looked at and, in a less-than-discreet tone, began to discuss my appearance.

'Oh, she doesn't look too good without her make-up on does she?'

'No, not at all as nice as she looks on the covers of magazines.'

'Look, she smiled! She can't be that unhappy about her children after all.'

What could I say? Nothing. I wasn't aware that my facial expression during an ordinary domestic function went a long way in the public's perception of my fight for the children, but I am now. To maintain a modicum of privacy I began to favour sunglasses and baseball caps when I left the house.

Entering the supermarket for the first time after the kidnap seemed far too normal. I felt a rising panic, a realisation that, like it or not, this was a step back into the real world that existed outside the ring of despair and grief that surrounded us. I didn't want to be there, I didn't want to get on with life, I craved nothing that a day-to-day existence had to offer – it held no value without Iddin and Shah. The supermarket was the place we would go to after school once a week, up and down the aisles with the children badgering me for this type of cereal or that type of biscuit as we purchased the week's supplies. I fought back tears and avoided most of the areas of the store that I had frequented with them. I still do. I was panic-stricken that I couldn't simply stop the world's clock until they came home to me.

And then I discovered that it was difficult to get through the shopping without being stopped every few yards and asked about the children. The people who hampered my progress had no idea that this activity, which they took for granted, was one of the hardest for me to tackle without my family. It struck at the very core of my role as mother and carer. Again, some people would offer support: they were praying for us or had written a letter to their MP, the Foreign Affairs Minister or the newspaper. But often there was another side to the interruptions, a voyeuristic undertone which soured any contact they made with me. It was the probing questions that unnerved me, women repeatedly telling me how sorry they were for me and the children, and then asking about my life with Bahrin, offering suggestions about the kind of deal they thought I could make with him. Some suggested I offer to accept the return of only one child; others offered the homilies 'At least you know they're alive' or 'They will come back to you when they're grown up'. I know I should thank God every second of the day that they are alive, but I know from experience what a mercurial existence it is to live with Bahrin on his terms and I fear for the essence of what makes Iddin and Shah unique. I raised them to be independent, thinking and enquiring individuals, to make decisions and evaluations about people by looking for the essential goodness within, not by the colour of a person's skin or his or her religion. I taught them to treat others in the way that they themselves wish to be respected.

When I am told that they will come back when they're adults, I find that cold comfort. The reality of that is too painful to contemplate. They have been prohibited by the Islamic Court from leaving Malaysia before they are eighteen years old, but they cannot legally obtain a passport without Bahrin's consent until the age of twenty-one. If Shahirah is married off at an early age, she will not be able to travel overseas without the permission of her husband. In any case, you don't have children and expect to miss all of their growing up, to miss out on the nurturing and the milestones that signpost their lives. Bahrin has shattered the expectations of life which Iddin and Shahirah had formed in their minds since they were old enough to walk. There will be no tooth fairy for Shah, no more Christmas trees, Easter egg hunts or Hallowe'en parties for either of them. Those things have been stolen from them by their own father without discussion, without asking them what they want, as arbitrarily and as easily as if he were swatting a fly.

And still the headlines kept on coming: PUSH TO ARREST PRINCE; MUM ATTACKS 'BUSY' EVANS; BUNGLE CLAIM IN KIDNAP PROBE; GILLESPIE CASE A GRIM WARNING; SEND HIM BACK!; RAJA BAHRIN WARNED OF EXTRADITION – POWERFUL FRIENDS; WHY I HAD TO ESCAPE: MY LIFE WITH A PRINCE – ABDUCTED CHILDREN'S MOTHER SPEAKS OUT.

I made yet another request, this time in writing, for a private interview with Senator Evans. He declined on the grounds that he was far too busy and that he already knew what issues I was going to raise with him. He must have been psychic. I personally think that he refused to meet me in person because he didn't want to be confronted by the human face of the situation. His reply, also in writing, was like throwing a brick wall up in front of my face. He wrote, 'I hope very much that you do succeed in your effort to gain access to your children, and that you find them well and happy when you do.' It was obvious from this last paragraph that I was on my own. The government was trying to wash its hands of the whole affair.

I made a tentative start back at work, compiling environmental reports for our weekly show. I had to go back on air, presenting the programme; it was a simple case of needing the money. The kidnap had drained us financially. I was very apprehensive as I could never be sure, no matter how carefully the talkback callers were vetted, what they would say to me on air. I worried that if someone mentioned the children and gave me their condolences, I'd break down and not be able to continue. Many of the regular listeners had written to me and their letters of encouragement often arrived just at the moment my strength needed boosting.

I started to recognise that a general numbness took hold of my heart when things became frenetic or too painful to face. I found I could lower this numbness like a mask to get me through the difficult periods but I also came to the realisation that, although I could lower the mask at will, it became increasingly difficult to raise it. I was settling into a kind of arm's-length coping. Everyone congratulated me on how well I was managing; it was a very important thing to cope and to be seen to be coping – only I didn't see anyone handing out the medals. People find it far more comfortable, and easy to deal with, if the impression that you're coping is there. Happy human beings, with only life's small hiccups to cause ripples in their orderly existences, tend to feel guilty around people who have suffered a tragedy. It makes them less so when they fall back on the belief that the fact you're coping means you're feeling no pain.

I pretend to cope when really I'm not. My whole being aches for the children, my nights are filled with their voices and their faces are my daydreams. I am a mother and yet I'm not. I am living and yet I'm not. What are my names? I've asked myself as I look into my reflection in the mirror. Do I still have a right to name myself as 'Jacqueline and Mummy'? Or should I put the latter one away?

October 1992
The retching finally ceased.

The headlines, however, continued: A SERIOUS ABSENCE OF HEART; WITHOUT HER CHILDREN; POLICE ON VERGE OF ABDUCT ARREST; DARING ESCAPE PLAN; GILLESPIE ABDUCTION REPORT DETAILS ELABORATE ESCAPE PLAN; POLICE FAILED TO STOP PRINCE; A WHITEWASH; BOLD KIDNAP DASH.

That month, many significant details come to light regarding both the way Iddin and Shah were abducted and who else was involved. The Senate report on the abduction was tabled in Parliament, amid a great deal of controversy and red faces on the part of the Australian Federal Police. The report, written by a senior Canberra bureaucrat, Graham Glenn, included evidence that I gave to him and revelations about the kidnap plan itself. The Justice Minister, Senator Tate, under whose ministerial portfolio came the Australian Federal Police, criticised them and said he shared 'misgivings' about the AFP's failure to alert Coastwatch after the children's disappearance. The Glenn report showed that Bahrin went to elaborate and complicated lengths to leave a false trail. He ensured that his personal possessions and various documents were left at the Victoria Hotel to give the impression that he and the children were only absent temporarily, accommodation was booked at a hotel in country Victoria and enquiries made with various bus lines.

The actual route taken out of Australia was a virtually non-stop 2,500-mile journey by car, commencing on 10 July, from Melbourne to Weipa, on the tip of the Cape York Peninsula in Queensland. On 12 July, the children were transported in separate vehicles for the drive to Cairns and from there transferred to a small truck owned by one of the accomplices. The children were secreted beneath a tarpaulin in thirty-degree heat. Between Melbourne and Cairns, Bahrin was aided by three people who travelled with him: two Singapore nationals, a man and a woman (who have never been named), and a sometime Western Australia resident, Bryan Walter Wickham, an immmigrant from Scotland and a man well known to police due to his links with prostitution and money laundering. Once in Weipa, it was necessary for them to go into hiding as they waited for repairs to be carried out on the cabin cruiser which had been purchased in the state of Western Australia and transferred to the remote port. The boat was fitted with long-range fuel tanks but still experienced mechanical problems. They sailed out of Weipa on 14 or 15 July and headed for Indonesia, but experienced engine trouble and were subsequently adrift in the Torres Strait channel of water for several days before contacting the Indonesian military for prearranged assistance.

The Glenn report was nothing more than a glorified whitewash, designed to allow the government to lay the whole matter of the children's abduction to rest. Senator Gareth Evans's lack of action was spineless and, with the Indonesian involvement so clear, his adoption of an ostrich-like stance deplorable.

Another round of requests for some form of access to Iddin and Shah went off to Bahrin's Melbourne solicitors. I followed his rules to the letter and only channelled my pleas via his lawyers, but there was still no reply.

I had another odd experience when I was in the supermarket with a friend for protection. In order to get a better look, a woman actually abandoned her shopping trolley and its contents to follow me around the store. She didn't say anything but her eyes took in every move that I made.

It was no longer a matter of taking someone with me just for moral support. The previous week, I had been attacked in the car park of the shopping centre. Suddenly I had been surrounded by a group of five Malaysian students, two girls in veils and three boys. They had backed me up against my car and started pushing me. When I had tried to get past, they had insulted me, hurling obscenities in Malay. It had been both frightening and anger-inducing. They had finally left me alone when I had begun to scream for help. After that, friends made me promise that I would not leave the house by myself.

Our house in Victoria Road, our first home together, was put on the market for auction. Financial problems stemming from the kidnap did not allow us the option of staying put. I felt torn apart knowing that the children wouldn't be able to come home to their house and their own rooms and was filled with a rush of panic when I contemplated dismantling their bedrooms and packing their belongings into cartons. It was as though I were losing another part of them. I found another house not far away but it was of little consolation. I wasn't rational, but I was very anxious and upset that we were unable to retain our telephone numbers when we relocated; I had a secret hope that one day Iddin would be able to gain access to a telephone and call home.

The new house we rented had a large garden and a play house as well; we chose it for the children on account of these features, but I couldn't help feeling bereft at the thought of leaving our home.

December 1992

The joy and expectancy at the prospect of Christmas was missing from our home that year. With Iddin and Shahirah gone there was nothing to celebrate but I was still determined that the Christmas tree would go up and the presents would be set out beneath it. Bahrin once robbed me of five Christmases and he was not going to do it again. The children still believed in Santa Claus so I kept the tradition alive for them. Christmas used to be such a happy time for our family but now I wondered how we were going to get through it. How would the children cope when they were confronted with their father's views on this Christian festival: a sinful, infidel custom, and me a sinful and immoral woman? I bought Shah and Iddin gifts, wrapped them and put them under the tree, afterwards placing them in a storage trunk for when they did come home. I wanted them to know that no matter how far away they were, they were still remembered by the people who loved them.

I never knew that it was possible to feel physical pain at the loss of one's children. I missed them so much. I missed their spindly legs wrapped around me and their arms around my neck. I missed their cuddles and their kisses. I even missed their dirty hands. But most of all I missed the smell of them. Their scent all but disappeared from their pillows and clothes after we moved. It was as though time was obliterating the reminders of their existence from our lives.

I managed to survive Christmas by going through the motions. The tree was decorated with the baubles the children had made over the years and I took a photograph of their pictures placed beneath the tree alongside a sign with the year printed on it.

Skye tried to fill the gap left by the children but none of us could pretend that we were a complete family around the dinner table. Rob Gell and Nicholas joined us and shared in our Christmas, such as it was. All our other friends filled the house on Christmas Eve, surrounding us with their love and bearing gifts to be put away for the children. I broke down in church on Christmas morning. St John's had been the scene of so many funny and happy family moments and this, combined with the traditional carols, was too much to bear. When the congregation stood to sing 'O Come All Ye Faithful' I heard Shah's voice as it had rung out the previous year, causing people to giggle and look our way. Last year Shah's interpretation had been, 'O come let us adore me', sung at full volume.

We collected Nanna from the nursing home in time for Christmas lunch. She was frail, so we had to carry her into the house and deposit her next to the tree. There she held court, exchanging presents and sipping her sherry. It almost broke my heart when she repeatedly asked for Iddin and Shah. I had to lie to her as the truth of their absence had been kept from her – I was afraid that the shock be too much.

On Christmas night I fell into bed exhausted but too frightened of the nightmares to allow sleep to overtake me. I lay still, imagining the possibility of scores of future Christmases without the children. The strain on my marriage was enormous. Iain had been so stoic, but his strength was wearing thin. He was dismissed as just a stepfather by some, but his life had been shattered as well. He's the one they called 'Daddy'. I remembered an incident with Iddin many months before. It had no doubt been prompted by a conversation he had overheard by chance. I had just collected the children from school and we were driving home when suddenly Iddin said: 'Mummy, I know the difference between a daddy and a father. Abah is my father and he made you pregnant with me and Shah, but a daddy is the one that gets up in the middle of the night when I'm frightened or sick and sits up until midnight and helps me with my school projects. And he teaches me to ride my bike and takes me round and stuff and takes me fishing too.' He was so clear on his opinion – he understood the definitions and the delineation between the two – and was so adamant that I let the conversation lie.

January 1993

Nanna died. I had no way of breaking the news to Iddin and Shah. I begged Bahrin's lawyers, and even rang Bahrin's office, but all my pleadings fell on deaf ears. I organised a memorial service for her at St John's. The altar was covered with the brightest, most riotous flowers I could buy in all of her favourite colours, and I later floated the arrangement out to sea from her favourite pier at St Kilda beach.

I don't think I have ever felt so alone. With Nanna gone I was irrevocably an adult. I could no longer bury my head in her lap and act the child when I needed comfort, or expect to feel her hand on my hair. If she could see what I was writing, she would lecture me about getting on with life, squaring my shoulders and moving on. Her motto was: 'We live in hope.' Now it is mine.

February 1993

I spent two weeks in Sydney with our close friends Marie and Michael. It was good to be in a different environment for a while and I also used the time to try to find another way to convince Senator Evans to meet with me. I resolved to ask Gough Whitlam, a former Australian Prime Minister, for some indication of where I should turn next. I contacted his office and explained that I was requesting guidance only, not political involvement. His secretary was extremely rude and told me that she thought I was wasting my time and, without even checking with him, she knew that he would have no inclination to communicate with me. Nevertheless I insisted that she kindly put my request to him. Ten minutes later she rang back and stated in a very cold voice that Mr Whitlam had asked her to convey to me that he felt it highly inappropriate that he speak to me – goodbye – clunk. There went my nanna's theory that Whitlam was the champion of the little people.

I next approached Bob Hawke, another recent Prime Minister. I contacted the Hawkes at their temporary home and spoke to his wife Hazel at some length. She was very polite and supportive during the first conversation, if somewhat reticent about the sort of advice her husband was in a position to give me, but she assured me that she would talk it over with Mr Hawke and get back to me. A day or so later she telephoned me at Marie's house and her attitude had gone through a decided change. She was fairly bristling with praise for Gareth Evans. After speaking with her husband, she told me, he had asked her to convey to me that they had known Senator Evans for many, many years as a close personal friend and that I must trust his judgement. 'If Gareth doesn't want to meet with you, it must be because he feels that it is for the best.' She told me that they trusted Gareth implicitly and therefore he must have had a very good reason for not seeing me, a reason that was too hard for me to understand.

As hard as it is to admit, I began to experience uncontrollable and mesmerising bouts of odd behaviour. I found that I had to bite my tongue whenever I witnessed a parent being overly angry with a child; I wanted to grab their arm and warn them that nothing in life is a certainty and that a child's presence in one's life is fragile and not indefinite. I worried about these irrational urges. I understood the psychological motivations but could not come to terms with them. Standing transfixed outside a children's shoe shop, drinking in the sight of parents and children shopping for new school shoes, I wished that I could do the same with my little ones. I did more than wish. I fantasised about the possible banter and conversations we would have as we made our choices.

It was the mundane, simple matters of daily life that cut through me like a knife. I would fight back a feeling that was not exactly jealousy but a gut-wrenching longing to step into someone else's shoes for a few seconds and parent their child. I went to see a movie, *Sleepless in Seattle*, with Marie and cried during the sad moments of the film when the characters discussed the loss of a much-loved woman. After the film was over, when we were walking to the car, I caught a glimpse of a father and son walking ahead of us. My heart flew up to my mouth and my breath stalled as my pulse began to race. I found myself quickening my pace and leaving Marie far behind so I could look at the little boy surreptitiously from a closer angle. The resemblance to Iddin was only fleeting, the shape of the boy's head and his colouring, but it was enough to trigger my hand to rise to stroke his head. I came to my senses quickly, pulled back to reality by the concern in Marie's voice as she reached me. I told no one about the incident and was thankful Marie had not been attuned to what I had done. I was mortified and bereft at the same time. What irrational action would my subconscious pull me towards next? Was I losing my mind?

March 1993

Iddin's tenth birthday came and went in February 1993 without any sign that Bahrin was relenting. Meanwhile, he told all and sundry that I had made no attempt to contact the children since they had been kidnapped. He didn't count all the nights I sat by the phone ringing Malaysia and begging anyone who would listen to let me speak to the children. His generous offer to allow me to send them a letter through his lawyers had stringent conditions attached: I was to write a non-emotive letter in which I was to refrain from asking the children to come home or telling them how much I missed them or loved them. Then, and only then, would my letter be considered and, if passed, handed on to the children.

Every year at Christmas and on their birthdays I purchased Iddin and Shah a special outfit of clothing for the occasion. I was determined to keep to this formula and, two days before Iddin's birthday on 15 February, set out determinedly to find the perfect choice. I planned to store the clothes for when he came home. I entered a large chain store and began to evaluate the brightly coloured garments, wondering which Iddin would choose for himself if he were standing by my side. Then it hit me, cutting through me and almost doubling me over with its intensity, a mixture of grief and total ignorance that I had never experienced before: I didn't know what size to buy. I had absolutely no knowledge about how big he was now, no idea if Shahirah had filled out or was much taller than she had been seven months earlier. I was their mother but I was ignorant about them. I, who had observed every change, every spurt of growth and every milestone of their lives since birth, couldn't make an ordinary purchase of clothing for either of them and be sure it would fit. It was a thing I had always done without much contemplation, an everyday occurrence taken for granted, and suddenly I couldn't do it any more. The enormity of this cathartic revelation made me lose the last vestige of control I had over my tears and I fell to my knees against a rack of tracksuits and cowered in their folds. A young mother stumbled over me minutes later, the concern reflected in her eyes quickly replaced by recognition and then curiosity.

'Mrs Gillespie, are you all right? Can I help you?'

'I don't know what size my children are. I wanted to buy my son some clothes for his birthday but I don't know his size,' I gulped between sobs.

She helped me to my feet and put her arms around me and held me as I gained control of myself again. Embarrassed beyond belief, I composed myself as hurriedly as possible, made my thanks and departed, keeping my head low to avoid the inquisitive glances that followed me.

Intellectually I understood what was happening to me, why I was behaving in these strange ways, but emotionally I was devastated by my reactions to the normality of the lives being led around me. Amputation of my own emotions might be the only way to get through this; I didn't know – there was no one to ask. I was muddling through the best way I could. Whether or not I'd make it past this period with my sanity intact I had no idea. I only knew that I had to be there when the children came home and that they would need a mother who was *compos mentis*, not one who was locked away in a padded cell.

The headlines continued: MUM'S ANGUISH; GILLESPIE CHILDREN APPEAR ON TV; PAIR BRAINWASHED; PRINCE'S WIFE SLAMS TALK OF EXTRADITION; ABDUCTOR PRINCE LACKS OFFICIAL AID; KIDNAP PRINCE MAY FACE TRIAL; RIFT LOOMS ON PRINCE WHO TOOK CHILDREN; BID TO ARREST KIDNAP PRINCE; MINISTERS ACT ON MUM'S PLEA; EXTRADITION BID ON KIDNAP PRINCE.

By early 1993, more than 220,000 people had added their signatures to the petitions circulating around Australia. This volume of public support precipitated a turnaround by the government: they finally announced they would be proceeding with a bid to extradite Bahrin from Malaysia to answer criminal charges under section 70A of the Family Law Act of Australia. Since the March 1993 date of the federal election had been announced, I had been pushing and needling the Labour government more strongly. I assumed that members of the opposition had added their voices to my criticism of the government's lack of action over the abduction. I publicly challenged both leaders of the major political parties to show they had a heart. An old adage says that a country's future is with its children and I agree. Any nation's most precious natural resource is its children and no nation can expect to strut the international stage posturing about human rights, atrocities and famine overseas unless it is mature enough and strong enough to protect its own future – its children.

* * *

On Friday, 6 March 1993, I sat in a television studio, cameras rolling to take in every nuance of my facial expressions, and watched my babies being paraded before the media like some performing circus act. Dressed in traditional Malay clothing, they made statements in Malay, a language that they had never spoken prior to their abduction. Iddin, arms folded across his chest and a look on his face of utter displeasure, stated in stilted Malay, 'I do not want to be a Christian.' Shahirah was then prompted by her father and said, again in Malay which lacked any fluency, 'I want to be a Muslim.' This performance was obviously a knee-jerk reaction by Bahrin to news of the impending extradition bid. How could he be so manipulative with his own children? After every utterance they made, the children glanced at him for approval, which he gave with a slight nod of his head. I felt physically ill. I began to weep uncontrollably as the host of the television programme tried to comfort me. All I wanted to do was wrap my arms around the children and tell them that they didn't have to perform for the cameras. It was just too much. The children should be left to live their lives as best they could. Bahrin and I could slog it out: we were adults and the children weren't weapons.

Doctor John Hewson, the then leader of the opposition, telephoned me on 8 March to pledge his support for my fight for the children. I still had not heard from the government, and Senator Evans still refused to speak to me.

An article which appeared in a major women's magazine sickened me because of its source. The daughter of one of my former friends sold personal photographs of me and Iddin to the magazine along with her story. Considering she was only nine years old when she knew me and I was a married woman of twenty, I can only suppose that this was a desperate attempt on her part for her fifteen minutes of fame.

April 1993

I agreed to an interview for Malaysian television in the vague hope that it might instigate some form of contact with the children if I could show the Malaysian Government that I didn't consort with the devil on a regular basis. The entire interview was conducted in Malay, which I found quite difficult as I was out of practice. Excerpts of my interview were eventually broadcast edited to pieces, with my words taken out of context and other questions dropped in. I had been advised not to trust them – and those who warned me had been proved right

And still more headlines: PHOTO THAT OUTRAGED KIDNAP MUM; MALAYSIAN PRINCE MAY FACE EXTRADITION; MAN HELD ON ABDUCTIONS; ABDUCT CASE ARREST; MALAYSIAN CHARGE HANGS OVER GILLESPIE; GOVERNMENT AVOIDS ROW WITH PRINCE; PRESSURE ON KIDNAP PRINCE.

In a surprise development, one of Iddin and Shah's kidnappers, Bryan Walter Wickham, Bahrin's paid accomplice, was apprehended by officers of the US Marshals' Department in Florida, USA, on 16 April. My first reaction was 'good old American know-how'. The initial information came to me via a late-night telephone call I received from Tim Pallesen, a staff writer with the *Palm Beach Post* newspaper.

Interpol – and, ironically, the media – had searched for Wickham all over the world from the Philippines (there it was suspected he had links to child prostitution) to Scotland, where Wickham had lived until he emigrated to Perth. He had left his children and his wife Sheila behind in Australia, although she proved to be more than capable of fending for herself. Demonstrating her skill as a sharp-tongued harridan, Sheila lashed out at me during interviews she gave and supported her husband's actions in the kidnap of my children. Neither she nor her husband had ever met me, Iddin and Shah prior to the abduction, but she fully condoned their illegal removal from the only secure home and family they had ever known. I suppose it was the gleam of all the cash and gold bullion paid to her husband for his part in the crime that eased any moral qualms – although one wonders whether Bryan Wickham has ever possessed any morals.

Wickham had been working in West Palm Beach, Florida, on various building sites since December 1992. From what I could gather, the FBI and US law enforcement agents had successfully pieced together his trail from fingerprints and a random vehicle registration check which some sharp-eyed officer had picked up as being connected to Wickham. Apparently, he had arrived in West Palm Beach in December 1992 and settled comfortably into an apartment provided by Mr Orville Rodberg, a local businessman, and his son, whose connection to Wickham was never explained. Complete with swimming pool and salubrious surrounds, Wickham had slipped into a sunny Florida lifestyle with great ease and little apparent complication.

Assistant US Attorney Thomas O'Malley ensured that the American proceedings went smoothly, so, with minimal delay following his arrest, Wickham was successfully extradited from the United States on kidnapping charges and arrived back in Australia for trial. He pleaded guilty to the abduction of Iddin and Shahirah and was sentenced on 5 May 1995 to eighteen months' imprisonment. Subsequently he would serve only nine months of his conviction with a probation period of nine months. The maximum penalty for this crime is usually three years per offence.

In court, Wickham told an extraordinary tale of deceit, double-crossing and eventual abandonment by Bahrin. He implicated the government of Indonesia and their military in the kidnap and maintained that he assisted Bahrin because of his own love of children. The man is a convicted criminal with alleged links to child exploitation, prostitution, tax evasion, money laundering and criminal cohorts – it makes my flesh creep to know that he was anywhere near my children. He destroyed Iddin and Shahirah's lives and those of my family. I don't think that his sentence was severe enough but I had no intention of pursuing the matter. I merely hoped that he would slither back under the rock from which he had crawled.

May 1993

The entire month of May was one of torturous turmoil and unrelenting battle.

On 7 May, our hopes were suddenly raised with the news that the Prime Minister of Malaysia, Mahathir Mohamed, had told a packed media conference that if Australia went via appropriate channels and followed correct procedures, his government would do nothing to block a bid for Bahrin's extradition.

Mother's Day was on Sunday, 9 May and Bahrin had a special gift prepared for me. In a disgusting interview staged inside a mosque, Iddin recited a litany of allegations about his life in Australia. Speaking in Malay, Iddin told the television reporter that I had repeatedly beaten him with a *rotan* and a belt and locked him and Shahirah below the ground in a secret room for days on end without food. My poor baby was also forced to add that Iain had also beaten and starved him. I wept as I watched Iddin's face and body language during this rehearsed speech. His upper body was locked rigid, the only movement came from his fingers playing nervously with his sleeve. His face was very tense and he did not raise his eyes from the floor. It was like watching footage of a hostage, a victim of some terrorist campaign, being forced to put his captor's views to the world. What did Bahrin want to achieve? By destroying the last vestiges of innocence the children had, he was taking away their emotional well-being and childhood.

Happy Mother's Day.

Thursday, 13 May brought another attack from a different quarter. The phone rang late that night and a man with an American accent asked to speak to me. He identified himself as the editor of a certain weekly magazine, a sister publication of a well-known USA newsstand favourite.

'Mrs Gillespie, I know you don't love your children, you just like the media attention.'

'I beg your pardon?'

'My reporter, Di Webster, has just interviewed your children for my magazine. Your daughter says that she hates you. Did you know that your daughter sings "I hate Jacqueline, I hate Jacqueline"? What do you have to say about that?'

'How dare you go anywhere near my children! They haven't even had the benefit of psychological counselling. I haven't even been allowed to speak to them since the kidnap. How dare you subject my children to an interview!'

He tried to badger me for a printable reply then and there, but I had no intention of giving him anything other than a piece of my mind. I was furious and when I slammed the phone down I was shaking all over and felt that familiar sensation of nausea creeping back. It was outrageous that the children had been probed and questioned by an untrained stranger whose only interest in them was a juicy story. It was then that I resolved to try to take some form of action in the Family Court to protect Iddin and Shah from media exploitation.

The next day we met with Lillian and John to discuss our options. John warned me that if I were to apply for a suppression order banning all publication of any interviews with Iddin and Shah, I would risk damnation by Australia's press. I told him that I didn't care, that I had spoken to a psychologist and that he had agreed that it was very emotionally damaging to the children to be questioned and probed by the media and asked to choose between parents. I explained to the lawyers that there was very little now that I could do for my children as a mother, but the one thing I could try to accomplish was to protect them from the media in its perverse search for the eternal new angle on a long-running story. If the children were still in Australia, no ethical journalist would even attempt to interview them, as it was automatically prohibited by law. We had also ascertained that Bahrin was charging a minimum of £8,000 per interview. I would not have my children sold to the highest bidder and then asked to perform.

My application to ban publication of any interviews or comments purporting to be made by the children was upheld by Justice Frederico on Friday, 14 May. For now they were safe; the incentive for journalists to poke around in my children's heads had been removed. It was useless to interview Iddin and Shah if the results couldn't be published. Notification of the publication restraints was faxed to every media outlet in Australia.

Iain and I flew to Sydney that night to attend business meetings and organise our work commitments. However, en route to the airport I was contacted on the car phone by the producer of a current affairs programme whose host I counted as a friend. The producer asked me to explain the motivation behind the new court order and went all out in his attempt to woo me into giving them an exclusive interview about the publication ban. I explained that it was impossible as we had to fly to Sydney. He in turn offered us overnight accommodation at a five-star hotel, a helicopter ride to the airport and first-class tickets to Sydney if we would appear on the programme that night and postpone our flight till the morning. I refused. We had been in court all day and were exhausted. Before the call was terminated, the producer casually said, 'You know you'll be accused of media manipulation by some of the press don't you? It could get ugly.'

'I'm prepared for that, but the children come first,' I replied.

On arrival in Sydney that night we were greeted by the news, hot off the media grapevine, that that very evening a television crew had arrived back from Terengganu after having filmed an interview with Iddin and Shahirah. The interview was going to be broadcast that weekend. We were informed the price that Bahrin had again extracted from the television network was £8,000.

The interview was broadcast minus the children's comments and the magazine hit the newsstands with portions of it blacked out. By the following Monday, as foretold, I was being accused of media manipulation, of having something to hide, of being frightened that the children were going to spill the beans about cruelty and, worse, that I didn't love my children at all – that I'd been glad about the kidnap and that my career had thrived as a result. That must be why we were teetering on the brink of financial ruin and why our radio programme had been cancelled.

But that Monday night had one more kick in store. I was publicly tongue-lashed and ripped to shreds on national television by a man whom I had admired and had counted as a friend. I was accused of milking the

Australian public for all it was worth, of being a master manipulator of the media and of various other sins. And all this because I had declined to give an exclusive interview to this programme. As I sat facing the television, listening to this diatribe, I felt my stomach heave and my body begin to go hot and cold. I couldn't believe the betrayal. At the very least the man could have rung me and asked me to explain my actions to him before he attacked me on air.

I was at such a low ebb that this attack hit me harder than any other chastisement I had received that day. I was a mum – what did they expect me to do? Allow them to chew my children up and spit them out with yesterday's headline? I sat rocking and howling on Marie's couch until I was hysterical. I allowed that man's attack to bring me very close to suicide that night. It seemed as if nothing positive were left in my life. I saw the futility of trying to explain my actions and the way my reputation as a journalist had been cut to ribbons. Only the tremendous understanding and patience of those around me that night pulled me back from the edge.

Soon after this episode, I followed a little girl down the street as she skipped happily beside her mother. I just wanted to recapture something of Shahirah's exuberance and store the memory away like a precious stone. The little girl chattered and skipped exactly as Shah had done beside me so many hundreds of times, and the tilt of her head resembled how Shah would often cock her head to one side when asking an earnest question. I made myself desist my pursuit after two hundred yards or so, mortified that I had been unable to quash my mesmerised reaction.

June 1993

It finally happened. The extradition brief against Bahrin went into preparation. I was called to give evidence before the magistrate handling the matter and swore a lengthy affidavit. In all, a total of eighty-six witnesses were questioned and their statements taken for the Commonwealth of Australia's case against Bahrin. They were finally acknowledging that Iddin and Shah's rights had been violated. In a strange way, this action was almost more significant morally than whatever the outcome would be.

Forty-five

November 1993
Much as I strained against it, some strands of life began
to intertwine into a narrow cord, spooling itself out
much further than my eye could see, tethering me to a
course which had little meaning without the children.
It wasn't from any real contrivance on my part but more
from a necessity to keep food on the table and a roof
over our heads that I also returned to work, on
documentaries. I found the interaction with outsiders
which researching a documentary demands quite
excruciating, and avoided most of the location shoots
and face-to-face interviews like the plague, keeping my
contact with strangers to a minimum.

There had been virtually no income for more than
twelve months following Iddin and Shahirah's abduction
as every moment had been dedicated to fighting and
lobbying for them – writing letters, making phone calls
and reading law books and case histories. The
superannuation had been cashed in, bits and pieces
disposed of and the old Jaguar sold to make ends meet.
All this had been particularly difficult for Iain, who
found himself providing a protective shield for me
against the world and, at the same time, found his
expectations eroded and his professional life in tatters.
I had changed as well, becoming driven in my quest for

the children and far more independent and single-minded in my isolation. For us both, but especially for Iain, rebuilding a career after an absence of a year and an unplanned presence in front of the camera instead of behind it was something that had never come into the equation of our marriage and the future we had mapped out just a few years earlier.

Going back to my old television network as a news anchor was a tentative process, and one which could only be undertaken after hours in 'dry' studio runs and under the watchful and supportive eye of the News Director, Neil Miller and a sympathetic camera crew. Having one's make-up applied and one's hair styled 'just so' seemed ridiculously incongrous when I knew that there was a real world outside the studio walls and that my own flesh and blood was somewhere far away. It was difficult to empathise with televison colleagues to whom nothing mattered bar the lapel of a suit sitting correctly, the latest ratings points or the new hairstyle they were contemplating.

During this mêlée of film-making and television run-throughs, the application for Bahrin's extradition from Malaysia, to stand trial in Australia for crimes committed under Section 70A of the Family Law Act of Australia, was rejected by the government of Malaysia. There was no explanation given by Prime Minister Mahathir, or anyone else from his government. It was, however, painfully apparent to any astute analyst of South-East Asian politics that Australia had simply let too much time go by before filing for Bahrin's extradition. Time was simply against us.

During the intervening months, Bahrin had assiduously cultivated a public persona as a devout Muslim, bearded and religiously garbed. Gone were the smartly tailored suits from Italy and England, the Paul Smith shirts, the handmade Italian shoes and the flashy cars; in their place was a publicly carried pistol and a ritual thumbing of his nose to all 'infidels' and Westerners. He poured money into building mosques which also showcased his architectural skills and used our children as the foundations on which to build a budding political and public profile. This was the strategy Bahrin employed and it was ultimately too risky politically for Mahathir to return my former husband to Australia for trial. Bahrin had cast his net in the direction of a constituency paddling in the shallows of fundamentalist religion with the efficiency of a commercial fishing trawler; to haul in his catch and destabilise the vaguely secular Islamic Malaysian Government was a simple matter indeed – if he chose to do so.

Later that month, I was informed via a newspaper clipping forwarded by the Foreign Affairs Ministry that Shahirah had been hospitalised with burns to the left side of her body, covering a substantial area between her neck and thigh. Her injuries were caused by a kettle full of boiling water being poured over her naked body by a servant as she sat in the bath. Apparently, the children had been moved to the city of Kuala Lumpur and the house Bahrin owned in the suburb of Petaling Jaya. It was never made clear if they had been accompanied by their father or Elmi. Perhaps they were supervised only by servants – I may never get the full story. What I do know is that there was no water heater installed in the bathroom where Shahirah was being bathed, hence her burns. A panic so intense gripped my stomach and made inhaling seem futile. My child was injured, in pain and held in a country where English was a second language. A few months earlier, before the abduction, my daughter spoke only English – how could she express herself proficiently when she was injured? I imagined her crying out for her mummy, terrified of the medical examinations and alone in a hospital room without me to hold and comfort her. Most of all, I wished I had been the one scalded and in pain, not my eight-year-old child.

Through subterfuge and badgering, I was able to find out to which hospital and ward Shahirah had been admitted. Hours spent on the telephone begging various nurses and doctors proved futile. No matter what shift of medical staff I encountered, none was willing to go against the royal directive that I have no contact with Shah or information about the state of her health. For two and a half days I dialled the hospital every couple of hours, desperately hoping that at the very least one of the members of staff I spoke to would have enough human decency and courage to pass on the message to a little girl that her mummy had telephoned, was worried about her and loved her very much. Not only was I refused all contact with Shah, I was also denied access to her medical records. No one I encountered had any backbone. Australian Embassy officials were also denied all information about her injuries.

Due to the intensity of the international media, Bahrin took it upon himself to discharge Shahirah from hospital after only a few days and took her on a nine-hour car journey back to Terengganu. He made a throwaway remark in reply to a journalist who had echoed my concern for our daughter and raised the possibility of scarring: 'Well, at least she's a Muslim girl and will always be covered.' At that moment I was so overwhelmed by white-hot rage that I could have cheerfully flayed Bahrin alive for his apparent callousness towards Shah.

With the publicity and media interest that this incident stirred up, and given evidence that this was probably going to be a pattern, I decided I couldn't read the news and be the news at the same time, and so I said goodbye to the Ten Network and any thoughts of news broadcasting for good.

Within weeks of this incident, I was approached to consider writing this book. Ruminating for hours on the proposition led me down thought tracks where I hadn't ventured since I was a child. I'd ceased writing many years earlier when my stepfather began to sexually abuse me; it was as if all the most telling words in my vocabulary would be my undoing if I continued to frame them into the poetry I had until point penned with joy and regularity. Even as a child of ten, I realised there was absolutely no way I could further compound the intrusion on my body by allowing it to shape itself into the written word and have my mind survive as well. To do so would be to relive every detail much better left dormant; it would have indelibly marked my betrayal in ink.

Eighteen years later, the prospect of writing about my life in Malaysia, and the abduction of Iddin and Shah, made me realise that up until that point, I had set myself tasks: breathing, eating, sleeping, bathing, fighting for the children, cooking, arguing with politicians, giving interviews to the media and attempting to work. Now I came to two realisations at once: how I habitually categorised life as 'before' and 'after', subconsciously referring to the kidnapping as the defining timeline of my life, and how I had recreated Iddin and Shahirah's bedrooms at my new house as if they would shortly walk through the door to take up residence. Years later, the trinkets and toys, books and baseball caps were beginning to gather dust and take on the aura of a shrine rather than a habitat.

My grief surrounded me like a dark cloud. It covered so many levels and, with so much time passing, I felt so guilty in my grief that I did my best to allow my friends to see evidence of my depression only in carefully rationed doses. Their lives had moved on, just as the seasons had; babies had been born and travels and relationships embarked upon. I truly felt that it wasn't fair to allow them to see that I was almost continuously in mourning and to drag them down along with me.

It was time. Time for accepting a shift in my perception of Iddin and Shah's sizes and likes and dislikes. Time to sort through their things, giving some away and packing into storage trunks their most beloved possessions, the items which told a story and held deeper memories. As I did this, tears streamed down my face unbidden, prompted by this tangible evidence held within my hands of the very essence of who my children were. And it was time to speak to an independent professional, someone who could assist me in understanding what the children had endured emotionally as a result of their abduction and to help me age them in my mind. The freedom to express my emotions without reservation was an enormous release, and one which I now saved for my appointments with a tremendously skilled and sensible psychotherapist, a clinical child psychiatrist who also specialised in grief counselling. Unfettered at last from the social niceties and sensitivities which had coloured all my conversations since the abduction of the children, I finally had the opportunity to dissect the torments sleep threw up for me and to rail against the platitudes people felt compelled to mouth in my direction, without fear of offence. This was a tremendously important foundation to have in place, for the next phase of life I was about to enter definitely required self-knowledge, equilibrium and a safety valve.

After carrying out intensive research about the crime of international parental child abduction, I came into contact with scores of parents around the globe who had lost their children to kidnap. Gradually, the idea of a television documentary began to formulate somewhere in the back of my mind. The title of the film came easily: *Empty Arms – Broken Hearts*.

I had begun my nosing around partly because of the isolation I felt. I was determined to use my research skills to obtain as much information and succinct knowledge of governmental response internationally as possible as ammunition in my fight for Iddin and Shahirah. The more contacts I made and legal histories I delved into, the more apparent it became that I was most definitely not alone as a parent whose children had been abducted. Instead of cases of parental child abduction being merely isolated incidents in a handful of rocky marital relationships and partnerships, the international statistics were ominously robust and rapidly increasing. Conservative estimates showed that well over 30,000 kidnapped children from Western nations alone were scattered and hidden in different parts of the world. These children were currently lost somewhere in diplomatic limbo and trapped in a legal void, victims of a crime of revenge. All of them had been taken to a strange country by a non-custodial parent and for the most part were cut off from all they once knew and loved.

Not many nations, I was to ascertain, kept centralised databases on the numbers of children abducted overseas, but according to Reunite, a British organisation responsible for assisting victims of child abduction, and the Lord Chancellor's Department, the United Kingdom was losing an estimated 1,400 children per annum. That's the equivalent of forty kindergartens suddenly being removed from the face of Britain. In France, the estimates put the number at a thousand 'dossiers', a term which is used to identify the individual family names and masks the probability that multiple siblings have been kidnapped in that year. Australia didn't keep comprehensive records, but official estimates stood at eighty to one hundred cases per year, and that number is still quite constant in this century as well. The United States of America won hands down in terms of sheer numbers, with a gigantic 367,000 'family abductions' every twelve months. That term pertains to the removal of a child or children by a family member across county lines, interstate or overseas without the permission of the parent with whom the child normally resides and without a voluntary return. Over eight hundred American children were taken overseas in a space of time slightly longer than a calendar year and fall under the heading of Hague Convention Abductions.

The Hague Convention on the Civil Aspects of Child Abduction is an international treaty which came into being in the mid-1980s to combat the escalating incidence of parental child abduction. In simple terms, a child taken from a country which is a signatory to the Hague Convention to another Hague Convention country must be automatically returned to his or her normal country of residence. It works rather like an extradition agreement and is not meant to be used to determine custody rights or other matters. Gradually, over the years, the Hague Convention has been adopted and ratified by more and more nations (in 1995, only forty-one nations were signatories; in 2006, the number has risen to fifty-six member states). Unfortunately, most of the Middle Eastern, African and Asian nations have refused to sign the treaty, which means that the children abducted to these places have no legal safety net to protect them and assist in their repatriation to their homelands. Quite a number of former European colonies and protectorates automatically refuse to return a child if the abducting parent is one of their own nationals – it is a strange form of what I now term 'post-colonial backlash'. And a significant sector of

European Union member states, although signatories to the Hague Convention, do not return children. In those cases it seems to be internal confusion about the rights of sovereignty versus the precedence of international treaties and self-determination which hampers the proper implementation of the Convention. Sometimes it is a strange form of nationalism tinged with racism or sexism which puts a spoke in the wheels of a child's future.

So there I sat, far too well informed for my own good, having tapped into the United Nations, the US State Department, the British Lord Chancellor's Department and countless other related agencies with the all-too-depressing statistics and red tape of international parental child abduction pressing in on me, tragic stories of children who had been denied what I identified as one of life's most basic of human rights – to know both one's parents. There were also scores of sometimes weeping parents pouring out their tales in long telephone calls from all around the globe. I also discovered another term to describe myself – I was now officially a 'left-behind parent'.

Over the time since my children had been kidnapped, I'd been accused of using the media to further their cause, and for that I make no apologies. Would a doctor stand idly by after an accident in which his or her own child had been injured and give no first aid, waiting ineffectually for an ambulance to arrive? I used the only skills I had to help my kids, and now it was time to give other children and parents a voice too, using those same skills. I wanted to create a cohesive documentary on what child abduction is and how it is dealt with around the world, I wanted to show what the social, emotional and political ramifications of such actions are and to try to educate parents not to use their children like cudgels with which to beat one another around the head. Hence the idea for the film.

In order to make *Empty Arms – Broken Hearts* a comprehensive documentary that wouldn't (I hoped) be parochial, a schedule for location filming was embarked upon that really necessitated an extra pair of feet, three more weeks, energy supplements and a lock pick. Perhaps an extra dose of sanity as well. By the time we finished filming, the crew and I had travelled to twenty-six locations, from Melbourne to Morocco, Paris to New York, England to Switzerland, over the course of four weeks. I became a world-class expert in avoiding excess baggage charges for the film equipment and savvy at negotiating myself out foreign jails, having been arrested in Monaco and Morocco whilst in pursuit of abductors and accomplices. That, and learning to bite my tongue as I listened to all the inane rhetoric espoused by the United Nations Committee on the Rights of the Child.

Chief Justice of the Family Court of Australia The Right Honourable Justice Alistair Nicholson was instrumental in opening many doors across to the globe to me – especially the chambers of the British judiciary. I will be incredibly grateful to him in perpetuity for encouraging me in my quest to change the position of the true victims of these international crimes of vengeance – the innocent children. I suspect that His Honour also hoped that I would channel some of my manic energies into an area that would sustain me in ways that ordinary life could not.

Choosing to make *Empty Arms – Broken Hearts* was not a very effective way to combat my yearning for Iddin and Shahirah. Everywhere I travelled, my thoughts would turn to them and the knowledge that, for the moment, the closest we could all be was the presence of their photographs pinned inside my pocket every day as I dressed for the filming ahead, a kind of talisman of faith. I remember seeing the Eiffel Tower for the first time one night from the window of my hotel, a strange crooked building on the Rue du Rivoli with minuscule balconies and creaking floors. The sky was that deep azure blue that only a European twilight can be and all of Paris seemed to glow golden. For a few moments my breath was taken away by the sheer beauty and enchantment of that magical city, and then my chest grew tight and the very absence of the children became a palpable void in my body. But somehow their spiritual presence, if not their physical presence, made my resolve strengthen each time I felt daunted and drained by the emotional roller-coaster of confrontations with officialdom and mutual tears with mothers and fathers who'd also been deprived of the joy of watching their children grow and mature.

How much strain, how much pressure can a relationship take before fissures begin to appear in its foundations? Certainly Iain and I were grappling with a myriad of issues as I pushed forward to simultaneously complete the manuscript of my book and the documentary. I had become strident and opinionated; I bore little sustained resemblance to the woman he married. I was very tired and just longed to sleep with my little ones snuggled up alongside me on a lazy Sunday morning. Will that ever happen again?

By the October after filming *Empty Arms – Broken Hearts*, it seemed I'd finally earned my battle stripes – or, at least, that was the unwritten text of an invitation I received to give a speech on parental child abduction at an international family law conference – again thanks to Justice Nicholson and his recommendations to the steering committee. Ironically, I had now crossed into the ranks of expert and was no longer perceived purely as a victim. With some trepidation, I embarked upon my first public-speaking engagement, so nauseous from nerves that I refrained from eating for twenty-four hours prior to standing behind the lectern. Quaking in my carefully chosen red suit and black suede shoes, I delivered my paper on the sociological effects of child abduction, never realising that it would be the first of many such seminars and conferences I would find myself attending.

Another Christmas loomed, taunting me with the children's absence. I placed their photographs under the tree and took another photo to mark the passing of time. Years, not months, had now passed since I had last seen or spoken to Iddin and Shah. I had missed their birthdays, Shah's teeth falling out and, most of all, their wonderful personalities and laughter. The pain hadn't eased but I had learned to cope with it for the most part. It's like having a gigantic apple corer taken to one's body and having a part of one's soul excised. I wander around with an enormous hole in my being, a thin membrane of coping covering the void. I've heard that amputees often retain a memory of a lost limb, feeling its presence and sensations; maybe that's what I experience.

These past years of the children's absence have been far more of an emotional minefield. The grieving continues in a vicious circle of ebbing and flowing tides that wash over me. I'm just not coping as well on certain levels as I did in the first year.

Epilogue

There is a strange irony that after so many years without being able to hold Iddin and Shah, I still expect to look over my shoulder and see them sitting on the sofa as I write this. Perhaps that's the true reflection of parenthood – the essence and reality of a child's existence remain as fresh and sweet as on the day one first held him or her, regardless of whether you're separated geographically or the child had gone.

I'm often awakened by what I think are the children's voices calling for me and feel compelled to get out of bed and look around the house. I know that this is just some kind of trick that my nightmares play on me, but the longing for them that surges through my body, the tangible ache I feel in my womb, tells me that the bond between them and me is not broken.

I will never think or say that Iddin and Shah belonged to me. They belong to no one but themselves. I sometimes think of them as precious gifts that were left with me for safekeeping to nurture, love and care for until fate took them away. They are as individual as snowflakes and infinitely more precious and pure than any self-centred wish I may have for myself. I can't subjugate my need for them, or the ache that overwhelms me to the point of drowning when I conjure up their voices in my head. But I can say this – no one can reinvent those two children I gave birth to; to even try would be an atrocity against their spirits. They are themselves, no matter how deeply they may have to bury their true feelings and identities, and, one day, I pray they will remember how to come home to me.

When I looked down on each of my children as babies, I remember that my thoughts flew ahead, calculating how old I would be when they walked for the first time, spoke for the first time and experienced the myriad of transitional phases on the way to adulthood and independence. I took for granted that I would watch them both grow taller than me; I assumed that I would bear witness to so many milestones in their lives. How wrong I was.

On reflection, the most important lesson I have acquired from all the madness of the past years is never to take anyone or anything for granted, especially one's children. The second is never to give up.

Two 'treasure chests' now fill one corner of my study, encapsulating the waiting and the hopes that I still hold for my son and daughter. Inside the massive trunks I place gifts, cards, photographs and letters to Iddin and Shah. These items mark the days and years of lost celebrations and anniversaries that they would have shared as loved members of our family had they still been with me. Friends and kind strangers also forward remembrances to me for the children, and I pray that one day I may open the boxes and give Iddin and Shahirah a hoarded and tangible legacy to their lost 'Australian' years.

The oddest things have happened in my life which have enabled me to make a little sense of a senseless situation. I have gained more confidence in my ability to write and would like to attempt to carve out a niche for myself as an author. Perhaps I'll succeed, perhaps not, but at least it gives me somewhere to put all the words which fill my head when I lie awake at night trying to find sleep.

During these long, short years I've discovered the worst and the best in other people, the obtuse and the compassionate. But most of all I've found a commonality of humanity around the world which gives me hope that international child abduction will abate – that is, a growing understanding amongst people that every race, creed and nationality holds a love for its children which has the capability, with education, to transcend self-centredness and revenge.

Iddin and Shahirah are now so much older than they were when they were taken from their home with me. I continue to request access to them but with no success. Neither do I receive replies to my letters or acknowledgements of the gifts I send. Since the day they were kidnapped, I have not been allowed to speak with them. My own grief has not eased but, like chronic pain, I have learned to live with it and accept that this truly is my existence.

Until the time I see my children again, I live in hope.

Jacqueline Pascarl

Glossary

Abah	father
Abang	title meaning older brother
Allah	Muslim God
angkat sumpah	palms of hands pressed together and raised to the forehead in obsequiousness
baju kebaya	two-piece traditional female dress: knee-length jacket with turn-back collar and long wraparound skirt
baju kurung	traditional two-piece female dress, translated as 'the dress cage'
baju melayu	traditional male dress consisting of a loose, long-sleeved, high-necked shirt without a collar, and trousers
Balai Police	police headquarters
bekeng	fierce
Bersanding	see *Istiadat Bersanding*
bomoh	witchdoctor with Islamic bent
bunga goyang	quivering artifical flowers made of gold metal on tiny springs, usually hair ornament

bunga telur	traditional commemorative gifts presented to wedding guests; literal translation: egg flower
dapur	kitchen outhouse
Datuk	knight of the realm
daulat tuanku	long live the King
dosar	sin
gin	genies
Hantar Belanjar	exchange of bridal gifts
Hari Raya	end of the fasting month of Ramadan
houries	scantily clad sex angels
ikan tendiri	tuna
Istana Badariah	Badariah Palace
Istana Maziah	Maziah Palace
Istiadat Berinai	royal henna ceremony
Istiadat Bersanding	solemn official sitting in state by bridal couple as part of traditional royal wedding
Istiadat Bersiram	royal ceremonial bathing ritual
jihad	Muslim holy war
kaffir	insulting terminology used in derogatory fashion to describe non-Muslims
kalong	jewelled necklace
kayu chengai	rich red-brown timber
Kampung Istana	palace village or precinct
kedukut	stingy
keling	derogatory term referring to the history of Indian Malaysians as imported slaves
kenang	bewitched
Khadi	Muslim legal official or indication of Islamic legal court order
Koran	Muslim holy book

kris	ceremonial dagger
Mak	mother
mat salleh	white man
nasib Tuhan	Will of God
Nobat	traditional royal Terengganu orchestra
orang darat	rural people
orang kampung	village people
Pahang	royal state
parlar	Muslim system of merit points gained for good deeds
pantan	dietary and behaviour code following pregnancy
Perak	royal state
Raja	prince or princess, ruler
Raja Muda	Crown Prince
Ramadan	month in the Islamic calendar when Muslims must fast from sunrise to sunset
rotan	long Malaysian whipping cane used for punishment
sampin	men's sarong worn around the waist over traditional *baju melayu*
saya terima	'I accept', phrase used in traditional weddings
songket	hand-woven fabric made from pure silk with gold thread
songkok	brimless oval fez-like hat worn by men
sunnat	non-compulsory actions undertaken under Islamic law including circumcision of females, or refined colloquial terminology for male circumcision

talil	solemn Islamic wake where prayers are said for the dead
tanjok	crownless turban fashioned from *songket* fabric
Tengku	title for prince or princess
tudum saji	woven rattan insect protectors
tukang urut	masseuse

Child Abduction Resource Information Internationally

Australia
The Empty Arms Network
email: emptyarmsaustralia@yahoo.com

Nicholes Family Lawyers
Specialists in parental child abduction issues and Hague
Convention law
Level 3, 224 Queen Street
Melbourne
Victoria 3000
Australia
Tel: +61 (0) 3 9670 4122
www.nicholeslaw.com.au
email: sally@nicholeslaw.com.au

Attorney General's Department
Canberra
Australia
Tel: +61 (0) 2 6250 6666
www.ag.gov.au

Department of Foreign Affairs and Trade
Canberra
Australia
1300 555 135 (24-hour hotline)
www.dfat.gov.au

Belgium
Missing Children International Network
Tel: +32 (84) 21 14 61
Fax: +32 (84) 22 13 94

Child Focus
Avenue Houba de Strooper 292
1020 Brussels
Belgium
Tel: +32 (0) 2 475 44 11

Canada
Missing Children's Society of Canada
Suite 219, 3501 – 23 Street NE
Calgary
Alberta T2E 6V8
Canada
Tel: +1 (403) 291 0705
Fax: + 1 (403) 291 9728
www.mcsc.ca
Email: rmorgan@mcsc.ca

France
Collectif de Solidarité aux Mères D'Enfants Enlevés
9 Rue des Chaillots
92190 Meudon
France
Tel: +33 (1) 45 34 49 10
Fax: +33 (1) 46 23 11 64
email: csmee@wanadoo.fr.

United Kingdom
Reunite International
PO Box 7124
Leicester LE1 7 XX
United Kingdom
Tel: +44 (0) 116 2556 234
Fax: + 44 (0) 116 2556 370
www.reunite.org
email: reunite@dircon.co.uk

United States of America
The National Center for Missing and Exploited Children
(US Central Authority for Incoming Cases)
Charles B Wang International Children's Building
699 Prince Street
Alexandria
Virginia 22314-3175
USA
Tel: +1 703 274 3900
Fax: +1 703 274 2200
Hotline: 1-800-THE-LOST (1 800 843 5678)
www.missingkids.com

Acknowledgements

I am probably one of the most fortunate people in the world, surrounded as I am by a large and selfless group of people who've sustained me with their love and generosity throughout the roller-coaster ride that my life has become and provided safe refuges in their hearts for me.

Thank you, Nanna, for straightening my steps; I miss you and love you.

To my beloved godparents, Auntie Connie and Uncle Kevin Coverdale – you have always been unstinting in your love and guidance. Without you both, I would have been a one-dimensional city slicker.

Deborah Gribble, Sue and Rob MacArthur, Marie Mohr, Mike Featherstone, Julie Jones and June Cann deserve thanks and an award for allowing me the respite I so often need.

Gratitude and love to my brilliant, tenacious legal representatives and friends Lillian Webb and John Udorovic, who have stood by me from the beginning. Special thanks to Joshua 'Can you use my surname?' Udorovic and Nadine Udorovic.

Thank you to Valerie 'We'll find a way' Hardy.

Sincere admiration for Mark Maddern, Jack Brown, Nick and Ben MacArthur and Jessica Watson-Munro – I couldn't imagine better friends for Iddin and Shahirah.

Thank you also to Heather and Graham Brown for our 'electricity', and Elizabeth Lew who lightened my workload and enabled me to sit down and write this book.

A heartfelt thank you must be said to my other solicitor and friend Nicholas Pullen of Holding Redlich Solicitors and Consultants, Sir Rupert and Lady April Hamer, Justice Bill Gillard (formerly QC), barrister John Cantwell, Noel Ackman QC, Murray and Frankie Nicoll, Dr Michael Jones, Neil Miller, Uncle Eric (Iddin and Shahirah's godfather and my dear friend), Michael Cremean, Andy and Kim Tavares, Michael Willesee, Rob and Nicholas Gell, David and Debbie Hirschfelder, Jeff Goldstein, Senator Rod Kemp, Bronwyn Bishop, Malcolm Fraser, Robert Hamilton, Torrance Mendez, Wayne Miller, Howard Sattler, Suzanne Monks, Mike Munro, Bert and Pattie Newton, Susan Duncan, John O'Loan, David Broadbent, Graeme Orr, Gavin McDougall, Richard and Joanne Waller, Geoff Barnes, Lindy Chamberlain-Creighton, Ramona Koval, Julie Clark and Richard Neville, Rea Francis and Simon Binks. Special thanks to Nene King.

To James Fraser, thank you for the boost and the belief that I could, perhaps, write.

Deborah Callaghan has evinced so much patience and support to get this edition of the book 'out there'; I'm glad I met you on the first edition. I have been more fortunate than most writers – I have struck two amazingly wonderful friends/literary agents in a single lifetime. Miss you always, Mr Anthony (with a 't' not a 'th') Williams.

I would also like to thank Bill Campbell and his wonderful team at Mainstream Publishing for deciding that an Australian woman's experiences still have relevance in a world fraught with uncertainties and fear, and that hope and tenacity guides us all – especially as parents. To Peter MacKenzie for his quiet support and an especially deep expression of gratitude to Fiona Brownlee due to her unwavering belief in this book and her friendship.

Abiding gratitude must also be expressed to the hundreds of kind people who wrote or telephoned with their encouragement and prayers in the fight for my children's human rights, along with the tens of thousands of Australians who added their signatures to the petitions that circulated around the nation. Added to this list must be the hundreds of people who stopped me on the street to wish our family well. Thank you all for giving back Iddin and Shahirah their identities and for strengthening my resolution.

The following is an extract from

SINCE I WAS A PRINCESS
The Fourteen-Year Fight to Find My Children

the sequel to

ONCE I WAS A PRINCESS

by
JACQUELINE PASCARL

Publication date: April 2007
ISBN 9781845962166
£17.99 (Hardback)

MAINSTREAM
PUBLISHING
www.mainstreampublishing.com

The wailing permeated my gut and travelled to that plateau just above the breasts where pain and empathy reside so closely. Even before I could pinpoint the location of its maker, I recognised the timeless cry as the sound of great loss and grief. I knew its origins well; I was familiar with its resonance and acquainted with its depth. In my past, I had myself been the originator of many such cries. It was a call to which there was no answer and no panacea – nor did it expect one. Its vibrations spread to my temples and the back of my skull, finally settling as a great unyielding lump in the back of my throat. As I stumbled across the rock-strewn terrain of the refugee camp, I thought how strange and yet somehow comforting it was that the aural marker of tragedy did not differ from one section of humanity to another.

High-pitched screams now punctuated the wails of grief, competing with the dull 'thump, thump' emitted by the rotors of a passing armoured helicopter. The chopper, carrying missiles, a reconnaissance team or some other NATO cargo, was visible only as a blackened presence against the night sky. This tract of land over which it passed was wedged between the battle zone of Kosovo and the bright lights of the Macedonian capital, Skopje, twenty miles down the unlit road. Our small sanctuary, just eleven minutes within the Macedonian border, provided a meagre haven for 27,000 displaced souls – women, children and men who had fled the armed conflict of Kosovo and the relentless pursuit of the Serbian military forces.

Stenkovec II was one of the three major processing and refugee camps in Macedonia set up under the protection of the United Nations High Commission for Refugees (UNHCR), and run on a day-to-day basis by CARE International, the global humanitarian aid and development agency. The camp was bleak and unforgiving, occupying a series of high-walled, rabbit-warren gullies, interconnected by excavated cuttings just wide enough for a tank to pass through. A minor hill at its core provided a small vantage point, up which children scrambled during the daylight hours and where an effort had been made by UNICEF to cobble together the semblance of a school and kindergarten. A former stone quarry which had until recently served as a heavy artillery and weapons range, the locale was devoid of trees, running water, electricity and sewerage.

The moon reflected off the battered face of my Swatch watch: 3.27 a.m. We had been unloading and processing these new busloads of refugees (or 'internally displaced persons', as the politically correct amongst us insisted on saying) since just after 1 a.m. The initial headcounts suggested about eight hundred souls had been crammed aboard six buses, each normally designated to carry fifty-five passengers.

Closing in on the weeping, I picked my way around to the rear of the huge khaki-coloured 'horse tents' – so named, I assumed, because the arm of the military which had donated them to the relief effort was a cavalry regiment. It was here that our new arrivals were to be sheltered. Each human being would be allotted a three-foot-wide space which would have to serve as sleeping quarters, living-room and storage space for whatever possessions they had managed to carry on their back or shove into an inadequate plastic shopping bag as they began their escape to safety. A requisite six feet between rows of people served as a central walkway between the two sides of a tent. These were the minimum space allowances under World Health Organisation and UNHCR guidelines during a time of emergency. This was the theory; but in practice nearly one hundred weary people would that night sleep in a tent meant to accommodate thirty, cheek by jowl with complete strangers in utter darkness. This was just one of the frustrating realities we faced as aid workers: we witnessed humanity at its lowest ebb forced to masquerade as sardines.

I checked each tent, trying to pinpoint the location of the grieving woman. The miner's lamp on my head bounced light off the startled faces peering back at me from the darkness. There was quiet sobbing in every shelter I visited, whispering, groaning and sometimes the whimpering of babies and children, but the sound I sought was on a different level, it had an entirely different intensity. Tangles of guy ropes and tent pegs running off our makeshift town hampered my path; I tripped and broke my fall by making a grab for the wire perimeter fence, and that is how I found her as my torch illuminated her feet, shod in battered tan high-heeled shoes. Knees drawn tightly up to her chest, she sat on the ground oblivious to my approach. Her brown gabardine skirt was heavily stained, that much I could see, and she now emitted guttural howls as she repeatedly banged her forehead with the heel of her hand. To witness such grief, and then to be capable of identifying it from the outside looking in, is an unspeakable invasion of a person. Even now, as I write, my chest compresses hard against my lungs and my eyes are drawn out of their sockets by the insight it affords. Her brown hair was short and streaked with blond, her hands and nails grubby and torn. The blouse she wore had once been white; she was dressed in a teacher's or secretary's garb, I guessed – average middle-class attire, but marred by what appeared to be dried blood and a few missing buttons. She was thirty plus, I guessed, around my own age – young enough, yet ancient if life has imploded all normalcy.

Grasping her pounding fist, I dragged it downwards as she threw back her head. Her jaw slackened with a huge expulsion of air and wailing from the back of her throat. Another woman emerged from the shadows, a grandmother, judging from the little girl clutching at her long cardigan. She spoke to me in Albanian, a tumble of words I couldn't understand. I tried a few words in Bosnian and there was a flicker of comprehension. The grandmother called to a teenage boy who had hung back against the tent wall.

Selma was the distressed woman's name, according to the boy translating the grandmother's words. Two days earlier, at a pre-border check by the Serbian paramilitary, she had been subjected to a body cavity search. The soldiers had found a roll of cash secreted on her person. Her punishment for attempting to smuggle cash out of Kosovo was the murder of her child.

Apparently, she was on her knees struggling to stop the thugs from tearing her seven-year-old son from her arms when one paramilitary grabbed her by the hair whilst another wrenched the small child's arms above his head, put a pistol to the base of his skull and pulled the trigger.

'His eyes, his eyes,' was what I now understood Selma sobbed as I held her tightly in both my arms, her head against my shoulder. The last image of her terrorised child had been seared into her mind with the efficiency of a precision laser, marking her as a mother shattered by its final brutality.

It was then, for the only time ever, that I broke the cardinal rule of aid work – never cry in front of your charges. Fuck that; I was crying with her not for her, and some of my tears were for the awfulness of our fellow human beings and the deeds of which they are capable.

The incongruity of my journey to that point in time was not entirely lost on me. How did I find myself wading through such violence, poverty, desperation and shining hope? I've often pondered the conundrum of an Australian mother of two becoming the common denominator between a refugee camp in the foothills of the Balkans, a child-literacy project amidst the Maasai of Kenya, hunky French paramedics, Parisian couture, heavy-duty army boots and an international furore over parental child abduction.

But the straight truth of the matter is that nothing surprises me much any more. A stiff vodka on ice sipped decorously in the private bar at the House of Lords or a muddy cup of coffee imbibed whilst squatting beside the casings of depleted uranium armaments aren't that different in terms of good conversation or company; and, besides, I now just accept the vagaries of life as a natural progression towards some distant point in the future. Years ago I had to make a choice: either to shut down my faculties, my heartbeat, my potential for joy, to wallow in unassuageable grief and torment, or to decide that I would survive and create a new life for myself by harnessing all my negative experiences into one positive and stubborn force and following the direction it homed in on. That was *the* single most important decision I have made since I was a princess.